M000279587

BARCELONA

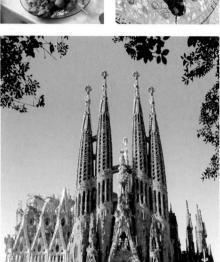

CONTENTS

Welcome to Rick Steves' Europe

Travel is intensified living—maximum thrills per minute and one of the last great sources of legal adventure. Travel is freedom. It's recess, and we need it.

I discovered a passion for European travel as a teen and have been sharing it ever since—through my bus tours, public television and radio shows, and travel guidebooks. Over the years, I've taught millions of travelers how to best enjoy Europe's blockbuster sights—and experience "Back Door" discoveries that most tourists miss.

This book offers a balanced mix of Barcelona's blockbuster sights and lesser-known gems. It's selective: Rather than listing dozens of tapas bars, I recommend only the best ones. And it's in-depth: My self-guided museum tours and city walks provide insight into Barcelona's vibrant history and today's living, breathing culture.

I advocate traveling simply and smartly. Take advantage of my money- and time-saving tips on sightseeing, transportation, and more. Try local, characteristic alternatives to expensive hotels and restaurants. In many ways, spending more money only builds a thicker wall between you and what you traveled so far to see.

We visit Barcelona to experience it—to become temporary locals. Thoughtful travel engages us with the world, as we learn to appreciate other cultures and new ways to measure quality of life.

Judging by the positive feedback I receive from readers, this book will help you enjoy a fun, affordable, and rewarding vacation—whether it's your first trip or your tenth.

Bon viatge! Happy travels!

Rick Steves

BARCELONA

If you're in the mood to surrender to a city's charms, let it be in Barcelona. The capital of Catalunya and Spain's second city, Barcelona bubbles with life—in its narrow lanes, pedestrian-friendly boulevards, elegant modern uptown, bohemian corners, and bustling market halls, and along its long beach promenade spiked with inviting beach bars (*chiringuitos*).

Like Los Angeles, Barcelona is basically flat, sloping gently from the foothills down to the sea. A large central square, Plaça de Catalunya, divides the older and newer parts of town. Above the square is the modern part called the Eixample. Below the square is the Old City and hilly Montjuïc, overlooking the harbor.

Barcelona is large (1.6 million people), though the Old City feels delightfully small. Its top sights are the cathedral, the Picasso Museum, and the fun-to-explore neighborhood itself. The Old City is made for strolling, from the broad, tree-lined Ramblas boulevard and the winding lanes lined with offbeat shops to the small squares ringed with cafés and dotted with palm trees. Make time to meander without a checklist.

Outside the Old City, the sights are scattered, but with a map and a willingness to figure out public transit (or take taxis), it's all manageable. If you have extra time and interest, consider day trips to Montserrat (for pilgrims), Sitges (for sun worshippers), and Figueres and Cadaqués (for Salvador Dalí fans).

The region of Catalunya, anchored by Barcelona, is proud-

Delightful Modernista architecture, at wavy La Pedrera and the colorful Palace of Catalan Music

ly Catalan and culturally different from Spain. You won't find bullfighting here, where it's banned—Barcelona turned its bullring into a shopping mall. Though Spanish is widely spoken in Catalunya, the native language is Catalan. This feisty region has chafed under rule by Spain over the years, especially during Francisco Franco's repressive dictatorship. Today, many Catalan people clamor for increased autonomy, while some agitate for independence.

In Barcelona, you'll see the evidence of its long history, from ancient Roman ruins (when the city was named Barcino) to medieval churches, twisty Gothic lanes, and monuments to Columbus and the sea trade. By the late 19th century, Barcelona had boomed into an industrial powerhouse.

This thriving city became a showpiece of innovative art and architecture. Talented Catalan architects, including Antoni Gaudí, forged the Modernista style and remade the city's skyline with curvy, fanciful buildings such as the dragon-roofed Casa Batlló and wavy La Pedrera, culminating in Gaudí's Sagrada Família, a gloriously avant-garde church under construction since 1882. Throughout the city, you'll glimpse Modernista architecture. Rows of ironwork balconies are punctuated with colorful, playful details: bay windows, turrets, hanging lanterns, flower boxes, carved reliefs, and painted tiles.

Pablo Picasso lived in Barcelona as a teenager—just as he

Circle Dances in Squares and Castles in the Air

From circle dancing to human towers, Catalans are proud of their distinctive cultural traditions.

For many, the slow-motion *sardana* dance is a patriotic display of Catalan unity, while for others, it's a fun chance to kick up their heels. To dance the *sardana*, participants form a circle, often on a public square. Holding hands with their arms raised, they gracefully step and hop to the music. The band consists of a long flute, oboes, strange-looking brass instruments, and a bongo-like drum.

All are welcome to join in, even tourists cursed with two left feet. Dances are held in the square in front of the cathedral on Sundays at 11:15 and many Saturdays at 18:00, except in August. (Put your day bag in the center of your circle, as other participants do, to guard against theft.)

Another Catalan tradition is the *castell,* a tower erected solely of people. Towers can be up to 10 humans high. The burliest form the base, supporting the *manilles* ("handles") who help haul others to the top, including the smallest of all, who becomes the steeple. Spotters cluster around the base in case anyone falls. *Castelleres* are judged on how quickly they build their towers and how fast they dismantle them. *Castells* pop up at festivals (such as Festa Major de Gràcia in mid-August and La Mercè in late September) and usually in the cathedral square on spring and summer Saturdays at 19:30.

Both traditions—the *sardana* and *castells*—require group participation, which is fitting for Catalunya, known for its community spirit. Keeping its traditions and language alive, Catalans proudly say, *"Visca Catalunya!"* (Long live Catalunya!) ◾

Catalan pride in living action: sardana *dancing and tower building*

The Miró mosaic on the Ramblas; strolling lush Gaudí-designed Park Güell

was on the verge of reinventing painting. Salvador Dalí and Joan Miró are among the world-changing 20th-century artists with ties to Barcelona. All three artists are represented by dedicated museums in Barcelona or nearby.

Perched on the sea, Barcelona itself is a work of art. Find a viewpoint to enjoy it, whether from a cable car, a cathedral rooftop, or Gaudí's colorful Park Güell.

In this coastal city, seafood is always on the menu, along with Spain's ever-present ham. Restaurants serve dinner late by our standards. To cope, do as the locals do, and dip into tapas bars in the early evening to enjoy Catalan small plates that can add up to an entertaining meal. Wash it all down with a *caña* (small beer), *crianza* (fine aged wine), or *cava* (sparkling wine). Then spill into the crowded streets to join the paseo, when everyone strolls in the cool of the evening.

Today's Barcelona is as vibrant as ever. Locals still hold hands and dance the everyone's-welcome *sardana* in front of the cathedral. Neighborhood festivals jam the events calendar. Barcelona's engaging culture is on an unstoppable roll in Spain's most cosmopolitan and European corner.

Barcelona by Neighborhood

Barcelona is a big city, but its major sights cluster in convenient zones. Travelers need only focus on a few areas: the Old City, the harbor/Barceloneta, the Eixample, and Montjuïc. Antoni Gaudí's Park Güell is north of the Eixample in the Gràcia district. Grouping your sightseeing, walks, dining, and shopping thoughtfully can save you lots of time and money.

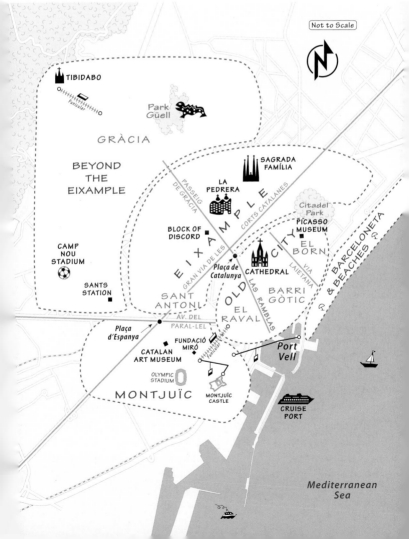

TOP NEIGHBORHOODS

Old City (Ciutat Vella)

This is the compact core of Barcelona—ideal for strolling, shopping, and people-watching—where you'll probably spend most of your time. It's a labyrinth of narrow streets that once were confined by the medieval walls. The lively pedestrian drag called the **Ramblas** goes through the heart of the Old City from Plaça de Catalunya to the harbor.

The Old City is divided into thirds by the Ramblas and Via Laietana, a vehicle-heavy thoroughfare running roughly parallel to the Ramblas. Between the Ramblas and Via Laietana is the characteristic **Barri Gòtic** (BAH-ree GOH-teek), with the cathedral as its navel. Locals call it "El Gòtic" for short. To the east of Via Laietana is the trendy **El Born** district (a.k.a. "La Ribera"), a shopping, dining, and nightlife mecca centered on the Picasso Museum and the Church of Santa Maria del Mar. To the west of the Ramblas is **El Raval** (rah-VAHL), enlivened by its university and modern-art museum. While rough-edged in places, it is the emerging foodie zone.

Harborfront

The old harbor, **Port Vell,** gleams with landmark monuments and new developments. A pedestrian bridge links the Ramblas with the modern Maremagnum shopping/aquarium/entertainment complex. On the peninsula across the quaint sailboat harbor is **Barceloneta,** a traditional fishing neighborhood with gritty charm and some good seafood restaurants. Beyond Barceloneta, a gorgeous man-made **beach** several miles long stretches east to the commercial and convention district called the **Fòrum.**

Trendy El Born (opposite); Ramblas vista; tapas bar; Port Vell waterfront bridge; street performer

Modernista Block of Discord (Eixample); Dalí art (Figueres); Cadaqués beach; Montjuïc towers; Montserrat (opposite)

Eixample

Above the Old City, beyond the bustling hub of Plaça de Catalunya, is the elegant Eixample (eye-SHAM-plah) district, its grid plan softened by cutoff corners. Much of Barcelona's Modernista architecture is found here—especially along the swanky artery Passeig de Gràcia, an area called **Quadrat d'Or** (Golden Quarter). To the east is the **Sagrada Família;** to the north is the **Gràcia** district and Antoni Gaudí's **Park Güell.**

Montjuïc

The large hill overlooking the city to the southwest is Montjuïc (mohn-jew-EEK), home to a variety of sights, including some excellent museums (Catalan Art, Joan Miró) and the Olympic Stadium. At the base of Montjuïc, stretching toward Plaça d'Espanya, are the former **1929 World Expo Fairgrounds,** with additional fine attractions (including the CaixaForum art gallery and the bullring-turned-mall, Las Arenas).

Day Trips

When you're ready to explore beyond Barcelona, you have good options: **Montserrat** is Catalunya's most important pilgrimage site, with a mountaintop Benedictine monastery (accessible by scenic and fun cable car or by rack railway).

Fans of surrealist artist Salvador Dalí can combine these two neighboring towns for a terrific day trip: **Figueres,** home to the best museum devoted to the artist—the Dalí Theater-Museum—and the beach town of **Cadaqués,** where the artist lived in the outstanding Salvador Dalí House and Garden.

Sitges, a popular resort and artists' haunt, boasts a charming Old Town and nine beaches connected by a promenade.

Planning and Budgeting

The best trips start with good planning. Here are ideas to help you decide when to go, design a smart itinerary, set a travel budget, and prepare for your trip. For general advice on sightseeing, accommodations, restaurants, and more, see the Practicalities chapter.

PLANNING YOUR TIME

As you read this book and learn your options...

Decide when to go.

Sea breezes off the Mediterranean and a generally warm climate make Barcelona pleasant for much of the year. Late spring and early fall offer the best combination of good weather, somewhat lighter crowds, long days, and plenty of tourist and cultural activities. You'll encounter hot, humid weather and the biggest crowds in July and August, and some shops and restaurants close down in August. Winter temperatures are far from freezing, but rainfall is abundant.

Work out a day-by-day itinerary.

The following day plans offer suggestions for how to maximize your sightseeing, depending on how many days you have. You can adapt these itineraries to fit your own interests. To find out what days sights are open, check the "Daily Reminder" in the Orientation chapter. Note major sights where advance tickets are required (or recommended) or a free Rick Steves audio tour is available.

Barcelona in One Day

For a relaxing day, stroll the Ramblas, visit the Sagrada Família and Picasso Museum, and have dinner in the El Born district. Or try the following ambitious plan (only possible with advance reservations).

9:00	From Plaça de Catalunya, follow my Barri Gòtic Walk and Barcelona Cathedral Tour. (Or follow my free Barcelona City Walk audio tour.)
11:00	Starting near the cathedral, take my El Born Walk to the Picasso Museum, stopping midway for a quick, early lunch at Santa Caterina Market.
12:30	Take my Picasso Museum Tour.
14:00	Catch a taxi or the Metro to the Sagrada Família.
14:30	Tour the Sagrada Família.
16:30	Hop a taxi or the Metro to the Diagonal Metro stop.
17:00	Take my Eixample Walk to Plaça de Catalunya. (To shorten the walk, stay on Passeig de Gràcia to see the main Modernista sights: La Pedrera and the Block of Discord.)
19:00	From Plaça de Catalunya, take my Ramblas Ramble to the harborfront.
Evening	From the harborfront (or any point along the Ramblas) take a taxi to a neighborhood with good tapas bars (which open early): Barceloneta (stroll the beach promenade), Barri Gòtic (around the cathe-

Barcelona icons: Gaudí's soaring Sagrada Família and a dish of succulent paella

Cathedral square; Ramblas paseo; street musicians; art shop in Barri Gòtic

dral), or lively El Born. Foodies can walk to nearby El Raval for cheaper, bohemian-chic eateries. Note that restaurants open late, around 21:00.

Barcelona in Two or More Days

With at least two days, divide and conquer the town geographically: Spend one day in the Old City (Ramblas, Barri Gòtic/cathedral area, Picasso Museum/El Born) and another on the Eixample and Gaudí sights (La Pedrera, Sagrada Família, Park Güell). If you have a third day, visit Montjuïc and/or side-trip to Montserrat.

With extra time, consider taking a hop-on, hop-off bus tour for a sightseeing overview (for example, the Bus Turístic blue route links most Gaudí sights and could work well on Day 2).

Day 1: Old City

9:00	Follow my Barri Gòtic Walk and Barcelona Cathedral Tour. (Or follow my free Barcelona City Walk audio tour.)
11:00	Browse the fun shops described in my Barri Gòtic Shopping Walk (see the Shopping chapter).
13:00	Explore El Born, following my El Born Walk, which starts near the cathedral. Drop into Santa Caterina Market for lunch.
15:00	Tour the Picasso Museum.
17:00	Stroll the Ramblas (follow my Ramblas Ramble and visit La Boqueria market).
Evening	For a tapas-bar dinner, choose among the neighborhoods listed in my one-day plan. Other possibilities include sightseeing (many sights are open late), concerts, or hanging out at a beach bar in Barceloneta.

Day 2: Modernisme

9:00	Take my Eixample Walk, touring La Pedrera and/or one of the Block of Discord houses—Casa Batlló or Casa Amatller. Have lunch along the way.
12:30	From Plaça de Catalunya, hop a taxi or Metro to the Sagrada Família.
13:00	Tour the Sagrada Família.
15:00	Choose among these options: Taxi to Park Güell for

more Gaudí. Or take the bus to Montjuïc (if you're not going to Montjuïc on Day 3) to enjoy the city view and your pick of sights. Or explore the harborfront La Rambla de Mar, the Old Port, and the beach scene.

Evening   Choose among the evening activities listed earlier.

Day 3: Montjuïc and Barceloneta

Tour Montjuïc, stopping at Fundació Joan Miró, Catalan Art Museum, and CaixaForum. Take the scenic cable-car ride down from Montjuïc to the port and spend the rest of the day at Barceloneta—stroll the promenade, hit the beach, and find your favorite beach bar for dinner.

Day 4

Consider these options: Visit the markets (La Boqueria and Santa Caterina—both closed Sun). Tour more sights (Palau Güell's Modernista interior, Barcelona History Museum, Frederic Marès Museum, Chocolate Museum, and more). Take a walking tour, bike tour, or cooking class. Relax or rent a rowboat in Citadel Park.

Days 5-7

With more time, choose among several day trips, including the mountaintop monastery of Montserrat, the beach resort town of Sitges, and the Salvador Dalí sights at Figueres and Cadaqués (reserve both in advance; see the Day Trips from Barcelona chapter).

Ham hocks at La Boqueria market; Montjuïc cable car with grand views

PLANNING YOUR BUDGET

Run a reality check on your dream trip. You'll have major transportation costs in addition to daily expenses.

Flight: A round-trip flight from the US to Barcelona costs about $900-1,500, depending on where you fly from and when.

Public Transportation: For a one-week visit, allow about $90 for Metro tickets and a couple of day trips by train. To get between Barcelona and El Prat airport, figure $15-80 round-trip, depending on which option you choose.

Budget Tips: To cut your daily expenses, take advantage of the deals you'll find throughout Barcelona and mentioned in this book.

AVERAGE DAILY EXPENSES PER PERSON

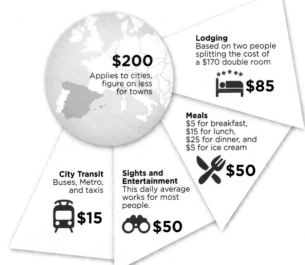

$200
Applies to cities, figure on less for towns

Lodging
Based on two people splitting the cost of a $170 double room
$85

Meals
$5 for breakfast,
$15 for lunch,
$25 for dinner, and
$5 for ice cream
$50

City Transit
Buses, Metro, and taxis
$15

Sights and Entertainment
This daily average works for most people.
$50

Use the city's public transportation, and visit sights by neighborhood for efficiency.

Buy an ArticketBCN pass and use it wisely (see page 27). Or visit only the sights you most want to see, and seek out free sights and experiences (people-watching counts).

Some businesses—especially hotels and walking-tour companies—offer discounts to my readers (look for the RS% symbol in the listings in this book).

Reserve your rooms directly with the hotel and book good-value rooms early. Some hotels offer a discount if you pay in cash and/or stay three or more nights (check online or ask). Rooms can cost less outside of peak season (which is summer for cheap hotels, winter for business-class hotels). And even seniors can sleep cheaply in hostels (most have private rooms) for about $30 per person. Or check Airbnb-type sites for deals.

It's no hardship to eat inexpensively in Barcelona. You can get tasty, affordable meals at sandwich shops, kebab stands, tapas bars, pizza shops, and international eateries. Shop the market halls and cultivate the art of picnicking in atmospheric settings.

When you splurge, choose an experience you'll always remember, such as a concert or a cooking class. Minimize souvenir shopping; focus instead on collecting wonderful memories.

Friendly hotel clerk; easy-to-use Metro system; detail of Sagrada Família facade (opposite)

BEFORE YOU GO

You'll have a smoother trip if you tackle a few things ahead of time. For more details on these topics, see the Practicalities chapter and RickSteves.com, which has helpful travel-tip articles and videos.

Make sure your travel documents are valid. If your passport is due to expire within six months of your ticketed date of return, you need to renew it. Allow 12 weeks or more to renew or get a passport. Be aware of any entry requirements; you may need to register with the European Travel Information and Authorization System (ETIAS) before you travel (quick and easy process; check https://travel-europe.europa.eu/etias_en). Get passport and country-specific travel info at Travel.State.gov.

Arrange your transportation. Book your international flights. Overall, Google Flights is the best place to start searching for flights. If you're traveling beyond Catalunya, figure out your transportation options: bus or train (and either a rail pass or individual train tickets), rental car, or a cheap flight. (You can wing it in Europe, but it may cost more.) Drivers: Consider bringing an International Driving Permit (sold at AAA offices in the US, www.aaa.com) along with your license.

Book rooms well in advance, especially if your trip falls during peak season or any major holidays or festivals.

Reserve ahead for key sights. Every visitor wants to see the same sights in Barcelona—the Picasso Museum, La Pedrera (Casa Milà), Sagrada Família church, Casa Batlló, and Park Güell—so it's essential to book in advance. While technically you can try to buy tickets at these sights (except Sagrada Família), I consider reservations mandatory in Barcelona.

Booking ahead is also a must to visit the Dalí sights in Figueres and/or Cadaqués.

Consider travel insurance. Compare the cost of insurance to the cost of your potential loss. Understand what protections your credit card might offer and whether your existing insurance (health, homeowners, or renters) covers you and your possessions overseas.

Manage your money. "Tap-to-pay" or "contactless" cards are widely accepted and simple to use. You may need your credit card's PIN for some purchases—request it if you don't have one. Alert your bank that you'll be using your debit and credit cards in Europe. You don't need to bring euros for your trip; you can withdraw euros from ATMs in Europe.

Use your smartphone smartly. Sign up for an international service plan, or rely on Wi-Fi instead. Download any apps you'll want on the road, such as maps, translators, and Rick Steves Audio Europe (see sidebar).

Pack light. You'll walk with your luggage more than you think. I travel for weeks with a single carry-on bag and a day pack. Use the packing checklist in the appendix as a guide.

Rick's Free Audio Tours and Video Clips

Rick Steves Audio Europe, a free app, makes it easy to download my audio tours and listen to them offline as you travel. For this book (look for the 🎧), free audio tours cover my **Barcelona City Walk** and **Eixample Walk.** The app also offers my public radio show interviews with travel experts from around the globe. Scan the QR code to find it in your app store, or visit RickSteves.com/AudioEurope.

Rick Steves Classroom Europe, a powerful tool for teachers, is also useful for travelers. This video library contains about 600 short clips excerpted from my public television series. Enjoy these videos as you sort through options for your trip and to better understand what you'll see in Europe. Check it out at Classroom.RickSteves.com.

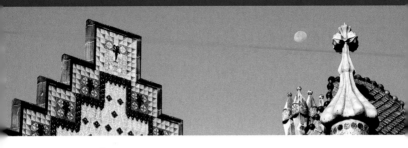

Travel Smart

If you have a positive attitude, equip yourself with good information (this book), and expect to travel smart, you will.

Read—and reread—this book. To have an "A" trip, be an "A" student. Note opening hours of sights, closed days, crowd-beating tips, and whether reservations are required or advisable. Check the latest at RickSteves.com/update.

Be your own tour guide. As you travel, get up-to-date info on sights, reserve tickets and tours, reconfirm hotels and travel arrangements, and check transit connections. Visit the local tourist information office (TI).

Outsmart thieves. Pickpockets abound in crowded places where tourists congregate. Treat commotions as smokescreens for theft. Keep your passport and backup cash and cards secure in a money belt tucked under your clothes; carry only a day's spending money and a card in your front pocket or wallet. Don't set valuable items down on counters or café tabletops, where they can be quickly stolen or easily forgotten.

Minimize potential loss. Keep expensive gear to a minimum. Bring copies or take photos of important documents (passport and cards) to aid in replacement if they're lost or stolen. Back up photos and devices to the cloud as you travel.

Beat the summer heat. If you wilt easily, choose a hotel with air-conditioning, start your day early, take a midday siesta at your hotel, and resume your sightseeing later. Churches offer a cool haven (though dress modestly—no bare shoulders or shorts). Take frequent ice cream breaks.

Guard your time and energy. Taking a taxi can be a good value if it saves you a long wait for a cheap bus or an exhausting walk across town. To avoid long lines, follow my crowd-beating tips, such as buying tickets in advance or sightseeing early or late (see the Nightlife in Barcelona chapter for a list of sights open late).

Be flexible. Even if you have a well-planned itinerary, expect changes, strikes, closures, sore feet, bad weather, and so on. Your Plan B could turn out to be even better.

Attempt the language. Many Catalans—especially in the tourist trade and in Barcelona—speak English, but if you learn some Catalan or Spanish, even just a few pleasantries, you'll get more smiles and make more friends. Apps such as Google Translate work for on-the-go translation help, but you can get a head start by practicing the survival phrases near the end of this book.

Connect with the culture. Interacting with locals carbonates your experience. Enjoy the friendliness of the Catalan people. Ask questions; most locals are happy to point you in their idea of the right direction. Set up your own quest for the best tapa, Modernista architecture, or street performer. Join the paseo and dance the *sardana*. When an opportunity pops up, make it a habit to say "yes."

Barcelona...here you come!

ORIENTATION TO BARCELONA

Bustling Barcelona is geographically big and culturally complex. Plan your time carefully, carving up the metropolis into manageable sightseeing neighborhoods. For efficiency, learn to navigate Barcelona by Metro, bus, and taxi. Make reservations in advance for Barcelona's most popular sights—otherwise, you may not get in at all. Armed with good information and a thoughtful game plan, you're ready to go. Then you can relax, enjoy, and let yourself be surprised by all that Barcelona has to offer.

This chapter offers helpful hints and details on Barcelona's tourist services, a rundown of your options for getting around, and recommendations for organized tours. For an overview of the city's neighborhoods and detailed day plans, see the previous chapter.

Apart from your geographical orientation, it's smart to orient yourself linguistically to a language distinct from Spanish. Although Spanish ("Castilian"/*castellano*) is widely spoken, the native tongue in this region is Catalan—nearly as different from Spanish as Italian (see the sidebar on page 28).

Overview

TOURIST INFORMATION

Barcelona's helpful TI has several branches (+34 932 853 832, www.barcelonaturisme.com). The primary TI is hidden beneath the main square, **Plaça de Catalunya** (daily 8:30-20:30, entrance just across from El Corte Inglés department store—look for red sign and take stairs down). Other branches are scattered around the city and generally have the same hours (some have shorter hours Sat-Sun). Locations include on **Pla de la Seu** in the Barri Gòtic (next to the Barcelona Cathedral), inside the base of the harborside

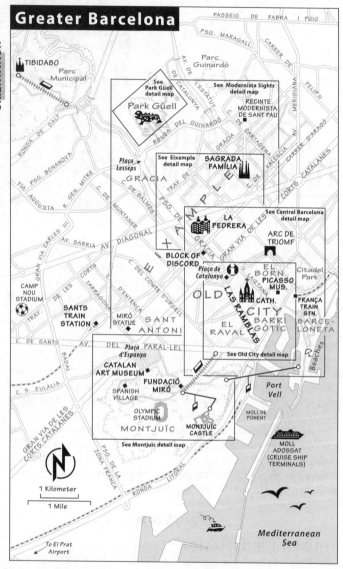

Greater Barcelona

PASSEIG   DE   FABRA   I   PUIG

PSG. MARAGALL

TIBIDABO

Parc Municipal

Parc Guinardó

See Park Güell detail map

See Modernista Sights detail map

RECINTE MODERNISTA DE SANT PAU

Park Güell

RONDA DEL GUINARDÓ

RONDA DE DALT

VIA AUGUSTA

Plaça Lesseps

See Eixample detail map

SAGRADA FAMÍLIA

GRACIA

See Central Barcelona detail map

LA PEDRERA

ARC DE TRIOMF

Citadel Park

BLOCK OF DISCORD

Plaça de Catalunya

EL BORN PICASSO MUS.

CAMP NOU STADIUM

SANTS TRAIN STATION

MIRÓ STATUE

SANT ANTONI

OLD CITY

CATH.

LAS RAMBLAS

BARRI GÒTIC

FRANÇA TRAIN STN.

BARCE-LONETA

EL RAVAL

Plaça PARAL·LEL

Plaça d'Espanya

CATALAN ART MUSEUM

FUNDACIÓ MIRÓ

SPANISH VILLAGE

OLYMPIC STADIUM

MONTJUÏC

MONTJUÏC CASTLE

See Old City detail map

Port Vell

Beaches

MOLL DE PONENT

MOLL ADOSSAT (CRUISE SHIP TERMINALS)

See Montjuïc detail map

N

1 Kilometer

1 Mile

To El Prat Airport

RONDA LITORAL

Mediterranean Sea

Columbus Monument, at the **airport** (terminals 1 and 2B), and at the **Sants train station.**

Smaller info kiosks pop up in touristy locales: on **Plaça d'Espanya,** in the park across from the **Sagrada Família** entrance, near the **Columbus Monument** (where the shuttle bus from the cruise port arrives), seasonally at the **Nord bus station,** at **cruise terminals** along the port, and on **Plaça de Catalunya.** Throughout the summer, red-jacketed tourist-info helpers appear in touristy parts of town; although they work for the hop-on, hop-off Bus Turístic, they are happy to answer questions.

The free **El Corte Inglés map,** provided at the store's Plaça de Catalunya customer service desk (just inside the entrance), is better than the TI's map.

TIs are handy places to buy tickets to most major sights (except the Picasso Museum). They also sell the **ArticketBCN** sightseeing pass, tickets for the Bus Turístic or TI-run walking tours (all described later), and tickets to FC Barcelona soccer games (men's and women's leagues).

Modernisme Route: A handy map showing all 120 of Barcelona's Modernista buildings is available online (www. rutadelmodernisme.com). The site also offers a great guidebook at bookstores throughout town (€12, 20-50 percent discounts at many Modernista sights—worthwhile if going beyond the biggies I cover in depth).

Sightseeing Passes: The **ArticketBCN** pass covers admission to six art museums and their temporary exhibits, letting you skip the ticket-buying lines. Sights include the recommended Picasso Museum, Catalan Art Museum, and Fundació Joan Miró (€38, valid 12 months; sold online, at participating museums, and at most TIs; www.articketbcn.org). If you visit three or more covered museums, this ticket can save you money and time. Just show your ArticketBCN to the ticket taker or at the info desk, and you'll get your museum ticket, which you can use to enter at any time (especially useful for Picasso Museum).

For most travelers, the **Barcelona Card** and the **Barcelona Card Express** are not worth the trouble.

Digital Publications: Good pretrip planning tools include *Time Out BCN Guide* (concise but thorough day-by-day list of events, www.timeout.com/barcelona) and *Barcelona Metropolitan* magazine (timely coverage of local topics and events, www. barcelona-metropolitan.com).

ARRIVAL IN BARCELONA

For more information on getting to or from Barcelona by train, plane, or bus, see the Barcelona Connections chapter.

HELPFUL HINTS

Book Ahead: To ensure you'll see Barcelona's top (and very crowded) sights—the Picasso Museum, La Pedrera (Casa Milà), Sagrada Família, Casa Batlló, and Park Güell—book timed-entry tickets online in advance. It's easy, it's cheap, and it's for your own good (and for Sagrada Família, it's required). Outside of Barcelona, guided tours of Dalí's house in Cadaqués

"You're Not in Spain, You're in Catalunya!"

This is a popular nationalistic refrain you may see on T-shirts or stickers around town. Catalunya is *not* the land of bullfighting and flamenco that many visitors envision when they think of Spain (visit Madrid or Sevilla for those).

The region of Catalunya, with Barcelona as its capital, has its own language, history, and culture. Its people—eight million strong—have a proud, independent spirit. Historically, Catalunya ("Cataluña" in Spanish, sometimes spelled "Catalonia" in English) has often been at odds with the central Spanish government in Madrid.

The Catalan language and culture were discouraged or even outlawed at various times, as Catalunya often chose the losing side in wars and rebellions against the kings in Madrid. In the Spanish Civil War (1936-1939), Catalunya was one of the last pockets of democratic resistance against the military coup of the fascist dictator Francisco Franco, who punished the region with four decades of repression. During that time, the Catalan flag was banned (locals showed their regional pride by flying their football team's flag instead).

Three of Barcelona's monuments are reminders of royal and Franco-era suppression. Citadel Park was originally a military citadel, constructed in the 18th century to keep locals in line. The Castle of Montjuïc, built for similar reasons, was the site of many political executions, including hundreds in the Franco era. The Sacred Heart Church atop Tibidabo, completed under Franco, was meant to atone for Barcelona's sins during the civil war—the main sin being opposition to Franco. Today, Catalunya is still divided: Some favor independence, while others are loyal to Spain (see "Independence for Catalunya?" on page 130).

To see real Catalan culture, look for the *sardana* dance or an exhibition of *castellers*. The main symbol of Catalunya is the

must be reserved in advance, and advance tickets are smart for the Dalí Theater-Museum in Figueres. Book as far ahead as possible for these sights (same-day tickets *may* be an option—but why risk it?).

When booking, aim for midafternoon or early evening, to avoid crowds: The city's major sites are busiest in the morning before 13:00 and during free entry times.

dragon slain by St. George ("Jordi" in Catalan)—the region's patron saint. You'll find dragons all over Barcelona, along with the Catalan flag—called the Senyera—with four horizontal red bars on a gold field. Why red stripes? According to legend, Wilfred the Hairy—a count of Barcelona and one of the founding fathers of Catalunya—was wounded in a ninth-century battle. A grateful neighboring king rewarded Wilfred's bravery with a copper shield and ran Wilfred's four bloody fingers across its surface, leaving four red stripes.

The Catalan language is irrevocably tied to the history and spirit of the Catalan people. After the mid-1970s end of the Franco era, the Catalan language made a huge comeback. Schools are now required to conduct all classes in Catalan; most school-age children learn Catalan first and Spanish second. While all Barcelonans speak Spanish, nearly all understand Catalan, three-quarters speak Catalan, and half can write it.

Most place names in this book are listed in Catalan. Here's how to pronounce some of the city's major landmarks:

Plaça de Catalunya	PLAH-sah duh kah-tah-LOON-yah
Eixample	eye-SHAM-plah
Passeig de Gràcia	PAH-sehj duh GRAH-see-ah
Catedral	KAH-tah-dral
Barri Gòtic	BAH-ree GOH-teek
Montjuïc	mohn-jew-EEK

When finding your way, these terms will be useful:

exit	*sortida* (sor-TEE-dah)
square	*plaça* (PLAH-sah)
street	*carrer* (kah-REHR)
boulevard	*passeig* (PAH-sehj)
avenue	*avinguda* (ah-veen-GOO-dah)

For more Catalan words, see the survival phrases in the appendix.

If you didn't book ahead, the TI may sell last-minute tickets to these sights (for a few extra euros).

Theft and Scam Alert: You have a better chance of being pickpocketed here—especially on the Ramblas—than anywhere else in Europe. The Sagrada Família (both inside and out), with its hordes of tourists gawking skyward, is also popular with pickpockets. Leave valuables in your hotel and wear a

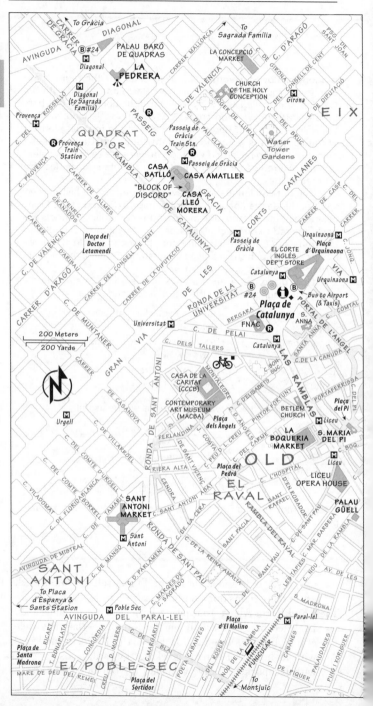

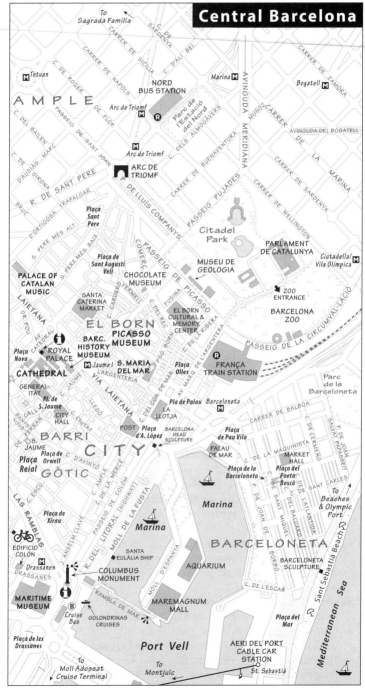

Central Barcelona

To Sagrada Família

CARRER DE SARDENYA

CARRER DE SICÍLIA

C. D'ALÍ BEI

Tetuan

C. DE ROGER

C. DE NÀPOLS

NORD BUS STATION

Marina

Bogatell

A M P L E

PASSEIG DE SANT JOAN

C. DE FLOR

Arc de Triomf

AVINGUDA MERIDIANA

MUÑOZ

CARRER DE ZAMORA

CARRER DE

AVINGUDA DEL BOGATELL

C. DEL BAILÉN

C. DE D'AUSIÀS MARC

GIRONA

C. DELS ALMOGÀVERS

CARRER DE LA MARINA

Arc de Triomf

CARRER DE BUENAVENTURA

CARRER DE SARDENYA

CARRER DE WELLINGTON

ARC DE TRIOMF

R. DE SANT PERE

DE LLUÍS COMPANYS

BRUC

D'ORTIGOSA

TRAFALGAR

PASSEIG PUJADES

Plaça Sant Pere

S. PERE MÉS ALT

S. PERE MÉS BAIX

Plaça de Sant Augustí Vell

PASSEIG DE SANT JOAN

PASSEIG DE PICASSO

Citadel Park

PARLAMENT DE CATALUNYA

Ciutadella/ Vila Olímpica

PALACE OF CATALAN MUSIC

SANTA CATERINA MARKET

CHOCOLATE MUSEUM

CARDERS

C. PEL'EC

VERMELL

MUSEU DE GEOLOGIA

ZOO ENTRANCE

LAIETANA

DR. POU

EL BORN

BARC. HISTORY MUSEUM

PICASSO MUSEUM

EL BORN CULTURAL & MEMORY CENTER

C. DE LA RIBERA

BARCELONA ZOO

PASSEIG DE LA CIRCUMVALLACIÓ

AV. CATEDRAL

Plaça Nova

ROYAL PALACE

CATHEDRAL

Jaume I

S. MARIA DEL MAR

L'ARGENTERIA

VIA LAIETANA

P.SG. BORN

C. DE LA ARGENTERIA

Plaça Olles

FRANÇA TRAIN STATION

Parc de la Barceloneta

GENERAL-ITAT

Pl. de S. Jaume

CALL

C. JAUME I

C. DE LA PRINCESA

AV. MARQ. L'ARGENTERA

BARCELONA HEAD SCULPTURE

C. FERRAN

BANYS NOUS

CITY HALL

C. CIUTAT

LLEDÓ

C. DEL COM DE MAR

Pla de Palau

LA LLOTJA

Barceloneta

CARRER DE BALBOA

P. DE JOAN SALVAT PAPASSEIT

S. JAUME

BARRI

Plaça de Orwell

C. D'AVINYÓ

POST Plaça d'A. López

CITY

Plaça de Pau Vila

PALAU DE MAR

Plaça de la Barceloneta

Plaça del Poeta Bosca

CARRER DE LA MAQUINISTA

P. DE CERMEÑO

MARKET HALL

Plaça Reial

GÒTIC

C. AMPLE

PASSEIG DE COLOM

C. DE LA MERCÈ

SANTA EULÀLIA SHIP

Marina

Marina

P. DE JOAN DE BORBÓ

C. DE SANT MIGUEL

C. DE L'ATLÀNTIDA

C. DEL BALUARD

C. DE SANT CARLES

To Beaches & Olympic Port

LAS RAMBLAS

C. ESCUD

Plaça de Xirau

R. DEL LITORAL (HIGHWAY)

J. ANSELM CLAVÉ

MOLL DE LA FUSTA

COLUMBUS MONUMENT

AQUARIUM

B A R C E L O N E T A

BARCELONETA SCULPTURE

Sant Sebastià Beach

EDIFICIO COLÓN

Drassanes

DRASSANES

MOLL D'ESPANYA

C. DE L'ESCAR

MARITIME MUSEUM

Cruise Bus

GOLONDRINAS CRUISES

RAMBLA DE MAR

MAREMAGNUM MALL

Plaça del Mar

Mediterranean Sea

Plaça de les Drassanes

To Moll Adossat Cruise Terminal

To Montjuïc

Port Vell

AERI DEL PORT CABLE CAR STATION

St. Sebastià

money belt. Whenever you pay with cash, count your change carefully.

Street scams are easy to avoid if you recognize them. Most common is the too-friendly local who tries to engage you in conversation. If a super-friendly man acts drunk and wants to dance because his soccer team just won, he's a pickpocket. Beware of thieves posing as lost tourists who ask for your help. Don't fall for any street-gambling shell games. Beware of groups of women aggressively selling flowers, people offering to clean a stain from your shirt, and so on. If you stop for any commotion or show on the Ramblas, put your hands in your pockets before someone else does. Assume any scuffle is a distraction by a team of thieves. On pedestrian streets, thieves on bikes are adept at swooping by and grabbing a purse or day bag you've placed right at your feet. But don't be intimidated... just be smart.

Personal Safety: Some areas feel seedy and can be unsafe after dark. Most crime is nonviolent, but muggings do occur. Certain parts of the Barri Gòtic (basically the two or three blocks directly south and east of Plaça Reial) and El Raval (just west of the Ramblas) can be dicey. One block can separate a comfy tourist zone from the junkies and prostitutes. If you use common sense in avoiding dark and lonely lanes, you should be fine.

Language Barrier: In posted information throughout the city (such as museum descriptions), you'll see Catalan first, followed by Spanish *(Castellano)* and English. Young people, the well educated, and people in tourism generally speak English in this very touristy city. The language someone favors can be a reflection of their political leanings.

Baggage Storage: Locker Barcelona is located just a few minutes' walk from Plaça de Catalunya. For weekends and holidays, book a locker in advance (cost depends on size, daily 8:30-22:30, shorter hours in winter, Carrer d'Estruc 36, +34 933 028 796, www.lockerbarcelona.com). For location, see the map on page 182.

Pharmacy: Pharmacies are sprinkled throughout the Barri Gòtic and Eixample: Look for a bright green illuminated cross. A 24-hour pharmacy is across from La Boqueria Market at #98 on the Ramblas.

Laundry: The clean-as-a-whistle **LavaXpres** is centrally located near recommended Plaça de Catalunya and Ramblas hotels (self-service, English instructions, daily 8:00-22:00, Passatge d'Elisabets 3, www.lavaxpres.com). **Speed Queen,** just off the Ramblas, is in a seedier neighborhood just down the street past Palau Güell (self-service, daily 7:00-23:00, Carrer Nou

Daily Reminder

Sunday: The Boqueria and Santa Caterina markets are closed. Some sights close early today, including the Olympic and Sports Museum (14:30), Camp Nou Stadium (14:30), the Catalan Art Museum (15:00), and the Palace of Catalan Music (15:30). Informal performances of the *sardana* national dance take place in front of the cathedral at 11:15 (none in Aug).

Some museums are free (and crowded) at certain times: Catalan Art Museum (first Sun of the month plus Sat after 15:00); Picasso Museum (first Sun of month plus Thu late afternoon-close); Maritime Museum (Sun after 15:00); and Barcelona History Museum and Frederic Marès Museum (first Sun of month plus other Sun from 15:00). Although free, these sights still require reservations, and slots often open only a few days in advance. I'd opt for another day when these places are less crowded.

The Magic Fountains come alive on summer evenings (June-Sept).

Monday: Many sights are closed, including the Picasso Museum, Catalan Art Museum, Palau Güell, Barcelona History Museum, *Santa Eulàlia* schooner (part of the Maritime Museum), Fundació Joan Miró, Frederic Marès Museum, El Born Cultural and Memory Center, and Olympic and Sports Museum. But most major Modernista sights are open today, including the Sagrada Família, La Pedrera, Park Güell, Casa Batlló, and Casa Museu Amatller.

Tuesday: All major sights are open.

Wednesday: All major sights are open. The Magic Fountains spout on summer evenings (June-Sept).

Thursday: All major sights are open. The Magic Fountains make a splash (March-Dec).

Friday: All major sights are open. The Magic Fountains light up Montjuïc (March-Dec).

Saturday: All major sights are open. Barcelonans often dance the *sardana* at 18:00 in front of the cathedral (none in Aug). The Magic Fountains dance March-Dec.

Late-Hours Sightseeing: For a list of sights open late, see the Nightlife in Barcelona chapter.

de la Rambla 19, +34 622 414 638). For both locations, see the map on page 182.

Bike Rental: Biking is a joy in Citadel Park and along the beach (suggested route on page 82), but it's stressful in the city center. Bike-rental shops are in just about every part of the city; I've listed only a few.

Barcelona Rent a Bike is located near Plaça de Catalunya (in the courtyard at Carrer dels Tallers 45). Both standard and e-bikes are available (daily, +34 933 171 970, www.barcelonarentabike.com).

A-Bike is near the Drassanes Metro stop, just a block from the Ramblas, and is a good place to pick up a bike for a trip to Barceloneta or Citadel Park (daily, standard and e-bikes, Carrer de Montserrat 8, +34 666 057 655, www.a-bike.es).

You'll see racks of government-subsidized "Bicing" **borrow-a-bikes** around town, but these are only for locals. Instead, check out the apps Donkey Republic and RideMovi (e-bikes), which offer rental bikes all over town.

GETTING AROUND BARCELONA

Barcelona's Metro and bus system is run by **TMB**—Transports Metropolitans de Barcelona (+34 932 987 000 or +34 932 148 000, www.tmb.cat).

It's worth asking for TMB's excellent Metro/bus map at the TI, larger stations, or the TMB info counter in the Sants train station. **Google Maps** is a great route planner for both Metro and bus riders. You'll also find a color map of useful public transportation routes in the back of this book.

Tickets and Multiride Cards: The Metro and local buses use the same ticket. A single-ride ticket *(bitllet senzill)* costs €2.40. One "ride" covers you for 1.25 hours of unlimited use on all Metro and local bus lines, as well as local rides on the Renfe and Rodalies de Catalunya train lines (including the ride to the train station) and the suburban FGC trains. Transfers made within your 1.25-hour limit are not counted as a new ride, but you must revalidate your multiride card whenever you transfer.

The T-Casual card (€11.35 for 10 rides) and the T-Dia card (€10.50 for 24 hours) are for individual travelers only. The T-Familiar card (€10 for 8 rides) is shareable as long as you stay together the entire journey (you'll be fined for riding without a ticket). Taking the Metro to or from the airport requires a separate €5.15 fare (more convenient by Aerobus shuttle—see the Connections chapter).

Multiday "Hola BCN!" travel cards cover unlimited travel for two or more days and include Metro service between the city and airport (€16.40/2 days, €23.80/3 days, €31/4 days, €38.20/5 days).

Tickets are sold on the TMB app (see next) and from easy-to-use machines at Metro stations and some bus stops. Most machines accept coins, bills, and credit/debit cards—just press "English" to start. On buses you can use **contactless** payment methods (credit card or phone), but not cash, to buy a single ticket.

TMB App: With the TMB app you can find your nearest station, get real-time transit updates, and buy tickets for all forms of public transit. The T-Mobilitat app is most useful on Android devices, where it allows tickets to be stored and validated directly on the phone. Non-Android phone users can make purchases in the app but must then collect and validate a T-Mobilitat smartcard at the station.

By Metro

The city's Metro, among Europe's best, connects just about every place you'll visit.

Among the several color-coded Metro lines, most useful for tourists is the **L3 (green)** line. Handy city-center stops on this line include (in order):

Sants Estació: Main train station

Espanya: Plaça d'Espanya, with access to the lower part of Montjuïc and trains to Montserrat

Paral·lel: Funicular to the top of Montjuïc

Drassanes: Bottom of the Ramblas, near Maritime Museum and Maremagnum mall

Liceu: Middle of the Ramblas, near the heart of the Barri Gòtic and cathedral

Plaça de Catalunya: Top of the Ramblas and main square with TI, airport bus, and lots of transportation connections

Passeig de Gràcia: Classy Eixample street at the Block of Discord; also connection to L2 (purple) line to Sagrada Família and L4 (yellow) line (described below)

Diagonal: Gaudí's La Pedrera

Lesseps: Closest stop for Gaudí's Park Güell

The **L4 (yellow)** line, which crosses the L3 (green) line at Passeig de Gràcia, has a few helpful stops, including **Jaume I** (between the Barri Gòtic/cathedral and El Born/Picasso Museum) and **Barceloneta** (at the south end of El Born, near the harbor action).

Riding the Metro: Before boarding, study a map (posted at Metro entrances, platforms, and aboard Metro cars) to get familiar with the system. Look for your line number and color, and find the end stop for your direction of travel. With a physical ticket, enter the Metro by inserting your ticket into the turnstile (with the arrow pointing in), retrieving it, and passing through. If you're using the T-Mobilitat app or smartcard, hold your phone or smartcard above the contactless symbol on the turnstile. Once inside, follow signs for your line and direction.

On board, most cars have handy lighted displays that indicate upcoming stops. Because the lines cross one another multiple times,

City of Festivals

Barcelona celebrates more festivals, markets, and street fairs than your average city. They dance the *sardana* (a circle dance), build *castells* (human pyramids), parade colorful *gegants* (giant puppets), and light up the night with fireworks displays called *correfoc* (fire run). Here's a roughly chronological rundown of Barcelona's most lively festivals.

Les Festes de Santa Eulàlia: Celebrating the patron saint of the city, this four-day festival features parades, dancing, *correfocs*, and many kid-friendly activities (mid-Feb, www.barcelona.cat/santaeulalia).

El Día de Sant Jordi: This celebration of St. George, the patron saint of Catalunya, is also Barcelona's version of Valentine's Day, when lovers and friends exchange books and flowers, and the streets are draped with the red-and-gold Catalan flag (April 23).

Corpus Christi: This festival, dating to 1320, contains traditional elements such as processions, music, and "dancing" eggs. The eggs, placed in flower-decorated fountains, spin ("dance") atop jets of water (late May/early June, www.barcelona.cat/culturapopular, click on "Festivals and Traditions").

Grec Festival de Barcelona: The city's premier summer arts festival has dance, theater, and music, with several events at Teatre Grec—a Greek-style amphitheater (usually July, www.barcelona.cat/grec).

Música als Parcs: Jazz and classical music fill the air in this popular series of evening concerts at city parks (June-Aug).

La Festa Catalana: This little spectacle of local folk traditions—human towers *(castells)*, giant puppets *(gegants)*, folk music, and dancing—happens spring and summer on the square in front of the cathedral (Saturdays at 19:30, May-Sept).

Festes de Sant Roc: The Barri Gòtic's biggest street party is filled with *gegants*, *sardana* dancing, street games, and fireworks (mid-Aug).

Festa Major de Gràcia: For eight days and nights, this festival features live music, *sardana* dancing, human pyramids, and traditional food and drinks (mid-Aug, www.festamajordegracia.cat).

La Mercè: Barcelona's main street festival is named after the city's patron saint, the Virgen de la Mercè. During the five-day festival, the city is filled with fireworks, music, an air show, human pyramids, a parade, and much more (late Sept, www.barcelona.cat/lamerce).

there can be several ways to make any one journey. (It's a good idea to carry a general map with you—especially if you're transferring.) Keep your Metro ticket until you've exited the system, just in case an inspector asks to see it.

Watch your valuables. If I were a pickpocket, I'd set up shop along the made-for-tourists L3 (green) line.

By Bus

Given the excellent Metro service, it's unlikely you'll spend much time on local buses (insert ticket in machine behind driver or use contactless pay options). Buses are useful, however, to get to Park Güell (bus #24), to connect the sights on Montjuïc, and to reach the beach.

By Taxi

Barcelona is one of Europe's best taxi towns. Save time by catching a cab (figure €10 from Ramblas to Sants station). Taxis are plentiful and honest, and cab rates are reasonable (€2.55 drop charge; €1.23/kilometer during the day; €1.51/kilometer 20:00-8:00, Sun, and holidays; €1 surcharge per large suitcase; €2.50 surcharge to/from Sants train station; and €4.50 surcharge for airport or cruise port). Similar to Uber, the **Taxi Barcelona & AMB** app lets you order a car and offers a fixed-price ride to your destination.

Tours in Barcelona

ON FOOT

🎧 To sightsee on your own, download my free Barcelona City Walk and Eixample Walk audio tours, which illuminate some of the city's top sights and neighborhoods (see page 22).

TI Walking Tours

The TI at Pla de la Seu (next to the Barcelona Cathedral) offers great guided walks through the **Barri Gòtic.** You'll learn the medieval story of the city as you walk through the cathedral neighborhood (€25, small discount if you buy online, daily at 10:00, 2 hours; buy online in advance—especially in summer when they sell out; otherwise buy ticket 15 minutes early at the TI desk—not from the guide; +34 932 853 832, www.barcelonaturisme.com).

The TI at Plaça de Catalunya offers a **Picasso** walk through the streets of his youth and early career, finishing in the Picasso Museum (€35, discount online, year-round Tue and Sat at 10:00 and 15:00, Thu at 10:00, 2 hours including museum visit). It's smart to reserve these walks in advance and double-check departure times with the TI (www.barcelonaturisme.com).

"Free" Walking Tours

A few companies offer "free" walks that rely on—and expect—tips to stay in business. These walks can be a fun, casual way to get your bearings. **Runner Bean Tours,** run by Gorka, Ann-Marie, and a handful of local guides, is reliable and well established. They offer two 2.5-hour, English-only walks, one on the Old City and the other covering Gaudí (daily at 11:00, Old City tour also at 16:30 April-Oct, +34 636 108 776, www.runnerbeantours.com). They also do an array of fixed-price tours, including for families.

Local Guides

These are three reliable and good local guides that I've enjoyed working with for years. They do both walking tours and visits to museums and sights (from about €250/3 hours): **Sònia Crespo** (+34 610 442 052, sonia@barcelonaexperts.com), **Mónica Sánchez Sabater** (+34 639 319 759, monicasanchezsabater@gmail.com), and **Mariona Prats** (+34 607 605 776, mariona@barcelonasustainabletours.com).

José Soler is a great and fun-to-be-with local guide who enjoys tailoring a walk through his hometown to your interests (€295/4 hours, +34 615 059 326, details at www.pepitotours.com, info@pepitotours.com). He and his driver also take small groups by car, van, or minibus on four-hour Barcelona highlights tours and tours outside the city (from €525); they can meet you at your hotel, the cruise port, or the airport.

Adi Mahler is a knowledgeable local guide giving tours of the Gothic Quarter with a focus on the history of Jews in Barcelona (€45/person for 2 hours, €80/person for 4 hours, adi_mahler@yahoo.co.uk, +34 633 400 142).

Live Barcelona is a team of professional, enthusiastic guides led by Cristina Sanjuán since 1997. They offer a variety of walking or chauffeured tours and can arrange cruise excursions and transfers (from €225/3 hours, +34 609 205 844, www.livebarcelona.com, info@livebarcelona.com).

ON WHEELS

Guided Bus Tours

Catalunya Bus Turístic runs excursions to nearby destinations, including some that are difficult to reach by public transportation. Trips run April to October and include The **Montserrat Tour** (€64, Mon-Fri at 10:00, 6 hours); **Easy Montserrat** (€52, Sun-Fri at 10:00, 6 hours, includes the rack railway); and **Salvador Dalí sights** in Figueres and Girona (€82, Tue-Sun at 8:30, 11 hours). Itineraries depart from the Nord bus station, close to the Triumphal Arch (live trilingual commentary in Catalan, Spanish, and English; €5 extra for a more in-depth English audioguide; no tours mid-Nov-late March, book online for 10 percent discount, +34 932 805 805, www.catalunyabusturistic.com).

Hop-On, Hop-Off Buses

The handy hop-on, hop-off **Bus Turístic** offers two multistop circuits in colorful double-decker buses that go topless in sunny weather and are useful as a once-over-lightly tour or simply to get around. The two-hour **blue route** covers north Barcelona (most Gaudí sights, departs from El Corte Inglés on Plaça de Catalunya). The two-hour **red route** covers south Barcelona (Barri

Gòtic and Montjuïc, departs from the Ramblas side of Plaça de Catalunya). All have headphone commentary and free Wi-Fi (daily 9:00-19:00, buses run every 20-30 minutes depending on season, www.barcelonabusturistic.cat). One-day (€33) and two-day (€44) tickets, which you can buy on the bus, at the TI, or cheaper online, offer discounts on the city's major sights and walking tours. Another company, **Barcelona City Tour,** offers a nearly identical service (same price and discounts, www.barcelona.city-tour.com).

Bike Tours

Barcelona Bike Tour offers 2.5-hour bike tours taking you from sight to sight, mostly on bike paths and through parks, with stop-and-go commentary in English (€30, daily at 10:00, limited to 10 people—reserve online in advance, Carrer Tallers 45, +34 933 171 970, www.barcelonaciclotour.com).

　　Barcelona eBikes offers daily themed tours, including Gaudí Highlights (€40, daily at 11:00), Sagrada Família (€69, daily at 11:00, includes admission), and a Picasso and Bohemian tour (€40, daily at 16:00). Tours start at their office in El Born (Plaça San Agustín Vell 16, +34 935 480 457, www.barcelonaebikes.com).

SPECIALTY TOURS AND ACTIVITIES

Spanish Civil War Tours

Nick Lloyd is the author of *Forgotten Places: Barcelona and the Spanish Civil War.* He and his guiding partner, Catherine Howley, are passionate teachers who take small groups on walks through the Old City to explain the social context and significance of the Spanish Civil War (1936-1939) in Barcelona. History buffs really love this tour (€25/person, Mon-Tue and Thu-Sat mornings, fewer in winter, 3 hours with an hour-long stop in a café for a sit-down talk, English only, https://thespanishcivilwar.com).

Cooking Classes and Food Tours

Cook & Taste offers group cooking classes in which you'll make and eat traditional dishes paired with local wines (group classes daily at 11:00 and 17:00, €70/person, €12 extra for guided La Boqueria or Santa Caterina visit offered Tue-Sat morning or Fri afternoon before the cooking class, Carrer Paradís 3, +34 933 021 320, www.cookandtaste.net). They also offer private classes and a chef-guided gastronomic tour of gourmet food and wine shops and La Boqueria.

Food Lovers Company guides carefully select traditional and atmospheric spots where you can sample high-quality seasonal specialties as they share personal insights on Barcelona and its cuisine (from €150/person, morning or evening tours, 4 hours, 6 people maximum, +34 635 604 290, www.foodloverscompany.com, hello@foodloverscompany.com). They also offer an all-day private winery tour in the nearby Penedés region that includes stops at two family-run wineries, with tastings, brunch, and transport in a private van.

The Barcelona Taste takes small groups on guided walks, making three stops in roughly three hours. They enthusiastically introduce you to lots of local treats and drinks. Options include a lunch tour (12:45-15:30) in the Eixample and evening tours (19:00-22:00) in the Gothic Quarter or the up-and-coming Poble Sec neighborhood (from €113/person, Mon-Sat, reserve early in season, www.thebarcelonataste.com).

SIGHTS IN BARCELONA

The sights listed in this chapter are primarily arranged by neighborhood for handy sightseeing. When you see a 📖 in a listing, it means the sight is covered in much more depth in one of my walks or self-guided tours. This is why some of Barcelona's greatest sights get less coverage in this chapter—we'll explore them later in the book, where you'll also find info on avoiding lines, saving money, and finding a decent bite to eat nearby. 🎧 Many of the following sights are also covered in my free Barcelona City Walk and Eixample Walk audio tours.

For the most popular sights (the Picasso Museum and the big Modernista sights—Sagrada Família, Park Güell, Casa Batlló, and La Pedrera), book tickets online well in advance. For general tips, see the "Sightseeing" section in the Practicalities chapter.

ON OR NEAR THE RAMBLAS

📖 For a self-guided walk down this pedestrian boulevard, see the Ramblas Ramble chapter. For food and drink recommendations nearby, see the Eating in Barcelona chapter.

▲▲The Ramblas

Meandering through the heart of the Old City is the Ramblas, Barcelona's most famous boulevard. Named for the long-gone stream *(rambla)* whose course it followed, the Ramblas flows from Plaça de Catalunya, past the core of the Barri Gòtic, to the harborfront Columbus Monument. Boasting a generous pedestrian strip down the middle,

Barcelona at a Glance

▲▲▲Picasso Museum Extensive collection offering insight into the brilliant Spanish artist's early years. **Hours:** Tue-Sun 10:00-20:00, Nov-April until 19:00, closed Mon year-round. See page 53.

▲▲▲Sagrada Família Gaudí's remarkable, unfinished church—a masterpiece in progress. **Hours:** Mon-Sat 9:00-20:00, Sun from 10:30; March and Oct daily until 19:00, Nov-Feb until 18:00. See page 64.

▲▲The Ramblas Barcelona's colorful, gritty, tourist-filled pedestrian thoroughfare. See page 41.

▲▲Palace of Catalan Music Best Modernista interior in Barcelona. **Hours:** Various tours run daily 9:00-15:30, plus frequent concerts. See page 54.

▲▲La Pedrera (Casa Milà) Barcelona's quintessential Modernista building and Gaudí creation. **Hours:** Daily 9:00-20:30, Nov-Feb until 18:30; nighttime visits also available. See page 62.

▲▲Park Güell Colorful Gaudí-designed park overlooking the city. **Hours:** Daily April-Oct 9:30-22:00 (last entry at 19:30), rest of the year 9:30 until sunset. See page 65.

▲▲Catalan Art Museum World-class showcase of this region's art, including a substantial Romanesque collection. **Hours:** Tue-Sat 10:00-20:00 (Oct-April until 18:00), Sun 10:00-15:00, closed Mon year-round. See page 75.

▲La Boqueria Market Colorful but touristy produce market just off the Ramblas. **Hours:** Mon-Sat 8:00-20:30, closed Sun. See page 44.

▲Palau Güell Exquisitely curvy Gaudí interior and fantasy rooftop. **Hours:** Tue-Sun 10:00-20:00, Oct-March until 17:30, closed Mon year-round. See page 44.

▲Maritime Museum A sailor's delight, housed in a medieval shipyard. **Hours:** Daily 10:00-20:00. See page 46.

▲Barcelona Cathedral Colossal Gothic cathedral ringed by distinctive chapels. **Hours:** Mon-Fri 9:30-18:30, Sat until 17:15, Sun 14:00-17:00; access may be limited during services. See page 50.

▲*Sardana* **Dances** Traditional dance in which Catalans join hands in a circle, celebrating their proud identity. **Hours:** Every Sun at 11:15, many Sat at 18:00, no dances in Aug. See page 50.

▲**Frederic Marès Museum** Quirky museum highlighted by Marès' collection of bric-a-brac from 19th-century Barcelona. **Hours:** Tue-Sat 10:00-19:00, Sun until 20:00, closed Mon. See page 50.

▲**Barcelona History Museum—Plaça del Rei** One-stop trip through town history, from Roman times to today. **Hours:** Tue-Sat 10:00-19:00, Sun until 20:00, closed Mon. See page 51.

▲**Santa Caterina Market** Fine market hall built on the site of an old monastery and updated with a wavy Gaudí-inspired roof. **Hours:** Mon-Sat 7:30-15:30, Tue and Thu-Fri until 20:00, closed Sun; shorter hours Tue and Thu in July-Aug. See page 56.

▲**Church of Santa Maria del Mar** Catalan Gothic church built by wealthy medieval shippers. **Hours:** Mon-Sat 10:00-20:30, Sun until 18:00. See page 56.

▲**Sant Antoni Market** Local-feeling 19th-century market complex at the center of the El Raval neighborhood. **Hours:** Mon-Sat 8:00-20:30, closed Sun, clothing stalls also closed Tue. See page 59.

▲**Casa Batlló** Gaudí-designed home topped with fanciful dragon-inspired roof. **Hours:** Daily 9:00-20:00. See page 60.

▲**Fundació Joan Miró** World's best collection of works by Catalan modern artist Joan Miró and his contemporaries. **Hours:** Tue-Sat 10:00-20:00, Sun until 18:00, shorter hours in winter, closed Mon year-round. See page 71.

▲**Magic Fountains** Lively fountain spectacle near Plaça d'Espanya. **Hours:** June-Sept Wed-Sun 21:30-22:30, April-May and Oct Thu-Sat 21:00-22:00, winter Thu-Sat 20:00-21:00 (no shows in drought conditions and Jan-Feb). See page 79.

▲**CaixaForum** Modernista brick factory now occupied by a cultural center featuring good contemporary art exhibits. **Hours:** Daily 10:00-20:00. See page 80.

▲**Barcelona's Beaches** Fun-filled, man-made beaches reaching from the harbor to the Fòrum. See page 82.

the Ramblas feels like a long street festival packed with people—mostly tourists—out browsing. Though it was once vibrant with flowers, a bird market, and newspaper stands, today it's mostly just a big, fun, international promenade with a fabled history. Halfway down is the booming La Boqueria Market.

▲La Boqueria Market

Barcelona has many characteristic market halls, but this is the most central—and the most crowded. Housed in a cool glass-and-steel structure, La Boqueria features a wide variety of produce and Catalan edibles for which you'll pay a premium. Still, La Boqueria's handy location right in the heart of the Old City makes it well worth a visit. For less touristy markets, consider Santa Caterina in El Born (with avant-garde architecture; see page 126), La Concepció in the Eixample (with a neighborhood vibe; see page 159), or Sant Antoni near El Raval (see page 59).

Cost and Hours: Free, Mon-Sat 8:00-20:30, best mornings after 9:00, closed Sun, many stalls shut down early on Mon, Rambla 91, +34 933 182 017, www.boqueria.barcelona.

▲Palau Güell

Just as the Picasso Museum reveals a young genius on the verge of a breakthrough, this early building by Antoni Gaudí (completed in 1890) shows the architect taking his first tentative steps toward what would become his trademark curvy style. Dark and masculine, with castle-like rooms, Palau Güell (pronounced "gway") was custom-built to house the wealthy Güell family and gives an insight into Gaudí's artistic genius. The rooftop has

his signature colorful tile mosaic chimneys and offers a panorama of the city. While some people will find this redundant if also visiting La Pedrera, others will appreciate this exquisite building for its delightfully loopy rooftop and far fewer crowds.

Cost and Hours: €12 ticket includes good audioguide; open Tue-Sun 10:00-20:00, Oct-March until 17:30, closed Mon year-round; last entry one hour before closing, rooftop closes when raining; guided tour in English Sat at 10:30; a half-block off the Ramblas at Carrer Nou de la Rambla 3, Metro: Liceu or Drassanes, +34 934 725 775, www.palauguell.cat.

Visiting the House: The parabolic-arch **entryways,** viewable from the outside, are the first clue that this is not a typical townhouse. For inspiration, Gaudí hung a chain to create a U-shape, then flipped it upside-down. The wrought-iron doors were cleverly designed so that those inside could see out, and light from the outside could get in—but not vice versa.

The Neo-Gothic **cellar,** with its mushroom pillars, was used as a stable—notice the rings on some of the posts used to tie up the horses (WCs are in the far corner).

A grand staircase leads to the **living space,** including a family room, dining room, and so on. Photos show how the Güell clan—with their textile riches—originally furnished the place. The intricacy of Gaudí's design work evokes the impossibly complex patterns that decorate great Moorish palaces. Step onto the terrace out back and look at the bay window, elaborately decorated in a sort of industrial fantasy.

The tall, skinny, atrium-like **central hall** fills several floors under a parabolic dome. Behind the grand, gilded doors is a personal chapel, which made it easy to instantly convert the hall from a secular space to a religious one.

Upstairs are Isabel Güell's bedrooms, rooms with period furniture, and a film telling the story of the two men behind this building: Gaudí and his patron, the building's resident and namesake, Eusebi Güell. At a time when most wealthy urbanites were moving to the Eixample, Güell decided to stay in the Old City.

The most dramatic space is the **rooftop;** Gaudí slathered the 20 chimneys and ventilation towers with bits of stained glass, ceramic tile, and marble to create a forest of giant upside-down ice-cream cones. Move around the rooftop, which follows the form of the parabolic dome you just saw inside, and admire the view of Barcelona from this high perch.

Plaça Reial

This genteel-feeling square, with palm trees and a pair of Gaudí-designed lampposts, is a welcoming open space in the otherwise enclosed Old City. You can sit down for a drink at one of the touristy bars, or just lean up against the fountain and take it all in.

LOWER RAMBLAS AND HARBORFRONT
▲Maritime Museum (Museu Marítim)

Barcelona's medieval shipyard, the best preserved in the entire Mediterranean, is home to an excellent museum near the bottom of the Ramblas. The museum's perma-
nent collection covers the salty history of ships and navigation from the 13th to the 20th century. Even if you choose not to pay for a full visit, the building is worth a look; interesting free exhibits are in the lobby (inside the main entrance facing the water), where you can get a glimpse of the building's interior.

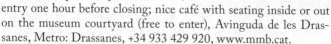

Cost and Hours: €10, free Sun from 15:00, ticket includes visit to *Santa Eulàlia* boat; open daily 10:00-20:00, last entry one hour before closing; nice café with seating inside or out on the museum courtyard (free to enter), Avinguda de les Drassanes, Metro: Drassanes, +34 933 429 920, www.mmb.cat.

Visiting the Museum: Scan the QR code at the ticket desk to access the audioguide. The building's cavernous halls evoke the 14th-century days when Catalunya was a naval and shipbuilding power, cranking out 30 huge galleys each winter. As in the US today, military and commercial ventures mingled as Catalunya built its trading empire.

Start your visit by going up the ramp to the right and into a screening room, where a **film** tells the history of shipyards and galleys. In the next room is a model of the shipyard buildings *(drassanes)*, which today have been converted into the Maritime Museum. Head into the next room and, on the far right, find a **model** of 15th-century Barcelona's waterfront. Notice the shipyard all the way to the left, the old medieval walls surrounding the city, and the Church of Santa Maria del Mar to the right.

Then head to the highlight: the impressively huge and rich-ly decorated replica of the royal galley of *Juan de Austria,* which fought in the 1571 Battle of Lepanto. To get a seagull's-eye view, go up the stairs to a raised platform at the bow and midship. Displays describe its history and daily life on a galley. At the stern of the boat, a screening room shows a five-minute first-person drama-tized video about galley life.

Several less-interesting boats are scattered around the halls. The *7 Vaixells, 7 Històries* (7 Boats, 7 Stories) exhibit delves into the boats' experiences with conflict, leisure, discoveries, cargo transport, pirating, travel, and technological advances.

Nearby: Your museum ticket includes entrance to the *Santa*

Eulàlia, an early 20th-century schooner docked a short walk from the Columbus Monument (otherwise €3; Tue-Fri and Sun 10:00-20:00, Sat 14:00-20:00, shorter hours Nov-March, closed Mon year-round). On Saturday mornings, you can sail around the harbor on the schooner for three hours (Sat 10:00-13:00, €15 for adults, €9 for kids 7-14, sign up online well in advance, www.mmb.cat).

Columbus Monument (Monument a Colóm)

Located where the Ramblas hits the harbor, this 200-foot-tall monument was built for the 1888 world's fair and commemorates Columbus' visit to Barcelona following his first trip to America. A tight four-person elevator takes you to a glassed-in observation area at the top for congested and average views (for better options, see the "Barcelona's Best Views" sidebar, later). A small and usually uncrowded TI is inside the base of the monument.

SIGHTS

Cost and Hours: Elevator-€8, daily 8:30-14:30, may stay open later when cruise ships are in town, Plaça Portal de la Pau.

Golondrinas Cruises

At the harbor near the Columbus Monument, tourist boats called *golondrinas* offer two unguided trips, giving you a view of Barcelona's (unimpressive) skyline from the water. The shorter version goes around the harbor in 40 minutes (€8, departures Sat-Sun 11:15-16:15). The hour-long cruise goes beyond the harbor (€10, departures daily 11:30-18:00, Sat-Sun also at 18:00, more in summer, fewer in winter, +34 934 423 106, www.lasgolondrinas.com).

BARRI GÒTIC

📖 For more details on this area and several of the following sights, see the Barri Gòtic Walk chapter or 🎧 download my free Barcelona City Walk audio tour.

Avinguda del Portal de l'Angel

This broad, traffic-free boulevard, which connects the modern Plaça de Catalunya to its historic cathedral district, is Barcelona's most well-trodden street. Although overrun with Spanish and international chain stores, its circa-1888 remodel has left it with a certain dignified air. Just off this drag, you'll discover humble old churches and the famous restaurant called Els Quatre Gats, where a young Picasso got his start. For tips on shopping along this street, see page 218.

SIGHTS

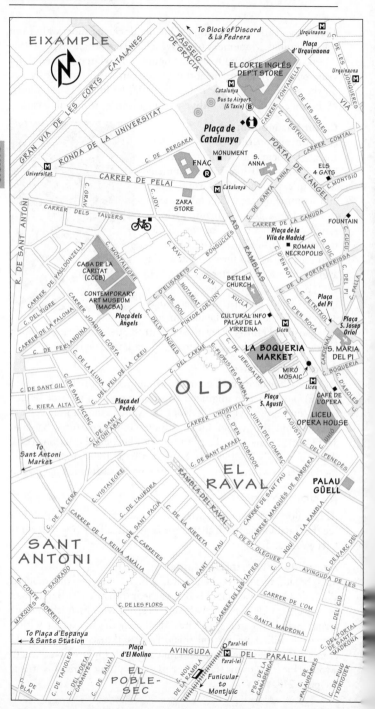

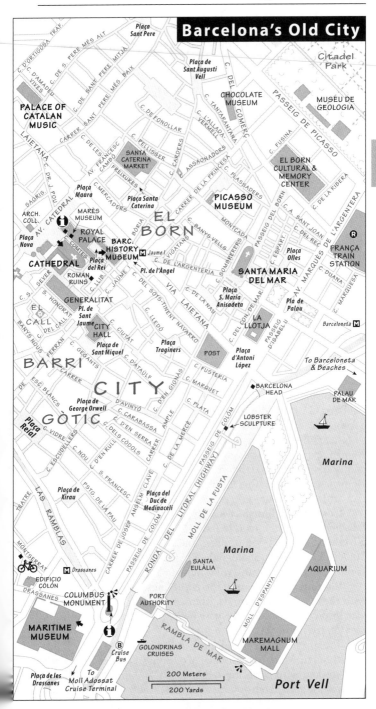

SIGHTS

Barcelona's Old City

Plaça Sant Pere

Citadel Park

C. D'ORTIGOSA TRAF.

C. C. DE S. PERE MÉS ALT

C. D'AMADEU VIVES

Plaça de Sant Augusti Vell

C. DEL COMERÇ

PASSEIG DE PICASSO

C. DE SANT PERE MÉS BAIX

CHOCOLATE MUSEUM

MUSÉU DE GEOLOGIA

PALACE OF CATALAN MUSIC

C. DE FONOLLAR

C. TANTARANTANA

C. L'ALLADA-VERMELL

CARRER SANT PERE MÉS BAIX

C. FUSINA

LAIETANA C. DR. J. POU

C. DE LES.FRANCESC CAMPO

C. PELLISSER

SANTA CATERINA MARKET

C. CARDERS

C. ASSAONADORS

EL BORN CULTURAL & MEMORY CENTER

C. DE LA RIBERA

SAGRIS.

AV. CATEDRAL

C. MERCADERS

C. FREIXURES

C. DE LA PRINCESA

C. FLASSADERS

Plaça Maara

Plaça Santa Caterina

C. BANYS VELLS

MONTCADA

PICASSO MUSEUM

PASSEIG DEL BORN

C. A. SANT-JOAN

C. DE L'ARGENTERIA

ARCH. COLL.

MARÈS MUSEUM

EL BORN

BORIA

C. VIGATANS

C. DEL REC

Plaça Nova

ROYAL PALACE

COMTES

BARC. HISTORY MUSEUM

Jaume I

FRANÇA TRAIN STATION

C. ESPART.

C. SOMBRERERS

SANTA MARIA DEL MAR

C. DUANA

CATHEDRAL

S. SEVER

C. JAUME I

Plaça del Rei

C. DE L'ARGENTERIA

Plaça Olles

C. MARQUESA

ROMAN RUINS

C. GLIUB

Pl. de l'Àngel

VIA LAIETANA

Plaça S. Maria Anisadeta

Pla de Palau

AV. MARQUÈS DE L'ARGENTERA

EL CALL

S. HONORAT

GENERALITAT

C. DE LA NAU

Barceloneta

BARRI

BANYS NOUS

DEL CALL

FERRAN

Pl. de Sant Jaume

CITY HALL

C. LLEDÓ

C. DEL SOTS-TINENT NAVARRO

C. DEL DORMER

LA LLOTJA

PASSEIG D'ISABEL II

C. GEGANTS

Plaça de Sant Miquel

Plaça Traginers

POST

Plaça d'Antoni López

To Barceloneta & Beaches

CARRER

C. D'ATAÜLF

C. CIUTAT

PALAU DE MAR

CITY

D'AVINYÓ

C. D'EN GIGNAS

BARCELONA HEAD

DE ESC. BLANCS

Plaça de George Orwell

C. CARABASSA

C. MARQUET

GÒTIC

G. VIDRELL

C. D'EN SERRA

AMPLE

C. PLATA

LOBSTER SCULPTURE

Plaça Reial

C. ESCUDELLERS

C. NOU

C. D'EN RULL

C. DELS CODOLS

C. DE LA MERCE

PASSEIG DE COLÓM

Marina

THEATRE

LAS RAMBLAS

Plaça de Xirau

PSTG. DE LA PAU

C. FRANCESC

ANSELM CLAVÉ

Plaça del Duc de Medinaceli

MOLL DE LA FUSTA

CARRER DE JOSEP

PASSEIG DE COLÓM

RONDA DEL LITORAL (HIGHWAY)

Marina

MONTSERRAT

Drassanes

SANTA EULÀLIA

AQUARIUM

EDIFICIO COLÓN

DRASSANES

COLUMBUS MONUMENT

PORT AUTHORITY

MOLL D'ESPANYA

MARITIME MUSEUM

MAREMAGNUM MALL

Plaça de les Drassanes

To Moll Adossat Cruise Terminal

Cruise Bus

GOLONDRINAS CRUISES

RAMBLA DE MAR

200 Meters

200 Yards

Port Vell

SIGHTS

▲Barcelona Cathedral (Catedral de Barcelona)

The city's 14th-century, Gothic-style cathedral (with a Neo-Gothic facade) has played a significant role in Barcelona's history—but as far as grand cathedrals go, this one is relatively unexciting. Still, it's worth a visit to see its richly decorated chapels, finely carved choir, tomb of Santa Eulàlia, and restful cloister with gurgling fountains and resident geese. Minor sights within include a rooftop terrace and an altarpiece museum.

Cost and Hours: €11 includes cathedral, choir, view terrace, museum, and cloister. Cathedral open Mon-Fri 9:30-18:30, Sat until 17:15, Sun 14:00-17:00; last entry 45 minutes before closing, access may be limited during services; +34 933 428 262, www.catedralbcn.org.

☐ See the Barcelona Cathedral Tour chapter.

▲*Sardana* Dances

If you're in town on a weekend, you can see the *sardana*, a traditional dance in which Barcelonans link hands and dance in a circle in an expression of their Catalan identity (Sun at 11:15, many Sat at 18:00, no dances in Aug, event lasts 1 hour, in Pla de la Seu square in front of the cathedral; for details, see the sidebar on page 7).

▲Frederic Marès Museum (Museu Frederic Marès)

This delightful and often overlooked museum, adjacent to the cathedral, features the eclectic collection of Frederic Marès (1893-1991), a local sculptor and packrat. The museum sprawls through several old Barri Gòtic buildings around a peaceful courtyard. It offers a fascinating look at ancient Roman statues from this region and is an exquisite warehouse of Romanesque and Gothic Christian art from Catalunya.

Cost and Hours: €4.20, free first Sun of the month and all other Sun from 15:00; open Tue-Sat 10:00-19:00, Sun until 20:00, closed Mon; audioguide-€1, Plaça de Sant Iu 5, Metro: Jaume I, +34 932 563 500, www.museumares.bcn.cat.

Visiting the Museum: The entire museum is well described with the essential audioguide. Think of the first two floors as private inspiration for Marès, whose own art can be found in his former library/studio on floor 3.

The top floor offers a glimpse at life in 19th-century Barcelona through Marès' fascinating "Collector's Cabinet"—an entire attic stacked with curiosities. This quirky and intimate collection features a dozen rooms of scissors, keys, irons, fans, nutcrackers, stamps, pipes, snuffboxes, opera glasses, pocket watches, bicycles, toy soldiers, dolls, and other bric-a-brac.

Plaça de Sant Jaume

This open-feeling square (a rarity in the tight Barri Gòtic) is flanked by the two most important administrative buildings in Catalunya: the Palau de la Generalitat (home of the autonomous Catalan government) and the Barcelona City Hall.

Roman Temple of Augustus (Temple Roma d'August)

Tucked inside a small medieval courtyard, four columns from an ancient temple of Augustus are a reminder of Barcelona's Roman origins. The temple, dating from the late first century BC, stood at one corner of the ancient forum quarter.

Cost and Hours: Free, Tue-Sat 10:00-19:00, Sun until 20:00, Mon until 14:00, Carrer del Paradís 10, +34 932 562 122, www.barcelona.cat/museuhistoria/en.

Plaça del Rei

Perhaps the best place in town to get a feel for Barcelona's faint connection to Old World royalty, this "Square of the Monarch" offers a good view of the Royal Palace, where Spanish kings and Catalan counts once resided. Although the palace complex is mostly closed to tourists, parts of the building are used for exhibits for the Barcelona History Museum.

▲Barcelona History Museum—Plaça del Rei (Museu d'Història de Barcelona)

At the Plaça del Rei branch of the city history museum (MUHBA for short), you'll see objects gathered from archaeological digs around Barcelona. But the real highlight is an underground labyrinth of excavated Roman ruins. Though the museum is housed in part of the former Royal Palace complex, you'll see only a bit of that grand space. Instead, the focus is on the exhibits on the basement level. You'll find English explanations and a handful of video screens showing what this site must have once looked like in ancient times.

Cost and Hours: €7; includes other MUHBA branches; free first Sun of month and all other Sun from 15:00; open Tue-Sat 10:00-19:00, Sun until 20:00, closed Mon; Plaça del Rei, enter on Carrer del Veguer, Metro: Jaume I, +34 932 562 122, www.barcelona.cat/museuhistoria/en.

Visiting the Museum: Start with the 10-minute introductory video in the **theater** (at the end of the ground floor). Then take an elevator down 65 feet (and 2,000 years—see the date spin back as you descend) to the **basement** to stroll the now-underground streets of Roman Barcino—founded by Emperor Augustus around 10 BC.

Barcelona: From Small to Sprawl

The city of Barcelona has grown with its history. The original Roman town from the time of Christ was contained inside the knot of streets clustered around today's cathedral and enclosed by an oval-shaped ring of Roman walls (stretching basically southeast from the square in front of the cathedral).

When Rome fell (around AD 476), the Christian Visigoths made the cathedral the center of town, and the populace remained huddled inside the Roman walls. During the Middle Ages, the city was ruled briefly by Moors (714-801) and Franks (ninth century). When the Counts of Barcelona unified Catalunya (10th century), the city began expanding. They built churches outside the Roman walls (or *extra muro*), each a magnet gathering a small community. By 1250, they needed to build a larger wall to contain these new settlers. This medieval wall stretched from Plaça de Catalunya to the sea, embracing the whole Old City. The hilltop of Montjuïc—outside the residential area—was topped with a harbor-guarding fortress.

Barcelona is a good example of how a city's architectural heritage rises and falls with economic times. In the 14th century, when the Mediterranean was the epicenter of trade, Barcelona thrived. That's why there are a lot of Gothic buildings here. After 1492, when the Age of Discovery opened up new sea routes, trade shifted to the Atlantic and away from Mediterranean ports. The following centuries saw little grand building in Barcelona.

Then, in the 19th century, Barcelona bounced back, powered by the Industrial Revolution. By 1850, the city was bursting at the seams. The outer wall was torn down and replaced by circular boulevards (named Rondas, meaning "to go around"). The city expanded in a regimented grid of modern boulevards—an urban waffle known as the Eixample. With affluence came big shots with big egos and plenty of money to finance the Modernista architectural wonders that now grace the city.

In 1992, Barcelona hosted the Summer Olympics, which accelerated modernization and stoked Barcelona's economy. In a brilliant move, organizers of the games housed much of the one-time rush of visitors on huge cruise ships, jump-starting a thriving cruise ship industry. Today, Barcelona is the leading cruise port in Europe, hosting about 900 cruise ships annually.

A big issue for the character of the city is the end of rent control for landowners and their tenants in the city center. Many charming shops that add character to the old quarter have been driven out of business, replaced by branches of corporate retailers. But the city's rising affluence has also kept it vibrant and colorful.

Today, Barcelona's population sprawls beyond city maps, creating a greater metropolitan area of some 5 million people—more than half of all the people in Catalunya.

The history is so strong here, you can smell it as you stroll across walkways over the excavated ruins of Roman Barcelona. This was a working-class part of town. The route leads through areas used for laundering clothes and dyeing garments, the remains of a factory that salted fish and produced *garum* (a fish-derived sauce used extensively in ancient Roman cooking), and facilities for winemaking. Next, wander through bits of a seventh-century early Christian church and an 11th-century bishop's palace that show Barcelona through its glory days in the Middle Ages. The final section downstairs takes you through Visigothic remains, including the octagonal font where Christians were baptized.

Finally, head upstairs to see a **model** of the city from the early 16th century. From here, you can enter **Tinell Hall** (part of the Royal Palace), with its long, graceful, rounded vaults and displays on local medieval history in a Mediterranean context. The nearby 14th-century **Chapel of St. Agatha** sometimes has free temporary exhibits.

With a little extra time, circle back to the innovative **"Barcelona Flashback"** exhibit one floor above the ticket desk. It's a refreshing display of objects, stories, and connections from the 20th century where participants are invited to interpret Barcelona's heritage on their own. Along the way, you'll find several unexpected terraces overlooking the Gothic Quarter.

EL BORN

El Born is home to the Picasso Museum, with narrow lanes sprouting from the neighborhood's main artery, Passeig del Born. 📖 For a neighborhood tour—including exhibits within the El Born Cultural and Memory Center and the interior of the Church of Santa Maria del Mar—see the El Born Walk chapter.

▲▲▲Picasso Museum (Museu Picasso)

Pablo Picasso may have made his career in Paris, but the years he spent in Barcelona—from age 14 through 23—were among the most formative of his life. It was here that young Pablo mastered the realistic painting style of his artistic forebears—and it was also here that he first felt the freedom that allowed him to leave that all behind and give in to his creative, experimental urges. When he left Barcelona, Picasso headed for Paris...and revolutionized art forever.

The pieces in this excellent museum capture that priceless moment just before this bold young thinker changed the world. While you won't find Picasso's famous later Cubist works here, you will enjoy a representative sweep of his early years. You'll also see works from his twilight years, as well as a roomful of works that reflect the childlike exuberance of an old man playing like a young kid on the French Riviera. It's the top collection of Picassos in his native country and the best anywhere of his early years.

Cost and Hours: €12 timed-entry ticket to permanent collection; free Thu late afternoon-close and all day first Sun of month—you must also reserve entry during free hours (up to 4 days ahead); open Tue-Sun 10:00-20:00, Nov-April until 19:00, closed Mon year-round; audioguide-€5, English-language tours run Tue at 15:00 and 16:00 and Sun at 11:00; confirm opening days and times online; Carrer de Montcada 15, +34 932 563 000, https://museupicassobcn.cat.

Advance Tickets Recommended: Buy online in advance to guarantee entry. If you have trouble with the museum's website, your next-best option is the ArticketBCN, which lets you skip the ticket-buying line and visit whenever you wish (ask museum staff when you arrive).

📖 See the Picasso Museum Tour chapter.

▲▲Palace of Catalan Music (Palau de la Música Catalana)

This concert hall, built in just three years, was finished in 1908. Its tall facade has many beautiful decorations, but its location—on

a narrow street that offers little perspective—makes it hard to appreciate from the outside. Still, the building, by Lluís Domènech i Montaner, boasts my favorite Modernista interior in town. Its inviting arches lead you into the 2,138-seat hall, which is accessible only with a tour (or by attending a concert). A kaleidoscopic skylight features a choir singing around the sun, while playful carvings and mosaics celebrate music and Catalan culture. If you're interested in Modernisme, this tour is one of the best experiences in town—and helps balance the hard-to-avoid focus on Gaudí as "Mr. Modernisme."

Cost and Hours: 50-minute **guided tour** in English—€20, runs daily on the hour 9:00-15:00, tour times may vary with performance schedule; 50-minute **audioguide tour**—€18, every 30 minutes until 15:30, you'll download an audio tour to your phone, bring your own earbuds/headphones; **self-guided tour**—€16, available 9:00-15:30, follow along with a printed brochure. Tickets are sold on the website, just inside the ornate entrance on Carrer de Sant Pere Més, and at the box office around the corner at Carrer Palau de la Música 4. Metro: Urquinaona, 10-minute walk from the Barcelona Cathedral or Picasso Museum, +34 932 957 207, www.palaumusica.cat.

Barcelona's Best Views

Barcelona's delightful architecture is best seen up close, but to fully appreciate the city's scenic beauty, take advantage of one of many panoramic viewpoints. Many require an admission fee, but some are free, such as Miramar park at Montjuïc. When deciding between viewpoints, target the ones that are already on your sightseeing route.

Cable Car: Although it's pricey and slow to load, the Aeri del Port cable car between Montjuïc and Barceloneta (in either direction) offers a dramatic moving panorama of the city. See page 70.

SIGHTS

Park Güell: Inviting, curvy benches along a spectacular terrace offer sweeping views of Barcelona from this foothills park (ticket required). Climb even higher to the Calvary hilltop for a free bird's-eye view of the park and city below. See the Park Güell Tour chapter.

Sagrada Família Towers: Elevators take you up the Nativity facade or the Passion facade for a good view of the city and a unique angle on this fascinating church (tickets required). See the Sagrada Família Tour chapter.

Montjuïc: Overlooking the port, this hilltop affords city views from its castle ramparts (ticket required) and Miramar viewpoint park (free), as well as from the Catalan Art Museum's terrace and stylish restaurant. See page 67.

El Corte Inglés: The gigantic department store on Plaça de Catalunya has a great view cafeteria on its ninth floor. See page 218.

La Pedrera: The rooftop of this Gaudí masterpiece offers up-close views of fairy-tale chimneys, plus a vista of the Eixample and the distant spires of the Sagrada Família (ticket required). See page 62.

Las Arenas Mall: Take a pay glass elevator or escalate for free (from inside the building) to the restaurant-ringed roof terrace atop this former bullring for views of the World Expo Fairgrounds and Montjuïc. See page 81.

Tibidabo: The city's highest peak offers almost limitless (but distant) city and Mediterranean views—if the weather and air quality cooperate. See page 66.

Barcelona Cathedral: An elevator (included in your entrance fee) takes you up to a view terrace for an expansive city view from the heart of the Barri Gòtic. See page 50.

Concerts: An excellent way to see the hall is by attending one of its frequent concerts (see website for details, box office +34 932 957 207). To see the Modernista main concert hall, be sure the show is being held in the **Sala de Concerts**—not the new Petit Palau hall.

▲Santa Caterina Market (Mercat de Santa Caterina)

This eye-catching market hall was built on the ruins of an old Dominican monastery, then renovated in 2006 with a wildly colorful, swooping, Gaudí-inspired roof and shell built around its original white walls (a good exhibition at the rear entrance provides a view of the foundations and English explanations). Come for the outlandish architecture but stay for the food and the local color (it lacks the tourist logjam of La Boqueria). It's one of my favorite lunch spots in town—either at the recommended **Cuines Santa Caterina** (with inviting restaurant seating inside and out) or at one of several tapas bars in the market. These tapas bars epitomize all that is good with this kind of eating in Spain.

Cost and Hours: Free; Mon-Sat 7:30-15:30, Tue and Thu-Fri until 20:00, closed Sun; shorter hours Tue and Thu in July-Aug; Avinguda de Francesc Cambó 16, +34 933 195 740, https://mercatsantacaterina.com.

▲Church of Santa Maria del Mar
(Basílica de Santa Maria del Mar)

This so-called "Cathedral of the Sea" was built entirely with local funds and labor in the heart of the wealthy merchant El Born quarter. Proudly independent, the church features a purely Catalan Gothic interior that was forcibly uncluttered of its Baroque decor by civil war belligerents.

Cost and Hours: Free entry during worship Mon-Sat 18:00-20:30 and Sun 10:00-13:00; otherwise entry is €5 (€10 to visit the rooftop) Mon-Sat 10:00-18:00 and Sun 14:00-18:00, when the interior is illuminated and you have access to the choir and the crypt. Guided rooftop tours generally run Sat-Sun on the hour during paid-entry times (€14, 1 hour, check for English tours and sign up at the door or on the website). Plaça Santa Maria, Metro: Jaume I, +34 933 102 390, www.santamariadelmarbarcelona.org.

El Born Cultural and Memory Center
(El Born Centre de Cultura i Memòria)

Occupying the cast-iron structure of a 19th-century market, the El Born Cultural and Memory Center hosts an exhibition devoted to Barcelona in the 18th century—including a Catalan rebellion in 1714, an active medieval archaeological site, and temporary exhibits.

Cost and Hours: Center—free and open Tue-Sun 10:00-

20:00, Oct-Feb until 19:00, closed Mon year-round; *Barcelona 1700* exhibit—€3, includes audioguide, English tours generally available Tue-Fri at 16:00; Plaça Comercial 12, https://elbornculturaimemoria.barcelona.cat.

Chocolate Museum (Museu de la Xocolata)

This museum—operated by the local confectioners' guild—tells the story of chocolate from Aztecs to Europeans via the port of Barcelona, where it was first unloaded and processed. It's a surprisingly serious museum, with good English information, some old chocolate-making equipment, and fancy audiovisual displays. But the history lesson is just an excuse to show off a series of remarkably ornate chocolate sculptures. These works of edible art—which change every year but often include such themes as Don Quixote or Gaudí's Sagrada Família—begin as store-window displays for Easter or Christmas. Once the holiday passes, the confectioners bring the sculptures here to be admired.

Cost and Hours: €6, free for kids 6 and under; Tue-Sat 10:00-19:00, Sun until 15:00, closed Mon; between Picasso Museum and Citadel Park at Carrer del Comerç 36, Metro: Jaume I, +34 932 687 878, www.museuxocolata.cat.

EL RAVAL AND NEARBY

Historically edgy El Raval is Barcelona's "new El Born"—a bohemian-chic magnet for the young and trendy and the foodie crowd. El Born, while still lots of fun, is well discovered, and higher rents are driving away small galleries and artisan shops (and opening the door to the big chains). Now El Raval (and the surrounding neighborhoods of Sant Antoni and El Poble-Sec) is the new frontier for legit local businesses. Once-congested streets are becoming pedestrian-only, lined with creative and fun-loving shops, cafés, bars, and restaurants. Entrepreneurs, artists, and chefs with more vision than money are finding their futures in El Raval.

El Raval Stroll

To explore this area, I'd follow this route (see map): From the top of the Ramblas, take a right on Carrer del Bonsuccés, which becomes Carrer d'Elisabets and leads to **the Museum of Contemporary Art** and Casa de la Caritat (a cultural center). Then turn left on Carrer dels Àngels to reach Carrer del Carme, where a right takes you to the community square at **Plaça del Pedró.**

Continue down Carrer de Sant Antoni Abat to the **Sant Antoni Market**—a massive 19th-century hall that's just inside the Sant Antoni neighborhood. Then follow tree-lined Ronda de Sant Pau to Carrer del Parlament, which ends at the Poble Sec Metro stop on wide Avinguda del Paral-lel. Cross this busy street into the **El Poble-Sec** neighborhood at the base of the Montjuïc hill. Fol-

SIGHTS

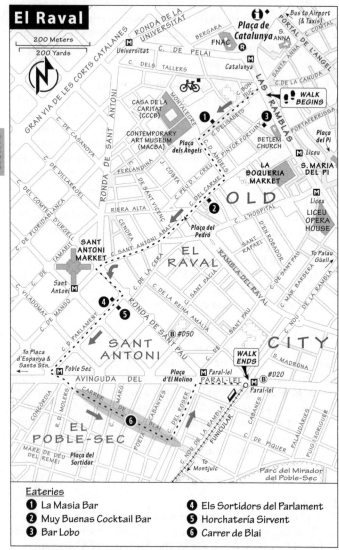

El Raval

200 Meters
200 Yards

Bus to Airport (& Taxis)
Plaça de Catalunya
FNAC
Universitat C. DE PELAI
Catalunya
WALK BEGINS
GRAN VIA DE LES CORTS CATALANES
RONDA DE LA UNIVERSITAT
BERGARA
C. DELS TALLERS
CASA DE LA CARITAT (CCCB)
CONTEMPORARY ART MUSEUM (MACBA)
Plaça dels Àngels
BETLEM CHURCH
Plaça del Pi
Liceu
S. MARIA DEL PI
LA BOQUERIA MARKET
O L D
Plaça del Pedró
EL RAVAL
LICEU OPERA HOUSE
To Palau Güell
SANT ANTONI MARKET
Sant Antoni
C I T Y
RONDA DE SANT PAU
#D50
WALK ENDS
SANT ANTONI
Plaça d'El Molino
Paral-lel
PARAL-LEL
#D20
Paral-lel
To Plaça d'Espanya & Sants Stn.
Poble Sec
AVINGUDA DEL PARAL-LEL
EL POBLE-SEC
FUNICULAR
Plaça del Sortidor
To Montjuïc
Parc del Mirador del Poble-Sec

Eateries
1 La Masia Bar
2 Muy Buenas Cocktail Bar
3 Bar Lobo
4 Els Sortidors del Parlament
5 Horchatería Sirvent
6 Carrer de Blai

low the pedestrian street Carrer de Blai (with cheap tapas bars) and Carrer del Roser to Metro Paral-lel. For eating recommendations along this route, see page 199.

Museum of Contemporary Art (MACBA)

The MACBA, perfectly situated in the trendy El Raval neighborhood, is an artistic community aimed at encouraging interest in contemporary art and culture. The museum hosts exhibits of various contemporary art from the second half of the 20th century to today, with a focus on learning and research.

Cost and Hours: €12; Mon and Wed-Sat 11:00-19:30, Sun until 15:00, closed Tue; Plaça dels Àngels 1, +34 934 813 368, www.macba.cat.

▲Sant Antoni Market (Mercat de Sant Antoni)

This sprawling market complex, spanning an entire block, was built near the former gate of Sant Antoni and was completed in 1882 (the same year work on the Sagrada Família began). Some of the food stalls have been run by the same families for generations: The Masclans family has been selling salted cod here since the market was inaugurated. A recent renovation brought the clothing stalls *(encats)* that once surrounded the market inside, lining the perimeter of the building. A popular outdoor flea market pops up here every Sunday, selling books, antiques, and other collectibles.

Unlike La Boqueria Market on the touristy Ramblas, Sant Antoini is a market made for locals (notice their shopping carts), and there are just a few eateries. **Casa Blanca,** in the center of the market, is a good choice for a sit-down meal.

Cost and Hours: Free; Mon-Sat 8:00-20:30, closed Sun, clothing stalls also closed Tue; Carrer del Comte d'Urgell 1, +34 934 263 521, www.mercatdesantantoni.com.

THE EIXAMPLE

For many visitors, Modernista architecture is Barcelona's main draw. And one name tops them all: Antoni Gaudí (1852-1926). Barcelona is an architectural scrapbook of Gaudí's galloping gables and organic curves. A devoted Catalan and Catholic, he immersed himself in each project, often living on-site. At various times, he called Park Güell, La Pedrera (Casa Milà), and the Sagrada Família home. For more on Gaudí and some of his contemporaries, and to learn about Modernisme, see the Eixample Walk chapter.

At the heart of the Modernista movement was the Eixample, a carefully planned "new town" just beyond the Old City with wide sidewalks, hardy shade trees, and a rigid grid plan cropped at the corners to create space and lightness at each intersection. Conveniently, all this new construction provided a generation of Modernista architects with a blank canvas for creating boldly experimental designs. At the edge of the Eixample is Gaudí's greatest piece of work, the yet-to-be-finished Sagrada Família.

Modernista Sights in the Eixample

In this section, I've focused on the big Modernista sights in the Eixample, starting at the center of this neighborhood with the **Block of Discord,** where three colorful Modernista facades com-

SIGHTS

pete for your attention: Casa
Batlló, Casa Amatller, and Casa
Lleó Morera (all on Passeig de
Gràcia—near the Metro stop of
the same name—between Carrer del Consell de Cent and Carrer d'Aragó). All were built by
well-known Modernista architects at the end of the 19th century. Because the mansions look

as though they are trying to outdo each other in creative twists,
locals nicknamed the noisy block the "Block of Discord." Of the
three houses, two are open to visitors—Casa Batlló and the less-
crowded Casa Amatller.

By the way, if you're tempted to snap photos from the middle
of the street, be careful—Gaudí died after being struck by a street-
car.

From the Block of Discord, you're four blocks from Gaudí's **La
Pedrera** and a quick subway ride from his **Sagrada Família.**

Even though Modernisme revolved around the Eixample,
traces of this style can also be found elsewhere. Other Modernista
highlights include Gaudí's **Park Güell,** where he put his colorful
stamp on 30 acres of greenery, **Palau Güell,** just off the Ramblas,
and **Casa Vicens** in the Gràcia district—the first house Gaudí designed. There's also Lluís Domènech i Montaner's **Palace of Catalan Music** in El Born and Josep Puig i Cadafalch's **CaixaForum** at
the base of Montjuïc.

For a tour of the Eixample, including a route that connects some of these sights, 📖 see the Eixample Walk chapter or
🎧 download my free Eixample Walk audio tour.

▲Casa Batlló

While the highlight of this Gaudí-designed residence is the roof,
the interior is also interesting—and much more over-the-top than
La Pedrera's. The house features
a funky mushroom-shaped fireplace nook on the main floor, a
blue and white ceramic-slath-
ered atrium, an attic with parabolic arches, and a dragon-inspired rooftop. The Gold ticket
includes a good (if long-winded)
virtual-reality guide on a tablet
that depicts the rooms as they
may have been.

Cost and Hours: €39 Blue ticket includes audioguide; €49

Modernista Sights

See detail map

Park Güell B #24

TERRACE — GAUDÍ HOUSE

B #116

Bus Turístic

#24 B

AVE. DE L'ESTATUT DE CATALUNYA

RECINTE MODERNISTA DE SANT PAU (FORMER HOSPITAL)

Sant Pau Dos de Maig

B DE DALT

Alfons X M

GUINARDÓ

C. DE L'ESCORIAL

Plaça Lesseps

Lesseps M B #116

CASA VICENS

Fontana M

Plaça del Sol

GRÀCIA

C. DEL TORRENT DE L'OLLA

DE L'OR

B Joanic #116 M

TRAVESSERA DE GRÀCIA

TRAVESSERA

AV. DE GAUDÍ

CARRER DE CARTAGENA

SAGRADA FAMÍLIA

Sagrada Família M

#50

C. DE MALLORCA

AV. DIAGONAL

HOTEL CASA FUSTER

CASA DE LES PUNXES

PALAU BARÓ DE QUADRAS

LA PEDRERA

Diagonal M

E I X A M P L E

C. DE VALÈNCIA

C. D'ARAGÓ

PSG. DE

COMPANYS

CARRER DE MUNTANER

AV. DIAGONAL

CARRER DE

FUNDACIÓ TÀPIES

PASSEIG DE GRÀCIA

Passeig de Gràcia M

CASA CALVET

ARC DE TRIOMF

Urquinaona

EL BORN

BLOCK OF DISCORD
CASA BATLLÓ,
CASA AMATLLER &
CASA LLEÓ MORERA

#24 B Catalunya

Plaça de Catalunya

VIA LAIETANA

PALACE OF CATALAN MUSIC

PICASSO MUSEUM

CARRER DEL COMTE D'URGELL

CARRER D'ENTENÇA

GRAN VIA DE LES CORTS CATALANES

BARRI GÒTIC

LAS RAMBLAS

OLD

Jaume I M

To Sants Station

SANT ANTONI MARKET

Miró Park

Plaça d'Espanya M Espanya

SANT ANTONI

EL RAVAL

Liceu M

CITY

PALAU GÜELL

Drassanes

COLUMBUS MONUMENT

Funicular to Montjuïc

To Moll Adossat (Cruise Ship Terminal)

AV. DEL PARAL·LEL

1 Kilometer

1 Mile

Gold skip-the-line ticket includes a hall with period furniture, virtual-reality tablet, and dizzying "Gaudí Dome" experience at the end; €45 early-entrance ticket promises fewer crowds (offered at 8:30 or 8:45). All tickets are timed entry—buy online in advance (€4 more at the door). Open daily 9:00-20:00, Passeig de Gràcia 43, +34 932 160 306, www.casabatllo.es.

Nighttime Visits and Concerts: Magic Night tickets include the same features as the Gold and Blue tickets above, but also a rooftop concert and a glass of *cava* (most nights in peak season at 20:00, €69 Blue ticket, €89 Gold ticket gets you a better seat).

Casa Museu Amatller

The middle residence of the Block of Discord, Casa Amatller was designed by Josep Puig I Cadafalch in the late 19th century for the Amatller chocolate-making family. Only viewable via a group tour, it features mostly original furniture, placed just as the owners had it when they lived there. Without a ticket, you can still admire the home's Neo-Catalan Gothic facade, with tiles and *esgrafiado* decoration, or step inside the foyer (free during open hours) to see the Modernista stained-glass door and ceiling and an elaborate staircase. Past the foyer is a café and chocolate shop, where you can taste Amatller hot chocolate with toast.

Cost and Hours: €17 for 45-minute visit with audioguide—generally on the hour and half-hour (daily 10:00-19:00, shorter hours in winter). A €20 one-hour guided English tour is offered daily at 10:00 and includes a gift of Amatller chocolate; Passeig de Gràcia 41, +34 932 160 175, www.amatller.org.

▲▲La Pedrera (Casa Milà)

One of Gaudí's trademark works, this house—built between 1906 and 1912—is an icon of Modernisme. The wealthy industrialist Pere Milà i Camps commissioned it, and while some still call it Casa Milà, most call it La Pedrera (The Quarry) because of its jagged, rocky facade. While it's fun to ogle from the outside, it's also worth going inside, as it's arguably the purest Gaudí interior in Barcelona—executed at the height of his abilities (unlike his earlier Palau Güell)—and it contains period furnishings. While Casa Batlló has a Gaudí facade and rooftop, these were appended to an existing building; La Pedrera, on the other hand, was built from the ground up according to Gaudí's plans. Your ticket includes entry to the interior (with the furnished apartment) and to the delightful rooftop, with its forest of tiled chimneys.

Cost and Hours: €25 timed-entry ticket includes good audioguide, buy online in advance (€3 more at the door); open daily 9:00-20:30, Nov-Feb until 18:30, nighttime visits available—see later; roof may close when it rains; at the corner of Passeig de Gràcia and Provença (visitor entrance at Provença 261), Metro: Diagonal, +34 932 142 576, www.lapedrera.com.

Avoiding Lines: Buy in advance online to guarantee entry. The €35 premium ticket allows you to arrive whenever you wish (no entry time) and skip all lines, including those for audioguides and the elevator. There's also an early-bird La Pedrera Sunrise guided tour at 8:00 (€39, certain days in peak season, details online).

Nighttime Visits: After-hours visits dubbed "La Pedrera Night Experience" include a guided tour of the building (but not the apartment), along with a rooftop light show and glass of *cava* (€38, usually daily 20:30-23:00, earlier in winter, book ahead). A nighttime combo-ticket (€45) includes the rooftop night experience plus the regular timed-entry daytime admission.

Concerts: On some summer nights, an evening rooftop concert series, "Summer Nights at La Pedrera," features live jazz and the chance to see the rooftop illuminated (€38, check website for details, book ahead).

Visiting the House: A visit covers three sections—the rooftop, the attic, and the apartment. Start by walking through the

fanciful, nature-inspired **courtyard.** Notice how the windows gradually get smaller as you look up to the top floors, allowing an equivalent amount of light and air to enter on the top floor as on the bottom floor.

Pick up your audioguide and head up the elevator to the bourgeois **apartment,** decorated as it might have been when the building was first occupied by middle-class urbanites (a short video explains Barcelona society at the time). Notice Gaudí's clever use of the atrium to maximize daylight in all the apartments.

Follow the signs to the **attic,** which houses a sprawling multimedia exhibit tracing the history of the architect's career, with models, photos, and videos of his work. It's all displayed under distinctive parabola-shaped arches. While evocative of Gaudí's style in themselves, the arches are formed this way partly to support the multilevel roof above. This area was also used for ventilation, helping to

keep things cool in summer and warm in winter. Tenants had storage spaces and did their laundry up here. In the 1940s there were actually 13 apartment units in this attic space.

Make your way to the jaw-dropping **rooftop,** where 30 chimneys and ventilation towers play volleyball with the clouds. (It could be that George Lucas got his inspiration for his Darth Vader helmet from the chimneys.) Look for the archway that frames the Sagrada Família in the distance, and study the layout of the city from mountain to sea. For a great view of Eixample city planning, look over into this block's central area, filled with gardens.

Back at the **ground level** of La Pedrera, poke into the dreamily painted original entrance courtyard.

▲▲▲Sagrada Família (Holy Family Church)

Gaudí's grand masterpiece sits unfinished in a residential Eixample neighborhood 1.5 miles north of Plaça de Catalunya. An icon of the city, the Sagrada Família boasts bold, wildly creative, unmistakably organic architecture and decor inside and out— from its melting Glory Facade to its skull-like Passion Facade to its rainforest-esque interior. Gaudí took over this project in 1883. It experienced some setbacks in the mid-20th century, but recent progress has been remarkable. The city has set a lofty goal of finishing by 2026, the centennial of Gaudí's death. Visitors get a close-up view of the dramatic exterior flourishes, the chance to walk through the otherworldly interior, and access to a fine  museum detailing the design and engineering behind this one-of-a-kind architectural marvel.

Cost and Hours: All tickets are timed-entry and must be purchased online in advance (no physical tickets sold on-site). All tickets include an audioguide (via an app). €26 ticket includes church, €30 ticket includes church and 50-minute live guided tour, €36 ticket includes church and one tower; €40 ticket includes church, guided tour, and one tower. Open Mon-Sat 9:00-20:00, Sun from 10:30; March and Oct daily until 19:00, Nov-Feb until 18:00; +34 932 080 414, www.sagradafamilia.org.

📖 See the Sagrada Família Tour chapter.

Recinte Modernista de Sant Pau
(former Hospital de la Santa Creu i Sant Pau)

This distinctive complex was designed in the early 20th century by Lluís Domènech i Montaner as a holistic hospital, with not only beds and wards but also gardens and a library. The hospital has since moved to new digs, and today the ensemble of buildings is preserved as a landmark of Modernista architecture. A short walk from the Sagrada Família, the building's interior and courtyards are well worth a look if you're in the area and a mega Modernista fan.

Cost and Hours: €16, €20 with audioguide; daily 10:00-18:30, until 17:00 in winter, guided tours in English available on request; Carrer de Sant Antoni Maria Claret 167, +34 935 537 604, www.santpaubarcelona.org.

BEYOND THE EIXAMPLE
▲▲Park Güell

Gaudí fans enjoy the artist's magic in this colorful park on the outskirts of town. While it takes a bit of effort to get here, Park Güell (Catalans pronounce it "gway") offers a unique look at Gaudí's style in a natural rather than urban context. Designed as an upscale housing development for early 20th-century urbanites, the park is home to some of Barcelona's most famous symbols, including a dragon guarding a whimsical staircase and a wavy bench bordering a panoramic view terrace supported by a forest of columns. Gaudí used vivid tile fragments to decorate much of his work, creating a playful, pleasing effect. The park contains the Gaudí House Museum, where Gaudí lived for a time (not worth the separate entry fee).

Cost and Hours: €10 timed-entry park admission. The only smart way to visit is to buy a ticket online in advance (tickets are sold at the park, but they often sell out and you'll wait in a long line). Open daily April-Oct 9:30-22:00 (last entry at 19:30), rest of the year 9:30 until sunset, +34 934 091 831, www.parkguell. barcelona.

Getting There: The easiest way to reach Park Güell—about 2.5 miles from Plaça de Catalunya—is to take a taxi (about €16). You can also ride bus #24 (direction: El Carmel) from Plaça de Catalunya to the Carretera del Carmel-Albert Llanas stop, a two-minute walk from my preferred side park entrance. Or, from Plaça de Catalunya, take the blue Bus Turístic and walk 10 minutes uphill to the park. It's also possible to ride the Metro (L3) to the Lesseps stop and walk 15 minutes, partly uphill.

🕮 See the Park Güell Tour chapter.

Tibidabo

Tibidabo comes from the Latin for "to thee I shall give," the words the devil used when he was tempting Christ. It's still an enticing offer: At the top of Barcelona's highest peak, you're offered the city's oldest fun-fair, a great spot for kids and—if the weather and air quality are good—an almost limitless view of the city and the Mediterranean. If you go mostly for the views, a cheaper "Panoramic View" ticket allows access to several classic rides (such as the carousel and airplane ride) at the entrance to the park.

Cost and Hours: Amusement park—€35, €14 for kids under 3'11" tall; Panoramic View zone—€19, €10.50 for kids under 3'11"; hours depend on season—generally July-Aug Wed-Sun 12:00-23:00, closed Mon-Tue, weekends only in off-season; lockers, café, +34 932 117 942, www.tibidabo.cat.

Getting There: The direct "TibiBus" (#T2A) runs from the Nord bus station to the park about every 10 minutes starting at 10:15 on days the park is open (€3). Get off at Plaça Dr. Andreu, where you'll see a handful of bars and restaurants. From there, take the funicular to the top (€12 round-trip, included if paying park admission). Public transit can get you there, but if your time is precious, the TibiBus or a taxi is a better value.

Camp Nou Stadium

The home turf of FC Barcelona men's soccer team is undergoing a €1.5 billion renovation to increase its capacity to 105,000 fans and add a roof. Visits normally include the club museum and a tour of the stadium, ending in a ground-level view of the pitch (and a big shop to buy official "Barça" gear). During construction visitors can tour the Barça Immersive Exhibit, which combines a museum tracing Barça club history (covering both the men's and women's teams) with virtual reality experiences. Check online to confirm details before visiting.

Cost and Hours: Barça Immersive Exhibit-€28, more in-depth (and pricier) options available for true fans; open daily 9:30-19:00, shorter hours off-season and on game days and the day before; Metro: Palau Reial or Collblanc, +34 902 189 900, www. fcbarcelona.com.

Soccer Games: During construction, FC Barcelona's men's team will play at Olympic Stadium (see listing, later). The women's team plays at Johan Cruyff Stadium, west of the center. Buy tickets from Barça's official website, at the stadium, or at the TI. Popular matches (such as those with Real Madrid or A.C. Milan) sell out quickly, in which case you could try online resellers Entradas.com or SportsEvents365.com.

MONTJUÏC

Montjuïc (mohn-jew-EEK, "Mount of the Jews"), overlooking Barcelona's hazy port, has always been a show-off. Ages ago, it was capped by an impressive castle. When the Spanish enforced their rule, they built the imposing fortress that you'll see the shell of today. The hill has also played an integral role in the construction of Barcelona's great structures—significant parts of the historic city, the cathedral, the Sagrada Família, and much more were all built with stones quarried from Montjuïc.

Montjuïc has also been prominent during the past century. In 1929, it hosted an international fair, from which many of to-day's sights originated. And in 1992, the Summer Olympics directed the world's attention to this pincushion of attractions once again. While Montjuïc lacks one knockout, must-see attraction, it is home to a variety of good sights. For art lovers, the most worthwhile destinations are the Fundació Joan Miró, Catalan Art Museum, and CaixaForum.

Sightseeing Strategies: I've listed these sights by altitude, from the hill-topping castle down to the 1929 World Expo Fairgrounds at the base of Montjuïc. If you're visiting them all, ride to the top by bus, funicular, or taxi, then visit them in this order so that most of your walking is downhill.

Here's one simple plan: From Metro Paral-lel, take the funicular up (included in your Metro ticket). Walk five minutes (left from exit) gradually downhill to the big white Fundació Joan Miró, five minutes more to the Olympic Stadium, and five more to the Catalan Art Museum. From there, descend the stairs to the Magic Fountains. Detour left (if interested) to the Mies Van der Rohe building, CaixaForum, and Spanish Village. Then return to the Magic Fountains and continue on to Plaça d'Espanya, Las Arenas mall, and a Metro stop to the rest of Barcelona.

Getting to Montjuïc: You have several choices. The simplest is to take a **taxi** directly to your destination (about €12 from downtown).

Buses also take you up to Montjuïc. From Plaça de Catalunya, bus #55 goes as far as Montjuïc's cable-car station/funicular. To get higher (to the castle), ride the Metro from Plaça de Catalunya to Plaça d'Espanya, then make the easy transfer to bus #150 to ride all the way up the hill. Alternatively, the red Bus Turístic will get you to the Montjuïc sights.

Another option is the **funicular** (covered by Metro ticket, runs every 10 minutes 9:00-22:00, shorter hours in winter). To reach it, take the Metro to the Paral-lel stop, then follow signs for *Parc Montjuïc* and the funicular icon—you can enter the funicular without using another ticket. (If the funicular is closed, you'll find a shuttle bus.) From the top of the funicular, turn left and walk gently downhill for the Fundació Joan Miró, Olympic Stadium,

SIGHTS

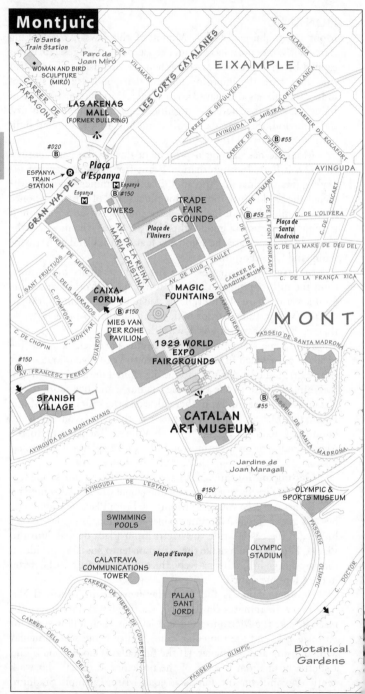

Montjuïc

To Sants Train Station

Parc de Joan Miró

WOMAN AND BIRD SCULPTURE (MIRÓ)

CARRER DE TARRAGONA

LES CORTS CATALANES

C. DE CALABRIA

C. DE VILAMARI

EIXAMPLE

LAS ARENAS MALL (FORMER BULLRING)

CARRER DE SEPÚLVEDA

FLORIDA BLANCA

AVINGUDA DE MISTRAL

CARRER DE ROCAFORT

CARRER DE C D'ENTENÇA

#D20 B

Plaça d'Espanya

ESPANYA TRAIN STATION R

Espanya M

GRAN VIA DE

TOWERS

AV. DE LA REINA MARIA CRISTINA

CARRER DE MÉXIC

C. DELS MORABOS

C. SANT FRUCTUÓS

C. D'AMPOSTA

C. DE CHOPIN

C. MONTFAR

M Espanya
B #150

Plaça de l'Univers

TRADE FAIR GROUNDS

C. DE TAMARIT

B #55

C. DE LA FONT HONRADA

C. DE LLEIDA

AVINGUDA

C. DE L'OLIVERA

C. DE

ELCART

Plaça de Santa Madrona

C. DE LA MARE DE DÉU DEL

CAIXA-FORUM

B #150

MIES VAN DER ROHE PAVILION

AV. DE RIUS I TAULET

MAGIC FOUNTAINS

CARRER DE JOAQUIM BLUME

CARRER DE LA GUÀRDIA URBANA

C. DE LA FRANÇA XICA

MONT

1929 WORLD EXPO FAIRGROUNDS

PASSEIG DE SANTA MADRONA

AV. FRANCESC FERRER I GUÀRDIA

#150 B

SPANISH VILLAGE

AVINGUDA DELS MONTANYANS

CATALAN ART MUSEUM

B #55

PASSEIG DE SANTA MADRONA

Jardins de Joan Maragall

AVINGUDA DE L'ESTADI

B #150

OLYMPIC & SPORTS MUSEUM

SWIMMING POOLS

Plaça d'Europa

CALATRAVA COMMUNICATIONS TOWER

CARRER DE PIERRE DE COUBERTIN

PALAU SANT JORDI

OLYMPIC STADIUM

PASSEIG OLÍMPIC

C. DOCTOR

CARRER DELS JOCS DEL 92

PASSEIG OLÍMPIC

Botanical Gardens

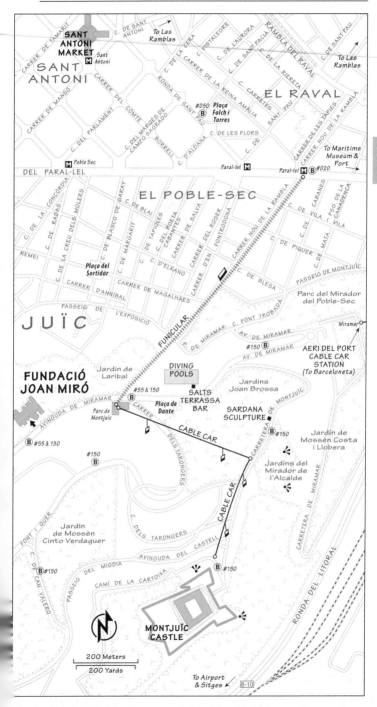

SIGHTS

C. DE SANT ANTONI

SANT ANTONI MARKET

To Las Ramblas

C. DE LA CERA

C. VISTALEGRE

C. DE L'AURORA

RAMBLA DEL RAVAL

C. DE SANT PAU

Ⓜ Sant Antoni

C. DE SANT PACIÀ

C. DE LA RIERETA

C. DE SANT PAU

SANT ANTONI

CARRER DE TAMARIT

CARRER DE MANSO

CARRER DEL PARLAMENT

CARRER DE LA REINA AMÀLIA

C. CARRETES

SANT PAU

EL RAVAL

CARRER DE MANSO

RONDA DE SANT PAU

#D50 **Plaça Folch i Torres**
Ⓑ

To Las Ramblas

CARRER DEL COMTE

C. DEL MARQÈS DE CAMPO SAGRADO

BORRELL

C. D'ALDANA

C. DE LES FLORS

C.

CARRER DE LES TÀPIES

CARRER NOU DE LA RAMBLA

C. DEL PARLAMENT

Ⓜ Poble Sec

DEL PARAL-LEL

Paral-lel **Ⓜ**

Paral-lel **Ⓜ** Ⓑ #D20

To Maritime Museum & Port

C. DE LA CONCÒRDIA

C. DE RABASSA

C. DE LA CREU DELS MOLERS

C. DE BLASCO DE GARAY

C. DE BLAI

EL POBLE-SEC

C. DEL POETA CABANYES

C. DE SALVÀ

CARRER DEL ROSER

CARRER NOU DE LA RAMBLA

C. DE CABANES

C. DE VILA I VILA

PSG. DE LA CANADENCA

REMEI

C. DE MARGARIT

C. DE TAPIOLES

C. D'ELKANO

CARRER D'EN FONTRODONA

C. DE PIQUER

C. DE MATA

Plaça del Sortidor

CARRER DE MAGALHÃES

CARRER D'EN FONTRODONA

C. DE BLESA

PASSEIG DE MONTJUÏC

CARRER D'ANNIBAL

CARRER DE MAGALHÃES

Parc del Mirador del Poble-Sec

PASSEIG DE L'EXPOSICIÓ

JUÏC

FUNICULAR

P. DE MIRAMAR C. FONT TROBADA

AV. DE MIRAMAR

Miramar

#150 Ⓑ

AV. DE MIRAMAR

AERI DEL PORT CABLE CAR STATION (To Barceloneta)

FUNDACIÓ JOAN MIRÓ

Jardí de Laribal

DIVING POOLS

SALTS TERRASSA BAR

Jardins Joan Brossa

AVINGUDA DE MIRAMAR
Ⓑ #55 & 150

CARRER

Plaça de Dante

CARRETERA DE MONTJUÏC

SARDANA SCULPTURE

Ⓑ #150

Jardí de Mossèn Costa i Llobera

Parc de Montjuïc

Ⓑ #55 & 150

CABLE CAR

CARRER DELS TARONGERS

CARRETERA DE MONTJUÏC

Jardins del Mirador de l'Alcalde

#150
Ⓑ

CABLE CAR

CARRETERA DE MIRAMAR

FONT I QUER

Jardí de Mossèn Cinto Verdaguer

C. DELS TARONGERS

AVINGUDA DEL CASTELL

PASSEIG DEL MIGDIA

Ⓑ#150

#150 Ⓑ

C. D'EN CAN VALERO

CAMÍ DE LA CARTOIXA

MONTJUÏC CASTLE

RONDA DEL LITORAL

N

200 Meters
200 Yards

To Airport & Sitges ←

B-10

and Catalan Art Museum. If you're heading all the way up to the Castle of Montjuïc, you can ride bus #150 or cable car from the top of the funicular (see castle listing, later).

For a scenic (if slow) approach to Montjuïc, you can ride the fun circa-1929 Aeri del Port **cable car** *(telefèric)* from the tip of the Barceloneta peninsula (across the harbor, near the beach) to the Miramar viewpoint park in Montjuïc. (Another station, along the port near the Columbus Monument, is closed.) The cable car is expensive, loads excruciatingly slowly (especially coming from the beach), and goes between two relatively re-

mote parts of town, so it's really not an efficient connection. It's only worthwhile for its sweeping views over town or to head back down to Barceloneta at the end of the day. Lines are shorter if you board in Montjuïc (€12.50 one-way, €20.00 round-trip, 3/hour, daily 10:30-19:00, June-Sept until 20:00, Nov-Feb 11:00-17:30, closed in high wind, +34 934 304 716, www.telefericodebarcelona.com).

If you're only visiting the Catalan Art Museum and/or Caixa-Forum, you can take the Metro to Plaça d'Espanya and **walk** up (primarily riding handy escalators).

Getting Around Montjuïc: Up top, it's easy and fun to walk between the sights—especially downhill. You can also connect the sights using the red Bus Turístic or one of the public buses. Bus #150 does a loop around the hilltop and is the only bus that goes to the castle; on the way up, it stops at or passes near the Caixa-Forum, Mies van der Rohe Pavilion, Spanish Village, Catalan Art Museum, Olympic Stadium, Fundació Joan Miró, the lower castle cable-car station/top of the funicular, and, finally, the castle. On the downhill run, it loops by Avinguda Miramar, the cable-car station for Barceloneta. Bus #55 connects only the funicular/cable-car stations, Fundació Joan Miró, and the Catalan Art Museum.

Castle of Montjuïc (Castell de Montjuïc)

The castle, which is pretty empty, is mostly worthwhile for the great city views from its ramparts. It was built in the 18th century with a Vauban-type star-fortress design by the central Spanish government to keep an eye on Barcelona and stifle citizen revolt. Until the late 20th century, the place functioned more to repress the people of Barcelona than to defend them. Being "taken to Montjuïc" meant you likely wouldn't be seen again. When the 20th-century dictator Franco was in power, the castle was the site of hundreds of political executions. But in 2010, Spain's Prime Minister José Luis

Rodríguez Zapatero, keeping a campaign promise, turned over control of the castle from Spain's national government to the city of Barcelona. These days it serves as a park, jogging destination, and host to a popular summer open-air cinema.

Beefy civil war-vintage cannons point visitors to grand Mediterranean vistas. Walk down to survey the boats in the harbor: Ships belonging to Grimaldi Lines, an Italian company, sail off to Genoa, Rome, and Sardinia; Mallorca ferries make the eight-hour trip to Barcelonans' big party escape; and the cruise-ship terminal is the busiest in Europe (Barcelona is the biggest port of embarkation for Mediterranean cruises). The seafront stretching far to the left was part of an Olympic project that turned a derelict industrial zone into a swanky stretch of promenades, beaches, and fancy condos. At the far right is Spain's leading port; you'll see containers stretching all the way to the airport.

Cost and Hours: €9, free first Sun of the month and all other Sun from 15:00; open daily 10:00-20:00, Nov-Feb until 18:00; €4 tours in English Sat-Sun at 13:00; www.bcn.cat/castelldemontjuic.

Getting There: To spare yourself the hike up, ride bus #150 to the base of the castle, catching it from Plaça d'Espanya, the top of the Montjuïc funicular, or various other points on Montjuïc. Or if the lines aren't too long, consider the much pricier **cable car** (Telefèric de Montjuïc), which departs from near the upper station of the Montjuïc funicular and offers excellent views (€10 one-way, €15 round-trip, runs daily June-Sept 10:00-21:00, shorter hours off-season).

▲Fundació Joan Miró

This museum has the best collection anywhere of works by Catalan artist Joan Miró (ZHOO-ahn mee-ROH, 1893-1983). Born in Barcelona, Miró divided his time between Paris and Catalunya (including Barcelona and his favorite village, Mont-roig del Camp). This building—designed in 1975 by Josep Lluís Sert, a friend of Miró and a student of Le Corbusier—was built

Joan Miró: The Freedom of Simplicity

Miró believed that everything in the cosmos is linked—colors, sky, stars, love, time, music, dogs, men, women, dirt, and the void. He mixed simple symbols of these things creatively, as a poet uses words. It's as liberating for the visual artist to be abstract as it is for the poet: Both can use metaphors rather than being confined to concrete explanations. Miró would listen to music and paint. It's interactive, free interpretation. He said, "For me, simplicity is freedom."

COPA DEL MUNDO DE FUTBOL ESPAÑA 82

Here are some tips to help you enjoy and appreciate Miró's art: First meditate on it, then read the title (for example, *The Smile of a Tear*), then meditate on it again. Repeat the process until you have an epiphany. There's no correct answer— it's pure poetry. Devotees of Miró say they fly with him and don't even need drugs. Psychoanalysts liken Miró's free-for-all canvases to Rorschach tests. Is that a cigar in that star's mouth?

to show off Miró's art. The museum displays an overview of Miró's oeuvre (as well as generally excellent temporary exhibits of 20th- and 21st-century artists). Consider renting the wonderful multimedia guide, which is well worth the extra charge.

If you don't like abstract art, you'll leave here scratching your head. But those who love this place are not faking it...they understand the genius of Miró and the fun of abstraction. Children probably understand it the best. Eavesdrop on what they say about the art; you may learn something.

Cost and Hours: €15, cheaper online; Tue-Sat 10:00-20:00, Sun until 18:00, shorter hours in winter, closed Mon year-round; 200 yards from top of funicular, Parc de Montjuïc, +34 934 439 470, www.fmirobcn.org/ca.

Services: The museum has a restaurant, café, and bookshop (all accessible without museum ticket).

Visiting the Museum: Follow the loosely chronological sequence of Miró works in Rooms 1 to 15. Temporary exhibits, featuring artists whose work connects to Miró's, are generally in Rooms 16 to 20 and Espai (Space) 13.

Room 1 (Sala Joan Prats): Young Miró is a sponge of different styles—Fauvism, Cubism, Catalan folk art, Impressionism (see the canvases of beaches and countryside), Orientalism *(Portrait of a Young Girl),* and whatever else he is exposed to. In 1920, he goes to Paris, dabbles in Dada, and socializes with Surrealists. Is Miró himself a Surrealist? Sort of. They share the same goal: circumventing the viewer's preconceptions about art and reality by juxtaposing unlikely items in order to short-circuit the brain.

Miró's early work does resemble Dalí's. But as his own idiosyncratic style evolves, Miró adds more and more abstraction to the mix. In his Green Paintings series (1925-1927), instead of placing photorealistic items against an otherworldly background (as Dalí would have), Miró arranges highly abstract symbols against a flat background. By 1925, Miró has left the figurative world behind and leaps wholeheartedly into the abyss—pushing the boundaries of abstraction. He paints a completely uninterpretable canvas...and then, just to be cheeky, titles it *Painting*.

SIGHTS

Rooms 2-10: In the 1920s, Miró, while attending literary groups in Paris, begins to merge poetry and painting. With the 1930s and the advent of the civil war, Miró temporarily becomes more figurative with his Wind Paintings. Recognizable monsters lurk threateningly. In the early 1940s, Miró flees the Nazi takeover of France and retreats to Spain. He becomes fixated on the heavens and produces his Constellations series—23 paintings of stars, moons, and other brightly colorful items cast against bright backgrounds.

By the late 1940s, Miró is becoming internationally appreciated, and within a few years, begins to do more public commissions. But going corporate doesn't tame Miró, as his works from the 1960s and 1970s demonstrate. If anything, he continues to refine his trademark style and strip everything down to basics. Star. Moon. Bird. Woman. (For Miró, "woman" means his wife, Pilar Juncosa, to whom he was dedicated for all his life. His last words—on his deathbed—were put in writing to his wife: "I love you.") Increasingly, Miró's works are intended as something to meditate on. Some of his best-known and most appreciated works date from this period and can't be found in any museum, but are scattered around the streets of Barcelona: in the middle of the Ramblas (see page 94); in the park behind the nearby Las Arenas mall (see page 81); and at the airport's old terminal (#2).

Room 11: The massive 400-square-foot *Tapestry of the Foundation*, which Miró designed for this space in 1979, has real texture—like a painting with thick brushstrokes. Notice Miró's trademark star and moon high above. (A different tapestry, which Miró custom-made for New York City's World Trade Center around this same period, was lost in the 9/11 terrorist attacks.)

In the hallway to the next room, look through the window to find the *Mercury Fountain*, by American sculptor Alexander Calder. This piece was created for the same 1937 exhibition at which Picasso premiered his seminal *Guernica*. Like Picasso's canvas, Calder's fountain was created to honor victims of the Spanish Civil War—in this case, the residents of Almadén, a mercury-mining town. Watch the liquid do its unpredictable thing as it drips and drops.

Room 12 (Sculpture Gallery): This gallery features several small bronze pieces by Miró. Ascend the ramp for a different angle. Nearby, find the stairs down to the Espai 13 installation space. Or continue to the end of the hall and downstairs to a room filled with pieces by other artists paying homage to Miró, plus a 15-minute film about Miró.

Second Floor: Return to earth with a visit to the terrace, where you'll find a modern sculpture gallery and views of the city. Inside there is a study center and good temporary exhibits (Rooms 16-20).

Olympic and Sports Museum (Museu Olímpic i de l'Esport)

This museum rides the coattails of the stadium across the street. You'll twist down a timeline-ramp that traces the history of the Olympic Games, interspersed with random exhibits about various sports. Downstairs you'll find exhibits designed to test your athleticism, a play-by-play rehash of the '92 Barcelona Olympiad, a commemoration of Juan Antonio Samaranch (the influential Catalan president of the IOC for two decades), a sports media exhibit, and a schmaltzy movie collage. High-tech but hokey, the museum is worth the time and money only for those nostalgic for the '92 Games.

Cost and Hours: €6, free for kids 7 and under; Tue-Sat 10:00-19:00 (Oct-March until 18:00), Sun 10:00-14:30, closed Mon year-round, skip the unnecessary audioguide, Avinguda de l'Estadi 60, +34 932 925 379, www.museuolimpicbcn.cat.

Olympic Stadium (Estadi Olímpic)

Barcelona's Olympic Stadium was originally built for the 1929 World Expo, but soon thereafter it played a big part in Barcelona's plan to host the "People's Olympiad." These games were to take place in July 1936 as an alternative to Hitler's Fascist Olympics, scheduled for that same summer in Berlin (and which Spain had planned to boycott). But just days before the Barcelona games were to begin, civil war broke out in Spain, and the event was canceled. Fifty-something years later, the stadium was updated and

expanded in preparation for the 1992 Summer Olympics. It was officially named for Catalan patriot Lluís Companys i Jover, the left-wing leader who was president when Spain's civil war began. Companys had pushed for the democratic alternative to Hitler's games; he was later arrested and executed by Franco.

The memorable XXV Olympiad kicked off here on July 25, 1992. At the opening ceremonies, an archer dramatically lit the Olympic torch—which still stands high at the end of the stadium overlooking the city skyline—with a flaming arrow.

Aside from the memories of the medals, the stadium offers little to see today. But if the doors are open, you're welcome to step inside. History panels along the railings overlooking the playing field tell the stadium's dynamic story. For much of 2024 the stadium will host FC Barcelona men's soccer while the team's home stadium, Camp Nou, undergoes renovation.

Nearby: Hovering over the stadium is the futuristic **Montjuïc Communications Tower** (designed by prominent Spanish architect Santiago Calatrava), originally used to transmit Olympic highlights and lowlights around the world.

▲▲Catalan Art Museum
(Museu Nacional d'Art de Catalunya)

The mission of this wonderful museum is to showcase Catalan art from the 10th century through the mid-20th century. Often called  "the Prado of Romanesque art" (and "MNAC" for short), it holds Europe's best collection of Romanesque frescoes and offers a good sweep of modern Catalan art. It's all housed in the grand Palau Nacional (National Palace), an emblematic building from the 1929 World Expo, with magnificent views over Barcelona, especially from the building's rooftop terrace.

Cost and Hours: €12, €20 combo-ticket includes Spanish Village, free Sat from 15:00 and first Sun of month; open Tue-Sat 10:00-20:00 (Oct-April until 18:00), Sun 10:00-15:00, closed Mon year-round; above Magic Fountains near Plaça d'Espanya—take escalators up; +34 936 220 360, www.museunacional.cat.

Eating: The museum hosts the chic and pricey Oleum restaurant with vast city views (€30 lunch *menu*, Tue-Sun 12:30-16:00, closed Mon). There's also a fine outdoor terrace café near the museum entrance (serving snacks with more city views; same hours as museum, closing time varies with Magic Fountains schedule) and a peaceful self-service restaurant hidden under the dome inside.

Rooftop Terrace: The rooftop terrace offers views across the city. It's free with your museum ticket (otherwise €2; same hours as museum). To reach the terrace from the main entrance, pass the WCs on the left and show your ticket to ride the elevator most of the way, then climb a few flights of stairs up to the terrace. To take an elevator the whole way, go to the far end of the museum, through the huge dome room, to the far-right corner.

Visiting the Museum: As you enter, pick up a map and download the audioguide app; bring your own earbuds or headphones. The left wing is Romanesque, and the right wing is Gothic, Renaissance, and Baroque. Upstairs is more Baroque, plus modern art, photography, coins, and more.

Romanesque: The MNAC's world-class collection of Romanesque (Romànic) art gives a rare glimpse into the medieval mind. Most pieces came from a handful of Catalan village churches clustered in a remote valley in the Pyrenees that thrived c. 1000-1300. These humble stone churches, passed over by the centuries, were rediscovered like time capsules in the 20th century. The art was moved to the museum (1920s) to save them from scavenging art dealers. A  series of **videos** shows the process of extracting the frescoes from the walls and moving them here.

In **Room 1,** you're greeted by a fresco of Mary painted in a re-created apse of one of the churches.

Room 2 has the collection's most lively and colorful murals, painted in a straightforward literal style. In the evocative *Stoning of St. Stephen*, unbelievers throw baked-potato-size rocks at Stephen (kneeling at right), who's comforted by a heavenly beam of light. In the room's other scenes, do a Romanesque scavenger hunt to find a camel, roving minstrels, a falconer, a row of horned birds, and other fantastic beasts.

In **Room 4,** one apse features saints in halos (Peter with his keys alongside Mary with a flaming chalice) and the countess who paid for the painting (lower right). The other apse has winged angels (seraphim) who appear to the prophets Isaiah (lower left) and Ezekiel (right), alongside Ezekiel's vision of the four-wheeled flaming chariot.

Rooms 5-7 focus on one of the most popular images in the medieval world: Christ in Majesty (a.k.a. the Pantocrator, or All

Powerful). Jesus is depicted inside an almond-shaped halo, seated on a throne, with one hand raised in blessing, the other holding an open Bible (often with the words *Ego sum lux mundi*—"I am the light of the world"). He's surrounded by either seraphim or the four symbols of the Evangelists. Christ is always easy to identify—he's the only one with a cross in his halo. Room 7 puts all the Romanesque elements together for a great in situ experience—a replica church, with Christ in Majesty in the apse and other Romanesque themes. Become a 12th-century peasant and let these images speak to you.

Browse through **Rooms 8-16,** seeing leafy column capitals, wooden crucifixes, and statues of Mary and the saints, until you spill back out into the main hall.

• *Cross the hall to the rooms of...*

Gothic Art: Picking up where Romanesque left off (c. 1300), fresco murals give way to vivid 14th-century wood-panel paintings of Bible stories. Make your way to **Room 26** (straight in, then to the left) and find the collection's highlight: a half-dozen paintings by the Catalan master Jaume Huguet (1412-1492), particularly his *Consagración de San Agustín (Consecration of Saint Augustine).*

These paintings (impressive enough on their own) were once part of a huge altarpiece—an estimated 40 feet tall and 30 feet wide—with some 20 paintings, done for a church in El Born. Huguet labored on the project for more than 20 years. The theme was the life of St. Augustine. It started with the painting of young Augustine (in black robe and red cap) dropping his pagan books to the floor as he realizes the truth and converts to Christianity. In other scenes, Augustine wears his golden robes and bishop's hat as he's shown preaching at a pulpit, disputing a heretic (in green, who tumbles to the ground before the power of Augie's words), kneeling to wash the feet of a pilgrim (who turns out to be Christ in disguise), and greeting a boy (who turns out to be a vision of young Jesus).

Huguet's masterpiece was the *Consecration* scene, where Augustine becomes bishop and is crowned with the hat. The details are incredible: the bright colors and gold leaf, the sober expressive faces, the brocaded robe with pictures of saints, and the early attempt at 3-D created by the floor tiles. Notice that this isn't simply a "painting"—it has a raised surface, like a cameo. It's a sheet of wood topped with molded stucco, then covered with paints and gold leaf. Nearby is Huguet's *Last Supper,* which was also part of the Augustine altarpiece. The details and faces here are astonishing. There's even an attempt at realistic 3-D: There are saints in front and saints in back, and some disciples pose in profile, some face-out, some from behind. But the table looks slanted, and the food is about to slide off.

• *The Gothic collection leads into...*

Renaissance and Baroque: Browse several rooms, watching as Renaissance artists make altarpieces more balanced and serene, with distant realistic backgrounds. You'll see Spain's golden age (Zurbarán, heavy religious scenes, and Spanish royals with their endearing underbites) and examples of Romanticism (dewy-eyed Catalan landscapes). Room 32 has El Greco's *Christ Carrying the Cross* and José de Ribera's saints with wrinkled foreheads. In addition, you'll find minor works by major—if not necessarily Catalan—masters like Velázquez, Goya, Tintoretto, Rubens, and Titian.

Rest of the Museum: The Gothic/Renaissance/Baroque exit spills out by the room of the huge **dome,** which once housed an ice-skating rink and now has a cafeteria. This was the prime ceremony room and dance hall for the 1929 World Expo.

From here, you can ride the glass elevator upstairs to the **modern art** section, which takes you on an enjoyable walk from the late 1800s to about 1950. It's kind of a Catalan Musée d'Orsay, offering a big chronological clockwise circle from Room 1, covering Symbolism, Modernisme, fin de siècle fun, Art Deco, and more. Find the early 20th-century paintings by Catalan artists Santiago Rusiñol and Ramon Casas, both of whom had a profound impact on a young Picasso (and, through him, on all modern art). Casas was also one of the financiers of Els Quatre Gats, the hangout of Modernista  artists; his fun Toulouse-Lautrec-esque works, including a whimsical self-portrait on a tandem bicycle, are crowd-pleasers. Also admire the central dome, which connects the modern art sections, and a mod 1978 tile panel that Miró created for the local headquarters of IBM.

Crossing over to the "Modern 2" section, you'll find more furniture (pieces that complement some of the empty spaces you may see if you visit Gaudí's buildings—including Gaudí-designed wooden chairs and a sofa), Impressionism, the shimmering landscapes of Joaquim Mir, and several distinctly Picasso portraits of women.

The museum also has a coin collection, seductive sofas scattered about, and several options for eating and views (described earlier).

1929 WORLD EXPO FAIRGROUNDS AND NEARBY

With the World Expo in 1929, Montjuïc morphed into an extravagant center for fairs, museums, and festivals. Nearly everything you see here dates from 1929 (the exceptions are Caixa-Forum and Las Arenas mall). The expo's theme was to demonstrate how electricity was about more than lightbulbs: Electricity powered the funicular, the glorious expo fountains, the many pavilion

SIGHTS

displays, and even the flame atop the fountain marking the center of Plaça d'Espanya (and celebrating the electric company that sponsored the show). If Barcelona is known for growing through big events, this certainly is a good example.

Standing at Plaça d'Espanya (or, better yet, on the rooftop terrace of the bullring mall—described later), look through the double-brick-tower gate, down the grand esplanade, and imagine it alive with fountains and lined by proud national pavilions showing off all that was modern in 1929. Today, the site is home to the Fira de Barcelona convention center. The Neo-Baroque fountain provides a brilliant centerpiece for Plaça d'Espanya.

Getting There: The fairgrounds sprawl at the base of Montjuïc, from the Catalan Art Museum's doorstep to Plaça d'Espanya. It's easiest to see these sights on your way down from Montjuïc. Otherwise, ride the Metro to Espanya, then use the series of stairs and escalators to climb up through the heart of the fairgrounds (eventually reaching the Catalan Art Museum).

▲Magic Fountains (Font Màgica)

Music, colored lights, and huge amounts of water make an artistic and coordinated splash in the evening near Plaça d'Espanya. Check ahead, as the fountains do not run when drought causes the city to restrict water usage.

Cost and Hours: Free 20-minute shows start every half-hour; June-Sept Wed-Sun 21:30-22:30, April-May and Oct Thu-Sat 21:00-22:00, winter Thu-Sat 20:00-21:00 (no shows in drought conditions and Jan-

Feb); from the Espanya Metro stop, walk toward the towering National Palace.

▲CaixaForum

The CaixaForum Social and Cultural Center is housed in one of Barcelona's most important Art Nouveau buildings. In 1911, Josep Puig i Cadafalch (a top architect
often overshadowed by Gaudí)
designed the Casaramona textile
factory, using Modernista design in an industrial rather than
a residential context. It func-
tioned as a factory for less than a
decade, then later served a long
stint as a police station under
Franco. Beautifully refurbished

in 2002, the facility reopened as a great center for bringing culture and art to the people of Barcelona.

Cost and Hours: €6, daily 10:00-20:00, Avinguda de Francesc Ferrer i Guàrdia 6, +34 934 768 600, www.caixaforum.es/barcelona.

Visiting the Center: From the lobby, signs point to *Sala 2, 3, 4,* and *5;* each typically hosts an outstanding temporary exhibition. Ride the escalator to the first floor, which features a modest but interesting exhibit about the history and renovation of the building. Then head into the appealing red-brick courtyard to access the exhibition halls. The sight features some English descriptions.

Take the stairs or elevator up to the Modernista Terrace (*Planta 2,* or look for signs to *Aula 1*). This terrace, boasting a wavy floor and bristling with fanciful brick towers, offers views over the complex and to Montjuïc. Enjoy the genius of Puig i Cadafalch's Modernista design, which provided state-of-the-art working conditions—natural light, good ventilation, and even two trademark towers filled with water (which could be broken to put out any factory fires). The various buildings (separated from each other to reduce the risk of fire) were built on terraces to level out the Montjuïc slope. Notice that there's no smokestack. This was one of the first electric-powered factories in town.

Mies van der Rohe Pavilion (Pabellón Mies van der Rohe)

Architecture pilgrims enjoy the pavilion that Ludwig Mies van der Rohe designed for the German exhibits at the 1929 expo. Although it was dismantled at the end of the fair, the building was heralded as a seminal example of modern architecture, and in the 1980s, the city reconstructed it on the original site. It's small and stripped-down—a strictly functional "Modernist" (i.e., decidedly *not* Modernista) structure. Unless you're a huge fan, skip the entry fee and simply walk around the pavilion to get a peek inside (including views of the "Barcelona Chair," the tubular steel and leather-cushioned chair that's become an icon of 20th-century furniture design).

Cost and Hours: €8, daily 10:00-20:00, Nov-Feb until 18:00, Avinguda de Francesc Ferrer i Guàrdia 7, +34 932 151 011, www.miesbcn.com.

Spanish Village (Poble Espanyol)

This five-acre model village was built as part of the 1929 expo to show off the cultural and architectural diversity in Spain. You'll see more than 100 building reproductions that show traditional architecture from all over Spain—all built in 1929. The village was mostly a shell to contain workshops and gift shops—and today, it still serves the same purpose. While extremely touristy and a bit tacky, many find it enjoyable. Craftspeople do their traditional thing (making guitars, blowing glass, crafting jewelry, and so on), and friendly shopkeepers offer tasty samples of traditional and local edibles. It's especially popular with rushed cruise groups eager to shop.

Cost and Hours: €14, €7 Tue-Sun from 20:00, €20 combo-ticket includes Catalan Art Museum; open Tue-Sun 10:00-24:00, Mon until 20:00, shorter hours Jan-Feb; www.poble-espanyol.com.

Getting There: It's best to take bus #150, as it's a long hike up from the main World Expo esplanade.

Las Arenas Mall

What do you do with a big bullfighting arena that's been sitting empty for decades? Make it a shopping mall. The grand Neo-Moorish Modernista *plaça de toros* functioned as an arena for bullfights from around 1900 to 1977, and then reopened in 2011 as a mall. It now hosts everything you'd expect in a modern shopping center: brand-name shops, a food-court basement, and a 12-screen cinema complex.

The **rooftop terrace,** with stupendous views of Plaça d'Espanya and Montjuïc, is ringed with eateries (reachable by external glass elevator for €1 or from inside escalators/elevators for free). Besides getting a bird's-eye perspective of the fairgrounds, you can gaze down at Parc de Joan Miró, which includes the giant sculpture *Woman and Bird (Dona i Ocell).* This was one of the works (along with the mosaic on the Ramblas) that the city commissioned from the artist to welcome visitors. Miró's sense of humor is evident—if the sculpture seems phallic, keep in mind that the Catalan word for "bird" is also slang for "penis."

Cost and Hours: Free; daily 10:00-22:00, Oct-May 9:00-21:00; outside elevator and restaurants open late year-round, Gran Via de les Corts Catalanes 373, Metro: Espanya, exit following *Sortida Tarragona* signs, www.arenasdebarcelona.com.

BEACHES AND NEARBY
▲Barcelona's Beaches

Barcelona has created a summer tourist trade by building a huge stretch of beach east of the town center. From Barceloneta, an un-

interrupted band of sand tumbles three miles northeast to the Fòrum. Before the 1992 Olympics, this area was an industrial wasteland nicknamed the "Catalan Manchester." Not anymore. The industrial zone was demolished and dumped into the sea, while sand was dredged from the seabed to make the pristine beaches locals enjoy today. Looking out to sea, you can't miss the W Hotel, shaped like a windblown sail, dominating a small peninsula.

The overall scene is great for sunbathing and for an evening paseo before dinner. It's like a resort island—complete with lounge chairs, volleyball, showers, WCs, bike paths, and inviting beach bars called *chiringuitos.* Each beach segment has its own vibe: Sant Sebastià (closest, popular with older beachgoers and families), Barceloneta (with many seafood restaurants), Nova Icària (pleasant family beach), and Mar Bella (attracts a younger crowd, clothing-optional).

Getting There: The Barceloneta Metro stop leaves you a long walk from the sand. To get to the beaches without a hike, take the bus. From the Ramblas, bus #59 will get you as far as Barceloneta Park; bus #D20 leaves from the Columbus Monument and follows a similar route. Bus #V15 runs from Plaça de Catalunya to the tip of Barceloneta (near the W Hotel).

Biking the Beach: For a break from the city, rent a bike and take the following little ride: Explore Citadel Park, filled with families enjoying a day out. Then roll through Barceloneta. This artificial peninsula was once the home of working-class sailors and shippers. From the Barceloneta beach, head up to the Olympic Village, where the former apartments for 13,000 visiting athletes now

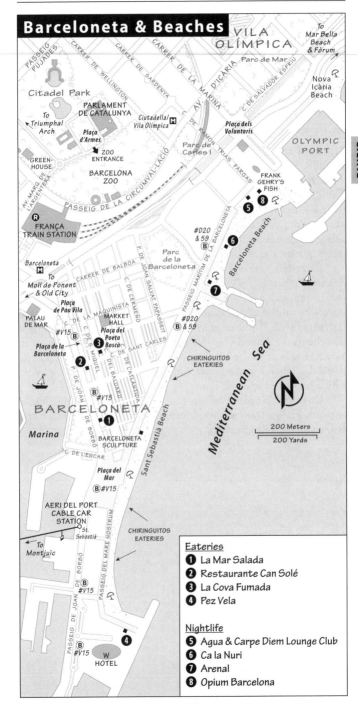

Barceloneta & Beaches

VILA OLÍMPICA

To Mar Bella Beach & Fòrum

PASSEIG PUJADES

CARRER DE WELLINGTON

CARRER DE SARDENYA

CARRER DE LA MARINA

CARRER DE L'ICÀRIA

AV. D'ICÀRIA

Parc de Mar

Nova Icària Beach

Citadel Park

To Triumphal Arch

PARLAMENT DE CATALUNYA

Plaça d'Armes

Ciutadella/ Vila Olímpica Ⓜ

AV. DE RAMON TRIAS FARGAS

C. DE SALVADOR ESPRIU

Plaça dels Voluntaris

OLYMPIC PORT

GREEN-HOUSE

ZOO ENTRANCE

BARCELONA ZOO

Parc de Carles I

FRANK GEHRY'S FISH

AV. MARQ. DE L'ARGENTERA

PASSEIG DE LA CIRCUMVAL·LACIÓ

Ⓡ FRANÇA TRAIN STATION

❺ ❽

❻ #D20 & 59 Ⓑ

Barceloneta Beach

Barceloneta Ⓜ

To Moll de Ponent & Old City

CARRER DE BALBOA

P. DE JOAN SALVAT PAPASSEIT

PASSEIG MARÍTIM DE LA BARCELONETA

Parc de la Barceloneta

Plaça de Pau Vila

PALAU DE MAR

C. DE LA MAQUINISTA

MARKET HALL

Plaça del Poeta Boscà

C. DE L'ALMIRALL CERVERA

C. DE SANT CARLES

#D20 & 59 Ⓑ

#V15 Ⓑ

C. DE SANT MIQUEL

❸

Plaça de la Barceloneta

❷

C. DEL BALUARD

C. DE L'ATLÀNTIDA

CHIRINGUITOS EATERIES

Mediterranean Sea

#V15 Ⓑ

BARCELONETA

P. DE JOAN DE BORBÓ

❶

Marina

BARCELONETA SCULPTURE

C. DE L'ESCAR

Sant Sebastià Beach

Ⓝ

200 Meters
200 Yards

Plaça del Mar

Ⓑ #V15

AERI DEL PORT CABLE CAR STATION

St. Sebastià

To Montjuïc

CHIRINGUITOS EATERIES

PASSEIG DEL MARE NOSTRUM

PASSEIG DE JOAN DE BORBÓ

Ⓑ #V15

Ⓑ #V15

❹

W HOTEL

Eateries
❶ La Mar Salada
❷ Restaurante Can Solé
❸ La Cova Fumada
❹ Pez Vela

Nightlife
❺ Agua & Carpe Diem Lounge Club
❻ Ca la Nuri
❼ Arenal
❽ Opium Barcelona

SIGHTS

house permanent residents. The village's symbol, Frank Gehry's striking "fish," shines brightly in the sun. A bustling night scene keeps this stretch of harborfront busy until the wee hours. From here you'll come to a series of man-made crescent-shaped beaches, each with trendy bars and cafés. If you're careless or curious (down by Mar Bella), you might find yourself pedaling past people working on an all-over tan. In the distance is the huge solar panel marking the site of the Fòrum shopping and convention center.

Citadel Park (Parc de la Ciutadella)

In 1888, Barcelona's biggest, greenest park—originally the site of a much-hated military citadel—was transformed for a Universal Exhibition (world's fair). The stately Triumphal Arch at the top of the park, celebrating the removal of the citadel, was built as the main entrance. Inside you'll find wide pathways, plenty of trees and grass, a zoo, a museum of geology, and a castle-like former restaurant for the fair (closed to the public).

Barcelona, one of Europe's most densely populated cities, suffers from a lack of real green space. This park is a haven and is especially enjoyable on weekends, when it teems with happy families (for more on the zoo and kids' activities in Citadel Park, see the Barcelona with Children chapter). Enjoy the ornamental fountain that the young Antoni Gaudí helped design, and consider a jaunt in a rental rowboat on the lake in the center of the park. Check out the tropical Umbracle greenhouse and the Hivernacle winter garden, which has a pleasant café-bar.

Cost and Hours: Park entry is free, daily 10:00 until dusk, north of França train station, Metro: Arc de Triomf, Barceloneta, or Ciutadella/Vila Olímpica.

RAMBLAS RAMBLE

From Plaça de Catalunya to the Waterfront

For more than a century, Barcelona's main boulevard has been a magnet for visitors. This one-hour stroll down the Ramblas goes from Plaça de Catalunya gently downhill to the waterfront, with an easy return by Metro.

Traditionally, the Ramblas was the place where locals flocked to buy flowers, lottery tickets, and a daily newspaper, or to enjoy a spot of shade while watching the world go by. But much of the local charm of the Ramblas has been taken over by sightseers, tacky trinkets, and lousy eateries. Many shops now cater to visitors more than locals, and the old neighborhood population has fled to more affordable homes in the suburbs. Still, if you come to Barcelona... you've got to ramble the Ramblas. (And if you stroll first thing in the morning, you'll find it more charming.)

The word "Ramblas" is plural; the street is actually a succession of five separately named segments. But street signs and addresses treat it as a single long street—"La Rambla," singular. This walk will help you see beyond the tourist crowds to discover the essence of the area. On the wide central sidewalk, you'll raft the river of tourism as you pass plenty of historic bits and pieces of this great city.

Orientation

Length of This Walk: Allow an hour. If you have less time, focus on the stretch between the Fountain of Canaletes and the Miró mosaic at Liceu. With more time, dip into La Boqueria Market.

When to Go: The Ramblas is two different streets by day and by night. To fully experience its yin and yang, walk it once in the evening and again in the morning, grabbing breakfast on a stool in a market café. Note that the Ramblas can be rowdy and off-putting late at night or after the Barça soccer team wins a match. Saturday is the best time to see La Boqueria Market.

Getting There: This walk begins at the Plaça de Catalunya end of the Ramblas, across the square from El Corte Inglés department store (Metro: Plaça de Catalunya).

La Boqueria Market: Mon-Sat 8:00-20:30, best mornings after 9:00, closed Sun, many stalls shut down early on Mon.

Palau Güell: €12; open Tue-Sun 10:00-20:00, Oct-March until 17:30, closed Mon year-round.

Columbus Monument: Elevator-€8, daily 8:30-14:30, may stay open later when cruise ships are in town.

Pickpockets: The Ramblas is prime hunting ground for pickpockets. Keep only today's spending money in your front pocket; secure your credit/debit cards, extra cash, and passport in your money belt.

Services: You'll find WCs at La Boqueria, beneath the statue at Plaça del Teatre, and at the Maremagnum mall at the end of this walk.

Get Oriented: Along the Ramblas, odd street numbers are on your right; even numbers are on the left.

Eating: The eateries here are tourist traps: Avoid them. But just off the street you'll find a few handy lunch spots, and the stalls of La Boqueria Market invite grazing. For details, see page 92.

The Walk Begins

• *Start your ramble on Plaça de Catalunya, at the top of the Ramblas.*

❶ Plaça de Catalunya

Dotted with fountains, statues, and pigeons—and ringed by grand buildings—this plaza is Barcelona's center. Plaça de Catalunya is the hub for the Metro, bus, air-port shuttle, and Bus Turístic. Of the region's 7.6 million Cata-lans, more than half live in great-er Barcelona. Plaça de Catalunya is their Times Square.

Geographically, the 12-acre square links the narrow streets of old Barcelona with the broad boulevards of the newer city (the Eixample). Four grand thoroughfares radiate from here: The Ramblas is the popular tourist promenade. Passeig de Gràcia, Barce-lona's answer to Paris' Champs-Elysées, has fashionable shops and

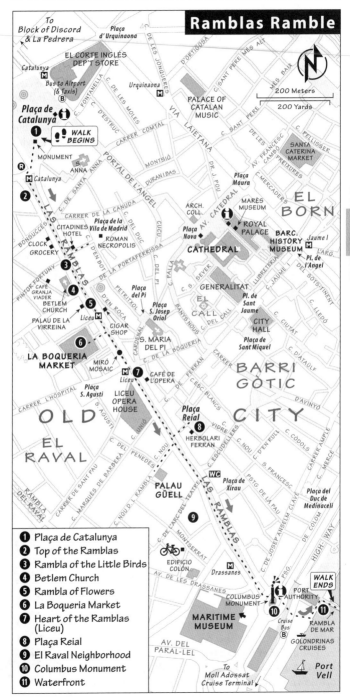

Ramblas Ramble

To Block of Discord & La Pedrera

Plaça d'Urquinaona

EL CORTE INGLÉS DEP'T STORE

Catalunya Ⓜ

Bus to Airport (& Taxis) Ⓑ

Plaça de Catalunya ⓘ

❶ WALK BEGINS

MONUMENT

Urquinaona Ⓜ

PALACE OF CATALAN MUSIC

200 Meters
200 Yards

Ⓡ

Ⓜ Catalunya

❷

S. ANNA

PORTAL DE L'ANGEL

MONTSIÓ

DURAN I BAS

D'ORTIGOSA

C. SANT PERE MÉS ALT

MÉS BAIX

C. PELLISSER

SANTA CATERINA MARKET

Plaça Maura

AV. FRANCESC CAMBÓ FREIXURES

EL BORN

CARRER DE LA CANUDA

Plaça de la Vila de Madrid

CITADINES HOTEL

CLOCK GROCERY

ROMAN NECROPOLIS

LAS RAMBLAS

❸

CAFÉ GRANJA VIADER

❹

BETLEM CHURCH

PALAU DE LA VIRREINA

Liceu Ⓜ ❺

CIGAR SHOP

LA BOQUERIA MARKET

❻

MIRÓ MOSAIC

ARCH. COLL.

Plaça Nova ◆

CATEDRAL

MARÈS MUSEUM

◆ ROYAL PALACE

BARC. HISTORY MUSEUM

Jaume I Ⓜ

Pl. de l'Angel

GENERALITAT

EL CALL

Plaça del Pi

Plaça S. Josep Oriol

S. MARIA DEL PI

Pl. de Sant Jaume

CITY HALL

Plaça de Sant Miquel

BARRI GÒTIC

Plaça S. Agusti

Ⓜ ❼ Liceu

CAFÉ DE L'OPERA

LICEU OPERA HOUSE

Plaça Reial

❽

HERBOLARI FERRAN

OLD CITY

EL RAVAL

CARRER L'HOSPITAL

PALAU GÜELL

WC

Plaça de Xirau

Plaça del Duc de Medinaceli

RAMBLA DEL RAVAL

❾

EDIFICIO COLÓN

LAS RAMBLAS

Drassanes Ⓜ

WALK ENDS

PORT AUTHORITY

❿ ⓫

RAMBLA DE MAR

COLUMBUS MONUMENT

MARITIME MUSEUM

AV. DE LES DRASSANES

Cruise Bus

GOLONDRINAS CRUISES

AV. DEL PARAL-LEL

To Moll Adossat Cruise Terminal

Port Vell

❶ Plaça de Catalunya
❷ Top of the Ramblas
❸ Rambla of the Little Birds
❹ Betlem Church
❺ Rambla of Flowers
❻ La Boqueria Market
❼ Heart of the Ramblas (Liceu)
❽ Plaça Reial
❾ El Raval Neighborhood
❿ Columbus Monument
⓫ Waterfront

RAMBLAS RAMBLE

cafés (and noisy traffic). Rambla de Catalunya is equally fashionable but cozier and more pedestrian-friendly. Avinguda del Portal de l'Angel (shopper-friendly and traffic-free) leads to the Barri Gòtic.

Plaça de Catalunya links the modern city with its past. In the 1850s, Barcelona tore down its medieval walls to expand the city, and this square was one of the first places to be developed. It once boasted curvy and decorative Modernista buildings (which still predominate in the Eixample district, just above the plaza), but during the Franco years, they were replaced with structures with stern, straight lines.

While Plaça de Catalunya is the center of Barcelona, it's also the cultural heart of the entire Catalunya region. At the Ramblas end of the square, the odd, inverted-staircase **monument** represents the shape of Catalunya. An inscription honors one of its former presidents, Francesc Macià i Llussà, who declared independence for the breakaway region in 1931. (It didn't quite stick.) Sculptor Josep Maria Subirachs, whose work you'll see at the Sagrada Família, designed it. These days, Catalans gather on the square by the tens of thousands to demonstrate passionately about whether Catalunya should be independent from Spain (for more on this political controversy, see page 130).

The venerable Café Zürich, just across the street from the monument, was once a popular downtown rendezvous spot. And the giant El Corte Inglés department store towering above the square (on the northeast side) has just about anything you might need.

• *Cross the street, head down about 30 yards, and pause to take in the scene.*

❷ Top of the Ramblas

The street called the Ramblas stretches before you, sloping gently downhill from here to the harbor. It's dotted with trees and ironwork lampposts, lined with fanciful buildings, paved with colorful mosaics, and trod upon by thousands of people both day and night.

Start with the ornate black and gold lamppost on your right. The base is a water tap called the **Fountain of Canaletes,** which has been a local favorite for more than a century. When Barcelona tore down its medieval wall and created this elegant promenade, this fountain was one of its early attractions. Legend says that a drink from the fountain ensures that you'll come back to Barcelona one day. Watch the tourists—eager to guarantee a return trip—struggle with the awkwardly high water pressure. The fountain is still a popular rendezvous spot and a gathering place for celebrations and demonstrations. Fans of the Barcelona soccer team party here after winning a big match; the fountain has been toppled many times by happy revelers climbing it. It's also a good spot to fill up your water bottle.

As you survey the Ramblas action, get your bearings for our stroll. You'll see the following features here and all along the way:

Wavy Tile Work: The pavement decorations represent the stream that once flowed here. *Rambla* means "stream" in Arabic, and this used to be a drainage ditch along one of the medieval walls enclosing the Barri Gòtic (to the left). Many Catalan towns, established where rivers approach the sea, have streets called "Ramblas." Today Barcelona's "stream" has become a river of humanity.

Skinny Balconies: Look up to see the city's characteristic shallow balconies. They're functional as well as decorative, with windows opening from floor to ceiling to allow light and air into the tight, dark spaces of these cramped old buildings.

Hardy Plane Trees: The deciduous trees lining the boulevard are known for their peeling bark and toughness in urban settings. They're ideal for the climate, letting in maximum sun in the winter and providing maximum shade in the summer.

Fixed Chairs: Nearby, notice the chairs fixed to the sidewalk at jaunty angles. It used to be that you'd pay to rent a chair here to look at the constant parade of passersby. Seats are now free, and it's still the best people-watching in town. Enjoy these chairs while you can—you'll find virtually no public benches or other seating farther down the Ramblas, only cafés that serve beer and sangria in just one (expensive) size: *gegant*.

ONCE Booths: Across from the fountain and a few steps down, notice the first of many booths along this walk that sell lottery tickets in support of ONCE, Spain's organization for the blind.

Soccer Souvenirs: You'll see soccer paraphernalia, especially the scarlet and blue of FC Barcelona—known as Barça. The team is owned by its more than 170,000 "members"—fans who buy season tickets, which come with a share of ownership. The team motto, "More than a club" *(Mes que un club)*, suggests that Barça represents not only athletic prowess but also Catalan cultural identity. This comes to a head during a match nicknamed "El Clásico," in which they face their bitter rivals, Real Madrid (whom many Barça fans view as stand-ins for Castilian cultural chauvinism).

• *Continue strolling.*

Walk 100 yards farther to #115, with an entrance flanked by two columns and a fine facade struggling to be noticed above the Ramblas ruckus. This marks the venerable **Royal Academy of Science and Arts building** (now home to a performing-arts theater). The building is emblematic of the city's striking architecture from the late 1800s—an industrial boom time that brought lots of construction. Look up: The clock high on the facade marks official Barcelona time—synchronize. The **Carrefour** supermarket next door has cheap groceries (at #113).

• *Remember that each of the Ramblas segments has its own name. You're now standing at what was the...*

❸ Rambla of the Little Birds (RIP)

A generation ago the Ramblas had a different kind of commerce. Locals came here for their newspapers, flowers, and even domestic pets. Traditionally, kids brought their parents here to buy birds, but also turtles and hamsters. But the clientele stopped coming and animal-rights groups lobbied to cut back on the stalls. Today, none of the traditional pet kiosks survive—and there's not a bird in sight. The commerce that remains is trinkets and drinks for hordes of tourists. Only the locals—and you—know the story behind the name for this stretch of the Ramblas, now lined with ice-cream and souvenir shops.

• *At #122 (the big, modern Citadines Hotel on the left), take a 100-yard detour through a modern passageway marked with the hotel's name to a restored...*

Roman Necropolis: Look down and imagine a 2,000-year-old road lined with tombs. Barcelona was founded about 10 BC by Romans, during the reign of Emperor Augustus, as the city of "Barcino," and this was the main road (Via Augusta) in and out of the walled town. (Today, the highway from Barcelona to France still follows the route laid out by this Roman thoroughfare.) In Roman cities, tombs were generally placed  along the roads outside the city walls. Emperor Augustus spent a lot of time on the Iberian Peninsula conquering new land, so the Romans were sure to incorporate Hispania into the empire's infrastructure.

Looking down at these ruins, you can see that Roman Barcino was about 10 feet lower than today's street level.

• *Return to the Ramblas and continue down 100 yards or so to the next cross street, Carrer de la Portaferrissa (on the left). Cross the street to see the* **decorative tile** *over a fountain still in use by locals. The scene shows what this spot looked like three centuries ago: There's the original city wall with its gate, and merchants are busy selling flowers, bananas, and, I believe, Barça T-shirts. Now cross the boulevard to the front of the big church.*

❹ Betlem Church

This imposing church is dedicated to Bethlehem, and for centuries locals have flocked here at Christmastime to see nativity scenes.

The church's diamond-shaped stonework is 17th-century Baroque: Check out the sloping roofline, ball-topped pinnacles, corkscrew columns, and scrolls above the entrance. This Baroque style, so common elsewhere in Europe, is unusual in Barcelona. That's because during the Baroque and Renaissance eras (1500-1800), Barcelona was broke. The city enjoyed two heydays: in the 1300s as a medieval sea-trading power, and in the 1800s during the prosperous Industrial Age. In between, Barcelona languished as New World discoveries shifted lucrative trade to the Atlantic, and the Spanish crown kept unruly Catalunya on a short leash. The church interior is stark, having been burned during the Spanish Civil War in the 1930s.

For a sweet treat, head around to the narrow lane on the far side of the church (Carrer d'en Xucla) to the recommended **Café Granja Viader,** which has specialized in baked and dairy delights since 1870. Step inside to see Viader family photos and early posters advertising Cacaolat—the local chocolate milk Barcelonans love.

• *Continue down the boulevard, through the stretch called the...*

❺ Rambla of Flowers

Pause at this charming section of the Ramblas to admire the nice apartment facades. This colorful block is lined with flower stands. Besides admiring the blossoms on display, gardeners covet the seeds sold here for varieties of radishes, greens, peppers, and beans seldom seen in the US—including the iconic green Padrón pepper of tapas fame (note that if you buy seeds, you're obligated to declare them at US customs when returning home).

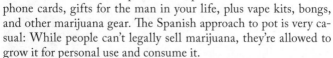

At #99 (on the right), the **Palau de la Virreina** sells last-minute tickets to dance and musical concerts.

At #97 (right), the **Casa Beethoven** shop is a cultural throwback to an earlier era, sedately selling music books, sheet music, and antiques like vinyl records.

On the left, at #100, **Tabacs Gimeno** has been selling cigars since the 1920s. Step inside and appreciate the dying art of cigar boxes and hand-crafted pipes. Go ahead, buy a Cuban (little singles for a couple of euros). As smoking has waned, shops like this have diversified. Tobacco shops sell stamps and phone cards, gifts for the man in your life, plus vape kits, bongs, and other marijuana gear. The Spanish approach to pot is very casual: While people can't legally sell marijuana, they're allowed to grow it for personal use and consume it.

• *A little farther on, across the street (opposite the Erotic Museum) is the arcaded entrance to Barcelona's great covered market, La Boqueria.*

❻ La Boqueria Market

This lively market hall is an explosion of *jamón* legs, bags of live snails, stiff fish, delicious oranges, and odd odors.

Since as far back as 1200, Barcelonans have bought their animal parts here. Taxes made it more costly to trade within the city walls, so the market, as were many in medieval times, was originally located just outside the city. It later expanded into the colonnaded courtyard of a now-gone monastery before being covered with a colorful arcade in 1850.

While tourists are drawn to the area around the main entry, locals know that the stalls up front pay the highest rent—and therefore inflate their prices and cater to out-of-towners. Skip the tempting but more expensive juices sold here and head to a booth farther in or along the sides.

The market and adjacent lanes are busy with tempting little eateries. Drop by a café for a *café con leche* or breakfast *tortilla española* (potato omelet). Once you get past the initial gauntlet, do some exploring. The small square on the north (uphill) side of the market hosts a farmers market in the mornings. Wander around—

as local architect Antoni Gaudí used to—and gain inspiration. Go on a scavenger hunt for some of these items:

Fresh, Local Produce: Stands show off seasonal fruits and vegetables that you'll see on menus. ("Market cuisine" is big at Barcelona restaurants—chefs come each morning to rustle up ingredients.) The focus here is on Spanish specialties like olives and saffron. The tubs of little green peppers that look like jalapeños are lightly fried for the dish called *pimientos de Padrón*. In  a culinary form of Russian roulette, a few of these mild peppers sometimes turn out to be hot—greeting the eater with a fiery jolt. In the fall, you'll see lots of mushrooms; in the winter, artichokes.

Certain food items are associated with a particular town—for example, anchovies from L'Escala, shrimp from Palamós, and so on. Among Catalans, this is a sort of code designating quality (like "Idaho potatoes" or "Washington apples").

Ham: Full legs of *jamón* (ham) abound. The many varieties of *jamón serrano* are distinguished by the type of pig they come from and what that pig ate. Top quality are *ibérico* (Iberian) and *bellota* (acorn eaters). Even by the slice these are very expensive, but gourmets pay €300 or more to go whole hock (see the "Sampling *Jamón*" sidebar on page 296).

Sausage: You'll see many types of the Catalan *botifarra* sausage. Some are ready to eat, while others must be cooked. *Chorizo* is the red Spanish sausage that's sometimes spicy (a rare bit of heat in an otherwise mild cuisine). A few meats are less common in American dishes, like rabbit and suckling pig. Beware: *Huevos de toro* means bull testicles—surprisingly inexpensive...and oh so good.

Seafood: The fishmonger stalls could double as a marine biology lab. In this Mediterranean city, people have come up with endless ways to harvest the sea. Fish is sold whole, not filleted—local shoppers like to look their dinner in the eye to be sure it's fresh. Count the many different types of shrimp (*gamba, langostino,* clawed *cigala*). Another popular treat is the tubular razor clam *(navaja).*

Cod: Some stalls specialize in dried salt cod *(bacalao)*. Historically, codfish—preserved in salt and dried—provided desperately needed protein on long sea voyages as Catalan merchants ventured far from their homes. Before it can be eaten, salt cod must be rehydrated, so it's sold either covered in salt or already submerged in water, to hasten the time between market and plate.

Olives: These are a keystone of the Spanish diet. Take a look at the 25 kinds offered at the Graus Olives i Conserves shop (center, at the back).

• *After you've scoped out the market, head back to the street and continue down the Ramblas.*

On your left, you're skirting the old Barri Gòtic neighborhood. Glance left through a modern cutaway arch for a glimpse of the medieval church tower of **Santa Maria del Pi.** This marks the Plaça del Pi and a great shopping street, Carrer Petritxol, which runs parallel to the Ramblas. Also nearby is the **Taverna Basca Iratí,** one of many user-friendly, Basque-style tapas bars in town, perfect for a quick pick-me-up on this walk).

On the right side of the Ramblas (at #83), find the highly regarded **Escribà bakery,** with its appealing Modernista facade: Look for the *Antigua Casa Figueras* sign arching over the doorway, mosaics of twining plants, a stained-glass peacock displaying his tail feathers, and undulating woodwork. In the sidewalk in front of the door, a plaque dates the building to 1902 (plaques like this identify historic shops all over town). Step inside the fine interior and indulge in a cream-filled *xuixo* pastry before continuing your ramble.

• *After another block, you reach the Liceu Metro station, marking the...*

❼ Heart of the Ramblas

At the Liceu Metro station's elevators, the Ramblas widens a bit into a small, lively square (Plaça de la Boqueria). Liceu marks the midpoint of the Ramblas between Plaça de Catalunya and the waterfront.

Underfoot, find the much-trod-upon **Joan Miró mosaic** in red, white, yellow, and blue. Miró was born and grew up right here in the Gothic Quarter. The mosaic's black arrow represents an anchor, a reminder of the

city's attachment to the ocean and a welcome to visitors arriving by sea (this is one of three Miró works welcoming visitors—there's also a mural at the airport and a sculpture at Sants train station). Miró's simple, colorful designs are found all over the city, from murals to mobiles to the CaixaBank logo. The best place to see his work is in the Fundació Joan Miró at Montjuïc (see page 71).

The surrounding buildings have playful ornamentation typical of the city. The **Chinese dragon** holding a lantern (at #82) decorates a former umbrella shop (notice the fun umbrellas perched high up). While the dragon may seem purely decorative, it's ac-

tually an important symbol of Catalan pride for its connection to the local patron saint, St. George (Jordi).

A few steps down (on the right) is the **Liceu Opera House** (Gran Teatre del Liceu), which hosts world-class opera, dance, and theater (box office left of main entrance, open Mon-Fri 10:00-19:00, Sat until 18:00, closed Sun). Opposite the opera house is **Café de l'Opera** (#74), an elegant stop for an expensive beverage. This bustling café, with Modernista decor and a historic atmosphere, boasts that it's been open since 1929, even during Spain's civil war.

RAMBLAS RAMBLE

• *We've seen the best stretch of the Ramblas; to cut this walk short, you could catch the Metro from here back to Plaça de Catalunya. Otherwise, let's continue to the port.*

Thirty yards along, pause and look left down a wide, straight street (Carrer de Ferran). Enjoy the view of elegant lamps, facades, and balconies as it leads to Plaça de Sant Jaume, the governmental center for both Barcelona and the region of Catalunya.

Head down the Ramblas another 50 yards (to #46), and turn left down an arcaded lane (Carrer de Colom) to the square called...

❽ Plaça Reial

Dotted with palm trees, surrounded by an arcade, and ringed by yellow buildings with white Neoclassical trim, this elegant square has a colonial ambience.

You'll find old-fashioned taverns *(cervecerías)*, modern bars with patio seating, and a Sunday coin-and-stamp market. Completing the picture are Gaudí's first public works (the two colorful helmeted lampposts).

This once-seedy part of town has been gentrified, making it more inviting and accessible. It's a lively hangout by day or by night (for after-dark options, see the Nightlife in Barcelona chapter). Big spaces like this (or the site of the Boqueria Market) often originated as monasteries. When these were dissolved in the 19th century, the government confiscated the land, turning the fine colonnaded squares into useful public spaces. To just relax over a drink and enjoy the scene, the **Ocaña cocktail bar** is a good bet.

• *Head back out to the Ramblas, and cross to the other side.*

A half-block detour down Carrer Nou de la Rambla brings you to **Palau Güell,** designed by Antoni Gaudí (on the left, at #3). Even from the outside, you get a sense of this innovative apartment, the first of Gaudí's Modernista buildings. As this is early Gaudí (built 1886-1890), it's darker and more Neo-Gothic than his more famous later work. The two parabolic-arch doorways and elaborate wrought-iron work signal his emerging nonlinear style. Completely restored in 2011, Palau Güell offers an informative look at a Gaudí interior (see the listing on page 44).

• *Return to the Ramblas and keep heading down the street.*

❾ El Raval Neighborhood

The neighborhood on the right side of this stretch of the Ramblas was nicknamed the Barri Xinès—the world's only Chinatown with nothing even remotely Chinese in or near it. The name was a prejudiced term broadly applied to any foreigner—whether from abroad or another part of Spain. The neighborhood's actual inhabitants were poor people from different backgrounds—Spanish, North African, and Gypsy (Roma). At night, the Barri Xinès was frequented by sex workers, drug pushers, and thieves, many of whom catered in one way or another to sailors wandering up from the port. Today, the Raval neighborhood is rapidly gentrifying (for a description of this area, see page 57).

At about this part of the Ramblas, you may see the first of the drag's surreal and goofy **human statues**—performers with creative and elaborate costumes. To enliven your ramble, drop coins into their cans (the money often kicks the statues into entertaining gear). Warning: Wherever people stop to gawk, pickpockets are at work.

All along the Ramblas you'll find *mantas,* sheets stretched out on the sidewalk with knockoffs of designer goods for sale. While police are supposed to run these vendors off and confiscate their merchandise, enforcement is lenient. It's almost a game: Police officers arrive, and vendors yank the strings attached to the four corners of their sheets, bundling their wares as they scatter. The police leave, and the vendors return.

The skyscraper to the right of the Ramblas is the 28-story Edi-

RAMBLAS RAMBLE

ficio Colón, built in 1970 as Barcelona's first high-rise. Nearby is the **Maritime Museum,** housed in what were the city's giant medieval shipyards.

• *Near the bottom of the Ramblas, take note of the Drassanes Metro stop, which can take you back to Plaça de Catalunya when you're ready. Up ahead is the...*

⑩ Columbus Monument

The 200-foot column honors Christopher Columbus, who came to Barcelona in 1493 after journeying to America. This Catalan

answer to Nelson's Column on London's Trafalgar Square (right down to the lions, perfect for posing with at the base) was erected for the 1888 Universal Exposition, an international fair that helped vault a surging Barcelona onto the world stage.

The base of the monument, ringed with four winged victories (taking flight to the four corners of the earth), is loaded with symbolism: statues and reliefs of mapmakers, navigators, early explorers preaching to Native Americans, and (enthroned just below the winged victories) the four regions of Spain. The reliefs near the bottom illustrate scenes from Columbus' fateful voyage. A tiny elevator ascends to the top of the column to a covered observation area for fine panoramas over the city (the entrance/ticket desk is in the TI, inside the base of the monument).

It's ironic that Barcelona celebrates this explorer; the "discoveries" of Columbus started 300 years of decline for the city, as

Europe began to face west, toward the Atlantic and the New World, rather than east, to the Mediterranean and the Orient. Within a few decades of Columbus, Barcelona had become a depressed backwater and didn't rebound until events like the 1888 Expo cemented its status as a comeback city.

• *Scoot across the busy traffic circle and continue straight ahead to the water's edge. Turn left, walk 50 yards, and find a pedestrian bridge that juts out over the harbor (with a wavy design and a wooden floor). Walk onto the bridge, then turn back and face the Columbus statue. This is a good spot to check out the...*

⑪ Waterfront

Survey Barcelona's bustling maritime zone. For more than 2,000 years, this harbor's trade has been the reason Barcelona is on the world map. Even today, the city is one of Europe's top ports, with many busy industrial harbors and several cruise terminals. (It's the busiest cruise port in the Mediterranean.) Despite the industrial activity, this low-impact stretch of seafront is clean, fresh, and people-friendly.

The wooden pedestrian **bridge** you're standing on is a modern extension of the Ramblas, called La Rambla de Mar ("Rambla of the Sea"). The bridge can swing out to allow boat traffic into the marina.

As you face Columbus, take in the sights. At the foot of the Ramblas are the docks with the *golondrinas* harbor-cruise boats (for details, see page 47). To the left of Columbus is the big Maritime Museum. Farther left, in the distance, is the majestic, 570-foot bluff of parklike **Montjuïc,** with sights and museums reachable by cable car (as you can see). To the right of the Columbus statue, the fanciful yellow Modernista-style building is the former port authority. Stretching to the right of that is a delightful promenade along the seawall of Barcelona's Old Port (Port Vell); it's worth a stroll. Along the promenade is a permanently moored historic schooner, the *Santa Eulàlia* (part of the Maritime Museum). Finally, over your right shoulder is Maremagnum, a modern shopping mall with a huge aquarium, restaurants, and piles of people. Its nighttime scene is rollicking and trendy.

Imagine: Near the end of the 20th century, this was a gloomy, depressed warehouse zone. But for the 1992 Olympics, city leaders refurbished the port area and rerouted a busy highway underground. Now the harbor is a fine space sprinkled with palm trees, restaurants, and eye-pleasing public art—a fitting gateway to the cosmopolitan city of Barcelona.

• *Your ramble is over. To get to other points in town, your best bet is to backtrack to the Drassanes Metro stop. Alternatively, you can catch bus #59 from the waterfront on Avenue Passeig de Colom (or take a cab) back to Plaça de Catalunya.*

To extend this walk, it's fun to stroll the length of the promenade to the iconic Barcelona Head *sculpture (by American Pop artist Roy Lichtenstein). This puts you right at the edge of El Born's shopping and restaurant area (*📖 *see the El Born Walk chapter). Or, from the* Barcelona Head, *circle back through Maremagnum, making a nice pedestrian loop around the marina.*

BARRI GÒTIC WALK

From Plaça de Catalunya to Plaça del Rei

Barcelona's Barri Gòtic (Gothic Quarter) is a bustling world of shops, bars, and nightlife packed into narrow, winding lanes and undiscovered courtyards. This is Barcelona's birthplace—where the ancient Romans built a city, where medieval Christians built their cathedral, where Jews gathered together, and where Barcelonans lived within a ring of protective walls until the 1850s, when the city expanded.

Today, this area of atmospheric tight lanes—nicknamed simply "El Gòtic"—is Barcelona's most historic neighborhood. It's a tangled yet inviting grab bag of grand squares, schoolyards, Art Nouveau storefronts, classy antique shops (especially along Carrer de la Palla), and musty junk stores. You'll encounter street musicians strumming Catalan folk songs and stroll among the lived-in balconies of the residents who make this a neighborhood.

Treat this self-guided walk from Plaça de Catalunya to Plaça del Rei as a historical scavenger hunt. You'll focus on the earliest chunk of Roman Barcelona right around the cathedral and explore some legacy sights from the city's medieval era.

Orientation

Length of This Walk: Figure 1.5 hours, not including entering sights.

When to Go: If you plan to enter the museums mentioned on this walk, avoid Monday, when some sights are closed.

Getting There: Start at the southeast corner of the Plaça de Catalunya (Metro: Plaça de Catalunya).

Church of Santa Anna: Free, usually Mon-Sat 10:00-12:00 & 16:00-18:00, Sun 10:00-14:00, Plazoleta de Santa Anna.

Barcelona Cathedral: €9, Mon-Fri 9:30-18:30, Sat until 17:15,

Sun 14:00-17:00—access may be limited during services. See the Barcelona Cathedral Tour chapter.

Old Main Synagogue: €4 to enter Mon-Fri 10:30-14:30 & 15:00-18:30 and Sun 10:30-15:00; free to enter Sun 16:00-19:00; closed Fri afternoons and Sat, shorter hours off-season; Carrer Marlet 5, +34 933 170 790, www.sinagogamayor.com.

Roman Temple of Augustus: Free, Tue-Sat 10:00-19:00, Sun until 20:00, Mon until 14:00.

Barcelona History Museum—Plaça del Rei: €7, free first Sun and other Sun from 15:00; open Tue-Sat 10:00-19:00, Sun until 20:00, closed Mon.

Tours: ∩ Download my free Barcelona City Walk audio tour, which covers portions of this walk.

Eating: For restaurants and tapas bars along the way, see page 196.

The Walk Begins

• *Start on Barcelona's grand main square,* **Plaça de Catalunya.** *From the northeast corner (between the giant El Corte Inglés department store and the Banco de España), head down the broad pedestrian boulevard called...*

❶ Avinguda del Portal de l'Angel

For much of Barcelona's history, this street was home to a major city gate. A medieval wall enclosed the city, and the entrance here—the "Gate of the Angel"—gave the street its name. An angel statue atop the gate purportedly kept Barcelonans safe from plagues and bid voyagers safe journey as they left the security of the city. Imagine the fascinating scene here at the Gate of the Angel, where Barcelona stopped and the Iberian wilds began.

Much later, this same boulevard (and much of the city) got a facelift in preparation for the 1888 Universal Exposition, the first international fair held in Spain. (The same event prompted construction of the Columbus Monument at the bottom of the Ramblas.) Improvements to the Gate of the Angel exemplify Barcelona's habit of spiffing itself up for big events. The city dressed up for another exposition in 1929 (Plaça d'Espanya fairgrounds) and again for the 1992 Olympic Games (sports facilities on Montjuïc and a rejuvenated waterfront).

Picture the traffic congestion here in the 1980s, before this street was closed to most motorized vehicles (if you visit in the morning you'll still dodge delivery trucks supplying stores). Today, you're elbow-to-elbow with shoppers cruising through some of the most expensive retail space in town. You'll notice branches of Zara, Oysho, Bershka, and Massimo Dutti, all founded by the same man (Amancio Ortega, among the richest people on the planet). He landed the best locations for his shops, each targeted to a different market segment.

Although today this street has been globalized and sanitized, a handful of businesses with local roots survive. On the right at the first corner (at #25), a blue-and-gold sign and appetizing display window mark **Planelles Donat**—long appreciated for its sweet *turró* (or *turrón*), an almond-and-honey candy that originated in the town of Xixona, in the coastal Alicante province. The shop is also popular for its ice cream, refreshing *orxata* (or *horchata*, an almond-flavored drink), and *granissat* (or *granizado*, ice slush). Imagine how historic shops like this one started, with artisans from villages camping out here in a vestibule of some big building, sell-

ing baskets of their homemade goodies—and eventually evolving into real shops.

• *A block farther down, pause at Carrer de Santa Anna to admire the Art Nouveau awning. From here, take a half-block detour to the right on Carrer de Santa Anna. At #32, go through a large entryway to the pleasant courtyard of the...*

BARRI GÒTIC WALK

❷ Church of Santa Anna

This austere Catalan Gothic church—a 12th-century gem—was part of a convent and still has its marker cross standing outside. To the left of the cross, approach the gate, where you can peek inside the fine cloister—an arcaded walkway around a leafy courtyard. Climb the modern stairs across from the church for views of the bell tower. Inside the church you'll find a bare Romanesque interior, topped with an octagonal wooden roof. At the back of the nave, the recumbent-knight tomb is of Miguel de Boera, renowned admiral of Charles V. (Let's hope his hands were not that large.)

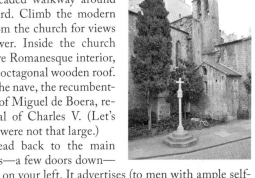

As you head back to the main drag, you'll pass—a few doors down—a **condom shop** on your left. It advertises (to men with ample self-esteem): *Para los pequeños placeres de la vida* ("For the little pleasures in life"). Spain is surprisingly liberal, considering that it was kept in a moralistic time-warp under the extremely conservative dictator Francisco Franco, who ruled from 1939 to 1975. In the generations

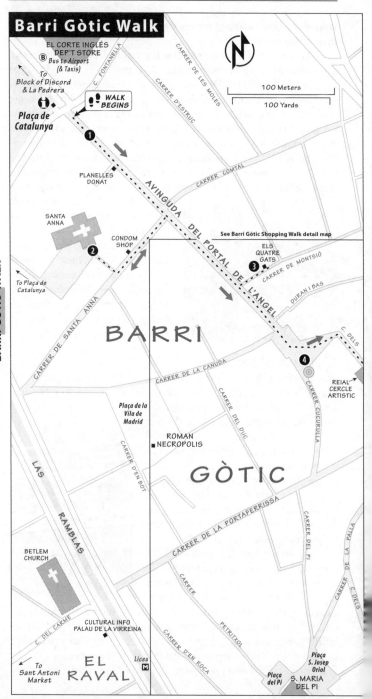

Barri Gòtic Walk

EL CORTE INGLÉS DEP'T STORE
Ⓑ Bus to Airport (& Taxis)

To Block of Discord & La Pedrera

Plaça de Catalunya

WALK BEGINS

C. FONTANELLA

CARRER DE LES MOLES

CARRER D'ESTRUC

100 Meters
100 Yards

PLANELLES DONAT

AVINGUDA DEL PORTAL DE L'ANGEL

CARRER COMTAL

SANTA ANNA

CONDOM SHOP

See Barri Gòtic Shopping Walk detail map

ELS QUATRE GATS

CARRER DE MONTSIÓ

DURAN I BAS

To Plaça de Catalunya

CARRER DE SANTA ANNA

BARRI

C. DELS

REIAL CERCLE ARTISTIC

CARRER DE LA CANUDA

Plaça de la Vila de Madrid

CARRER DEL DUC

CARRER CUCURULLA

ROMAN NECROPOLIS

GÒTIC

LAS RAMBLAS

CARRER D'EN BOT

CARRER DE LA PORTAFERRISSA

CARRER DEL PI

CARRER DE LA PALLA

C. DELS

BETLEM CHURCH

CARRER

CULTURAL INFO PALAU DE LA VIRREINA

C. DEL CARME

CARRER D'EN ROCA

PETRITXOL

Plaça S. Josep Oriol

To Sant Antoni Market

EL RAVAL

Liceu Ⓜ

Plaça del Pi

S. MARIA DEL PI

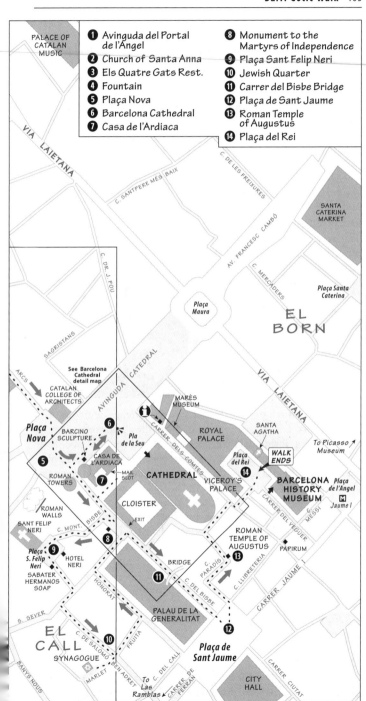

1. Avinguda del Portal de l'Àngel
2. Church of Santa Anna
3. Els Quatre Gats Rest.
4. Fountain
5. Plaça Nova
6. Barcelona Cathedral
7. Casa de l'Ardiaca
8. Monument to the Martyrs of Independence
9. Plaça Sant Felip Neri
10. Jewish Quarter
11. Carrer del Bisbe Bridge
12. Plaça de Sant Jaume
13. Roman Temple of Augustus
14. Plaça del Rei

BARRI GÒTIC WALK

since Franco, the major Catholic issues (contraception, abortion, divorce, cohabitation, and so on) have swung to the liberal side.

Take a moment here on Carrer de Santa Anna to notice little details. Look up at pulleys (handy in buildings with no elevators). See the ironwork buildings with fine old entrances and cheaper facades (with plasterwork fashioned into fake columns). Note how all the buildings maxed out their late-19th-century height limits. Here (and around town), you may see the *estelada* flag—red and gold with a blue triangle and white star—a symbol of Catalan separatists.

• *Backtrack to Avinguda del Portal de l'Angel and continue down the street. At Carrer de Montsió (on the left) side-trip a half-block to...*

❸ Els Quatre Gats

This restaurant (at #3) is a historic monument, tourist attraction, nightspot, and recommended eatery (see listing on page 196). It's

famous for being the circa-1900 bohemian-artist hangout where Picasso nursed drinks with friends and had his first one-man show. The building itself, by prominent architect Josep Puig i Cadafalch, represents Neo-Gothic Modernisme. Take a look around the corner from the entrance—it looks more like a medieval church or a castle, with pointed arches, windows with stone tracery, and gargoyles peeking from the stonework.

Stepping inside, you feel the turn-of-the-century vibe. Even if you don't eat or drink here, you can check out the vintage photos on the wall and take a quick look around (ask *"Solo mirar, por favor?"*). Rich Barcelona elites and would-be avant-garde artists looked to Paris (not Madrid) for cultural inspiration. This place was clearly influenced by Paris' Le Chat Noir, a cabaret/café and the hangout of Montmartre intellectuals. Like Le Chat Noir, Els Quatre Gats even published its own artsy magazine for a while. The story of the name? When the proprietor told his friends that he'd stay open 24 hours a day, they said, "No one will come." Using a popular Catalan phrase, they told him, "It'll just be you and four cats."

• *Return to and continue down Avinguda del Portal de l'Angel. You'll soon reach a fork in the road and a building with a...*

❹ Fountain

The blue and yellow tilework, a circa-1918 addition to this even older fountain, depicts ladies with big jugs of water. Picture the scene here back in the 17th century. No one had indoor plumbing, and the neighborhood women would gather to fill their big crocks and take them home. This fountain was especially important as the last watering stop for horses before leaving town. Even until 1940, about 10 percent of Barcelonans still

got their water from fountains like this.

• *Shoppers will feel the pull of wonderful little shops down the street to the right. But be strong and take the left fork, down Carrer dels Arcs. Rounding the corner, you'll pass the* **Reial Cercle Artístic,** *hosting exhibitions by Catalan artists (free, daily 10:00-14:00 & 15:00-20:00). Continue and enter the large square called...*

❺ Plaça Nova

As you enter the square, you can't miss the prickly steeple of the Barcelona Cathedral (which we'll visit shortly). But first, take in a few other sights.

Two bold **Roman towers** flank a street leading off the square. These once guarded the entrance gate of the ancient Roman city of Barcino. The big stones that make up the base of the (reconstructed) towers are actually Roman. Near the base of the left tower, **modern bronze letters** spell out "BARCINO." The city's name may have come from Barca, one of Hannibal's generals, who is said to have passed through during Hannibal's roundabout invasion of Italy. At Barcino's peak, the **Roman wall** (see the section stretching to the left of the towers) was 25 feet high and a mile around, with 74 towers. It enclosed a population of 4,000.

One of the towers has a bit of reconstructed **Roman aqueduct** (notice the streambed on top). In ancient times, bridges of stone carried fresh water from the distant hillsides into the walled city.

Opposite the towers is the modern **Catalan College of Architects** building (Collegi d'Arquitectes de Barcelona), which is, ironically for a city with so much great architecture, quite ugly. The frieze was designed by Picasso (1962) in his distinctive simplified style. With just a few squiggly stick-figures, Picasso captured

The Barri Gòtic Through History

As you tour the Old City, you'll see elements from every layer of Barcelona's 2,000-year history. There are ancient Roman ruins from when this was the important provincial capital of Barcino, enclosed within a circular wall. After Rome fell around the year 500, Barcelona remained vibrant while much of Europe floundered in darkness. Centered around the cathedral, a hive of merchants and artisans populated the twisty lanes of the Gothic Quarter, or "Barri Gòtic."

Barcelona thrived in the 1200s and 1300s as a cosmopolitan seaport. Later, that tradition of international trade made the city a natural port of call for none other than Christopher Columbus. (We'll see reminders of him along this walk.) By the late 1800s, the city had boomed into an industrial powerhouse. It became the cradle of a new artistic style—Modernisme—which produced fanciful Neo-Gothic buildings like El Quatre Gats restaurant and the facade of the Barcelona Cathedral. That energetic spirit is still alive today. It's obvious in the shops in this quarter, in the Catalan independence movement, and in the 24/7 energy of the Barri Gòtic's café culture.

traditional Catalan activities. If you check out all three sides of the building, you'll see scenes suggesting music, bullfighting, sea trade, and the *sardana* dance. The branch-waving kings represent the giant puppets *(gegants)* paraded through the streets during local festivals (see sidebar, page 36). Picasso spent his formative years (1895-1904, age 14-23) here in the Old City. He drank

with fellow bohemians at Els Quatre Gats and frequented brothels a few blocks from here on Carrer d'Avinyó ("Avignon")—which inspired his influential Cubist painting *Les Demoiselles d'Avignon*. Picasso's hunger to be on the cutting edge propelled him from the Barri Gòtic to Paris, where he eventually remade modern art.

• *Immediately to the left as you face the Picasso frieze,* **Carrer de la Palla** *is another inviting shopping street (described in the Shopping in Barcelona chapter). But let's head left through Plaça Nova to take in the mighty...*

❻ Barcelona Cathedral

The facade is a virtual catalog of Gothic motifs. There's the pointed arch over the entrance and the stained-glass windows with elaborate stone tracery. Statues of robed saints stand in niches, and winged angels teeter on the octagonal bell towers. And the whole thing is topped with three tall steeples. These pointy spires are meant to give the impression of a church flickering with spiritual fires. This was the Gothic style called Flamboyant—meaning "flame-like."

This has been Barcelona's holiest spot for 2,000 years. The Romans built their temple of Jupiter right here. In AD 343, that pagan temple was replaced by a Christian cathedral. Around the year 1000, that building was replaced again, this time by a Romanesque-style church. The current Gothic structure was started around 1300, during the medieval glory days of the Catalan nation, and finished in 1450. But the much newer facade, dating from the 1800s, is in the Neo-Gothic style of Modernisme. That part of the construction was capped in 1913 with the central spire, 230 feet tall. So, in a way, the cathedral is evidence of Barcelona's two "golden ages"—its seaport heyday in the 1300s, and its 19th-century revival.

The square in front of the cathedral, **Pla de la Seu,** is flanked on the left by a building housing a small TI and the Diocesan Museum of Barcelona. This area is where Barcelonans dance the *sardana* on weekends (see page 7). If there's no dancing, you may see a street musician. The city strictly regulates buskers and gives permits only to quality performers at designated points like this one.

📖 The cathedral's interior—with its vast space, peaceful cloister, and many ornate chapels—is worth a visit (see the next chapter). If you interrupt this tour to visit the cathedral now, you'll exit the cloister a block down Carrer del Bisbe. From there you can circle back to the right, following the wall of the cathedral to visit stop #7—or skip #7 and step directly into stop #8.

As you stand in the square facing the cathedral, look far to your left to see the multicolored, wavy canopy marking the roofline of the **Santa Caterina Market.** The busy street between here and the market—called Via Laietana—is the boundary between the Barri Gòtic and the funkier, edgier **El Born** neighborhood.

• *For now, return to the Roman towers and pass between them to head up Carrer del Bisbe. Take an immediate left, up the ramp to the entrance of...*

Gegants

Anyone who's experienced a festival in Barcelona can't have missed the dancing costumed giants bobbing and swinging to the music. These *gegants* (*gi-gantes* in Castilian) first ap-peared in Corpus Christi cele-brations back in the 14th century and were modeled on biblical themes. Over time the puppets lost their strictly reli-gious identities and came to also represent royalty, local lu-minaries, and historical fig-ures, as well as simple, every-day people.

Gegants rise to a height of 10 to 12 feet, and sometimes even taller. Their heads and arms are made of papier-mâché and are attached to a framework of wood or aluminum that's covered by the character's costume. The whole rig is then car-ried by a puppeteer who, hidden inside, is linked to the frame-work with a harness. As the puppeteer dances and spins, the puppet's arms swing freely through the air.

Often seen along with the *gegants* are the comical *cap-grossos* ("big heads")—costumed characters with oversized papier-mâché heads.

➐ Casa de l'Ardiaca

It's free to enter this mansion that was once the archdeacon's res-idence and now functions as the city archives (closed Sun). The elaborately carved doorway is Renaissance. To the right of the doorway is a carved mail slot by 19th-century Modernista archi-tect Lluís Domènech i Mon-taner. Enter a small courtyard with a fountain. Notice how the century-old palm tree seems to be held captive by urban man. Next, step inside the air-condi-

tioned lobby of the city archives, where—along the back of the ancient Roman wall—there are often free exhibits. At the left end of the lobby, go through the archway and look down into the stair-well for a peek at more impressive Roman stonework. Back in the courtyard, climb to the balcony for views of the cathedral steeple and gargoyles. From this vantage point, note the small Romanesque chapel on the right (the only surviving 13th-century bit of the cathedral) and how it's dwarfed by the towering cathedral.

• *Return to Carrer del Bisbe and turn left. After a few steps, you reach a small square with a bronze statue ensemble.*

❽ Monument to the Martyrs of Independence

Five Barcelona patriots—including two priests—calmly receive their last rites before being garroted (strangled) for resisting Na-poleon's occupation of Spain in the early 19th century. They'd been out-raged by French atroci-ties in Madrid (depicted in Goya's famous *Third of May* painting in Madrid's Prado Museum). Accord-ing to the plaque mark-ing their mortal remains,

these martyrs to independence gave their lives in 1809 *"por Dios, por la Patria, y por el Rey"*—for God, country, and king.

Tiles flanking the monument tell the story: On the far left, the patriots receive their last communion in prison. On the near left, they're escorted out of the citadel—that hated symbol of for-eign occupation. On the near right is the execution scene. See the three doomed men huddled with their priests below the instru-ments of their coming execution: ropes and a ladder. Priests, con-sidered privileged, were strangled, while the common people were hung. (Spain last used the garrote in 1974, and France last used the guillotine in 1977. Europe is generally appalled that the US still executes people.) After their execution, all the martyrs were buried across the way in the cathedral cloister.

The plaza offers interesting views of the cathedral's towers. Opposite the square is the cathedral's exit through the cloister.

• *Exit the square down tiny Carrer de Montjuïc del Bisbe (to the right as you face the martyrs). This leads to the cute...*

❾ Plaça Sant Felip Neri

This shaded square serves as the play-ground of an elementary school and is often bursting with energetic kids speaking Catalan (just a couple of gen-erations ago, this would have been ille-gal and they would be speaking Span-

ish). It's a fun scene to enjoy at a respectful distance (no photos of the children, please).

The Church of Sant Felip Neri, which Gaudí attended, is still pocked with bomb damage from the Spanish Civil War. As a stronghold of democratic, anti-Franco forces, Barcelona saw a lot of fighting. The shrapnel that damaged this church was meant for the nearby Catalan government building (Palau de la Generalitat, which we'll see later on this walk).

Just as the Germans practiced their new air force technology in Guernica in the years leading up to World War II, the fascist friends of Franco (both German and Italian) also helped bomb Barcelona from the air. As was the fascist tactic, a second bombing followed the first as survivors combed the rubble for lost loved ones. A plaque on the wall (left of church door) honors the 42 killed—mostly children—in that 1938 aerial bombardment.

In the medieval tangle of the Barri Gòtic, people gathered densely within the city's protective walls, leaving very few open spaces—except for cemeteries clustering around churches. Many squares, like this one, started out as cemeteries. They later became open spaces when, with the Enlightenment (c. 1800) and modern concern for hygiene, graveyards were moved outside of town.

The buildings here were paid for by the guilds that powered the local economy. The shoemakers guild (to the right of the arch where you entered the square) is decorated above the windows with reliefs depicting boots.

• Grab a beverage and stay a while (the posh **Hotel Neri** serves drinks overlooking the square). Or exit the square past the fun **Sabater Hermanos** artisanal soap shop, and head down Carrer de Sant Felip Neri. At the T-intersection, turn right onto Carrer de Sant Sever, then immediately left on Carrer de Salomó Ben Adret. You've entered the...

⑩ Jewish Quarter (El Call)

In Catalan, a Jewish quarter goes by the name El Call—literally "narrow passage," for the tight lanes where medieval Jews were forced to live under the watchful eye of the nearby cathedral. (Some believe El Call comes from the Hebrew *kahal*, which means congregation.) At the peak of Barcelona's El Call, some 4,000 Jews were crammed into just a few alleys in this neighborhood.

Walk down Carrer de Salomó Ben Adret, and pass through the charming little square (a gap in the dense tangle of medieval buildings cleared by another civil war bomb), where you will find a few cafés. Take the next lane to the right (Carrer de Marlet). On the right is the (literally) low-profile, four-foot-high entrance to what in the Middle Ages was likely Barcelona's **main synagogue** (L'Antiga Sinagoga Mayor).

The structure dates from the third century, but it was destroyed during a brutal pogrom in 1391. The city's remaining Jews were expelled in 1492, and artifacts of their culture—including this synagogue—were forgotten for centuries. In the 1980s, a historian tracked down the synagogue using old tax-collection records. Another clue that this was the main synagogue: In accordance with Jewish traditions, it stubbornly faces east (toward Jerusalem), putting it at an angle at odds with surrounding structures. The sparse interior includes access to two small subterranean rooms with Roman walls topped by a medieval Catalan vault. Look through the glass floor to see dyeing vats used for a shop that later occupied this site.

• *From the synagogue, start back the way you came but then continue straight ahead, onto Carrer de la Fruita. Pause and look around. Imagine life here centuries ago. The place was filled with life, with people hauling water and selling goods from small carts, kids running around, and carriages banging against stony corners. These tight lanes, like deep canyons, are in the shade for all but a few minutes a day.*

At the T-intersection, turn left, then right, to find your way back to the Martyrs statue. From here, we'll turn right down Carrer del Bisbe to the...

⓫ Carrer del Bisbe Bridge

This has been a main street since the days of ancient Barcino. The Romans built straight streets on a rectangular grid plan, and this one led to their town center.

Arching across Carrer del Bisbe is a medieval-looking skybridge. This structure—reminiscent of Venice's Bridge of Sighs—connects the Catalan government building (on the right) with what was the Catalan president's ceremonial residence (on the left). Though the bridge appears to be centuries old, it was constructed in the 1920s by Catalan architect Joan Rubió (a follower of Gaudí), who also did the carved ornamentation on the buildings.

Check out the carved decor on the bridge and (even more) on the buildings. You'll see jutting angels, dragons, centaurs, skulls, goddesses, old men with beards, climbing vines, and coats of arms. The delicate facade a few steps farther down on the right is much older. It marks the 15th-century entry to the government palace.

• *Continue along Carrer del Bisbe to...*

⑫ Plaça de Sant Jaume

This stately central square of the Barri Gòtic takes its name from the Church of St. James (in Catalan: Jaume, JOW-mah) that once stood here. After the church was torn down in 1823, the square was fixed up and rechristened "Plaça de la Constitució" in honor of the then decade-old Spanish constitution. But the plucky Catalans never embraced the name, and after Franco, they went back to the original—even though the church is long gone.

Set at the intersection of ancient Barcino's main thoroughfares, this square was once a Roman forum. In that sense, it's been the seat of city government for 2,000 years. Today it's home to the two top governmental buildings in Catalunya: Palau de la Generalitat and, across from it, the Barcelona City Hall.

For more than six centuries, the **Palau de la Generalitat** (on the uphill side of the square) has housed the offices of the autonomous government of Catalunya.

It always flies the Catalan flag next to the obligatory Spanish one. Above the building's doorway is Catalunya's patron saint—St. George (Jordi), slaying the dragon. The dragon (which you'll see all over town) is an important Catalan symbol. From these balconies, the nation's leaders (and soccer heroes) greet the people on momentous days. The square is often the site of festivals or demonstrations, from a single aggrieved citizen with a megaphone (the phone company billed me twice!) to riotous thousands (demanding independence from Spain, for instance).

Facing the Generalitat across the square is the **Barcelona City Hall** (Casa de la Ciutat). It sports a statue (in the niche to the left of the door) of a different James—

"Jaume el Conqueridor." The 13th-century King Jaume I is credited with freeing Barcelona from French control, granting self-government, and setting it on course to become a major city. He was the driving force behind construction of the Royal Palace (which we'll see shortly).

Locals treasure the independence these two government buildings represent. In the 20th century, when Barcelona opposed the dictator Franco, he retaliated by abolishing the regional government and (effectively) outlawing the Catalan language and customs. Two years after Franco's death in 1975, joyous citizens packed this square to celebrate the return of self-rule.

Look left and right down the main streets branching off the square; they're lined with ironwork streetlamps and balconies draped with plants. Carrer de Ferran, which leads to the Ramblas, is classic Barcelona.

In ancient Roman days, when Plaça de Sant Jaume was the town's central square, two main streets converged here—the Decumanus (Carrer del Bisbe—bishop's street) and the Cardus (Carrer de la Llibreteria/Carrer del Call). The forum's biggest building was a massive temple of Augustus, which we'll see next.

• *Facing the Generalitat, exit the square going up the second street to the right of the building, on tiny Carrer del Paradís. Follow this street as it turns right. When it swings left, pause at #10, the entrance to the...*

⓭ Roman Temple of Augustus (Temple Roma d'August)

You're standing at the summit of Mont Tàber, the Barri Gòtic's highest spot. A plaque on the wall by the entrance reads: "Mont Tàber, 16.9 meters" (elevation 55 feet). At your feet, a millstone inlaid in the pavement also marks a momentous spot. It was here that the ancient Romans founded the town of Barcino around 12 BC. They built a *castrum* (fort) on the hilltop, protecting the harbor, and this temple to honor their emperor, Augustus.

Go inside for a peek at the last vestiges of the imposing Roman temple. All that's left are four columns and some fragments of the transept and its plinth (good English info on-site). The huge columns, dating from the late first century BC, are as old as Barcelona itself. They were part of the ancient town's biggest structure, dedicated to Augustus, who was worshipped as a god. These Corinthian columns (with deep fluting and topped with leafy capitals) were the back corner of a 120-foot-long temple that extended from here to Barcino's forum... Plaça de Sant Jaume (where you just were).

• *Continue down Carrer del Paradís one block. When you bump into the back end of the cathedral, pause to notice how amazingly well-preserved the cityscape is here, under an assembly of gargoyles.*

Take a right, going down Carrer de la Pietat/Baixada de Santa Clara. (Is that a unicorn gargoyle on the side of the church? A unigoyle?) Go 100 yards until you emerge into a square called...

⑭ Plaça del Rei

This square is a great place to end our walk, as it calls up Barcelona's medieval golden age. The buildings enclosing the square recall the city's medieval past. Face the central section (topped by a five-story addition) which was the core of the **Royal Palace** (Palau Reial Major). A vast hall on its ground floor once served as the throne room and reception room. From the 13th to the 15th century, the Royal Palace housed Barcelona's counts as

well as the resident kings of Aragon. One of those kings of Aragon, Ferdinand, married Isabel, queen of Castile, creating the united country of Spain. In 1493, here in this Royal Palace, they hosted a triumphant Christopher Columbus, accompanied by six New World natives (whom he called "*indios*") and several pure-gold statues. King Ferdinand and Queen Isabel welcomed him home and honored him with the title "Admiral of the Oceans."

To the right and up the stairs is the palace's church, the 14th-century **Chapel of Santa Agatha,** where royalty worshiped. The venerable church sits atop the foundations of a Roman wall (entrance included in Barcelona History Museum admission; see page 51).

To the left is the **Viceroy's Palace** (Palau del Lloctinent). It was built in the 1500s for the right-hand man of the Spanish monarch, who was now located in far-off Castile. So, in a way, this building represents the rise of Spain and the decline of Aragon, Catalunya, and the city of Barcelona. Catalunya was swallowed up into greater Spain, the Royal Palace was demoted to a small regional residence, and Barcelona declined.

Step into the interior courtyard, a delightful Renaissance space with a fine staircase, a coffered wood ceiling, and an imposing bronze door sculpted by Josep Maria Subirachs (who is also responsible for the Passion Facade at the Sagrada Família). Over the years, this building served as the local headquarters of the Spanish Inquisition. It currently houses the historical archives of the crown of Aragon. Among their treasures is the so-called **Santa Fe Capitulations**—the 1492 contract between Columbus and the Catholic Monarchs that set the terms for his upcoming sea voyage. (The document is rarely on display but there's often a poster of it on the courtyard wall.)

Ironically, Columbus' discoveries changed Barcelona forever. Spain shifted its focus to the New World, away from Barcelona and its Mediterranean trade routes. The political center moved to

Madrid, and while Spain enjoyed its golden age, Barcelona spiraled downward. By the 1700s, it was a dirty, cramped city, crowded within the medieval walls of the Barri Gòtic. But Catalunya would rise again. In the 1800s, Barcelona became Spain's industrial engine; the city expanded and beautified itself. There was renewed interest in the Catalan language and culture. Today, Barcelona is a vibrant international metropolis. And, in the Barri Gòtic, the proud spirit of Catalunya lives on.

• *Our walk is over. While you're here, you could check out the Plaça del Rei branch of the* **Barcelona History Museum,** *starring some excavated Roman ruins. (For a peek*

at the Roman streets without going in, look through the low windows lining the square.)

It's easy to get your bearings by backtracking to either Plaça de Sant Jaume or the cathedral. The Jaume I Metro stop is two blocks away (leave the square on Carrer del Veguer and turn left). From here, you could head over to the Santa Caterina Market to browse for lunch before tackling my El Born Walk. Or simply wander through more of this area, enjoying Barcelona at its Gothic best.

BARRI GÒTIC WALK

BARCELONA CATHEDRAL TOUR

Although Barcelona's cathedral doesn't rank among Europe's finest (and frankly, barely cracks the Top 20), it's still important and easy to visit. This quick tour introduces you to the cathedral's highlights: its vast nave, rich chapels, elaborately carved choir, tomb of Santa Eulàlia, and oasis-like cloister. Other sights inside are the view terrace and a little museum.

Orientation

Cost & Hours: €11 includes cathedral, choir, view terrace, museum, and cloister. Keep your ticket handy as you will need it to enter each area. Cathedral open Mon-Fri 9:30-18:30, Sat until 17:15, Sun 14:00-17:00; last entry 45 minutes before closing. Note that access may be limited during services.

Information: +34 933 428 262, www.catedralbcn.org.

Dress Code: The dress code is strictly enforced; don't wear tank tops, shorts, or skirts above the knee.

Getting There: The huge, can't-miss-it cathedral is in the center of the Barri Gòtic on Pla de la Seu (Metro: Jaume I). It's easy to splice your cathedral visit into my Barri Gòtic Walk (see the previous chapter).

Getting In: The main entrance faces Pla de la Seu.

Tours: ∩ Download my free Barcelona City Walk audio tour, which includes a tour of the cathedral interior. Or scan the QR code at the entrance for a downloadable audioguide.

Church Services: Mass is generally in Catalan, with a single noon service in Spanish (also in Spanish at 18:00 Sat-Sun).

Length of This Tour: Allow 30 minutes—more if visiting the view terrace and museum.

Visitor Services: A tiny pay WC is in the center of the cloister.

BACKGROUND

This has been Barcelona's holiest spot for 2,000 years. The Romans built their Temple of Jupiter here. In AD 343, the pagan temple was replaced with a Christian cathedral. That building was supplanted by a Romanesque-style church (11th century). The current Gothic structure was started in 1298 and finished in 1450, during the medieval glory days of the Catalan nation. The facade was humble, so in the 19th century the proud local bourgeoisie (enjoying a second golden age) redid it in a more ornate, Neo-Gothic style. Construction was capped in 1913 with the central spire, 230 feet tall.

The Tour Begins

• *Enter the cathedral and look up.*

❶ Nave

The spacious church is 300 feet long and 130 feet wide. Tall pillars made of stone blocks support the crisscross vaults. Each round keystone where the arches cross features a different saint. Typical of many Spanish churches, there's a choir—an enclosed area of wooden seats in the middle of the nave, creating a more intimate space for worship and isolating the elite who could actually

get close to the altar and hear the sermons. The Gothic church also has fine stained glass, ironwork chandeliers, a 16th-century organ (left transept), tombstones in the pavement, and an "ambulatory" floor plan, allowing worshippers to amble around to the chapel of their choice.

❷ Side Chapels

The nave is ringed with 28 chapels. Besides creating worship spaces, the walls defining these chapels serve as interior buttresses supporting the roof (which is why the exterior walls are smooth, without the normal Gothic buttresses outside). Barcelona honors many of the homegrown saints found in these chapels with public holidays.

From the 13th to 15th century, these side chapels were simply moneymakers for the church. After the Black Death ravaged the population—and the economy—the church rented chapels to guilds to function as private offices, which came with the medieval

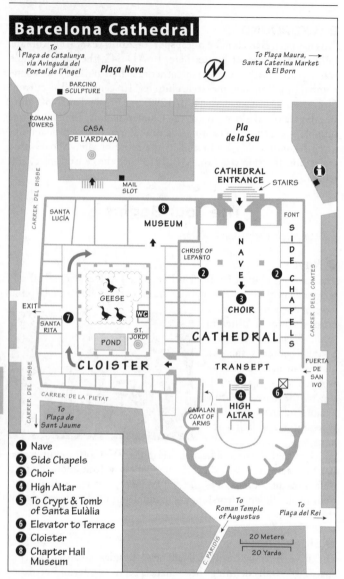

Barcelona Cathedral

To Plaça de Catalunya via Avinguda del Portal de l'Angel

Plaça Nova

To Plaça Maura, → Santa Caterina Market & El Born

BARCINO SCULPTURE

ROMAN TOWERS

CASA DE L'ARDIACA

Pla de la Seu

CARRER DEL BISBE

MAIL SLOT

CATHEDRAL ENTRANCE

STAIRS

SANTA LUCÍA

MUSEUM **8**

FONT

1

N A V E

S I D E   C H A P E L S

CHRIST OF LEPANTO

2

2

CARRER DELS COMTES

EXIT

GEESE

WC

3

CHOIR

SANTA RITA

7

POND

ST. JORDI

CATHEDRAL

CLOISTER

←

TRANSEPT

PUERTA DE SAN IVO

CARRER DEL BISBE

CARRER DE LA PIETAT

To Plaça de Sant Jaume

CATALAN COAT OF ARMS

5

4

HIGH ALTAR

6 ☒

BARCELONA CATHEDRAL

1 Nave
2 Side Chapels
3 Choir
4 High Altar
5 To Crypt & Tomb of Santa Eulàlia
6 Elevator to Terrace
7 Cloister
8 Chapter Hall Museum

To Roman Temple of Augustus

To Plaça del Rei

C. PARIDIS

20 Meters
20 Yards

equivalent of safety-deposit boxes and a notary public (documents signed here came with the force of God). Notice how the iron gates are more than decorative—they were protective. The rich ornamentation was sponsored by local guilds. Think of it: The church was the community's most high-profile space, and these chapels were a kind of advertising to illiterate worshippers.

The church is still fundraising. Candles, which aren't free, power your prayers. As you visit the chapels, employ one or more electronic candles. Pop in a coin and you'll turn on a candle. Or save your coins to light a real candle, which you can buy at the main entrance, or in the cloister gift shop (often not displayed—ask).

• *We'll walk past a few of these chapels, just to get a sense of them. Begin by heading to the back-left corner (over your left shoulder as you enter the main door).*

The chapel at the back corner of the nave has an old **baptismal font** that once stood in the original fourth-century church. The Native Americans that Columbus brought back to town were supposedly baptized here.

• *Work your way down the left aisle.*

The first chapel along the left wall is dedicated to **St. Severus,** the bishop here way back in AD 290.

The second chapel was by, for, and of the local **shoe guild.** Notice the two painted doors with shoes above them that lead to the back office. As the patron of shoemakers was St. Mark, there are plenty of winged lions in this chapel.

• *Cross the nave over to the large chapel in the back-right corner and work your way, one chapel at a time, down that side of the church.*

This chapel (reserved for worship) features the beloved **Christ of Lepanto** crucifix. They say the angular wooden figure of Christ, which swings to the left, leaned to dodge a cannonball during the history-changing Battle of Lepanto (1571), which stopped the Ottomans (and Islam) from advancing into Europe.

• *Now head down the right aisle.*

The next chapel has a statue of **St. Anthony** holding the Baby Jesus. His feast day (January 17) is one of many celebrated in the city with an appearance by the *gegants* (giant puppets), a street fair, horse races, and a blessing of pets.

The third chapel honors a 20th-century bishop, **San Josep Oriol,** who survived an assassination attempt in the cathedral cloister.

The golden fourth chapel is for **St. Roch** (at the top, pointing to his leg wound, above St. Pancraç), whose feast day is celebrated joyously in the Barri Gòtic in mid-August.

The fifth chapel has a black-and-white sideways statue of **St. Ramon (Raymond) of Penyafort** (1190-1275), the Dominican Bishop of Barcelona who heard Pope Gregory IX's sins and is the patron saint of lawyers (and, therefore, extremely busy). Ramon figures into the city's biggest festival, La Mercè, since he had a miraculous vision of the Virgin of Mercy.

A few chapels down, the eighth chapel is worth a look for its over-the-top golden altarpiece decor nearly crowding out **Bishop Pacià**—considered one of the Church fathers (c. AD 310-391).

• *Now, head to the choir—straight ahead from the church's main doors.*

❸ Choir

The 15th-century choir *(coro)* features ornately carved stalls. During the standing parts of the Mass, the chairs were folded up, but

VIPs could still lean on those little wooden ledges. Each was creatively carved and—since you couldn't sit on sacred things— the artists were free to enjoy some secular and naughty fun here. In 1518, the stalls were painted with the coats of arms of Europe's nobility. They gathered here as members of the Knights of the Golden Fleece to honor Charles V, king of Spain, who was making his first trip to the country he ruled. Like a proto-United Nations, they also discussed how to work together to defend Europe from the Turkish threat. Check out the detail work on the impressive wood-carved pulpit near the altar, supported by flying angels.

• *At the front of the church stands the...*

❹ High Altar

Look behind the altar (beneath the crucifix) to find the bishop's chair *(cathedra)*. As a cathedral, this church is the bishop's seat— hence its Catalan nickname of *La Seu*. To the

left of the altar is the organ and the elevator up to the terrace (included in your ticket). To the right of the altar, the wall is decorated with Catalunya's yellow-and-red coat of arms. Under that, the two wooden coffins on the wall contain two powerful counts of Barcelona (Ramon Berenguer I and his third wife, Almodis), who ordered the construction of the 11th-century Romanesque cathedral that preceded this structure.

• *Descend the steps beneath the altar, into the crypt, to see the...*

❺ Tomb of Santa Eulàlia

The marble and alabaster sarcophagus (1327-1339) contains the remains of Santa Eulàlia. The cathedral is dedicated to this saint.

Thirteen-year-old Eulàlia, daughter of a prominent Barcelona family, was martyred by the Romans for her faith in AD 304. Murky legends say she was subjected to 13 tortures. First she was stripped naked and had her head shaved, though a miraculous snow-fall hid her nakedness. Then she was rolled down the street in a barrel full of sharp objects. After further torments failed to kill her, she was crucified on an X-shaped cross—a symbol you'll find carved into pews and seen throughout the church.

The relief on the coffin's side tells her story in three episodes: she preaches Christianity to the pagan Roman ruler; he orders her to die (while she pleads for mercy); and she's crucified on the X-shaped cross. As one of Barcelona's two patron saints, Eulàlia is honored with an annual festival (with *gegants,* fireworks, and human towers) in February.

• *The* ❻ *elevator in the left transept takes you up to the rooftop* **terrace** *for an expansive city view.*

Otherwise, exit through the right transept to enter the...

❼ Cloister

The cloister's arcaded walkway surrounds a lush circa-1450 court-yard. Ahhhh. It's a tropical atmosphere of palm, orange, and magnolia trees; a fish pond; trickling fountains; and squawking geese.

From within the cloister, look back at the **arch** you just came through, an impressive mix of Romanesque (arches with chevrons, from the earlier church) and Gothic (pointy top).

The nearby **fountain** has a tiny statue of St. Jordi (George) slaying the dragon. Jordi is one of the patron saints of Catalunya and by far the most popular boy's name here. During the Corpus Christi festival in June, kids come here to watch a hollow egg dance atop the fountain's spray.

As you wander the cloister (clockwise), check out the **coats of arms** as well as the **tombs** in the pavement. These were for rich merchants who paid good money to be buried as close to the altar as possible. A few pavement stones here and there have the symbols of their trades: scissors, shoes, bakers, and so on. The cloister had

a practical economic purpose. The church sold out its chapel space, and this opened up an entire new wing to donors. A second floor was planned (look up) but not finished.

The resident **geese** have been here for at least 500 years. There are always 13, in memory of Eulàlia's 13 years and 13 torments. Other legends say they're white as a symbol of her virginity. Before modern security systems, they acted as alarms. Any commotion would get them honking, alerting the monk in charge. Faithful to tradition, they honk to this very day.

Farther along the cloister, next to the door, the **Chapel of Santa Rita** (patron saint of impossible causes) usually has the most candles. In the next corner of the cloister is the barrel-vaulted **Chapel of Santa Lucía,** a small 13th-century remnant of the earlier Romanesque cathedral. It's quite dark, as churches were before the advent of Gothic style. People hoping for good eyesight (Santa Lucía's specialty) pray here. Notice the especially nice eyes in the painted statue of Lucía.

• *At the far end of the cloister, you'll find the...*

❽ Chapter Hall Museum (Museu de la Sala Capitular)

The little museum has the six-foot-tall 14th-century **Great Monstrance,** a ceremonial display case for the communion wafer. Made of gold and studded with jewels, it's really three separate parts: a church-like central section, topped with a crown canopy, standing on a golden chair. This huge monstrance with its wafer is paraded through the streets during the Corpus Christi festival. Nearby is a gold-plated silver statue of Santa Eulàlia, carrying the X-shaped cross she was crucified on. An 11th-century baptismal font from the Romanesque church is also on view.

The next room, the Sala Capitular, has several altarpieces, including a **pietà** by Bartolomé Bermejo (*Desplà*, 1490). An anguished Mary cradles a twisted Christ against a bleak, stormy landscape. It's unique in Spanish art for its Italianesque, Renaissance 3-D. Rather than your basic gold backdrop, this has a strong foreground (the mourners), middle distance (the cross), and background (the city and distant hills). The kneeling donors who paid for the painting are photorealistic, complete with reading glasses and five o'clock shadows. These are just two of the countless Barcelona faithful who helped make their cathedral great.

• *Our tour is over. Go in peace.*

EL BORN WALK

From Via Laietana to the Waterfront

The neighborhood called El Born (a.k.a. "La Ribera") is bohemi-an-chic, with funky shops, upscale cafés and wine bars, a colorful market hall, unique boutiques, gritty bars and nightclubs, and one of Barcelona's top museums, exhibiting the early works of Picasso. Anchored by the Church of Santa Maria del Mar and just a short stroll from the waterfront, El Born is a rewarding quarter to ex-plore and a welcome escape from the sightseeing grind.

Back when Barcelona was Barcino—a walled Roman town—this area was farmland. As the city sprawled beyond its walls, El Born was established.

With its proximity to the harbor, El Born became the neigh-borhood of sailors, shippers, and skilled craftsmen. During the medieval city's trading heyday, wealthy shipping magnates built grand mansions and a local church, Santa Maria del Mar, that ri-valed the cathedral.

But all that came crashing down in 1714, when the Spanish crown crushed Catalan resistance to Madrid's rule and, in a show of force, razed a big chunk of this district to erect an imposing citadel (now a delightful park). The focus of the city shifted west, to the Barri Gòtic, and El Born became a largely forgotten backwater.

In recent years, as tourists have overrun the Barri Gòtic, El Born has regained attention. While it has gentrified and is now one of the city's most in-demand residential areas, El Born retains a pleasantly rough-around-the-edges appeal. Its tight lanes are still lined with innovative one-off shops that often make what they sell. Although we'll cover some history, this walk includes some entic-ing boutique streets; think of it as a route for making your own discoveries.

Orientation

Length of This Walk: About one hour, not including shopping stops.

When to Go: Sightseers and shoppers should do this walk during the day. But to take advantage of the neighborhood's lively night scene, go in the late afternoon/early evening to visit the sights, then stay for dinner and nightlife. By the way, if your answer to "when to go" was "10 years ago"—you're right. El Born is no longer the city's most happening place—the "next El Born" is the Raval neighborhood and the surrounding area, including Sant Antoni and Poble-Sec (described on page 57).

Getting There: This walk begins at the Barcelona Cathedral. The closest Metro stop is Jaume I.

Santa Caterina Market: Mon-Sat 7:30-15:30, Tue and Thu-Fri until 20:00, closed Sun; shorter hours Tue and Thu in July-Aug.

El Born Cultural and Memory Center: Center—free and open Tue-Sun 10:00-20:00, Oct-Feb until 19:00, closed Mon year-round; *Barcelona 1700* exhibit—€3, English tours generally available Tue-Fri at 16:00, Plaça Comercial 12, https://elbornculturaimemoria.barcelona.cat.

Picasso Museum: €12 timed-entry ticket—book online in advance; free Thu late afternoon-close and all day first Sun of month (must also reserve entry during free hours, up to 4 days ahead); open Tue-Sun 10:00-20:00, Nov-April until 19:00, closed Mon year-round; confirm opening days and times online; see the Picasso Museum Tour chapter.

Church of Santa Maria del Mar: Free during worship Mon-Sat 18:00-20:30 and Sun 10:00-13:00; otherwise entry is €5 (€10 to visit the rooftop) Mon-Sat 10:00-18:00 and Sun 14:00-18:00, when the interior is illuminated and you have access to the choir and crypt; Plaça Santa Maria.

The Walk Begins

• *Our walk starts in front of the Barcelona Cathedral. As you stand facing the church, head left toward the Santa Caterina Market. You'll see its colorful, undulating roof in the distance. To get there, you'll cross...*

❶ Via Laietana

This traffic-choked street slices through Barcelona's Old City. It marks the boundary between the Barri Gòtic (behind you) and El Born (in front of you). When the road was built in 1908, Barcelona was turning its back on its Gothic past and racing into its Moderni-

El Born Walk

100 Meters
100 Yards

SANT
To Palace
of Catalan
Music

PERE

WALK
BEGINS
Plaça
Maura ❶

To Cathedral
Main Entrance

CHOCOLATE
MUSEUM

To
Citadel
Park

SANTA
CATERINA
MARKET ❷

CHAPEL ❸
Placeta
d'en Marcús
Plaça Santa
Caterina

BAR
DEL PLA

EL BORN
CULTURAL &
MEMORY CENTER ❻

PICASSO
MUSEUM

MOCO
MUSEUM
TAPEO ❺
EL
XAMPANYET
CASA
GISPERT ❼

ROYAL
PALACE
Plaça
del Rei
BARC.
HISTORY
MUSEUM
CATHEDRAL

EL
BORN

Plaça
de l'Àngel

SANTA
MARIA
DEL MAR ❾ ❿ ❽

To
Ramblas

BARRI
GÒTIC

Plaça
Olles
Pla de
Palau ⓫

CAFÉS EL
MAGNÍFICO
S. Maria
Anisadeta

BOTIFARRERIA
DE SANTA
MARIA

LA VINYA
DEL SENYOR

VILA
VINATECA
LLOTJA
DE MAR

❶ Via Laietana
❷ Santa Caterina Market
❸ Capella d'en Marcús
❹ Carrer de Montcada
❺ Passeig del Born
❻ El Born Cultural &
Memory Center
❼ Shopping Streets
❽ Monument of Catalan Indep.
❾ Church of Santa Maria del Mar
❿ Shopping Detour
⓫ Pla de Palau
⓬ Barcelona Head

POST

Plaça
d'Antonio
López

WALK
ENDS

To
Old Port &
Columbus
Monument

⓬

To
Barceloneta
& Beaches

BARCELONA
HEAD
SCULPTURE

sta future—and hundreds of historic buildings were torn down to create this new artery. (The most treasured structures, nicknamed "traveling buildings," were saved—taken down one brick at a time and reassembled in a more workable location.) Fortunately, even as much of Barcelona modernized, El Born retained much of its medieval character and the low-key charm we're about to see.

• *Across Via Laietana, continue ahead to the crazy building that looks like it's wearing a giant, colorful sunhat.*

❷ Santa Caterina Market

While tourists swarm the more famous La Boqueria Market on the Ramblas, Santa Caterina is a lively dose of local color, still primarily serving its neighborhood. This is the place to buy *jamón* and cheese with fewer crowds and less tourist markup.

Check out the exterior. The market was originally built atop the ruins of an old monastery in 1845 to keep El Born's blue-collar workers well fueled with quality foods. A 2006 renovation added the swooping roof and a shell around its original arcaded white walls. The roof's bright colors evoke Gaudí and the colorful produce within.

Its Catalan architect, Enric Miralles, is best known for designing the Scottish parliament building in Edinburgh—an unlikely connection that's also oddly fitting, since both the Catalans and the Scots consider themselves "nations without states."

Enter and browse your way to the far left end. Inside are beautifully lit produce stalls with mouthwatering presentations and surprising variety (one stall displays 20 kinds of tomato). There are lots of tempting eateries—locals eat before shopping so as not to overbuy. For tips on where to eat in the market, see page 198.

As you exit at the far left end, find the archaeological area (with diagrams and English explanations) of the old monastery. (If the market is closed, you can reach this spot by looping around the left side to the back.) You're standing in what was once the sacristy, located just off the apse of the monastery's church.

• *Leaving the market, angle left and continue down narrow Carrer d'en Giralt el Pellisser, a lane of tiny boutiques and cafés. Look up and see the neighborhood. At the T-intersection, turn right, where you'll immediately find a tiny church.*

❸ Capella d'en Marcús

This humble Romanesque chapel, from the 1100s, is supposedly the oldest church in town. Made of stone and topped with two small bells, it was a neighborhood center where El Born's working-class medieval folk would pause to share the news. Back then, this part of El Born was where guilds—the laborers specializing in a particular trade—were located. The streets were named after the types of trades plied there, like beltmakers (the street you are on—Carrer dels Carders) or tanners (on Carrer dels Assaonadors, behind the church).

The chapel stands at what was once a major intersection. Across the street from its front door, above the plaque for #1, notice the sign with the horse and the word *entrada* (entrance). This is an old-fashioned one-way sign, marking the direction of carriage

traffic in this tight tangle of
lanes. Along the right side of the
chapel, at the far end of the tiny
square, find the sign's twin, *salida* (exit), above the street sign for
Carrer dels Assaonadors. You'll
spot signs like these all over El
Born and the Barri Gòtic.

• *Passing between the chapel and
the recommended Bar del Pla, continue straight down the lane called
Carrer de Montcada.*

❹ Carrer de Montcada

After one block, glance right at Carrer de la Princesa to notice its
many lively bars. If you turned right here, you'd go to the Jaume I
Metro stop, Barri Gòtic, and cathedral area.

Instead, cross Princesa and continue straight ahead, entering the most historic stretch of Carrer de Montcada. This was the
medieval neighborhood's main street, connecting the blue-collar
tradesmen's quarter (where we were) with the wealthy merchant
district near the waterfront (up ahead). El Born's rich and famous
built their mansions here. The street is lined with rustic stone pala-
zzos with elaborately carved windows and wide-arched entrances
leading to interior courtyards.

Carrer de Montcada has become the most touristy street in El
Born thanks to the **Picasso Museum** (on the left), which sprawls
through five mansions laced together (formerly owned by the noble
Montcada family, who give the street its name). Even without a
ticket, you can generally pop into the museum courtyards and
make out the typical mansion layout: built around a quiet, interior
open-air courtyard with servants' quarters on the ground floor and
staircases up to the living rooms above.

Continuing down the street, pause at the **Moco Museum** (at
#25, worth a look if you are interested in contemporary art) to see
another historic palazzo. There's yet another at #20 (right) with its
rainspout gargoyles. As the street widens up, you'll find palm trees,
other art galleries, cafés, shops, and restaurants (mostly touristy,
though I recommend El Xampanyet and Tapeo).

• *At the end of the street, you'll pop out onto a long square stretching to
the left.*

❺ Passeig del Born

This long square—actually a "passeig," or boulevard—has been
El Born's center for a thousand years. At one end of the square is
the neighborhood church; at the other is the neighborhood market
hall. Enjoy the square's cobbled pavement, tree-lined ambience,

ironwork lanterns, apartments with small balconies, and handful of fine stone medieval facades.

Passeig del Born grew as a neighborhood center because (as we'll see) it was located very close to the waterfront, where all the commercial action was. Sailors, traders, merchants, and travelers came here, all looking for a meal, a drink, a church to worship at, and a place to shop. In medieval times, Passeig del Born served as a jousting square (as its Roman circus-esque shape indicates), giving it the name "El Born," from an old Catalan word for "tournament." Eventually the square's name was given to the entire district that grew up around it.

Over the centuries, the Passeig has hosted festivals, religious processions during Holy Week, Inquisition-era heretic burnings, carnival celebrations, and other public spectacles. These days, Passeig del Born is a popular springboard for exploring inviting tapas bars, fun restaurants, and nightspots in the narrow streets all around.

• *At the far end of Passeig del Born is the former market hall, now known as the...*

❻ El Born Cultural and Memory Center

This vast iron-and-glass construction once housed the El Born produce market, which not only served this neighborhood but was a major distribution point for the entire city. In 1971, the merchants moved their wholesale business to the suburbs, and the neighborhood went into a steep decline. Only in the last decade or so has El Born revived.

Today, the market hall has reopened as the El Born Cultural and Memory Center, an exhibition and event space (free to enter). The first such iron-and-glass structure in town, the 1876 building was inspired by similar market halls that were then the rage in France.

Visiting the Center: When the hall was renovated in the 20th century, workers discovered remains of the Old City below. Belly up to the railing and look down at the exposed excavations and foundations. This was the neighborhood around the year 1700. In the central zone (near the cultural center's entrance), you can make out a cobbled plaza flanked by houses and shops. In the area to the left, a canal brought in water, near where the laundry was located. A nearby street (still in the left zone) was once lined with guitar-making shops, and there's a rectangular 17th-century paddleball court. Heading over to the right zone, find the round vat of a brandy distillery and the all-important ice house, for stocking snow shipped in from nearby mountains to refrigerate food. Yes, this was clearly a vibrant neighborhood—until the tragic events of 1714.

Information plaques explain the story, which still resonates

Independence for Catalunya?

In much of Spain, you'll find four languages on ATM screens, and all are native to Spain: Spanish (of course), Euskara (used by the northern Basques), Galician (of the Celtic northwest), and Catalan. It suggests that regional differences are strong—and the thirst for local independence thrives.

The roots of the Catalan independence movement go back to—well, really, medieval times, when Catalunya was a self-ruling country. After their defeat in the War of Spanish Succession in 1714, the Catalans chafed under Castilian control. Then, in 1978, when post-Franco Spain adopted its modern constitution, Catalunya was granted special autonomy as a "nationality." Catalans began energetically reviving their long-suppressed language and customs.

By the 21st century, the movement was growing. When the Spanish government tried to clarify that "nationality" didn't really mean political autonomy so much as cultural heritage, it only stoked separatism. Spain's 2008 banking crisis threw more gas on the fire, as hardworking Catalans resented bailing out the Madrid establishment. By 2010, Barcelona commonly witnessed demonstrations of a million people peacefully chanting, singing, and waving their red-and-yellow flags.

The case for independence is multifaceted. First, of course, is Catalunya's unique heritage and language. Then there's the economy: Catalans see their wealthy region as carrying the rest of the country on its back. Politically, Catalunya is generally more liberal than the rest of Spain. Catalans tend to view the national government as incompetent and out of touch with local needs (Catalunya's more-progressive measures are frequently vetoed).

In 2014, Catalans held a referendum and voted to leave Spain...only to have the national government nullify the referendum as unconstitutional. In response, in 2015, Catalunya's government voted to begin the secession process...but that too was

with locals. In the early 1700s, Barcelona's Catalan patriots took advantage of the chaos of the War of Spanish Succession to rise up against their Spanish overlords. But Barcelona fell in 1714, and the Spaniards suppressed the rebellion brutally. Residents were forced to destroy their homes and use those very stones to build a citadel for the Spanish just east of here (now a park). The citadel came with a one-kilometer buffer zone, so no buildings were allowed where the market stands today.

A permanent display called *Barcelona 1700* brings that age to declared unconstitutional.

Things came to a head in 2017. The Catalan people once again voted for independence, and their parliament declared Catalunya a sovereign nation. This time, though, Spain cracked down—hard. They sent thousands of police to break up demonstrations, spy on activists, and arrest ringleaders. The Catalan parliament was dissolved, and politicians who favored independence were charged with sedition and imprisoned. Catalan President Carles Puigdemont fled to Brussels to avoid arrest.

At first, Spain's heavy-handed tactics brought an angry backlash, even from nonseparatists. But over time, the crackdown worked. Demonstrations slowly dwindled from the thousands to the hundreds. And, in a bid to ease tensions, the Spanish government eventually pardoned many jailed separatists (though others remained fugitives).

The independence roller coaster has left Catalans exhausted—and divided. While all Catalans support regional pride, they're sharply split over exactly what that means. Some still favor outright secession, while others simply want more federal autonomy. Many fear that talk of secession scares off business, and others are loath to leave the security of the Spanish fold. The Catalan press has one perspective, while the Madrid media has another. The unfortunate thing about the independence votes so far is that they're all or nothing, while many Catalans are somewhere in the middle.

The sad result is that in everyday political discourse, name-calling has become common: Are you a "fascist" (Spanish nationalist) or a "politically correct" secessionist, a "collaborator" or a "seditionist"? Catalans have become less likely to talk openly, turning to less-divisive topics (not unlike the political dynamic in the US today). A Catalan friend told me that the real victim is the Catalan people. He misses the good old days when, on the feast of St. Jordi, the roses given in his honor were all red—not (as now) yellow, the color of protest.

Only time will tell what the future holds for Catalunya. Though the independence movement is dormant for now, it's far from dead. And Catalan pride remains as strong as ever.

life with paintings, artifacts, and videos (buy tickets from the info point near the entry; includes audioguide explaining the excavations). There are usually other temporary exhibits to explore as well.

• *If you want to make an interesting and delicious detour, the* **Chocolate Museum** *is just two blocks from here (see page 57). Otherwise, from the cultural center, backtrack into Passeig del Born and turn left on the arcaded Carrer del Rec. This part of El Born has a high concentration of...*

❼ Shopping Streets

Fashion boutiques populate the area around **Carrer del Rec.** Take the first right turn, down **Carrer de l'Esparteria,** a great shopping street. On the side lanes, you can see local "fashions" flapping in the breeze from characteristic wrought-iron balconies. While strict building codes prohibit people from drying laundry outside in most of the city, an exception is made for El Born—since parts of this medieval quarter lack interior courtyards.

As elsewhere in El Born, most street names are tied to a particular craft or product. An "*esparteria*" is a place where things (like baskets) made from esparto grass are woven; Carrer de la Formatgeria (third street on the right) was home to the cheesemakers.

Stick with Esparteria; the lane jogs slightly left and becomes Carrer dels Ases. Pause at **Carrer de Malcuinat,** literally "the street of bad cooking." Looking left, you'll notice you're just a block off what was once the bustling old port. In the Middle Ages, unpretentious eateries here served fill-the-tank meals to undiscerning sailors who were fresh off the boat. These days, restaurants here range from decent to tourist trap (there's even an Irish pub).

• *Turn right down the short Carrer de Malcuinat, emerging at a big square with the...*

❽ Monument of Catalan Independence

The square is called Plaça del Fossar de les Moreres ("The Burial Place of the Mulberry Trees"). The lone mulberry tree and modern monument honor a 300-year-old massacre that's still fresh in the Catalan consciousness. On September 11, 1714, the Bourbon king Philip V, ruling from Madrid, completed a successful 14-month siege of Barcelona (the "Catalan Alamo"). In retaliation for the local resistance to Bourbon rule, he massacred Catalan patriots. From that day on, the king outlawed Catalan language, culture, and institutions, kicking off more than two centuries of cultural suppression. For example, no university was allowed in Barcelona from 1720 to 1850. To establish his hold, the king demolished homes in what was then the fishermen's  quarter (much of this area, especially around the El Born Cultural and Memory Center) and built a gigantic citadel. The suddenly homeless seafarers were moved to the tight, grid-planned Barceloneta area that juts into the harbor just east of here. Meanwhile, besides this depopulation of El Born, the neighborhood declined further as shipping shifted west, to the Barri Gòtic's harbor at Port Vell.

This square marks the site of a mass grave of the massacred Catalans. The **eternal flame** burns atop this monument, and this 18th-century 9/11 remains a sobering anniversary for Catalans, who still harbor a grudge against the Bourbon king. When heading to the toilet, they say, "I'm going to Philip's house."

Here or elsewhere in El Born, you may see displayed the *estelada* **flag,** the symbol of Catalan separatists: It features the typical red-and-gold horizontal stripes of the Catalunya flag, but with a blue triangle and white star on the hoist side. This design comes from the flag of a former Spanish colony that fought hard for its independence—Cuba. It's a provocative image to Spaniards who want to keep Catalunya in their country.

• *The hulking building dominating this square is the Church of Santa Maria del Mar. Turn left and walk to the small square in front of the church.*

❾ Church of Santa Maria del Mar

This 14th-century church, the proud centerpiece of El Born, is where shipwrights and merchants came to worship. It was dubbed "Del Mar" (meaning "of the sea"), as it was right near the water's edge when it was built. Proud shippers built this church in less than 60 years, so it has a harmonious style that is considered pure Catalan Gothic. Located outside the city walls, this was a defiantly independent symbol of neighborhood pride; to this day, it's fully supported not by the Church or the city, but by the community.

Exterior: The church, with its twin lighthouse-like towers, has an impressively ornate facade. On the big front doors, notice the figures of workers who donated their time and sweat to build the church. The stone they used was quarried at Montjuïc and carried across town on the backs of porters called *bastaixos*. Although they've always been celebrated by residents, their work is now more widely appreciated following the release of the historical novel *Cathedral of the Sea* (2006), which tells the story of the church's construction from the perspective of an ambitious *bastaixo*.

Inside the Church: Stepping inside, take in the nave. The church is stripped down—naked in all its Gothic glory. The treelike columns with their extreme vertical thrust inspired Gaudí (the influence on the columns inside his Sagrada Família church is obvious). As within the Barcelona Cathedral, here you see the characteristic

Indulgences near the Church

The colorful neighborhood around the Church of Santa Maria del Mar offers plenty of inviting places to eat, drink, and shop (with recommended eateries nearby—see page 197). Explore!

For liquid and gourmet food souvenirs, try **Vila Viniteca,** a wine shop with (they claim) the widest selection in Barcelona (Mon-Sat 8:30-20:30, closed Sun, Carrer dels Agullers 7—as you face the church, it's buried about 100 yards away in the streets over your right shoulder, +34 937 777 017). Across the lane is their gifty-edibles shop, with a wild cheese selection. To go with your wine and cheese, try the very Catalan sausage *botifarra* from **La Botifarreria de Santa Maria.** Take a number and join the locals in line; be sure to ask for *botifarra* that doesn't require cooking (Mon-Sat 9:30-14:30 & 17:00-20:30, closed Sun; Carrer Santa Maria 4, +34 933 199 123).

A caffeine jolt awaits at **Cafés El Magnífico,** selling what's reputed to be the city's best coffee beans and takeout coffee (Mon-Sat 10:00-20:00, closed Sun, one block up Carrer de l'Argenteria at #64—immediately to the left as you face the church's front door, +34 933 193 975). For a fragrant snack, head to **Casa Gispert,** which has been roasting nuts in the same wood-fired oven since 1851. Drop in to enjoy the aroma of fire-roasted nuts and pick up a snack (Mon-Sat 10:00-14:00 & 16:00-20:00, closed Sun; facing front door of church, circle around left side and walk almost all the way to the end—store is on the left at Carrer dels Sombrerers 23, +34 933 197 535).

Catalan Gothic buttresses flying inward, defining the chapels that ring the nave. Brilliant stained glass—most notably the rose window over the main entry—floods the interior with soft light.

The church was once highly decorated with Baroque frills. But during the Spanish Civil War (1936-1939), when the Catholic Church sided with the conservative forces of Franco, working-class leftists took their anger out on this church. They torched the interior, and it burned for 11 days straight—destroying all its wood furnishings and decor (carbon still blackens the ceiling). Since then, some things have been replaced; the local sculptor Frederic Marès began the restoration. At the altar, there's a statue of St. Mary of the Sea, to whom this church is dedicated. Just as 16th-century sailors left models of their ships at the altar for Mary's protection, even today, a classic old Catalan ship remains at Mary's feet.

• *If you've seen enough, you can end your walk now and give in to El Born's many buyable and edible temptations (see sidebar for ideas). A good place to start is around the left side of the church ("left" as you face the main facade), on a side street called Carrer dels Banys Vells, which makes for an excellent...*

❿ Shopping Detour

Follow Carrer dels Banys Vells all the way up to Carrer de la Princesa; a bunch of great shops hide along the lanes branching off to the left. Many of them have workshops where the goods for sale are actually produced. You'll see small boutiques, leather stores, one-of-a-kind dress shops, and art studios. The warren of streets wedged between here and Carrer de l'Argenteria are particularly interesting and an easy place to score cool finds, including handmade clothing, accessories, and bags.

• *Backtrack to the Church of Santa Maria del Mar. Facing the main facade, turn right and head down Carrer d'Espaseria. You'll pop out at...*

⓫ Pla de Palau

Goods arriving from the harbor were received and traded on this square. The hulking building on your right (with columns and a triangular pediment) is the **Llotja de Mar,** or commercial exchange. It originated in medieval times as a place to trade fish and goods brought in on boats. Then, as Barcelona grew into a major shipping center and El Born was its ritziest neighborhood, the Llotja went from trading fish and livestock to becoming one of Europe's first stock exchanges. From the late 17th through late 20th century, the building also housed the prestigious Barcelona Arts and Crafts School, providing state-subsidized instruction to budding artists—including Pablo Picasso and Joan Miró.

• *From Llotja de Mar, cross the wide street (Passeig d'Isabel II) and turn right to walk under the shaded arches of the big arcaded building. At the busy intersection at the end of the arcade, you'll come face-to-face with the...*

⓬ *Barcelona Head*

This sculpture, created for the 1992 Summer Olympics by American Pop artist Roy Lichtenstein, instantly became an icon of the city. Depicting a woman's head in an abstract style, it brings together the colors of Miró, the tiles of Gaudí, the Cubism of Picasso, and the trademark dots of Lichtenstein. He created paintings that have

EL BORN WALK

the look of a comic strip, blown up to a size where you can see individual printing color dots.

The grand main post office stands across the main avenue. Also nearby is a giant, whimsical **lobster sculpture** waving hello. Designed by Javier Mariscal, this cheery crustacean is just one more piece of invigorating public art on Barcelona's fine waterfront. In fact, El Born, with its history, shops, and galleries, is itself a veritable open-air art museum.

• *Barcelona's inviting waterfront beckons. From here, you could continue into the neighborhood of Barceloneta and the beach (or consider renting a bike for a pedal down the beach promenade—see page 39). Or walk along the delightful art-lined promenade next to the Old Port (bristling with sailboats) to the Columbus Monument at the bottom of the Ramblas.*

PICASSO MUSEUM TOUR

Museu Picasso

This museum has the best collection in Spain of the work of Pablo Picasso (1881-1973), and the best collection anywhere of his earliest works. The Spaniard Picasso spent his formative years (from age 14 to 23) in Barcelona, and a visit to this museum intimately reveals the young man finding his way as an artist. By experiencing his youthful, realistic art, you can better understand his later, more challenging art and more fully appreciate his genius.

Picasso's personal secretary, Jaume Sabartés, amassed many examples of his friend's work and bequeathed them to Barcelona. The artist, happy to have a museum showing off his work in the city of his youth, added to the collection over the years. The museum and artworks are now housed in several connected Catalan Gothic palaces in the El Born neighborhood.

Orientation

Cost and Hours: €12 timed-entry ticket to permanent collection, more with special exhibits, book tickets and confirm hours in advance online; Tue-Sun 10:00-20:00, Nov-April until 19:00, closed Mon year-round.

Free Entry: The museum is free—and crowded—Thu late afternoon until close and all day on the first Sun of the month. You must reserve entry during free hours online (up to four days in advance).

Information: +34 932 563 000, https://museupicassobcn.cat.

Reservations and Ticketing Tips: Buy a **timed-entry ticket** in advance at the museum website. While tickets are sold at the door, there's nearly always a long line and the museum often sells out.

The museum's website can be temperamental—keep trying. If you're unsuccessful, buy an **ArticketBCN** when you arrive (for pass details, see page 27), which allows you to enter the galleries whenever you wish (if you already have a pass, notify museum staff when you arrive).

The museum's busiest times are mornings before 13:00, all day Tue, and during free entry times. Day-of tickets (when available) are also sold online (must purchase at least 2 hours before your visit).

Getting In: The galleries sit one floor above a free-to-enter court-yard. Tickets are sold at the center ground-floor entry at #19.

Getting There: The museum is on Carrer de Montcada; from the Jaume I Metro stop, it's a five-minute walk. It's a 10-minute walk from the cathedral and many parts of the Barri Gòtic.

Tours: The 1.5-hour audioguide (€5) offers descriptions for 51 paintings. English-language tours are available Tue at 15:00 and 16:00 and Sun at 11:00.

Length of This Tour: Allow at least an hour.

Services: The ground floor has a required bag check, a bookshop, and WC.

Cuisine Art: Along Carrer de Montcada in either direction are several recommended tapas bars: With your back to the museum, a few steps to the left are **El Xampanyet** and **Tapeo,** while to the right (across Carrer de la Princesa and up a block) is **Bar del Pla.** For details about these and other characteristic places nearby, see page 198.

The Tour Begins

The Picasso Museum's collection of nearly 300 paintings is presented more or less chronologically. With good text panels in every room providing context, it's easy to follow the evolution of Picasso's work. This tour (like the museum itself) is arranged by the stages of his life and art. Don't be surprised if a painting described here is not on view. Individual paintings are rotated in and out constantly (to keep it interesting for locals and repeat visitors). But the themes and chronology remain constant.

Boy Wonder (Room 1)

Pablo's earliest art is realistic and earnest. His work quickly advanced from childish pencil drawings (from about 1890), through a series of technically skilled **art-school works** (copies of plaster feet and arms), to oil paintings of impressive technique. Pablo was born in 1881, so you can easily calculate how amazingly young he was when he painted these works. His **portraits**—of grizzled peasants, family members, and himself (at age 15)—demonstrate surprising psychological insight. Because his dedicated father—himself a cu-

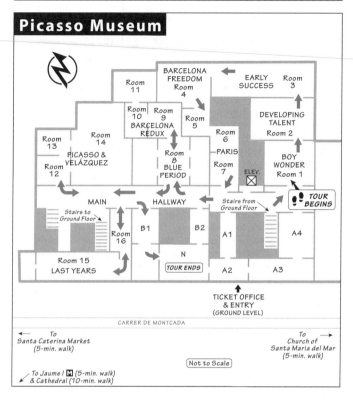

Picasso Museum

BARCELONA
FREEDOM
Room 4

EARLY
SUCCESS — Room 3

Room 11

Room 10 | Room 9
BARCELONA
REDUX

Room 5

DEVELOPING
TALENT
Room 2

Room 14

Room 13

PICASSO &
VELÁZQUEZ

Room 12

Room 8
BLUE
PERIOD

Room 6

PARIS
Room 7

ELEV. ⊠

BOY
WONDER
Room 1

👣 TOUR
BEGINS

MAIN

HALLWAY

Stairs from
Ground Floor

Stairs to
Ground Floor

Room 16

B1

B2

A1

A4

N

Room 15
LAST YEARS

TOUR ENDS

A2

A3

TICKET OFFICE
& ENTRY
(GROUND LEVEL)

CARRER DE MONTCADA

← To
Santa Caterina Market
(5-min. walk)

To →
Church of
Santa Maria del Mar
(5-min. walk)

To Jaume I Ⓜ (5-min. walk)
& Cathedral (10-min. walk)

Not to Scale

rator and artist—kept everything his son ever did, Picasso must have the best-documented youth of any great painter. Though Pablo dabbled in landscapes, still lifes, and everyday scenes, he was always, first and foremost, a painter of people.

Developing Talent (Room 2)

Pablo moved to Barcelona at age 14. During a summer trip to Málaga (his birthplace and boyhood home) in 1896, he experimented with a series of fresh, Impressionistic-style landscapes (relatively rare in Spain at the time). As a 15-year-old, Pablo dutifully entered art-school competitions. A case along the wall shows off his art-school studies, Barcelona scenes from 1896 (allowing you to see the city through Picasso's eyes), and classical studies of the human body.

His first big work, *First Communion,* tackled a prescribed religious subject, but Picasso made it an excuse to paint his family. His sister Lola was the model for the communicant, and the man beside her has the face of Picasso's father. Notice Lola's exquisitely painted veil. This piece was heavily influenced by the academic style of local painters.

Pablo Picasso (1881-1973)

Pablo Picasso was the most famous and, for me, the greatest artist of the 20th century. Always exploring, he became the master of many styles (Cubism, Surrealism, Expressionism) and of many media (painting, sculpture, prints, ceramics, assemblages). Still, he could make anything he touched look unmistakably like "a Picasso."

Born in Málaga, Spain, Picasso was the son of an art teacher. At a very young age, he quickly advanced beyond his teachers. Picasso's teenage works are stunningly realistic and capture the inner complexities of the people he painted. As a youth in Barcelona, he fell in with a bohemian crowd that mixed wine, women, and art.

In 1900, at age 19, Picasso started making trips to Paris, and he moved there four years later. He absorbed the styles of many painters (especially Henri de Toulouse-Lautrec) while searching for his own artist's voice. His paintings of beggars and other social outcasts show the empathy of a man who was himself a poor, homesick foreigner. When his best friend, Spanish artist Carlos Casagemas, committed suicide, Picasso plunged into a **Blue Period** (1901-1904). The dominant color in these paintings matches their melancholy mood and subject matter (emaciated beggars, hard-eyed pimps).

In 1904, Picasso got a steady girlfriend (Fernande Olivier) and suddenly saw the world through rose-colored glasses—the **Rose Period.** He was further jolted out of his Blue Period by the "flat" look of the Fauve paintings being made around him. Not satisfied with their take on 3-D, Picasso played with the "building blocks" of line and color to find new ways to reconstruct the real world on canvas.

At his studio in Montmartre, Picasso and his neighbor Georges Braque worked together, in poverty so dire they often didn't know from where their next bottle of wine was coming. And then, at age 25, Picasso reinvented painting. Fascinated by the primitive power of African tribal masks, he drew human faces with simple outlines and almond eyes. Intrigued by his girlfriend's body, he sketched Fernande from every angle, then experimented with showing several different views on the same canvas. A hundred paintings and nine months later, Picasso gave birth to a monstrous canvas of five nude, fragmented prostitutes with mask-like faces—*Les Demoiselles d'Avignon* (1907).

This bold new style was called **Cubism.** With Cubism, Picasso shattered the Old World and put it back together in a new way. The subjects are somewhat recognizable (with the help of the titles), but they're built with geometric shards (let's call them "cubes")—it's like viewing the world through a kaleidoscope of brown and gray. Cubism presents several different angles of the subject at once—say, a woman seen from the front and side simultaneously, resulting in two eyes on the same side of the nose. Cubism showed the traditional three dimensions, plus Einstein's new fourth dimension—the time it takes to walk around the subject to see other angles.

In 1918, Picasso married his first wife, Olga Kokhlova. He then traveled to Rome and entered a **Classical Period** (1920s) of more realistic, full-bodied women and children, inspired by the three-dimensional sturdiness of ancient statues. While he flirted with abstraction, throughout his life Picasso always kept a grip on "reality." His favorite subject was people. The anatomy might be jumbled, but it's all there.

Though he lived in France and Italy, Picasso remained a Spaniard at heart, incorporating Spanish motifs into his work. Unrepentantly macho, he loved bullfights, seeing them as a metaphor for the timeless human interaction between the genders. The horse—clad with blinders and pummeled by the bull—is just a pawn in the battle between bull and matador. To Picasso, the horse symbolizes the feminine, and the bull, the masculine. Spanish imagery—bulls, screaming horses, a Madonna—appears in Picasso's most famous work, *Guernica* (1937). The monumental canvas of a bombed village summed up the pain of Spain's brutal civil war (1936-1939) and foreshadowed the onslaught of World War II.

At war's end, Picasso left Paris, his wife, and his emotional baggage behind, finding fun in the **south of France.** Sun! Color! Water! Freedom! Senior citizen Pablo Picasso was reborn, enjoying worldwide fame. He lived at first with the beautiful young painter Françoise Gilot, mother of two of his children, but it was another young beauty, Jacqueline Roque, who became his second wife. Dressed in rolled-up white pants and a striped sailor's shirt, bursting with pent-up creativity, Picasso often cranked out a painting a day. Picasso's Riviera works set the tone for the rest of his life. They're sunny, lighthearted, and childlike; filled with motifs of the sea, Greek mythology (fauns, centaurs), and animals; and freely experimental in their use of new media. His simple drawing of a dove holding an olive branch became an international symbol of peace.

Picasso made collages, built "statues" out of wood, wire, ceramics, papier-mâché, or whatever, and even turned everyday household objects into statues (like his famous bull's head made of a bicycle seat with handlebar horns). **Multimedia** works like these have become so standard today that we forget how revolutionary they once were. His last works have the playfulness of someone much younger. As it is often said of Picasso, "When he was a child, he painted like a man. When he was old, he painted like a child."

Picasso's relatives star in a number of portraits from this time. You may find a touching portrait of his mother, with a cameo-like face and fine details in her white blouse. Find the portrait of his aunt **Tía Pepa,** painted in Málaga in 1896 (this and other family portraits are frequently rotated). It's said Picasso painted this in less than a day. Notice how ably he captured the toughness of his aunt. Look at Picasso's signature on some paintings in this room. Spaniards keep both parents' surnames, with the father's first, followed by the mother's: Pablo Ruiz Picasso.

Early Success (Room 3)

In the large, classically painted *Science and Charity* (1897), Picasso used realistic means to represent subjects of social concern—a technique typical of the social realism movement of the late 19th century. The doctor (modeled on Pablo's father) represents science. The nun represents charity and religion. From the hopeless face and lifeless hand of the sick woman, it seems that Picasso believes nothing will save her from death. Pablo painted a little perspective trick: Walk back and forth across the  room to see the bed stretch and shrink. Three small studies (to the left) show the preparatory work Picasso did for this major painting.

Science and Charity won second prize at a fine-arts exhibition, earning Picasso the chance to study in Madrid. Stifled by the stuffy art school there, he hung out instead in the Prado Museum and learned by copying earlier Spanish masters, especially Diego Velázquez, with whom he developed a virtual friendship. An example of Picasso's impressive mimicry is sometimes displayed in this room—a nearly perfect copy of a **portrait of Philip IV** by Velázquez. (Near the end of this tour, we'll see a much older Picasso riffing on another Velázquez painting.)

In this room you'll also see outdoor views of Madrid (mostly in Retiro Park) and rural village scenes. In 1898 Pablo fell sick and was sent to convalesce in the mountain village of Horta de Sant Joan. Away from his father and the conservative art establishment in Madrid, his creative spirit was freed. You can sense that Picasso was finding his artistic independence as he painted these landscapes and scenes of village life. The artist later credited his time at Horta de Sant Joan as an important step in his artistic evolution.

Barcelona Freedom (Room 4)

After regaining his health, Picasso returned to Barcelona in 1900.

Art Nouveau was all the rage there. Upsetting his dad, he quit art school and fell in with an avant-garde crowd. These bohemians congregated daily at Els Quatre Gats ("The Four Cats," a popular restaurant to this day—see page 104). Picasso even created the **menu cover** for this favorite hangout. Further establishing his artistic freedom, he painted often dark and brooding **portraits** of his new friends (including Carlos Casagemas and Jaume Sabar-

tés, who later became Picasso's personal assistant and donated the foundational works of this museum). Still a teenager, Pablo exhibited his first one-man show—a series of neighborhood sketches in the style of Toulouse-Lautrec—at Els Quatre Gats in 1900.

Paris (Rooms 6-7)

In 1900 Picasso made his first trip to Paris, a city bursting with life, light, and love. Dropping the paternal surname Ruiz (which is a kind of Spanish "Smith"), Pablo established his commercial brand name: simply "Picasso." Here the explorer Picasso went bohemian and befriended poets, prostitutes, and artists. He began sampling the contemporary art styles around him: He painted **cancan dancers** like Toulouse-Lautrec, **still lifes** like Paul Cézanne, brightly colored **Fauvist** works like Henri Matisse, and Impressionist **landscapes** like Claude Monet (you may see examples on the walls of this room). In *The Waiting (Margot),* the subject—with her bold outline and strong gaze—pops out from the vivid, mosaic-like background. Picasso was learning Cézanne's technique of "building" a figure with "cubes" of paint—a step toward Picasso's invention of Cubism.

Blue Period (Room 8)

Picasso would travel to Paris several times before settling there permanently in 1904. The suicide of his best friend Casagemas, his own poverty, and the influence of new ideas linking color and mood led Picasso to abandon jewel-bright color for his Blue Period (1901-1904). He cranked out stacks of blue art just to stay housed and fed. With blue backgrounds (the coldest color) and depressing subjects, this period was revolutionary in art history. Now the artist was painting not what he saw, but what he felt. Painting misfits and street people, Picasso, like Velázquez and Toulouse-Lautrec before him, revealed the beauty in ugliness.

During a visit back to Barcelona, Picasso painted a nighttime view over the **rooftops** of the city. His palette is still blue, but here we see proto-Cubism...five years before the first real Cubist painting.

Rose Period

Picasso finally lifted out of his funk after meeting a new lady, Fernande Olivier (a bronze bust of her from 1906 may be on view). He moved out of the blue and into the happier Rose Period (1904-1907), dominated by soft pink and reddish tones. Other than the *Portrait of Bernadetta Bianco,* the museum is weak on Rose Period works.

Cubism

Pablo's role in the invention of the groundbreaking Cubist style (with his friend Georges Braque) is well known—at least I hope so, since this museum has no true Cubist paintings. What made the style revolutionary is that it's free from conventional perspective. A Cubist work gives not only the basic shape of a subject—it shows every aspect of it simultaneously. The technique of "building" a subject with "cubes" of paint simmered in Picasso's artistic stew for years. The idea was to simultaneously see several 3-D facets of the subject.

Barcelona Redux (Rooms 9-10)

Picasso spent six months back in Barcelona in 1917 (yet another girlfriend, a Russian ballet dancer, had a gig in town). The paintings in these rooms demonstrate the artist's irrepressible versatility: He had already developed Cubism, but he also continued to play with other styles. In *Woman with Mantilla,* we see a little Post-Impressionistic Pointillism in a portrait that is as elegant as a classical statue. Nearby, *Gored Horse* has all the anguish and power of his iconic *Guernica* (painted years later).

Remember that this museum has very little from the most famous and prolific "middle" part of Picasso's career—basically, from his adoption of Cubism to his sunset years on the French Riviera. (To fill in the gaps in his middle career, see the sidebar in this chapter.)

Picasso and Velázquez (Rooms 12-14)

Whoosh. We've skipped ahead a few decades in Picasso's life, and suddenly he is 40 years older. We left him at age 36 in 1917. Now it's 1957 and he's 76. As a mature artist, Picasso had few peers. He turned to the great Old Masters for inspiration.

He decided to make a series of works related to what many consider the greatest painting by anyone, ever: Diego Velázquez's *Las Meninas.* The 17th-century original (in Madrid's Prado Muse-

Velázquez's Las Meninas *(left) inspired many versions by Picasso (right).*

um) depicted the young maids of honor (or *meninas*) of the Spanish royal court. Heralded as the first completely realistic painting, *Las Meninas* became, centuries later, an obsession for Picasso.

Pablo, who had great respect for Velázquez, painted more than **40 interpretations** of the masterwork, and donated all of them to the museum, which rotates the version on display. He seemed to enjoy a relationship of equals with Velázquez, and like artistic soul mates, the two geniuses sparred and teased. Picasso deconstructed Velázquez and then injected light, color, and perspective as he improvised on the earlier masterpiece. In Picasso's big, black and white version, he more or less re-created Velázquez's painting in its entirety. But here, the king and queen (reflected in the mirror in the back of the room) are hardly seen, while the painter—the great Velázquez—towers above everyone. In other paintings in the series, Picasso uses vibrant color and focuses on details—one maid of honor or a pair of them, or zeroes in on just their faces. Browse the various studies (in Rooms 13-14), a playground of color and perspective. See the fun Picasso had playing paddleball with Velázquez's tour de force—filtering Velázquez's realism through the kaleidoscope of Cubism.

Last Years (Room 15)

Picasso spent the last 36 years of his life living simply in the south of France. He said many times that "paintings are like windows open to the world." We see his sunny Riviera world: With simple black outlines and Crayola colors, Picasso painted sun-splashed nature, peaceful doves, and the joys of the beach. He's enjoyed life with his second (and much younger) wife, Jacqueline Roque.

His last works have the playfulness of someone much younger. As is often said of Picasso, in his youth he was taught to see the world like an adult, and in his golden years he enjoyed seeing and portraying the world with the freedom of a child.

Nearby (in Rooms B1, N, and B2), you'll see how in his later years Picasso became a master of other media besides painting. With his **ceramics,** he made bowls and vases in fun animal shapes, decorated with simple motifs. You'll also find **portraits of Jaume Sabartés,** whose initial donation made this museum possible.

Picasso died with brush in hand, still growing as an artist. Sadly, since he vowed never to set foot in fascist, Franco-ruled Spain, Picasso never returned to his homeland...and never saw this museum. But to the end, Picasso continued exploring and loving life through his art.

EIXAMPLE WALK

From the Top of Passeig de Gràcia to Plaça de Catalunya

Literally "The Expansion," the Eixample is where Barcelona spread when it burst at the seams in the 19th century. Rather than allowing unchecked growth, city leaders funneled Barcelona's newfound wealth into creating a standardized yet refreshingly open grid plan—quite the opposite of the claustrophobic Gothic lanes that had contained locals for centuries.

The creation of the Eixample coincided with a burst in architectural creativity as the great Modernista builders Antoni Gaudí, Lluís Domènech i Montaner, and Josep Puig i Cadafalch adorned Barcelona's new boulevards with fanciful facades. It was a perfect storm of urban planning, unbridled architectural innovation, Industrial Age technology, ample wealth, and Catalan cultural pride.

This walk takes you gently downhill through the Eixample's "Golden Quarter" (Quadrat d'Or) to see two of the city's Modernista musts—the Block of Discord and La Pedrera (Casa Milà)—as well as several other sights. We'll wind through some pleasant, relatively untouristy residential neighborhoods that showcase modern Barcelona's unusual street plan, inviting restaurant and shopping options, and everyday life in this elegant quarter.

Orientation

Length of This Walk: Allow one hour (more if you tour the sights).

Getting There: This walk starts at the Diagonal Metro station.

La Pedrera (Casa Milà): €25 timed-entry ticket—buy online in advance, daily 9:00-20:30, Nov-Feb until 18:30; see page 223 for nighttime visits, tours, and other ticketing options.

Casa Batlló: €39 "Blue" timed-entry ticket includes audioguide—buy online in advance; daily 9:00-20:00, nighttime visits and concerts most peak season evenings at 20:00; see page 61 for additional ticketing options.

Casa Museu Amatller: €17 for 45-minute visit with audioguide, generally on the hour and half-hour (daily 10:00-19:00, shorter hours in winter), €20 one-hour English tour offered daily at 10:00; see page 62 for details.

La Concepció Market: Mon and Sat 8:00-15:00, Tue-Fri until 20:00, closed Sun, Carrer de Aragó 313-317.

Church of the Holy Conception: Free, daily 8:00-13:00 & 17:00-21:00, enter at Carrer de Roger de Llúria 70, through the cloister, if entrance on Carrer d'Aragó is locked.

Tours: ∩ Download my free Eixample Walk audio tour.

Eateries: La Concepció Market is the handiest spot on this walk for a tasty, budget bite. Several fine tapas bars and restaurants are on or near this route (see page 199).

BACKGROUND

Barcelona boomed in the 1800s, with its population doubling (from a half-million to a million) over the course of one century. After a long period of stagnation—caused by changing sea-trading routes and political repression from Madrid—the city was finding new success. Catalunya's abundant coal deposits and many rivers were powering lucrative textile mills. The factories brought workers from all over Spain and beyond. By 1850, Barcelona was becoming an industrial powerhouse.

Unfortunately, Barcelona was all jacked up with nowhere to grow. Two hundred thousand residents were still crammed into the Barri Gòtic. It was a slum of steep and crowded tenements where disease was rampant, the air was choked with coal soot, and the quality of life was miserable. It was clear there was only one solution—expansion *(eixample)*.

Other European cities (like Paris, Vienna, and Copenhagen) were dealing with similar growing pains by tearing down antiquated defensive walls, draining moats, and converting the unused land into circular boulevards, parks, and housing.

But because the Madrid government was still wary of a Catalan uprising, Barcelona by law had to stay within its medieval walls. Finally, in 1854, Queen Isabella II allowed the city to tear down the old walls and expand northward. Because very little existed outside the Old City, urban planners had a blank slate.

Civil engineer Ildefons Cerdà (1815-

1876) ~~proposed~~ a carefully plotted, remarkably modern plan. It would be an efficient grid of streets that would surround the convoluted tangle of Barcelona's Old City. He added a unique twist to the usual rectangular grid. By snipping off the corners of buildings, he created light and spacious octagonal "squares" at every intersection.

Work began in 1860 on Cerdà's progressive plan. In his vision, each block-square district of the Eixample would have all the services its residents would need: hospital, park, market, schools, and day-care centers. Restrictions on the height, width, and depth of buildings ensured that sunlight would reach every dwelling unit. The hollow space found inside each "block" of apartments would form a neighborhood park. Cerdà's vision proved to be an urban-planning success story.

The birth of the Eixample also coincided with two other important moments in the city's history: The revival of Catalan cultural pride (the Renaixen-ça) and the emergence of Catalunya's version of Art Nouveau—Modernisme (see the sidebar). These progressive movements found expression not only in enlightened urban planning but also in the beauty built into the buildings.

Rich and artsy big shots bought plots along the Eixample grid and hired some of the best and brightest architects in the business, including Antoni Gaudí. It's no accident that Modernista mansions come with big bay windows and outlandish decoration: The people who paid for them wanted both to be seen and recognized for their forward-thinking embrace of the new art. They built as close to the center as possible—that's why the most distinctive buildings are near Passeig de Gràcia.

Today's Eixample remains Barcelona's upscale and genteel uptown. The heart of the Eixample is the Quadrat d'Or, or "Golden Quarter," with the richest collection of Modernista facades...and the richest residents. As you walk through the streets, peek into the big, ornate iron and glass doorways of almost any apartment building to see the eclectic decorative entrance halls and old-fashioned elevators. This remains one of the city's most desirable neighborhoods.

The Walk Begins

• *Begin at the Diagonal Metro stop. Take the Passeig de Gràcia exit and surface at the street of the same name.*

❶ Passeig de Gràcia (Top End)

Stand at the head of this broad boulevard and gaze downhill. This is the Eixample's grand, 50-yard-wide, tree-lined "main street," which runs through the heart of the district. At the far end—seven blocks down—is Plaça de Catalunya, where we'll end our walk.

Passeig de Gràcia was built as a kind of Champs-Elysées of Barcelona. The richest folks built their mansions along here (as we'll see). It was a place to dress up, promenade in your carriage, linger for a drink at a café, or shop at a high-fashion boutique. Gazing around, it's clear that the street still retains that same chic character. International high-fashion stores abound, like Dolce & Gabbana, Jimmy Choo, and Montblanc.

Passeig de Gràcia actually dates back to pre-Eixample times, when it was a narrow (but aptly named) path to the town of Gràcia. That former town is now the neighborhood of **Gràcia,** just a couple of blocks uphill from here, across Avinguda Diagonal. Gràcia is known for its old-time character, narrow streets, and upper-middle-class intellectual feel, with many design schools and a youthful scene.

• *Before moving on, if you're a Modernista completist, it's just a short walk from here to three more fine buildings—"extra credit" for those fascinated by this era (see the sidebar, "A Modernista Detour," for directions).*

  Otherwise, stroll gently downhill along Passeig de Gràcia for a block or two. On your left will be the unmistakable wavy stone facade of...

❷ La Pedrera (a.k.a. Casa Milà)

Of all the over-the-top mansions built in the Eixample, this one was the most daring. A wealthy developer and his wealthier wife hired the city's most famous architect, Antoni Gaudí, and gave him a free hand. Even today, this Gaudí exterior laughs down on the crowds filling Passeig de Gràcia. La Pedrera ("The Quarry") has a much-photographed roller coaster of melting-ice-cream eaves. It remains Barcelona's quintessential Modernista  building and was Gaudí's last major commission (1906-1910) before he dedicated his final years to the Sagrada Família.

The building has an iron structural skeleton to support its weight (a new construction technique at the time). Gaudí's planned statues of the Virgin Mary and archangels were vetoed by the owner.

The best views of La Pedrera are from kitty-corner across the street. From there, notice the century-old elegance of this fancy neighborhood. The ornate metal streetlamps (from 1906) were originally gas-lit. At the base of the lampposts, spot the two little doors curbside—these were actually equipped with wood-burning ovens to heat benches for aristocratic bums. Across the street, notice the circular stone sofa corralling a plane tree.

• *From Passeig de Gràcia, turn right on Carrer de Provença and go one block. Each block is exactly 250 meters (so walking around the block is exactly one kilometer). As you stroll, look up and appreciate the details. You'll pass posh shops and apartments with nice bay windows in this exclusive neighborhood. Notice the dedicated bike lane and the long lines of parked motor scooters. To maintain the Eixample's quality of life, car traffic is restricted, so locals find other ways to get around. At the first corner you'll find the Mauri pastry shop—where it's always teatime for local grandmothers. But we're turning left on...*

❸ Rambla de Catalunya

First, pause to notice the cut-off corners of the intersection. Octagonal intersections like this showed off the fine building facades, allowed for freer traffic movement, and gave citizens some breathing room in the crowded city.

Now head down Rambla de Catalunya—a narrow, manageable street with a median strip lined with inviting cafés. The boutiques along here are still upscale, but generally more local and unique than those on the main drag.

The area a few blocks to the west of here (around Carrer d'Aribau) is a center of the local gay community, earning it the nickname "Gayxample."

Rambla de Catalunya has many classy buildings. After a block, on the left (at #78), you'll find the elaborately carved **Casa Juncosa**. It was built in 1909, around the same time as Gaudí's La Pedrera, from similar materials—stone and iron—but its curved balconies and bay windows show the touch of a more traditional architect. If open, peek inside to see the atrium leading to condos and say *hola* to the doorman.

Despite the great architectural variation in their facades, most Eixample homes were used identically: The entire building was owned by one family who lived on the high-ceilinged middle level and rented out the floors above and below. Shops and businesses occupied the ground floor; tenants lived on the less grand floors higher up. Throughout the Eixample, you'll see that the first floor

Modernisme and the Renaixença

Modernisme is Barcelona's unique contribution to the Europe-wide Art Nouveau movement. Meaning "a taste for what is modern"—such as streetcars, electric lights, and big-wheeled bicycles—this free-flowing organic style lasted from 1888 to 1906.

Broadly speaking, there were two kinds of Modernisme (otherwise known as Catalan Art Nouveau). Early Modernisme has a Neo-Gothic flavor, clearly inspired by medieval castles and towers—logically, since architects wanted to recall the days when Barcelona was at its peak. From that starting point, Antoni Gaudí branched off on his own, adding the color and curves we most associate with the look of Barcelona's Modernisme.

The aim was to create buildings that were both practical and decorative. To that end, Modernista architects experimented with new construction techniques. Their most important material was concrete, which they could mold to curve and ripple like a wave and enliven with brightly colored glass and tile. Their structures were fully modern, but the decoration was a clip-art collage of natural images, exotic Moorish or Chinese themes, and fanciful Gothic crosses and knights to celebrate Catalunya's medieval glory days.

It's ironic to think that Modernisme was a response against the regimentation of the Industrial Age—and that all those organic shapes were only made possible thanks to Eiffel Tower-like iron frames. As you wander through the Eixample looking at all those fanciful facades and colorful, leafy, blooming shapes in doorways, entrances, and ceilings, remember that many of these homes were built at the same time as the first skyscrapers in Chicago and New York City.

Underpinning Modernisme was the Catalan cultural revival movement called the Renaixença. Across Europe, it was a time of national resurgence. It was the dawn of the modern age, and downtrodden peoples—from the Basques to the Irish to the Hungarians to the Finns—were throwing off the cultural domination of other nations and celebrating what made their own culture unique. Here in Catalunya, the Renaixença encouraged everyday people to get excited about all things Catalan—from their language, patriotic dances, and inspirational art to their surprising style of architecture.

Eixample Walk

GRÀCIA

EIXAMPLE

To Sagrada Família

Verdaguer Ⓜ

CARRER DE CÓRSEGA

C. DEL ROSSELLÓ

AVINGUDA DIAGONAL

CARRER DE GIRONA

CARRER DE BAILÈN

CASA DE LES PUNXES

WALK BEGINS

PALAU BARÓ DE QUADRAS

CUBIÑÁ◆

ⓑ#24
Ⓜ Diagonal

LA PEDRERA (CASA MILÀ)

CARRER MALLORCA

LA CONCEPCIÓ MARKET

❻

CARRER D'ARAGÓ

VALÈNCIA

CHURCH OF THE HOLY CONCEPTION

❶

❷

CENTRE CULTURAL LA CASA ELIZALDE

❺

CARRER DE

❼

Ⓜ Girona

MAURI PASTRIES

C. PROVENÇA

PASSEIG DE GRÀCIA

J. MURRIA QUEVIURES GROCERY

C. DE ROGER

C. DEL CONSELL DE CENT

C. DE DIPUTACIÓ

QUADRAT D'OR

CASA JUNCOSA

PASSEIG DE GRÀCIA TRAIN STN.

Ⓡ

TOWER

PASS. MEDIEVIGO

PASSATGE PERMANYER

C. DE LLÚRIA

200 Meters

RAMBLA

FUNDACIÓ TÀPIES

❸

CASA BATLLÓ

Ⓜ Passeig de Gràcia

BLOCK OF DISCORD

C. DE PAU CLARIS

200 Yards

SERVEI ESTACIÓ

❹

GADGETS & THINGS

DE

CASA AMATLLER

CASA LLEÓ MORERA

PASSEIG DE GRÀCIA

Passeig de Gràcia

CATALANES

CATALUNYA

COMEDIA THEATER

Ⓜ

❽

EL CORTE INGLÉS DEPT. STORE

❶ Passeig de Gràcia (Top End)

❷ La Pedrera (a.k.a. Casa Milà)

❸ Rambla de Catalunya

❹ Block of Discord

❺ Carrer de València

❻ La Concepció Market

❼ Church of the Holy Conception

❽ Passeig de Gràcia (Bottom End)

❾ Plaça de Catalunya

GRAN VIA DE LES CORTS

RONDA DE LA UNIVERSITAT

WALK ENDS

#24 & D-50 ⓑ

Catalunya Ⓜ

❾

Plaça de Catalunya

Ⓜ Universitat

OLD

FNAC

CITY

up is usually taller and more elaborate than the rest—often with balconies or bay windows that higher floors are lacking. (Most of these houses predate the elevator; after that convenience was invented and widely installed, penthouse living became popular.) Many houses have two doors—one for the owners and another for the upstairs tenants. Most house blocks had an interior garden courtyard for ventilation and light, although over time many of these spaces have been covered over by one-story structures or parking lots.

Because the Eixample was developed during the Renaixença of local culture, you'll spot decorative Catalan themes such as St. George—the local patron saint—slaying the dragon.

Not all the architecture of this neighborhood is artful. In fact, lots of tasteless buildings, erected in the 1970s, punctuate the older elegance. Locals are fully aware that when a building hits the age of 50, it becomes protected—and many of the greatest eyesores of the Eixample are about to reach that threshold, at which time they will become a permanent part of the cityscape. Also notice how many buildings have what locals call "caps." A mayor in the 1980s allowed landowners to add extra floors to older buildings; many structures have a simple addition capping an otherwise elegant facade.

A block farther down, cross Carrer d'Aragó and turn left for a better view of the **Fundació Antoni Tàpies** (on the left). This brick building with a crazy hairdo of fanciful ironwork (called "The Cloud and the Chair" by Antoni Tàpies) was designed by one of the holy trinity of Modernista architects, Lluís Domènech i Montaner. It serves as a nice introduction to the more famous Modernista buildings we're about to see and sums up the  credo of the movement: modern brick, iron, and glass materials; playful decorative motifs; and a spacious, functional, and light-filled interior.

• *Continue along on Carrer d'Aragó. For a fun little stop, pop into the hardware craft store* **Servei Estació** *(at #270). Two floors up, they have an open terrace in the back with self-serve coffee from where you can peek at the back side of the Block of Discord. Continue down Carrer d'Aragó to Passeig de Gràcia; turn right (downhill) and take in the view from the corner. This begins the city block of Modernista facades known as the...*

❹ Block of Discord (Illa de la Discòrdia)

One block, three buildings, three creative Modernista architects, and a lot of visual commotion—that's the Block of Discord. Over a short span of time, the big names of Catalunya's bold Art Nouveau architectural movement erected innovative facades along this one short stretch of Passeig de Gràcia. Although each architect has better works elsewhere in town, this is a convenient place to see their sharply contrasting visions side by side. In fact, the whole block is a jumble of delightful architectural whimsy. Reliefs, coats of arms, ironwork, gables, and bay windows adorn otherwise ordinary buildings.

A Modernista Detour

Several Modernista buildings are clustered near the Diagonal Metro stop. To reach them, cross Avinguda Diagonal, and continue two long blocks on Passeig de Gràcia. Where the street curves around the tree-lined median, you'll find the **Hotel Casa Fuster,** a fine Modernista building by Lluís Domènech i Montaner. The hotel's Café Vienés hosts a weekly jazz night (for details, see the Nightlife in Barcelona chapter).

Backtrack to Diagonal to reach two works by Josep Puig i Cadafalch. Take a left (go east) down the busy Diagonal bou-

levard. After a block, you reach the **Palau Baró de Quadras** (Diagonal 373, on the right across the street). Puig i Cadafalch's plateresque facade (in Spain's medieval "silverwork" style of intricate decoration) celebrates a time when Catalunya was powerful, and the statues flanking the door—of St. George defeating the dragon—make the building's Catalan pride even more evident. Today the building houses the Institut Ramón Llul, a public cultural center dedicated to promoting Catalan language and culture (www.llull.cat). You can walk into the foyer and peek at some of the interior for free.

Continuing down another block and a half, Diagonal leads to the distinctively turreted Casa Terrades (at #416, on the left)—better known as **Casa de les Punxes** ("House of Spikes"). Here Puig i Cadafalch lassoed together what had been three separate buildings into one large complex, wrapping them in a fanciful Gothic castle cloak (no inside access). The turrets, spires, balconies, and ceramic tiles celebrate Catalan culture.

• *Work your way down the block, beginning with the unmistakably Gaudí-style facade that's situated one building in from the corner.*

Casa Batlló (#43)

The most famous facade on the block is Antoni Gaudí's green-blue, ceramic-speckled Casa Batlló (pronounced BAHT-yoh). It's thought that Gaudí based the work on the popular legend of St. George (Jordi) slaying the dragon: The humpback roofline suggests a crest-

ing dragon's back, and the smallest, top balcony is shaped like a rosebud (a rose is said to have grown in the place where St. George spilled the dragon's blood). The building's tibia-like pillars and skull-like balconies evoke the dragon's victims. Look at the first-floor bay window. If you squint (and perhaps smoke some pot, the consumption of which is legal here, by the way), you might see a bat with outstretched wings, relating to a Catalan folk legend. Notice also the random broken tiles, a Gaudí trademark that only later became appreciated. The tiled roof has a soft-ice-cream-cone turret topped with a cross. But some see instead a Mardi Gras theme, with mask-like balconies, a facade flecked with purple and gold confetti, and the ridge of a harlequin's hat up top. The inscrutable Gaudí preferred to leave his designs open to interpretation.

Before moving on, turn 180 degrees and look across the boulevard to see the linear iron-framed apartment building at #52—structurally the same as Casa Batlló. In 1904, when Gaudí was hired to renovate Casa Batlló, it looked like that.

• *Next door is...*

Casa Amatller (#41)

Josep Puig i Cadafalch completely remodeled this house for the Amatller family. The facade features a creative mix of three of

Spain's historical traditions: Moorish-style pentagram and vine designs; Gothic-style tracery, gargoyles, and bay windows; and the step-gable roof from Spain's Habsburg connection to the Low Countries. Notice the many layers of the letter "A": The house itself (with its gable) forms an A, as does the decorative frieze over the bay window on the right side of the facade. Within that frieze, you'll see several more A's sprouting from branches (*amatller* means "almond tree"). The reliefs above the smaller windows show off the hobbies of the Amatller clan: Find the little animals holding the early box camera, the open book, and the amphora jug (which the family collected). Look through the second-floor bay window to see the corkscrew column. You can step inside the interior courtyard for a sense of the livability of a residence like this, with its braided columns, marble floors, pink walls, wood-beam ceiling, and stone staircase topped with eagles. As you leave, note the servants' door on the right, ornamented with St. George and the dragon.

For another dimension of Modernisme, peek into the ground-floor windows of the Bagués Masriera shop and notice the slinky pieces of Spanish Art Nouveau jewelry.

• *Continue down the street to the end of the block. On the corner, you'll find...*

Casa Lleó Morera (#35)

This Modernista house is not open to the public, but you can admire its paella-like mix of styles from the outside. It's the work

of the architect Lluís Domènech i Montaner, who also designed the Palace of Catalan Music. The lower floors have classical columns and a bay window reminiscent of a Greek temple. (Notice the real marble column—supporting nothing but some aristocrat's ego—placed for all to see behind the bay window.) Farther up are Gothic balconies of rosettes and tracery, while the upper part has faux Moorish stucco work. The whole thing is ornamented with fantastic griffins, angels, and fish. Flanking the third-story windows, four muses, representing the fine arts, hold exciting inventions of the day—the camera, lightbulb, and gramophone—demonstrating just how modern these homeowners were in this age of Modern-isme.

• *From here, cross the street and backtrack up the Block of Discord, enjoying a more distant view of the facades. Take time to notice the swirling sidewalk (by Gaudí), the nice benches slathered with broken white tile mosaics, and the arcing ironwork streetlamps (by other architects).*

Turn right on Carrer d'Aragó. Go one block and turn left on Carrer de Pau Claris, then right onto...

❺ Carrer de València

A half-block down (on the right at #302) is the **Centre Cultural La Casa Elizalde**. This city center is a hive of creative and personal growth activities. You're welcome to explore the building, which often has free temporary exhibits on art or community life. Head into the passage, noticing the community bulletin board listing classes and events. Continuing down the hall, you'll pop out into an appealing interior courtyard with benches. Look up and around the buildings for a taste of the typical inner patios that are a quiet sanctuary from the busy Eixample streets. (Upstairs there's more, including WCs: women, first floor; men, second floor.)

Continue down Carrer de València to the next intersection, with a couple of interesting facades. On the right is the classic Modernista grocery of **J. Murria Queviures**. This old-fashioned gourmet deli is stocked with pricey ingredients for a top-end picnic.

Modernista Masters: Gaudí and Beyond

Yes, you'll hear plenty about Gaudí, but he's merely one of many who contributed to the architectural revolution of Modernisme. Here's a rundown of the movement's talented stars.

The Stars of Modernisme

Antoni Gaudí (1852-1926), Barcelona's most famous Modernista artist was a proud descendant of four generations of metalworkers. He incorporated ironwork into his architecture and came up with novel approaches to architectural structure and space. Gaudí's work strongly influenced his younger Catalan contemporary, Salvador Dalí. Notice the similarities: While Dalí was creating unlikely and shocking juxtapositions of surrealistic images, Gaudí did the same in architecture—using the spine of a reptile for a banister or a turtle-shell design on windows. Entire trips (and lives) are dedicated to seeing the works of Gaudí, but on a brief visit, the highlights include his great unfinished church, the Sagrada Família; the La Pedrera, Casa Batlló, and Palau Güell mansions; and Park Güell, his ambitious and never-completed housing development.

While Gaudí gets most of the attention and certainly was a remarkable innovator, these next two architects are just as important—and perhaps more purely representative of the Modernista style.

Lluís Domènech i Montaner (1850-1923), a professor and politician, was responsible for some major civic buildings, including his masterwork, the Palace of Catalan Music, and the sprawling Sant Pau hospital complex (Recinte Modernista de Sant Pau). Domènech i Montaner also designed Casa Lleó Morera on the Block of Discord and Casa Fuster (now a luxury hotel), along with several works in the small towns of Canet de Mar and Comillas.

Breathe deep to smell the cheese aging in the cellar. The vintage ad outside, facing the corner—dubbed *La Mona y el Mono (The Classy Lady and the Monkey)*—advertised anise liquor to Modernista-era clients.

Farther down, almost to the end of the block, on the left at #293 is a fine Modernista building with wrought-iron railings and matching bay windows. Unfortunately, that's followed by a modern brick monstrosity that breaks up the Eixample harmony. Across the street (#320), step into the **Navarro flower shop.** It's open daily 24 hours so there's just no excuse if a loved one is deserving flowers. Take a fragrant stroll, looping deep into the shop.

Josep Puig i Cadafalch (1867-1956) was a city planner who oversaw the opening up of Via Laietana through the middle of the Old City, the redevelopment of Montjuïc for the 1929 World Expo, and a redesign of the monastery at Santa Maria de Montserrat. Later he flourished as a Modernista architect, best known for the manor houses Casa de les Punxes and Casa Amatller on the Block of Discord. He also designed the brick Casaramona factory complex (now the CaixaForum exhibition space) and Casa Martí—the home for the Modernista hangout bar Els Quatre Gats, which became a cradle of sorts for the whole movement.

Supporting Cast

All the architects worked with a team of people who made real contributions. For example, Gaudí's colleague **Josep Maria Jujol** (1879-1949) is primarily responsible for much of what Gaudí became known for—the broken-tile mosaic decorations (called *trencadís*) on Park Güell's benches and La Pedrera's chimneys.

Joan Martorell i Montells (1833-1906) was a professor, mentor, and employer of a young Gaudí. Although an accomplished architect, Martorell's most important role was as a facilitator for his prized student: He oversaw the committee that hired Gaudí to build Sagrada Família and introduced Gaudí to his most important benefactor, **Eusebi Güell** (1846-1918). Güell used his nearly $90 billion fortune to bankroll Gaudí and others, much as the Medici financed Michelangelo and Leonardo da Vinci. Güell's name still adorns two of Gaudí's most important works: Palau Güell and Park Güell.

Continue a few steps more to the intersection, with the twin-turreted Municipal Conservatory of Barcelona on the corner. You'll often see students hurrying into this city-run music academy with violin cases on their backs.

• *Continue another half-block down Carrer de València. On the right is the entrance to...*

❻ La Concepció Market

While it has many of the same features as La Boqueria (on the Ramblas) and the Santa Caterina Market (in El Born), this market (with a modern supermarket in the basement and a garage below that) has virtually zero tourists. Pass the delightful flower market crowding the sidewalk and walk through the building, from one end to the other. It's a good place to sample local cheeses, buy olives, pick up some fruit, or sit at a counter for cheap, ultra-fresh tapas.

Ponder the fact that in just a few blocks, we've passed a municipal building, a school, and a market. This is very much in keeping with the original vision for the Eixample as a series of self-sufficient neighborhood zones with easy access to important services. Each neighborhood here is served by a market like this one.

• *Exiting the market at the far end, turn right on Carrer d'Aragó. At the intersection with Carrer del Bruc, notice (on the right) the detailed iron gate and columns. This is the entrance to the Seu del Districte Eixample at #311—the Eixample's own branch of City Hall. Peek in the doors to see the traditional* gegants, *giant puppet-like figures paraded around the city on special days (they're called* gigantes *in Castilian).*

Now, cross Carrer del Bruc and continue another half-block, to the church. Step inside. (If it's locked, enter via the cloister, just ahead and around the corner.)

❼ Church of the Holy Conception (Basílica de la Puríssima Concepció)

This purely Gothic, 14th-century church once stood in the Old City. But when the city walls came down as part of Barcelona's expansion, a few historic churches like this one were moved, brick by brick, to new locations in the 1870s. The bell tower came from a different Gothic church. (These relocated historic structures are nicknamed "traveling buildings.")

Step inside and take a seat. Ahhhh. The interior has many classic features of Barcelona Gothic: gray stone, interior buttresses forming side chapels, statues of many local saints, intricate chandeliers, and crisscross vaults on the ceiling culminating in medallions with more local saints. A statue of Mary crowns the prickly Gothic altar.

Exit the church midway up the nave, to the left. This leads you outside into a delightful 15th- and 16th-century cloister. The slender columns and delicate arches mingle with palm, banana, magnolia, and orange trees to create a peaceful oasis.

• *From the cloister, return to Carrer d'Aragó, turn right and follow it back to the big and busy Passeig de Gràcia (and the Block of Discord). There turn left, and head straight downhill to the end of this walk. Up ahead, an angel atop a monumental building says, "Plaça de Catalunya is this way."*

❽ Passeig de Gràcia (Bottom End)

As we saw earlier, this main street of the Eixample was once prime real estate for stately residences. But times change, and this stretch of Passeig de Gràcia shows the encroachment of the modern world.

As the city continued to grow and real estate was at a premium, it became more lucrative to tear down those mansions and replace them with multi-story apartments and businesses. The domed building topped with an angel on a phoenix went up in the 1920s for an insurance company. A block down (by the fountain), one of the few surviving original mansions was converted to the **Comedia movie theater.**

As you walk down Passeig de Gràcia, see how the elegant 19th-century Eixample melds into the 21st-century city. Softly rounded buildings give way to stern rectangular skyscrapers. Now travel the final stretch down to the sprawling Times Square of this country, Plaça de Catalunya.

❾ Plaça de Catalunya

Dotted with fountains, statues, and pigeons—and ringed by grand buildings—this plaza is Barcelona's center. Plaça de Catalunya, where four great thoroughfares cross, is the heart of the city. Historically, Plaça de Catalunya links the modern city with its past. As you cross this square and slip back into the Old City, those last 500 feet take you back 500 years. You can step back into the Barri Gòtic knowing you've seen the best of Barcelona's ambitiously modern town, the Eixample.

SAGRADA FAMÍLIA TOUR

Architect Antoni Gaudí's most famous and awe-inspiring work is this unfinished, super-sized church. With its cake-in-the-rain facade and otherworldly spires, the church is not only an icon of Barcelona and its trademark Modernisme, but also a symbol of its greatest practitioner. As an architect, Gaudí relied on the foundation of the classics, nature, and religion, and this church represents all three.

Gaudí labored on Sagrada Família for 43 years, from 1883 until his death in 1926. Nearly a century on, people continue to toil to bring Gaudí's designs to life. There's something inspirational about a community of committed people with a vision who've worked on a church that wouldn't be finished in their lifetimes—as was standard in the Gothic age. The progress of this remarkable building is a testament to the generations of architects, sculptors, stonecutters, fundraisers, and donors who shared Gaudí's astonishing vision. After paying the admission price (becoming a partner in this building project), you will actually feel good. If there's any building on earth I'd like to see, it's the Basílica de la Sagrada Família...finished.

Orientation

Cost: All tickets are timed-entry and must be purchased online in advance (no physical tickets sold on-site). €26 ticket includes church, €30 ticket includes church and 50-minute tour with live guide, €36 ticket includes church and one tower, €40 ticket includes church, guided tour, and one tower. All tickets include the app and audioguide.

Hours: Mon-Sat 9:00-20:00, Sun from 10:30; March and Oct daily until 19:00, Nov-Feb until 18:00.

Information: +34 932 080 414, www.sagradafamilia.org.

La Sagrada Família App: When you book online, you'll receive a link to the official La Sagrada Família app with audioguide, which can be downloaded to your phone. You can also access your ticket (or buy tickets) via the app.

When To Go: The church is always busy, but late afternoon and early evening tend to be less crowded—and also the best time to catch the "golden hour" when light floods through the stained-glass windows.

Getting There: The Metro stop Sagrada Família puts you right on the church's doorstep. Exiting toward Plaça de Gaudí (follow silhouette logos of the church) will save a little walking.

Getting In: If you show up without a ticket, try scanning the posted QR code to buy online on the spot. Carefully note your assigned entry time. You can enter the church from 15 minutes before your ticketed time and up to 30 minutes after. Make your way to the Nativity Facade side, show your ticket (either on your phone or printed out), and go through security.

Sharp items like pocketknives must be checked (you'll get a claim number to pick up your item upon exiting through this side). All hats must be removed.

Church Services: Mass (in various languages) is held every Sunday at 9:00; those who actually want to worship here are admitted at no charge. Entry to the church begins at 8:00, but lines can form as early as 6:30.

Towers: The €36 and €40 tickets include access to one tower. (If tickets including a tower visit are sold out online, check at the info kiosk near the Passion Facade for last-minute availability.) Towers can close when windy or rainy (if that happens, the tower portion of your ticket will be refunded).

Elevators on opposite sides of the church take you partway up the towers—one on the Passion Facade, and one on the Nativity Facade. The elevators only go up—to get down, you'll use a tightly wound, narrow staircase with 400 steps. The **Passion Facade elevator** takes you up a bit higher, and the stairs to come down are slightly wider than those descending from the **Nativity Facade elevator.** The facades are not joined, so it isn't possible to cross from one facade to the other. From either side, you'll have great views of the city and a gargoyle's-eye perspective of the loopy church.

Baggage Check: Day bags are allowed in the church but are scanned. Backpacks are not allowed in the towers: Small lockers are available at each elevator when the towers are open (lockers only for tower ticket holders).

Length of This Tour: Allow 1.5 hours.

Eating: It can be difficult to find a decent bite in this touristy area. The recommended **Forn de Pa Puiggrós** (a 5-minute walk north, at Avinguda de Gaudí 39) and **Granja Petitbo** (a 10-minute walk south, at Passeig Sant Joan 82) are good cafés nearby.

Nearby: Inviting parks flank the two completed facades.

The Tour Begins

• *Before entering the church, start on the far side of the pond in the park that faces the Nativity Facade (where the entry lines are located). From there, you're back far enough to take in the entire towering facade. This is a great place to take a photo and take in the...*

❶ View of the Exterior from Beyond the Pond

Stand and imagine how grand this church will be when completed. The eight 330-foot spires topped with crosses are just a fraction of this mega-church. When finished, it will have 18 spires. Rising above the spires are four taller towers, dedicated to the four **Evangelists** and topped with giant figures: an angel for Matthew, a lion for Mark, an ox for Luke, and an eagle for John. A tower dedicated to **Mary** rises still higher—400 feet—with an

illuminated crystal star at its top. And in the very center of the complex will stand the grand 560-foot **Jesus tower,** topped with a cross that will shine like a spiritual lighthouse, visible even from out at sea.

The **Nativity Facade**—where tourists enter today—is only a side entrance to the church. The grand main entry, through the Glory Facade, will be around to the left. To accommodate the church's planned entrance esplanade, a nine-story apartment building will have to be torn down. (This is an ongoing controversy as authorities negotiate with landowners.)

The three facades—Nativity, Passion, and Glory—will chronicle Christ's life from birth to death to resurrection. Inside and out, a goal of the church is to bring the lessons of the Bible to the world. Despite his boldly modern architectural vision, Gaudí was fundamentally traditional and deeply religious. He designed the Sagrada Família to be a bas-

Sagrada Família

To Recinte
Modernista
de Sant Pau
& **9**

AVINGUDA DE GAUDÍ

Pond

Plaça de Gaudí

20 Meters
20 Yards

#D50 **B**

Sagrada Família **M**

☒ Elevator

M Sagrada Família

CARRER DE MALLORCA

1 ⚐

TOUR BEGINS

FENCE

ENTRANCES

CARRER DE LA MARINA

EXIT

BRONZE MODEL

2 ⚐

N A T I V I T Y   **F A C A D E**

WC

☒ **3** INFO KIOSK

SPIRES

CLOISTER

VIDEO THEATER ■

VIEW OF GAUDÍ'S ■ TOMB

T
R
A
N
S
E
P
T

CARRER DE PROVENÇA

AMBULATORY

CHOIR

BRONZE DOOR

4 **N A V E** ⚐ **5**

G L O R Y   F A C A D E

UNFINISHED ESPLANADE

SACRISTY

SPIRES

CLOISTER

☒

P A S S I O N   **F A C A D E** WC

MUSEUM ENTRANCE

6 ⚐

INFO
■ KIOSK   EXIT

8

7 SCHOOL

Sagrada Família **M**

FENCE

CARRER DE SARDENYA

T

C. DE MALLORCA

To
10

Plaça de la Sagrada Família

Tour
1 View of the Exterior
2 Nativity Facade
3 Church Atrium
4 Interior
5 Glory Facade
6 Passion Facade
7 School
8 Ramp to Museum

Eateries
9 To Forn de Pa Puiggrós
10 To Granja Petitbo

tion of solid Christian values in the midst of what was a humble workers' colony in a fast-changing city.

When Gaudí died, the only section that had been completed was the Nativity Facade (with its themes of birth and new life). Notice the dove-covered Tree of Life on top, with playful little creatures carved into nooks and crannies throughout, and a white pelican at the bottom. Because it was believed that this noble bird would feed its young with its own blood, the pelican

A Dream Made Real

For over 140 years, Barcelona has labored to bring Antoni Gaudí's vision to reality. The present architect has been at it since 2012. The work is funded exclusively by private donations and entry fees.

Like Gothic churches of medieval times, the design has evolved over the decades. At heart, it's Gothic, a style much admired by Gaudí. He added his own Art Nouveau/Modernisme touches, guided by nature and engineering innovations. Today the site bristles with cranking cranes, rusty forests of rebar, and scaffolding. Sagrada Família offers a fun look at a living, growing, bigger-than-life building.

Sagrada Família Timeline

1882: The church is begun in Gothic-revival style by architect Francisco de Paula del Villar.

1883: Paula del Villar quits, and Antoni Gaudí is hired—and completely re-envisions the church's design.

1892: Gaudí begins the Nativity Facade.

1914: Gaudí turns his attention exclusively to the Sagrada Família.

1925: The first bell tower is completed.

1926: Gaudí dies, with the project about 20 percent complete.

1936-1939: The Spanish Civil War halts all work; the crypt is burned, along with many of Gaudí's plans.

1950s: Building resumes in earnest with the start of the Passion Facade.

1976: The four Passion spires are finished, bringing the total of completed spires to eight (out of 18 planned).

1980s: Computer technology is introduced, greatly accelerating the pace of construction.

2000: The nave roof is completed.

2005: Passion statues are completed.

2010: Crossing vaults are finished (enclosing the roof), and Pope Benedict XVI dedicates the church as a basilica.

2016: Construction begins on the towers of the Evangelists, Mary, and Jesus.

2021: Tower of Mary is finished.

2026: The church likely won't be complete by the 100th anniversary of Gaudí's death, but the Tower of Jesus should be.

?? Make a date to attend the dedication with your kids...to teach them a lesson in delayed gratification.

was a common symbol in the Middle Ages for the self-sacrifice of Jesus.

The Nativity Facade's four spires are dedicated to apostles, and they repeatedly bear the word "sanctus," or holy. Their colorful ceramic caps symbolize the miters (formal hats) of bishops. The shorter spires (to the left) symbolize the Eucharist (communion), alternating between a chalice with grapes and a communion host with wheat.

The rest of the church, while inspired by Gaudí's long-range vision, has been designed and executed by others. This artistic freedom was amplified in 1936, when civil war shelling burned many of Gaudí's blueprints. Supporters of the ongoing work insist that Gaudí, who enjoyed saying, "My client [God] is not in a hurry," knew he wouldn't live to complete the church and recognized that later architects and artists would rely on their own muses for inspiration. Studying the various plans and models in the museum below the church, it's clear that Gaudí's plan evolved dramatically the longer he worked. And the plan continues to evolve to this day.

• *Keep an eye on the time. About 15 minutes before your assigned time slot, join the line to enter the church complex. Pass through security, then walk up the stairs to the viewing plaza in front of the Nativity Facade. Check out the small* **bronze model** *of how the church might look when completed. Then stand as far back as you can to take in this facade.*

❷ Nativity Facade

This is the only part of the church essentially finished in Gaudí's lifetime (although the architect had intended for this facade to be painted). The four spires decorated with his naturalistic sculpture mark this facade as unmistakably part of his original design. Mixing Gothic-era symbolism, images from nature, and Modernista asymmetry, the Nativity Facade is the best example of Gaudí's original vision, and it established the template for future architects.

Cleverly, this attractive facade was built and finished first to bring in financial support for the project.

The theme of the facade, which faces the rising sun, is Christ's birth. A statue above the doorway shows Mary, Joseph, and Baby Jesus in the manger, while a curious cow and donkey peek in. It's the Holy Family—or "Sagrada

Família" (literally "sacred family")—to whom this church is dedicated. Flanking the doorway are the three Magi and adoring shepherds. Other statues at this height show Jesus as a young carpenter (far right), the Holy Family fleeing to Egypt (far left), and angels playing musical instruments. Much higher up, in the arched niche, Jesus crowns Mary triumphantly.

The doors in the middle of the facade were designed by head sculptor Etsuro Sotoo. Born in Japan, Sotoo visited Barcelona for the first time in 1978 and fell in love with the project. He worked hard to become a part of it and even converted to Catholicism. Go up to the bronze doors and examine the surface, covered with small colorful bugs and leaves.

• *If your ticket includes a tower or a guided tour, a guard will direct you to your elevator or tour meeting point. Otherwise, enter the ❸ church atrium through Sotoo's doors. Continue to the center of the church, near the altar, to survey the magnificent...*

❹ Interior

Typical of even the most traditional Catalan and Spanish churches, the floor plan is in the shape of a Latin cross, 300 feet long and 200 feet wide. Ultimately, the church will accommodate 8,000 worshippers. The crisscross arches of the ceiling (the vaults) show off Gaudí's distinctive engineering. The church's roof and flooring were completed in 2010—just in time for Pope Benedict XVI to arrive and consecrate the church.

Part of Gaudí's religious vision included a love for nature. He said, "Nothing is invented; it's written in nature." Like the trunks of trees, these **columns** (56 in all) blossom with life, complete with branches, leaves, and knot-like capitals. The columns vary in color and material—brown clay, gray granite, dark gray basalt.

Partway up, the columns angle off to form many **arches.** Gaudí's starting point was the medieval Gothic pointed arch, which he altered to achieve maximum weight-bearing effect.

Light filtering through the stained-glass windows has the dappled effect of a rainforest canopy. Notice how splashes of color breathe even more life into this amazing space. The morning light shines in through blues, greens, and other cool colors, whereas the evening light glows through reds, oranges, and warm tones. Gaudí envisioned an awe-inspiring symphony of colored light to encourage a contemplative mood.

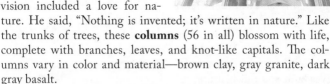

At the center of the church stand four main **columns,** each marked with an Evangelist's symbol and name in Catalan: angel (Mateu), lion (Marc), bull (Luc), and eagle (Joan). These columns support a ceiling **vault** that's 200 feet high—and will also support the central steeple (the Jesus tower with the shining cross). It will be the tallest church steeple in the world, though still a few feet shorter than the city's highest point at the summit of Montjuïc hill, as Gaudí believed that a creation of man should not attempt to eclipse the creation of God.

The Holy Family is looking down from on high: Jesus is above the altar, Mary is in the left transept, and Joseph in the right transept.

To the right, behind the high altar, peer down to see a surprisingly traditional space—the 19th-century Neo-Gothic building that Gaudí was originally hired to finish. Today this is a **crypt** holding the tomb of Gaudí himself. A few steps away are two small theaters in adjacent side chapels. One shows a short video about the architect and his work. Immediately behind the altar (possibly accessed from the other side) is a small chapel for prayer and meditation.

• *Walk through the forest of massive columns to the opposite end of the church. The view from here is best for appreciating the majesty of the building's interior. (A big mirror is placed here to make admiring the ceiling easier.) Notice the statues representing, once again, the four Evangelists. These are models of the sculptures placed on the pinnacles of the four exterior towers dedicated to each Evangelist. Suspended high above the nave, the U-shaped **choir** can seat a thousand singers, who will eventually be backed by four organs.*

Doors here will one day open to the...

❺ Glory Facade

While you can't go out what will one day be the main entrance, you can study a life-size image of the **bronze door** intended for this spot, emblazoned with the Lord's Prayer in Catalan and surrounded by "Give us this day our daily bread" in 50 languages. If you were able to exit through the actual door, you'd be face-to-face with drab, doomed apartment blocks. In the 1950s,

the mayor of Barcelona, figuring this day would never really come, sold the land destined for the church project. Now the city must buy back these buildings to fulfill Gaudí's vision of a grand esplanade leading to this main entry. Four towers will rise. The facade's sculpture will represent how the soul passes through death, faces the Last Judgment, avoids the pitfalls of hell, and finds its way to eternal glory with God. Gaudí purposely left the facade's design open for later architects—and maybe the current neighbors will have a say. Stay tuned.

• *Head back up the nave and exit through the left transept. To the left, notice the second **elevator** up to the towers. To the right, stroll through the **sacristy**, where you will find benches, candelabras, and sacristy furniture designed by Gaudí. Before exiting, look down at the fine porphyry **floor** with scenes of Jesus' entry into Jerusalem. Now head outside and down the ramp. Step away to take in the...*

❻ Passion Facade

Judge for yourself how well Gaudí's original vision has been carried out by later artists. The Passion Facade's four spires were designed by Gaudí and completed (quite faithfully) in 1976. But the lower part was only inspired by Gaudí's designs. The sculptures intended for this facade were interpreted freely and sternly (also controversially) by Josep Maria Subirachs (1927-2014), who completed the work in 2005.

Subirachs tells the story of Christ's torture and execution. The various scenes—Last Supper, betrayal, whipping, and so on—zig-zag up from bottom to top, culminating in Christ's crucifixion over the doorway. The  style is severe and unadorned, quite different from Gaudí's signature naturalism. Large letters high above spell out "Iesus Nazarenus Rex Iudæorum" (Jesus the Nazarene, King of the Jews). The bone-like archways are closely based on Gaudí's original designs. And Gaudí had made it clear that this facade should be grim and terrifying.

The facade is full of symbolism. A stylized Alpha and Omega carving is over the door (which faces the setting sun). Jesus, hanging on the cross, has hair made of an open book, symbolizing the word of God. To the left of the door is a grid of numbers, always adding up to 33—Jesus' age at the time of his death. The distinct face of the man below and to the left of Christ (in profile, next to what looks like two stormtroopers) is a memorial to Gaudí.

• *Now, for a fun little break from all this church architecture, head into the small building outside the Passion Facade. This is the...*

❼ School

Gaudí erected this school for the children of the workers building the church. Today, it displays a replica classroom and old photos of school activities during Gaudí's time.

• *Back outside, head down the* ❽ *ramp, where you'll find WCs and the entrance to the...*

Museum

Housed in what will someday function as the church crypt, the museum takes you through the past, present, and future of Sagrada Família's development.

It starts with a photo of the master himself and a timeline illustrating how construction has progressed from Gaudí's day until now. Walking the hall, you'll pass pieces of Gaudí's original plaster model of the church (damaged during Spain's civil war; on the left), and his reconstructed studio (also on the left). Compare Gaudí's old-fashioned space with a nearby photo of the current team, working with the latest technology.

In a room at the end of the hall, four plaster models show the evolution of Gaudí's thinking (clockwise from left): 1) the Neo-Gothic design by the church's first architect, Francisco de Paula del Villar; 2) Gaudí's re-envisioned plan, with a nave formed of narrow parabolic arches; 3) a plan with the middle story opened up; and 4) finally, an even more open plan with tree-like columns fanning out at the top.

Exploring further, past a gift shop, you'll find exhibits dedicated to the sculptor Subirachs and the stained-glass artist Joan Vila-Grau; an exhibit about nature as inspiration for architecture; and a small theater showing a worthwhile nine-minute movie. Sit down and enjoy this fine review of all you've seen.

You'll also find an intriguing "hanging model" for Gaudí's unfinished Church of Colònia Güell (in a suburb of Barcelona), with a design similar to that of Sagrada Família. The model demonstrates the architect's use of gravity to calculate how the arches would support the church. Wires dangle like suspended chains, forming perfect hyperbolic arches. Attached to these are weighted bags representing the load the arches must support. Flip these arches over, and they can bear the heavy weight of the roof.

Gaudí lived on the site of Sagrada Família for more than a decade and is buried here in the Neo-Gothic 19th-century crypt. You can look (steeply) down at his tomb. There's a move afoot to beatify Gaudí and make him a saint. Gaudí prayer cards provide words of devotion. Perhaps someday his tomb will be a place of pilgrimage.

Back in the main hall, peer into the actual workshop where artists employ the latest technology (such as 3-D printing) to test ideas and create models.

The final part of the museum has photos of Pope Benedict XVI's 2010 visit and consecration of the church, as well as dedications to the architects and sculptors who have worked on this project.

From here, step outside. You can either leave the complex through a gift shop (on the right), or circle left and upstairs to return to the church, exiting through the Passion Facade.

Once outside, look back and pause for a moment to pay homage to the man who made all this possible. Gaudí—a faithful Catholic whose medieval-style mysticism belied his career as a Modernista architect—was certainly driven to greatness by his passion for God.

• *Our tour is over. From here, you have a few options.*

Return to Central Barcelona: *It's simple to hop on the Metro back to the* **center.** *Bus #D50 goes to the heart of the* **Eixample** *(corner of Gran Via de les Corts Catalanes and Passeig de Gràcia).*

Visit Park Güell: *The park sits nearly two (uphill) miles to the northwest. By far the easiest way to get there is by taxi (around €12).*

Walk to the former Hospital de la Santa Creu i Sant Pau: *It's an easy stroll to this often-overlooked Modernista masterpiece (Recinte Modernista de Sant Pau; see page 64). With the Nativity Facade at your back, walk to the near-left corner of the park across the street. Then walk about 10 minutes along Avinguda de Gaudí, a pleasantly shaded, café-lined pedestrian street, to reach the Sant Pau sight. This area is also a good place for a post-church meal (see "Eating" at the beginning of this chapter).*

PARK GÜELL TOUR

Tucked in the foothills at the edge of Barcelona, this fanciful park—designed by Antoni Gaudí—combines playful architecture, inviting spaces, and a one-of-a-kind terrace offering sweeping views over the rooftops of the city.

Big crowds swarm the park's Monumental Zone with all its iconic Gaudi features: A grand staircase monitored by a colorful dragon, a forest of columns supporting a spectacular view terrace, and an undulating balcony slathered in tile shards.

Outside the Monumental Zone, the rest of the park contains the Gaudí House Museum, the Calvary viewpoint, a picnic area, and a pleasant network of nature trails and fascinating viaducts.

No matter which area of the park you visit, you'll see Barcelonans and tourists alike enjoying themselves. Park Güell is simply a fine place to take a break from a busy city where green space is relatively rare.

Orientation

Cost: €10 timed-entry park admission. The only smart way to visit is to buy your ticket online in advance (tickets are sold at the park, but they often sell out and you'll wait in a long line).

Hours: April-Oct 9:30-22:00, last entry at 19:30; rest of year 9:30 until sunset.

Information: +34 934 091 831, www.parkguell.barcelona.

When to Go: To avoid the biggest crowds, visit as early in the day as possible or after 18:00. You can enjoy the park at twilight from April-Oct, when it stays open until 22:00 (last entry at 19:30).

Getting There: Park Güell is about 2.5 miles from Plaça de Catalunya, beyond the Gràcia neighborhood in Barcelona's foot-

PARK GÜELL

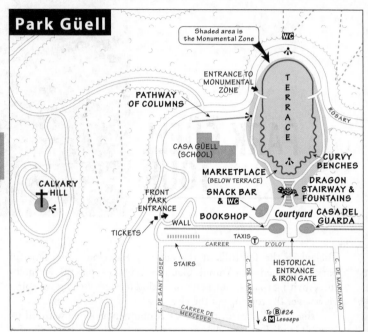

Park Güell

Shaded area is the Monumental Zone

WC

ENTRANCE TO MONUMENTAL ZONE

PATHWAY OF COLUMNS

TERRACE

ROSARY

CASA GÜELL (SCHOOL)

CURVY BENCHES

MARKETPLACE (BELOW TERRACE)

DRAGON STAIRWAY & FOUNTAINS

CALVARY HILL

FRONT PARK ENTRANCE

SNACK BAR & WC

BOOKSHOP

Courtyard

CASA DEL GUARDA

TICKETS

WALL

TAXIS

D'OLOT

CARRER

C. DE SANT JOSEP

STAIRS

C. DE LARRARD

HISTORICAL ENTRANCE & IRON GATE

C. DE MARIANAO

CARRER DE MERCEDES

To B #24 & M Lesseps

hills. If asking for directions, ask for "Park Gway" (sounds like "parkway").

From downtown, a **taxi** (about €16) is the easiest way to get directly to the park's entrance. Public transit options leave you within walking distance: Take **bus #24** (direction: El Carmel) from the southwest corner of Plaça de Catalunya, next to the Desigual shop, ride 30 minutes, and get off at the Carretera del Carmel-Albert Llanas stop, a two-minute walk to my preferred park entrance. Also from Plaça de Catalunya, the blue **Bus Turístic** drops you about four blocks from the Carretera del Carmel entrance (10-minute uphill walk). Or you can ride the **Metro** (L3) to the Lesseps stop and walk 15 minutes, partly uphill.

Getting In: The park has a dizzying number of entrances (a few near the top are reserved for locals). I prefer starting at the side entrance on Carretera del Carmel (near the bus #24 stop) and ending at the Monumental Zone. At all entrances you'll find a ticket office, WCs nearby, and plenty of park staff to help orient you. Signage inside can be confusing, so pick up a map to supplement the one in this book. Hang on to your ticket; you'll need it when you exit (you can exit anywhere).

Length of this Tour: An hour is plenty to see the Monumental Zone, but the park is a pleasant place to explore. I'd allow an additional 30 to 60 minutes to stroll the grounds.

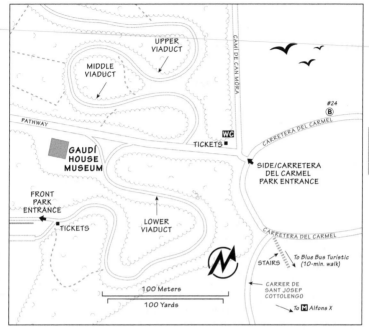

PARK GÜELL

Gaudí House Museum: €5.50, daily 9:30-20:00, Oct-March 10:00-18:00, tickets easily available at the door, www. casamuseugaudi.org.

Eating: Options are limited. There's a simple **snack bar** with tables by the historical entrance. A few basic **cafés** are on the streets leading to the historical entrance. If you've packed a **picnic** (a good idea), you can eat anywhere outside the Monumental Zone.

OVERVIEW

Gaudí intended this 30-acre garden to be a high-end community with 60 upscale residences. Funded by his frequent benefactor Eusebi Güell, he began work on the project in 1900; however, the project stalled in 1914, with the outbreak of World War I, and it never resumed. Only two houses were built, neither designed by Gaudí (one is now the Gaudí House Museum). Be thankful that the housing development faltered—as a park, this place is a delight. It offers a novel peek into Gaudí's eccentric genius in a setting that's wonderfully in keeping with the naturalism that pervades his work.

Many sculptures and surfaces in the park are decorated with colorful *trencadís* mosaics—broken ceramic bits rearranged into new patterns. This Modernista invention, made of discarded tile, dishes, and even china dolls from local factories, was an easy, cheap, and aesthetically pleasing way to cover curvy surfaces like benches and columns. Most of the mosaics you see in the park are by Gaudí's collaborator, Josep Maria Jujol.

The Tour Begins

• *This tour assumes you're arriving at the side entrance on Carretera del Carmel. If you have extra time to explore the park beyond the Monumental Zone, head off to the right to enjoy some of Gaudí's viaducts, or stroll to the opposite side of the park to take in the view from Calvary Hill (described later).*

If, instead, you're heading directly to the Monumental Zone, continue straight along the path. On the left you'll soon see the...

Gaudí House Museum

This pink house with a steeple was Gaudí's home for 20 years. Designed by a fellow architect (not Gaudí), it was originally built as a model home to attract prospective residents. Gaudí himself lived here from 1906 until 1925. His belongings are mostly gone, but the house is now a museum with some quirky Gaudí furniture, and it offers an idea of what the envisioned housing development might have been (but it's not worth the entry fee for most travelers).

The lane connecting this house to the view terrace, called the **Rosary Pathway,** is lined with giant stone balls that represent the beads of a rosary. During the years he lived here, the reverent Gaudí would pray the rosary while walking this path.

• *Continue along the path, curving behind the view terrace to the **Monumental Zone** entrance where you'll walk onto the...*

View Terrace (Nature Square)

Sit on a colorful bench and enjoy one of Barcelona's best views. (Find the Sagrada Família in the distance.) The terrace is ringed by a 360-foot-long bench that functions as both a balustrade and a seat, designed to fit your body just so. Supposedly, Gaudí enlisted a construction worker as his guinea pig to figure out exactly where to place the lumbar support. To Gaudí, this terrace evoked ancient Greek theaters that burrowed scenically into the  sides of hills—but it is more like an ancient Greek agora, a wide-open meeting place, jammed with people feasting on the view.

Gaudí engineered a catchment system to collect rainwater hitting this plaza and funnel it through the columns of the market below to an underground cistern. The collected water was used to irrigate the surrounding gardens and power the park's fountains. Notice the lion's-head gargoyles and the big stone droplets that cling to the outside edge of the terrace, which hint at this hidden function.

From here, as you face the city, **Calvary Hill** is high up on your right, hidden behind trees. Atop it stands a stubby stone tower with three crosses, meant to evoke where Jesus was crucified. Gaudí envisioned Park Güell as a metaphor for the soul's progress: starting low, but toiling upward toward spiritual enlightenment. And indeed, the park's higher paths seem to converge to lead pilgrims to this summit. The tower rewards those who huff up with grand views over Barcelona and its bay.

• *Head toward the staircase on the right side of the terrace. The big pink house flanking the stairs is where Eusebi Güell lived. Now a **school**, this house predates the park project and was not designed by Gaudí. As you walk down the stairs, stop to explore the...*

Pathway of Columns

Gaudí drew his inspiration from nature, and this arcade is like a surfer's perfect tube. Both structural and aesthetic, it is one of many clever double-decker **viaducts** that Gaudí designed for the grounds: vehicles up top, pedestrians in the portico down below. Gaudí intended these walkways to remind visitors of the pilgrim routes that crisscross Spain (such as the famous Camino de Santiago).

• *Continue down the stairway and into the...*

Marketplace (Hypostyle Room)

This space was designed to house a **produce market** for the neighborhood's inhabitants. Eighty-six Doric columns—each lined at the base with white ceramic shards—populate the marketplace and add to its vitality. (Their main job, though, is to hold up the view terrace above.) Shards of white ceramic also cover the multiple domes of the ceiling. The four giant mosaic decorations overhead represent the four seasons. Notice the hook in the middle of each one, where a lantern could be hung.

• *Next you'll come to the top of the grand...*

Dragon Stairway

Twin staircases curve downward, separated by three **fountains** stacked between them. The first, at the top of the steps, is an icon of the park—and of Barcelona: a smiling dragon, slathered in colorful tile. Next is a red-and-gold Catalan shield, with the head of a serpent poking out. The third fountain is rocky and leafy, typical of Gaudí's naturalism.

The **two grottos** flanking the stairs were functional: One was a garage for Eusebi Güell's newfangled automobiles; the other was a cart shelter.

• *At the bottom of the dragon stairway you'll come to the...*

Historical Entrance

Enjoy Gaudí's historical front entrance with its palm-frond **gate** and gas lamps on either side, made of wrought iron. Gaudí's dad

was a blacksmith, and he always enjoyed this medium.

Two Hansel-and-Gretel gingerbread lodges flank this former entrance, signaling to visitors that the park is a magical space. One building houses a bookshop; the other is home to the skippable **La Casa del Guarda,** a branch of the Barcelona History Museum (entry included with your ticket). The sparse exhibit inside has no real artifacts—just videos about Gaudí's building methods and old movies of the age. But true Gaudí fans should take a close look at the structure, as it's one of the few built examples of his ideas for simple housing.

Rest of the Park

Like any park, this one is made for aimless rambling, and you are free to stay as long as you like. As you wander, consider that, as a high-end housing development, Gaudí's project flopped (back then, high-society ladies didn't want to live so far from the cultural action). But a century later, as a park, it's a magnificent success.

• *You have several options for returning to the city center. **Taxis** wait outside the exit on Carrer d'Olot. Or, walk five minutes downhill on Carrer de Larrard to Travessera de Dalt to catch **bus #24.** The blue **Bus Turístic** stops at 7 Avinguda de la Mare de Déu de Montserrat—a 10-minute walk downhill from the side park entrance. For the **Metro**, it's a 15-minute walk to the Lesseps Metro stop.*

SLEEPING IN BARCELONA

Choosing the right neighborhood in Barcelona is as important as choosing the right hotel. All of my recommended accommodations are in safe areas convenient to sightseeing. The area around Plaça de Catalunya, Barcelona's central square, is filled with business-class hotels. Near the Ramblas—the city's pedestrian boulevard—you'll find cheaper, less-refined places with more character. For Old World charm, stay in Barcelona's Old City. For an uptown feel, sleep in the Eixample.

Barcelona is Spain's most expensive city, but if you do your homework you can still find reasonably priced rooms. Fancy, business-class hotels have hard-to-pin-down prices that fluctuate with demand. In summer and on weekends, supply often far exceeds the demand, and many of these places cut prices. Cheaper hotels offer ramshackle charm year-round. For some travelers, short-term, Airbnb-type rentals can be a good alternative; search for places in my recommended hotel neighborhoods.

I rank accommodations from **$** budget to **$$$$** splurge. For the best deal, contact hotels directly by phone or email. When you book direct, the owner avoids a commission and may be able to offer a discount. Book well in advance for peak season or if your trip coincides with a major holiday or festival (see the appendix). Note, though, that Barcelona can be busy any time of year. For more details on reservations, short-term rentals, and more, see the "Sleeping" section in the Practicalities chapter.

NEAR PLAÇA DE CATALUNYA

These hotels are on big streets within two blocks of Barcelona's exuberant central square, where the Old City meets the Eixample. Some of my recommended hotels are on Carrer Pelai, a busy street; for these, request a quieter room in back.

$$$$ Hotel Catalonia Plaça Catalunya has four stars, an elegant old entryway with a modern reception area, splashy public spaces, slick marble and hardwood floors, 150 comfortable rooms, and a garden courtyard with a pool a world away from the big-city noise. It's a bit pricey for the quality of the rooms—you're paying for the posh lobby (air-con, elevator, a half-block off Plaça de Catalunya at Carrer de Bergara 11, Metro: Catalunya, +34 933 015 151, www.cataloniahotels.com, catalunya@cataloniahotels.com).

$$$$ Hotel Midmost is an oasis a little west of Plaça de Catalunya. It has 56 rooms with luxurious, four-star style; a seaside-lounge-inspired rooftop terrace; and a mini pool to relax (family rooms, air-con, elevator, Carrer de Pelai 14, Metro: Universitat, +34 935 051 100, www.hotelmidmost.com, info@hotelmidmost.com).

$$$ Hotel Denit is a small, stylish, 36-room hotel on a quiet pedestrian street two blocks off Plaça de Catalunya. It's chic, minimalist, and fun: Guidebook tips decorate the halls, and the rooms are sized like T-shirts, from small to extra-large (includes breakfast, air-con, elevator, Carrer d'Estruc 24, Metro: Catalunya, +34 935 454 000, www.denit.com, info@denit.com).

$$$ Hotel Reding, on a quiet street a 10-minute walk west of the Ramblas and the Plaça de Catalunya action, is a slick place with a fun lobby and 44 basic but mod rooms on color-themed floors at a reasonable price (air-con, elevator, Carrer de Gravina 5, Metro: Universitat, +34 934 121 097, www.chicandbasic.com/en/hotel-reding-barcelona, reding@chicandbasic.com).

$$$ Hotel Lleó (YAH-oh) is well run, with 92 big, bright, and comfortable rooms; a great breakfast room; and a generous lounge with minimalist decor (air-con, elevator, small rooftop pool, Carrer de Pelai 22, midway between Metros: Universitat and Catalunya, +34 933 181 312, www.hotel-lleo.com, info@hotel-lleo.com).

$$ Hotel Ginebra is a modern version of the old-school *pension,* with 18 rooms on the third floor of a classic well-located building at the corner of Plaça de Catalunya (RS%—use code "HGinebra-RickSteves", family rooms, no breakfast, air-con, elevator, Rambla de Catalunya 1, Metro: Catalunya, +34 932 502 017,

SLEEPING

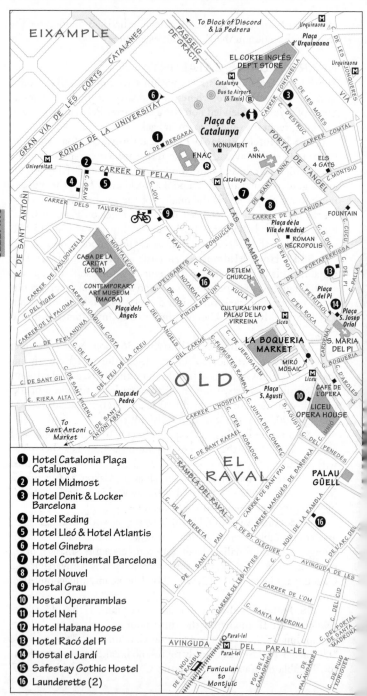

1 Hotel Catalonia Plaça Catalunya
2 Hotel Midmost
3 Hotel Denit & Locker Barcelona
4 Hotel Reding
5 Hotel Lleó & Hotel Atlantis
6 Hotel Ginebra
7 Hotel Continental Barcelona
8 Hotel Nouvel
9 Hostal Grau
10 Hostal Operaramblas
11 Hotel Neri
12 Hotel Habana Hoose
13 Hotel Racó del Pi
14 Hostal el Jardí
15 Safestay Gothic Hostel
16 Launderette (2)

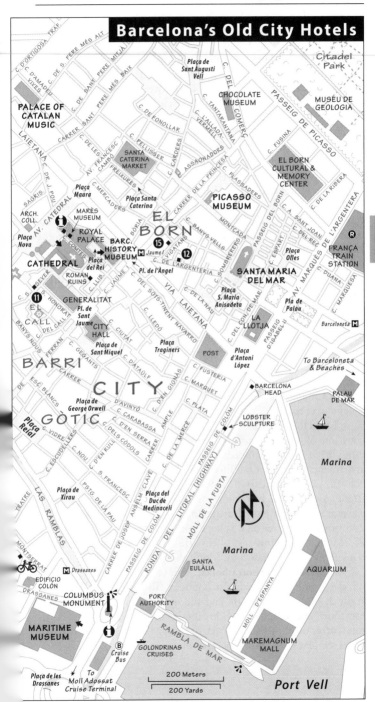

Barcelona's Old City Hotels

SLEEPING

www.hotelginebra.com.es, info@hotelginebra.com.es, Brits Alfred and Ivon).

$$ Hotel Atlantis is solid, with 50 big, nondescript, dated rooms and fair prices for the location (includes breakfast, air-con, elevator, Carrer de Pelai 20, midway between Metros: Universitat and Catalunya, +34 933 189 012, www.hotelatlantis-atbcn.com, info@hotelatlantis-bcn.com).

ON OR NEAR THE RAMBLAS

These places are generally family-run, with ad-lib furnishings, more character, and lower prices.

$$$ Hotel Continental Barcelona, in a building overlooking the top of the Ramblas, offers classic, tiny view-balcony opportunities if you don't mind the street noise. Its 40 rooms are quite comfortable and the quiet terrace out back is a world away from the Ramblas action. Choose between your own little Ramblas-view balcony (where you can eat your breakfast) or a quieter back room. J. M.'s (José María's) free breakfast and all-day snack-and-drink bar are a plus (RS%, air-con, elevator, Ramblas 138, Metro: Catalunya, +34 933 012 570, www.hotelcontinental.com, barcelona@hotelcontinental.com).

$$$ Hotel Nouvel, in an elegant, Victorian-style building on a handy pedestrian street, is less business oriented and offers more character than the others listed here. It boasts royal lounges and 78 comfy rooms (air-con, elevator, Carrer de Santa Anna 18, Metro: Catalunya, +34 933 018 274, www.hotelnouvel.es, info@hotelnouvel.com).

$$$ Hostal Grau is a homey, family-run, and extremely eco-conscious hotel with custom recycled furniture and organic bedding. It has 25 crisp, impeccable, and well-priced rooms (and four apartments perfect for families) a few blocks off the Ramblas in the colorful university district. Double-glazed windows keep it quiet (some rooms with balconies, strict cancellation policy, air-con, elevator, cozy communal areas and kitchen available for guests, 200 yards up Carrer dels Tallers from the Ramblas at Ramelleres 27, Metro: Catalunya, +34 933 018 135, www.hostalgrau.com, bookgreen@hostalgrau.com, Monica).

$$$ Hostal Operaramblas, with 68 simple rooms 20 yards off the Ramblas, is fresh and modern. The street can feel a bit seedy at night, but it's safe and the hotel is very secure (RS%—use code "operaramblas," no breakfast, air-con in summer, elevator, Carrer de Sant Pau 20, Metro: Liceu, +34 933 188 201, www.operaramblas.com, info@operaramblas.com).

MORE OLD CITY HOTELS

These accommodations are buried in Barcelona's Old City, mostly in the Barri Gòtic.

$$$$ Hotel Neri is posh, pretentious, and sophisticated, with 22 pricey rooms spliced into the ancient stones of the Barri Gòtic, overlooking an overlooked square (Plaça Sant Felip Neri) a block from the cathedral. It has modern art on the bedroom walls, dressed-up people in its gourmet restaurant, and high-class service (air-con, elevator, small rooftop deck, Carrer de Sant Sever 5, Metro: Liceu or Jaume I, +34 933 040 655, www.hotelneri.com, info@hotelneri.com).

$$$ Hotel Habana Hoose, a funky fusion of Scottish punk and Cuban influences, has a boutique feel and eclectic décor in its 43 rooms and public spaces. It's a good value located in the El Born district on a pedestrianized street between the cathedral and Church of Santa Maria del Mar (air-con, elevator, Carrer de l'Argenteria 37, 50 yards from Metro: Jaume I, +34 935 956 505, www.chicandbasic.com/barcelona/en, habanahoose@chicandbasic.com).

$$$ Hotel Racó del Pi, part of the H10 hotel chain, is a quality, professional place with a generous inner courtyard and 37 modern, bright rooms. It's located on a wonderful pedestrian street immersed in the Barri Gòtic (air-con, quieter rooms in back, around the corner from Plaça del Pi at Carrer del Pi 7, three-minute walk from Metro: Liceu, +34 933 426 190, www.h10hotels.com, h10.raco.delpi@h10hotels.com).

$$$ Hostal el Jardí offers 45 tight, plain rooms on a breezy square. Many rooms come with petite balconies (for an extra charge). It's a good deal only if you value the quaint-square-with-Barri-Gòtic ambience—you're paying for the location. Book well in advance (air-con, elevator, some stairs, halfway between Ramblas and cathedral at Plaça Sant Josep Oriol 1, Metro: Liceu, +34 933 015 900, www.eljardi.com, reservations@eljardi.com).

EIXAMPLE

For an uptown, boulevard-like neighborhood, sleep in the Eixample, a 10-minute walk from the Ramblas action. Most of these places use the Passeig de Gràcia or Catalunya Metro stops. Because these stations are so huge—especially Passeig de Gràcia, which sprawls underground for a few blocks—study the maps posted in the station to establish which exit you want before surfacing.

$$$$ Hotel Granvía, filling a palatial, brightly renovated 1870s mansion, offers a large, peaceful sun patio and several comfortable common areas. Its 58 spacious rooms are modern and luxurious (RS%—free breakfast for Rick Steves readers who book direct, family rooms, air-con, elevator, Gran Via de les Corts Cat-

SLEEPING

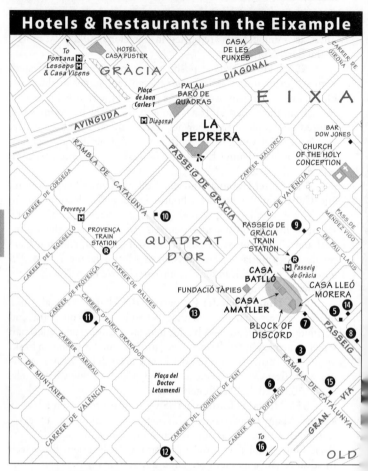

Hotels & Restaurants in the Eixample

alanes 642, Metro: Passeig de Gràcia, +34 933 181 900, www. hotelgranvia.com, hgranvia@nnhotels.com).

$$$$ Hotel Yurbban Trafalgar is a small, classy boutique hotel with 56 rooms and a chic-minimalist decor. Their rooftop bar, tiny pool, and views alone are worth the price of your stay (air-con, free self-service laundry, gym, near the Palace of Catalan Music at Carrer de Trafalgar 30, a long block from Metro: Urquinaona, +34 932 680 727, www.yurbbantrafalgar.com, trafalgar@yurbban. com).

$$$ Hotel Continental Palacete, with 22 rooms (some very small), fills a 100-year-old chandeliered mansion. With flowery wallpaper and ornately gilded stucco, it's gaudy in the city of Gaudí, but it's also friendly, quiet, and well located. Guests have unlimited access to an all-day snack-and-drink bar (RS%, includes breakfast, air-con, two blocks northwest of Plaça de Catalunya at

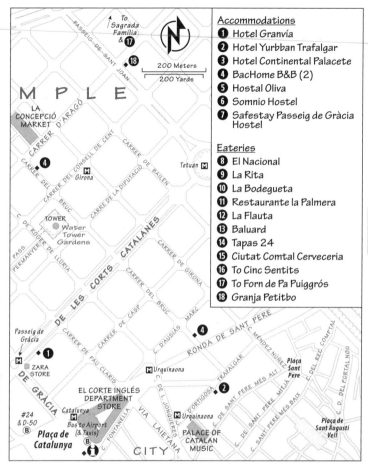

To
Sagrada
Família
&

200 Meters
200 Yards

Accommodations
❶ Hotel Granvía
❷ Hotel Yurbban Trafalgar
❸ Hotel Continental Palacete
❹ BacHome B&B (2)
❺ Hostal Oliva
❻ Somnio Hostel
❼ Safestay Passeig de Gràcia Hostel

Eateries
❽ El Nacional
❾ La Rita
❿ La Bodegueta
⓫ Restaurante la Palmera
⓬ La Flauta
⓭ Baluard
⓮ Tapas 24
⓯ Ciutat Comtal Cerveceria
⓰ To Cinc Sentits
⓱ To Forn de Pa Puiggrós
⓲ Granja Petitbo

SLEEPING

corner of Rambla de Catalunya and Carrer de la Diputació, Rambla de Catalunya 30, Metro: Passeig de Gràcia, +34 934 457 657, www.hotelcontinental.com, palacete@hotelcontinental.com).

$$ BacHome B&B has two bright and comfortable locations in traditional Eixample buildings on Carrer del Bruc. BacHome Terrace (at #14, +34 620 657 810) has 10 rooms and a pleasant outdoor terrace. BacHome Gallery (#96, +34 608 350 965) has seven rooms and common areas with big windows looking out onto the city (no breakfast, air-con, elevator, Clara and Barbara, Metro: Urquinaona, www.bachomebarcelona.com, reservations@bachomebarcelona.com).

$$ Hostal Oliva, family-run with care, is an old-school place with 16 basic, bright, high-ceilinged rooms. It's on the fourth floor of a classic old Eixample building—with a beautiful mahogany elevator—in a perfect location, just a couple of blocks above Plaça de

Catalunya (no breakfast, air-con, corner of Passeig de Gràcia and Carrer de la Diputació, Passeig de Gràcia 32, Metro: Passeig de Gràcia, +34 934 880 162, www.hostaloliva.com, info@hostaloliva.com).

$$ Somnio Hostel, on the low end of this range, has nine simple private rooms with shared bathrooms (no breakfast, air-con, Carrer de la Diputació 251, second floor, Metro: Passeig de Gràcia, +34 932 725 308, www.somniohostels.com, info@somniohostels.com).

OTHER ACCOMMODATIONS
Hostels

¢ **Safestay Hostels:** These well-run hostels offer plenty of opportunities to meet other backpackers (www.safestay.com). Both locations enforce quiet hours after 23:00. **Safestay Gothic Hostel** rents 130 beds in the Barri Gòtic, a block from the Picasso Museum (roof terrace, Carrer Vigatans 5—see the "Barcelona's Old City Hotels" map, Metro: Jaume I, reception +34 932 687 808, safestaygothic@safestay.com). **Safestay Passeig de Gràcia Hostel** has 400 beds in the heart of the Eixample (bar, kitchen, Passeig de Gràcia 33, Metro: Passeig de Gràcia, +34 932 156 538, receptionbcnpdg@safestay.com).

Apartments

Many Barcelona residents see turn-key vacation rentals as damaging to the fabric of traditionally residential neighborhoods, especially when they're rented to rowdy bachelor/bachelorette parties. I like to counterbalance this trend by treating my temporary Barcelona home—and neighbors—with a little extra courtesy.

Consider a short-term rental if you're traveling as a family, in a group, or staying several days. Sites such as Airbnb and VRBO let you correspond directly with property owners or managers. Or consider one of the agencies listed below. For more information on renting apartments, see page 290 in the Practicalities chapter.

Midtown Apartments (www.midtownapartments-barcelona.com, midtownapartments@nnhotels.com) are an extension of the Hotel Granvia (listed earlier) and offer 30 top-notch apartments and a pool. **Friendly Rentals** (www.friendlyrentals.com) has a number of listings in Barcelona (and other European cities). Local agencies include **Top Barcelona Apartments** (http://top-barcelona-apartments.com) and **MH Apartments** (www.mhapartments.com). **Cross-Pollinate** represents B&Bs and apartments in a handful of European cities, including Barcelona (US tel. +1 800 270 1190, www.cross-pollinate.com, info@cross-pollinate.com).

EATING IN BARCELONA

Barcelona, the capital of Catalan cuisine, offers a tremendous variety of colorful places to eat, ranging from workaday eateries to homey Catalan bistros *(cans)*, crowded tapas bars, and avant-garde restaurants. Good restaurants in Barcelona benefit from talented chefs who aren't afraid to experiment, the relative affluence of the region, and the availability of good, fresh ingredients—especially fish and seafood.

My favorites—grouped by neighborhood and handy to the sights—are practical, characteristic, affordable, and lively. To avoid bad, overly touristy restaurants, a good rule of thumb is not to eat (or drink) on the Ramblas or Passeig de Gràcia.

Some Barcelona eateries specialize in tapas (serving small plates throughout the afternoon and evening), while others are more formal restaurants (with generous portions, no tapas, and service that starts much later than the American norm). I recommend eateries in both categories and some that combine both options. At many, expect a busy tapas scene at the bar, along with restaurant tables where larger plates can be enjoyed family-style.

Catalan tapas menus most often include seafood (cod, hake, tuna, squid, and anchovies), delicious local olives, and a traditional sausage called *butifarra*. In restaurants, you'll see Catalan favorites such as *fideuà*, a thin, flavor-infused noodle served with seafood—a kind of Catalan paella—and *arròs negre,* black rice cooked in squid ink. *Pa amb tomàquet* is the classic Catalan way to eat bread—toasted white bread with olive oil, tomato, and a pinch of salt. It may be served free with your plate and also used to make sandwiches. While the famous cured *jamón* (ham) is more Spanish than it is Catalan, you'll still find lots of it in Catalunya (see the "Sampling *Jamón*" sidebar on page 296). All this food is accompanied by local beers, wines, and, of course, the beloved sweet vermouth.

EATING TIPS

I rank eateries from $ budget to $$$$ splurge. For more advice on eating in Barcelona, including ordering, tipping, adapting to the Spanish eating schedule, and typical cuisine and beverages, see the "Eating" section of the Practicalities chapter. I've tried to make this information appropriately Catalan—as opposed to just Spanish with a Barcelona accent.

Hours: As in the rest of Spain, the people of Catalunya eat late—lunch around 14:00 (and as late as 16:00) and dinner after 21:00. The earliest you can go to a restaurant for dinner is about 20:00, when the place is empty or filled with tourists. Going after 21:00 is better, but if you wait too late it can be hard to get into popular restaurants. Note that some restaurants close for a few weeks in the summer, when the owners take a vacation.

Although tapas are served throughout the day, the real action begins late—21:00 or after. For less competition at the bar, go early or on Monday and Tuesday (but check to see if the place is open, as many close on Sunday or Monday).

Bread and Water: Most places don't automatically give you bread with your meal. If you ask for it, you'll usually receive *pa amb tomàquet* (bread with tomato spread), and you will be charged. Barcelona's tap water is safe to drink and free, but some bar owners are rather insistent on not serving it to their clientele, as it doesn't taste particularly good. For details on how to ask for water, see page 302.

Local-Style Tapas: Catalans have an affinity for Basque culture, so you'll find a lot of Basque-style tapas places here, where they lay out bite-size tapas (called *pintxos* or *pinchos*) on the countertop. These places are user-friendly, as you are free to take what you want and you don't have to look at a menu or wait to be served; just grab what looks good, order a drink, and save your toothpicks (they'll count them up at the end to tally your bill). I've listed several of these bars (including Taverna Basca Irati and Sagardi Euskal Taberna), but there are many others. Look for *vasco* or *euskal* (both mean "Basque")—or just keep an eye out for places with lots of toothpicks. You'll also find traditional Catalan tapas bars and *bodegas* (originally a name denoting wine cellars but preserved as many *bodegas* evolved into restaurants).

Market Halls: Try eating at one of Barcelona's covered market halls at least once—either at La Boqueria (on the Ramblas) or Santa Caterina (in El Born). I far prefer Santa Caterina, as La Boqueria is so touristy now. It's hard to walk through any market and not pick up something—either traditional or fun and touristy. Sant Antoni (in El Raval) is another great market to visit, but there are fewer eating options.

Catalan in Restaurants: Catalan and Spanish (in that order) are the official languages of Barcelona. While menus are usually in both languages, and many times English as well, these days—with the feisty spirit of independence stoked—you may find some menus in just Catalan, or Catalan and English without Spanish. I've given most food terms in Spanish and added Catalan where helpful. For terms in Spanish and Catalan, consult the "Tapas Menu Decoder" on page 300 and the list of drink terms on page 299.

In any Catalan bar or restaurant, an occasional *"si us plau"* (please) or *"moltes gràcies"* (thank you very much) goes a long way with the locals. An *"adéu"* (good-bye), *"que vagi bé"* (have a good one!), or, in the evening, *"bona nit"* (good evening/night) on your way out the door will certainly earn you a smile. And, as they say in Catalan, *"Bon profit!"* (Bon appétit!)

NEAR THE RAMBLAS

The entire length of the Ramblas itself is a tourist trap with bad food, weak drinks, and rip-off prices. But within a few steps of the Ramblas, you'll find several handy lunch places, an inviting market hall, and some good vegetarian options.

Lunching Simply yet Memorably near the Ramblas

Although these places are enjoyable for a lunch break from sightseeing, many are also open for dinner.

$$ Taverna Basca Irati serves 40 kinds of hot and cold Basque *pintxos* for €2.50 each. These are small open-faced sandwiches—a baguette slice topped with something tasty. Muscle in through the hungry crowd, get an empty plate from the waiter, and then help yourself at the bar (you'll be charged by the number of toothpicks left on your plate when you're done). Wash down your food with Rioja (full-bodied red wine), Txakolí (sprightly Basque white wine), or cider (daily, a block off the Ramblas, behind arcade at Carrer del Cardenal Casañas 17, Metro: Liceu, +34 933 023 084).

EATING

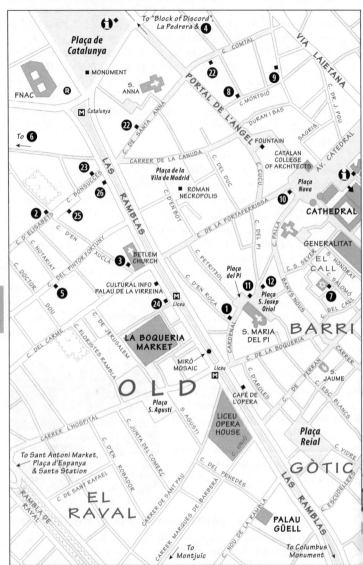

Near the Ramblas
1 Taverna Basca Irati
2 Restaurant Elisabets
3 Café Granja Viader
4 To El Corte Inglés
5 Biocenter
6 To Flax & Kale, Teresa Carles
  & Muccis Pizza

Barri Gòtic
7 La Vinateria del Call
8 Els Quatre Gats
9 Onofre
10 Bilbao Berria La Barra
11 Bar del Pi
12 El Drac de Sant Jordi
13 Carrer de la Mercè Tapas Bars

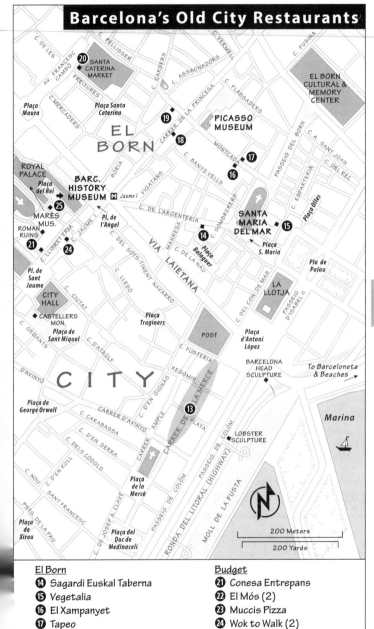

Barcelona's Old City Restaurants

El Born
- ⑭ Sagardi Euskal Taberna
- ⑮ Vegetalia
- ⑯ El Xampanyet
- ⑰ Tapeo
- ⑱ Can Cisa/Bar Brutal
- ⑲ Bar del Pla
- ⑳ Cuines Santa Caterina & Tapas Bars

Budget
- ㉑ Conesa Entrepans
- ㉒ El Mós (2)
- ㉓ Muccis Pizza
- ㉔ Wok to Walk (2)
- ㉕ Buenas Migas (2)
- ㉖ Supermarket

EATING

EATING

Budget Meals Around Town

Bright, clean, and inexpensive **sandwich shops** proudly hold the cultural line against the fast-food invasion that has hamburgerized the rest of Europe. You'll see two big Catalan chains (Bocatta and Pans & Company) everywhere, serving mass-produced McBaguettes ordered from a multilingual menu. I've had better luck with hole-in-the-wall sandwich shops—virtually as numerous as the chains—where you can see exactly what you're getting. Good alternatives include **Conesa Entrepans** (on Plaça de Sant Jaume) and the good local chain **El Mós,** with speedy service, fresh ingredients, and long hours daily (two locations near Plaça de Catalunya, at Carrer Comtal 12 and Carrer Santa Anna 9).

Kebab places are also a good, super-cheap standby; you'll see them all over town. Another popular budget option is the **empanada**—a pastry turnover filled with seasoned meat and vegetables. In basic restaurants and bars, you'll often find **daily lunch specials** *(menú del día)* for about €15. And you can always graze cheaply in bars offering an array of affordable **tapas** and individual bites called **pintxos** (or *pinchos*).

For other options, try **Muccis Pizza,** with good, fresh pizza slices and empanadas (two locations just off the Ramblas, at Bonsuccés 10 and Valldonzella 1). **Wok to Walk** makes tasty food for people on the run, serving up noodles and rice in takeaway containers with your choice of meat and/or veggies and finished with a savory sauce (convenient branches near Plaça de Sant Jaume and Liceu Metro station). **Buenas Migas** is another Barcelona chain serving focaccia, quiche, salads, and pastas (locations include behind the cathedral at Baixada de Santa Clara 2, at Plaça de la Sagrada Família 17, and off the Ramblas at Plaça del Bonsuccés 6).

$$ Restaurant Elisabets is a rough little neighborhood eatery packed with antique radios. It's popular with young locals and tourists alike for its €14.50 "home-cooked" three-course lunch special. Survey what those around you are enjoying and order what looks best. Locals put up with the brusque service for the tasty food (Mon-Sat lunch only, closed Sun and Aug, reservations smart, 2 blocks west of Ramblas on far corner of Plaça del Bonsuccés at Carrer de les Ramelleres 3, Metro: Catalunya, +34 933 175 826, www.elisabets1962.com).

$$ Café Granja Viader is a quaint time capsule, family-run since 1870. They boast about being the first dairy business to bottle and distribute milk in Spain. Specializing in baked and dairy treats, toasted sandwiches, and light meals, this place is ideal for a traditional breakfast. Or indulge your sweet tooth: Try a glass of *orxata* (or *horchata*—*chufa*-nut milk, summer only), *llet mallorquina* (Majorca-style milk with cinnamon, lemon, and sugar), *crema catalana* (crème brûlée, their specialty), or *suis* ("Swiss"—hot chocolate with a snowcap of whipped cream). *Mel i mató* is fresh cheese with honey...very Catalan (closed midday 14:00-17:00 and all day Sun, a block off the Ramblas behind Betlem Church at Carrer d'en Xuclà 4, Metro: Liceu, +34 933 183 486).

Cafeteria on Plaça de Catalunya: For a quick, affordable lunch with an almost 360-degree view, the ninth-floor cafeteria at **$$ El Corte Inglés** can't be beat. Grab a tray and browse; there's always fresh paella and the food is often cooked to order (Mon-Sat until 21:00, closed Sun except in summer, Metro: Catalunya, +34 933 063 800).

Picnics: Shoestring tourists buy groceries at **El Corte Inglés** (supermarket in basement) and **Carrefour Market** (Mon-Sat 9:00-21:00, closed Sun, Ramblas 113, Metro: Liceu).

La Boqueria Market: If you're in La Boqueria and ready for lunch, a snack, or a drink, several high-energy bars would love to take your money. For more on La Boqueria, see the "Ramblas Ramble," on page 92. For a less-touristy market hall, try Santa Caterina in El Born (described later).

Vegetarian Eateries near the Ramblas

$$ Biocenter, a Catalan soup-and-salad restaurant busy with local vegetarians, takes its cooking very seriously. They serve a generous portion of *pa amb tomàquet* (weekday lunch specials, daily, Sun until 16:00, two blocks off the Ramblas at Carrer del Pintor Fortuny 25, Metro: Liceu, +34 933 014 583).

$$ Flax & Kale is a top-end vegetarian place; the nearby campus gives it a university vibe. As its name suggests, this place serves seriously healthy dishes and juices in a delightful, spacious indoor setting, but I prefer to join the locals on the first-floor terrace—ask about it (daily, five-minute walk from the top of the Ramblas at Carrer Tallers 74, +34 933 175 664). Its sister location, named for the founder, **Teresa Carles,** is also good but has a more forgettable setting (daily, closer to the Ramblas, just off Carrer Tallers at Carrer Jovellanos 2, Metro: Universitat or Catalunya, +34 933 171 829).

BARRI GÒTIC

These eateries populate Barcelona's atmospheric Gothic Quarter, near the cathedral.

Restaurants

$$$ La Vinateria del Call, buried deep in the Jewish Quarter, is one of the oldest wine bars in town. It offers a romantic restaurant-style meal of tapas with fine local wines at a candlelit table. They have more than 100 well-priced wines, including a decent selection of Catalan wines at €3.50 a glass. Three or four plates of their classic tapas will fill two people (open Tue-Sat for lunch and dinner and Sun for dinner only, closed Mon, reservations smart, with back to church, leave Plaça de Sant Felip Neri and walk two short blocks to Carrer de Salomó Ben Adret 9; Metro: Jaume I, +34 933 026 092, http://lavinateriadelcall.com).

$$$ Els Quatre Gats ("The Four Cats") was once the haunt of the Modernista greats—including a teenage Picasso and architect Josep Puig i Cadafalch, who designed the building. You can snack or drink at the bar or head to the back for a sit-down meal. While touristy (less so later), the food and service are good and the prices are fair (closed Mon, live music most evenings, just steps off Avinguda del Portal de l'Angel at Carrer de Montsió 3, Metro: Catalunya, +34 933 024 140).

$$$ Onofre, owned and run by Marisol and Ángel, is a tiny wine bar (20 wines by the glass) with a handful of simple tables behind walls of wine bottles. Foodie but without pretense, it has a good mix of locals and tourists and a fun, creative, accessible menu—be adventurous and try the brandy foie shavings (closed Sun, near the Palace of Catalan Music, Carrer de les Magdalenes 19, +34 933 176 937).

$$ Bilbao Berria La Barra is a hardworking tapas bar, like its Basque sisters around town. It faces the cathedral, with tables outside on the square, and sells little open-faced sandwiches and fun bites buffet-style for around €2.50 per toothpick. Grab a plate and pick what you want (long hours daily, Plaça Nova 3, +34 933 170 124).

On Plaça de Sant Josep Oriol: To enjoy the most inviting square in the Gothic Quarter with a meal, consider these simple eateries (open daily), both with cramped tables inside and a few tables on the square: **$$ Bar del Pi** serves salads, sandwiches, and tapas in a traditional space. **$ El Drac de Sant Jordi** has a fun budget formula—€12 for any four tapas, a drink, and a tiny dessert. It's a good option for those who want to dine early.

EATING

Tapas on Carrer de la Mercè in the Barri Gòtic

This area lets you experience a rare, unvarnished bit of old Barcelona with great *tascas*—colorful local tapas bars. Get small plates (for maximum sampling) by asking for "tapas," not the bigger "*raciones*." Glasses of red wine *(vino tinto)* go for about €1. And though trendy uptown restaurants are safer and better-lit, and come with English menus and less grease, these places will stain your journal. The neighborhood's dark, the regulars are rough-edged, and you'll get a glimpse of a crusty Barcelona from before the affluence hit.

Of the many bars on Carrer de la Mercè, I'd visit these three: **$ Bar Celta** (marked *la pulpería*, at #9); **$ La Plata** (#28); and **$ Bodega del Gòtic,** at the north end of Carrer de la Mercè (#46).

EL BORN

El Born sparkles with eclectic and trendy as well as subdued and classy little restaurants hidden in the small lanes surrounding the Church of Santa Maria del Mar. While I've listed a few well-established tapas bars that are great for light meals, to really dine, simply wander around for 15 minutes and pick the place that tickles your gastronomic fancy. Consider starting off your evening with a glass of fine wine at one of the *enotecas* on the square facing the Church of Santa Maria del Mar (such as **La Vinya del Senyor**). Sit back and admire the pure Catalan Gothic architecture. Many restaurants and shops in this area are closed on Mondays. For all these eateries, use Metro: Jaume I.

Near the Church of Santa Maria del Mar

$$ Sagardi Euskal Taberna offers an array of Basque goodies—tempting *pintxos* and *montaditos* (small open-faced sandwiches) at €2.50 each—along its huge bar. Ask for a plate and graze (just take whatever looks good). Wash it down with Txakolí, a Basque white wine poured from the spout of a huge wooden

barrel into a glass as you watch (daily, Carrer de l'Argenteria 62, +34 933 199 993).

$$ Vegetalia, facing the Monument of Catalan Independence and the Church of Santa Maria del Mar, is a basic vegetarian diner with a cheery, healthy-feeling interior and a few outdoor tables (good three-course lunch special, daily, Plaça del Fossar de les Moreres, +34 930 177 256).

Near the Picasso Museum

$$ El Xampanyet ("The Little Champagne Bar") is a colorful family-run bar with a fun-loving staff (Juan Carlos, his mom, and other relatives). They specialize in tapas and anchovies—and their cheap homemade *cava* (Spanish champagne) goes straight to your head. Don't be put off by the seafood from a tin: Catalans like it this way. A *sortido de fumats* (assorted plate of small fish) with *pa amb tomàquet* makes for a fun meal. This place is filled with tourists by day but jam-packed with locals after dark. The scene is lively and the space is small—lines start forming early, so be prepared to wait (same price at bar or table, closed Sat for dinner and Sun-Mon for lunch, a half-block beyond the Picasso Museum at Carrer de Montcada 22, +34 933 197 003).

$$ Tapeo is a mod, classy alternative to the funky Xampanyet across the street. It serves high-end tapas at a long, sit-down bar and tiny tables with stools. This small space fills quickly so go early to get a seat (daily, Carrer de Montcada 29, +34 933 101 607).

$$$ Can Cisa/Bar Brutal is a creative and edgy bohemian-chic place with a young, local following. It serves a mix of Spanish and Italian dishes with an emphasis on wines—especially natural wines, with plenty available by the glass (Mon-Thu dinner only, Fri-Sun lunch and dinner, Carrer de la Princesa 14, +34 932 954 797).

$$$ Bar del Pla is a favorite near the Picasso Museum. This classic bar—overlooking a tiny crossroads next to Barcelona's oldest church—serves traditional Catalan dishes, *raciones,* and tapas. Their *croquetas,* mushrooms with wasabi, and crispy oxtail with foie gras are highlights (closed Sun, reservations smart; leaving the Picasso Museum, head right two blocks past Carrer de la Princesa to Carrer de Montcada 2; +34 932 683 003, www.bardelpla.cat).

At Santa Caterina Market

$$ Cuines Santa Caterina, bright and modern, has shared tables under the open rafters of a modern market hall. There's also a handy tapas bar and fine self-service outdoor seating on the square. Their menu—with vegetarian, international, and Mediterranean dishes, all made from market-fresh and seasonal ingredients—cross-references everything on an innovative grid (outside tables OK for both restaurant and tapas bar, daily, Avinguda de Francesc Cambó 16, +34 932 689 918).

$ Tapas Bars: Several lively tapas bars in the market are great for a quick and characteristic bite. Sitting here at one of these bars, immersed in the local scene, nets you a cheap and wonderful meal along with great market memories.

EL RAVAL AND NEARBY

Adventurous eaters will find a good selection of intriguing places to try in and around the El Raval district. The Sant Antoni market hall has a few options. For locations, see the map on page 58.

$$ La Masia Bar, a rough-around-the-edges dive, is located close to the Ramblas in the old Chinese neighborhood. It serves cheap tapas and beer to a local crowd in a tiny interior (closed Sun, Carrer d'Elisabets 16, +34 639 008 021).

$$$ Muy Buenas Cocktail Bar, with a charming 1928 Modernist interior, stands out in this neighborhood. Stop in for a drink at the classy bar or reserve ahead for the small dining room (daily, Carrer del Carme 63, +34 938 072 857).

$$$ Bar Lobo is a hip, modern place serving breakfast and tapas to a sophisticated crowd. Sit in the bright interior or outside on a lively square (daily, Carrer del Pintor Fortuny 3, +34 934 815 346).

$$$ Els Sortidors del Parlament is a rustic but high-end, trendy tapas bar with an inviting menu and a curated wine list (closed Wed, Carrer del Parlament 53, +34 934 411 602).

$ Horchatería Sirvent, famous for its *horchata*, feels like an old-fashioned ice cream parlor. The family takes great pride in the top-quality products they've been making by hand since 1920 (closed in winter, Carrer del Parlament 56, +34 934 412 720).

$$ Carrer de Blai is a long pedestrian-only stretch of thriving bars and youthful restaurants where you can eat tapas for half what you'd pay in El Born. **La Tasqueta de Blai** (#15) is a good choice with plenty of premade tapas to graze on.

EIXAMPLE

The people-packed boulevards of the Eixample are lined with appetizing eateries featuring breezy outdoor seating. Choose between a real restaurant or an upscale tapas bar (for the best variety, I prefer Rambla de Catalunya). For locations, see the "Hotels & Restaurants in the Eixample" map on page 186.

Restaurants

$$ El Nacional is a greenery-filled gastronomic destination with four restaurants (specializing in tapas, meat, and seafood) and four bars under one elegant roof. This former garage, a popular after-work hangout for locals, is a great choice for an early dinner or drink. Walk around to survey your options (long hours daily, follow romantically lit passageway to Passeig de Gràcia 24, +34 935 185 053, www.elnacionalbcn.com).

$$ La Rita is a fresh and dressy little restaurant serving Catalan and Mediterranean cuisine near the Block of Discord. Their €14 lunch and €25 dinner fixed-price meal specials are a great value. Arrive early...or wait (daily, near corner of Carrer de Pau Claris and Carrer d'Aragó at d'Aragó 279, a block from Metro: Passeig de Gràcia, +34 934 872 376).

$$ La Bodegueta is an atmospheric below-street-level bodega serving hearty wines, homemade vermouth, *anchoas* (anchovies), tapas, and *flautas*—sandwiches made with flute-thin baguettes. The three-course lunch special (weekdays only) with wine is a deal. A long block from Gaudí's La Pedrera, this makes a fine sightseeing break—and on a nice day, you can dine outside in the median of the boulevard under shady trees (daily, Sun from 17:00, at intersection with Carrer de Provença, Rambla de Catalunya 100, Metro: Provença, +34 932 154 894).

$$$ Restaurante la Palmera serves a mix of Catalan, Mediterranean, and French cuisine in an elegant room with bottle-lined walls. This untouristy place offers great food, service, and value—for me, a very special meal in Barcelona. They have three zones: the classic main room, a more forgettable adjacent room, and a few outdoor tables. I like the classic room. Reservations are smart (creative €30 six-plate *degustation* sampler at lunch only; closed Sun-Mon; Carrer d'Enric Granados 57, at the corner with Carrer Mallorca, Metro: Provença, +34 934 532 338, www.lapalmera.cat).

$$ La Flauta fills two floors with enthusiastic eaters (I prefer the ground floor). It's fresh and modern, with a fun, no-stress menu featuring small plates, creative *flauta* sandwiches, and a €16 three-course lunch deal. Consider the list of *tapas del día*. Good wines by the glass are listed on the blackboard, and solo diners get great service at the bar (closed Sun, upbeat and helpful staff, no reservations, just off Carrer de la Diputació at Carrer d'Aribau 23, Metro: Universitat, +34 933 237 038).

$ Baluard, one of Barcelona's most highly regarded artisan bakeries, has many locations around the city (the original is in Barceloneta). Line up with the locals to get a loaf of heavenly bread, a pastry, or a slice of pizza (daily, Sun until 15:00, Carrer de Valencia 246, +34 932 550 556).

Tapas Bars
Many trendy and touristic tapas bars in the Eixample offer a cheery welcome and slam out the appetizers. These two are particularly

handy to Plaça de Catalunya and the Passeig de Gràcia artery (closest Metro stops: Catalunya and Passeig de Gràcia).

$$$ Tapas 24 makes eating fun. This local favorite, with a few street tables, fills a spot a few steps below street level with happy energy, funky decor, and good yet pricey tapas. Along with daily specials, the menu has all the typical standbys and quirky inventions. The *tapas del día* list is particularly good. The owner, Carles Abellan, is one of Barcelona's hot chefs; although his famous fare isn't cheap, you can enjoy it without going broke. Prices are the same whether you dine at the bar, at a table, or outside. Come early or wait (daily, just off Passeig de Gràcia at Carrer de la Diputació 269, +34 934 880 977).

$$ Ciutat Comtal Cerveceria is an Eixample favorite with an elegant bar and tables plus good seating out on the Rambla de Catalunya for all that people-watching action. It's packed after 20:00, when you'll likely need to put your name on a list and wait. While it has no restaurant-type menu, the varied list of tapas and *montaditos* is easy, fun, and high-quality, and it includes daily specials (daily, facing the intersection of Gran Via de les Corts Catalanes and Rambla de Catalunya at Rambla de Catalunya 18, +34 933 181 997).

Out-of-the-Way Splurge

$$$$ Cinc Sentits ("Five Senses"), a 20-minute walk southwest of the Eixample, toward Montjuïc, is my gourmet recommendation for those who want to dress up and spend more money. At this chic, minimalist, snooty place, all the attention goes to the fine service and beautifully presented avant-garde cuisine inspired by Catalan traditions and ingredients. Expect fixed-price meals only—no à la carte. The *menú curt* includes 8 courses (€149) and the *menú degustació* has 10 courses (€169); both are unforgettable extravaganzas. Each comes with a wine-pairing option (€89-99 extra). Reservations are essential (Tue-Sat seatings at 13:30 & 20:30, closed Sun-Mon, Carrer d'Entença 60, Metro: Rocafort line 1, or a 5-minute walk from Metro: Plaça de Espanya, +34 933 239 490, www.cincsentits.com).

Cafés near Sagrada Família

Choices around the Sagrada Família are very touristy; walk a little beyond the crush for a better value.

$ Forn de Pa Puiggrós, a family-run bakery, offers good sandwiches a five-minute walk north on the pedestrian-friendly Avinguda de Gaudí (closed Sun, at #39, +34 934 36 23 04).

$ Granja Petitbo, a 10-minute walk south at the corner of Passeig de Sant Joan and Carrer D'Arago, has the standard tapas but throws in some American favorites too: burgers, eggs rancheros, and lasagna (daily, Passeig de Sant Joan 82, + 34 935 31 31 98, http://granjapetitbo.com).

BARCELONETA AND THE BEACH

The nearest Metro stop to this former sailors' quarter is Barceloneta; the bus will get you closer—the best ones are #V15 (catch it at Plaça de Catalunya or along Via Laietana), #59 (from the top of the Ramblas), or #D20 (from the Columbus Monument). For locations, see the "Barceloneta & Beaches" map on page 83.

At the Center of Barceloneta

The main square of Barceloneta (Plaça del Poeta Boscà) is homey, with a 19th-century iron-and-glass market, families at play in the park, and lots of hole-in-the-wall eateries and bars. The main drag, Passeig de Joan de Borbó, faces the city and is lined with many interchangeable seafood restaurants and cafés.

$$$ **La Mar Salada** is a traditional seafood restaurant with a slightly modern twist and both indoor and outdoor seating with some water views (weekday fixed-price lunch, closed Sun for dinner and all day Tue, Passeig de Joan de Borbó 59, +34 932 212 127).

$$$$ **Restaurante Can Solé,** serving seafood since 1903, hides on a nondescript lane between the square and the marina one block off the harborfront promenade. This venerable yet homey restaurant draws a celebrity crowd, judging by the autographed pictures of the famous and not-so-famous that line the walls (closed Sun for dinner and all day Mon, Carrer de Sant Carles 4, +34 932 215 012, www.restaurantcansole.com).

$$ **La Cova Fumada,** at the far end of the main square from the big market hall, is a popular, good-value choice for brunch or tapas in a neighborhood family setting (outdoor tables, Mon-Fri until 15:00, Sat until 13:00, Thu-Fri also 18:00-20:00, closed Sun, Carrer del Baluard 56, +34 932 214 061).

On the Beach

The *chiringuito* tradition of funky eateries lining Barcelona's beach now has serious competition from trendy bars and restaurants. My favorites are at the far south end near the towering Hotel W.

$$$$ **Pez Vela** is the top-end option with a fashionable local crowd and its own DJ (long hours daily, Passeig del Mare Nostrum 19, +34 932 216 317).

BARCELONA WITH CHILDREN

Barcelona is a great place to travel with kids; it's bubbling with inexpensive, quirky sights and an infectious human spirit. Sure, there's an amusement park, a zoo, and a science museum, but your kids will have an adventure simply wandering down the city's tangled streets. And when it's time for a break, Barcelona has one of Europe's best urban beach scenes.

Trip Tips

PLAN AHEAD
Involve your kids in trip planning. Have them read about the places that you may include in your itinerary (even the hotels you're considering) and let them help with your decisions.

Where to Stay
- Choose hotels in an area with wide, strollable streets, small parks, and a family-friendly feel—try Eixample or Barceloneta.
- If you're staying a week or more, or if your kids love playing in the sand, consider renting an apartment near one of Barcelona's many beaches.
- Aim for hotels with restaurants, so older kids can go back to the room while you finish a pleasant dinner.
- Barcelona's hotels often give price breaks for kids. Most have some sort of crib you can use.
- Your kids will thank you for avoiding the few remaining hotels without air-conditioning.

What to Bring

- If traveling with infants, plan on bringing or buying a light stroller for neighborhood walks, and a child backpack for riding the Metro.
- Bring your own drawing supplies and English-language picture books, as these supplies can be pricier in Europe.

EATING

Your kids may be surprised to find out that Catalan food is nothing like Mexican food back home. Picky eaters may have a hard time with *jamón*, deep-fried dishes, and strange seafood. Try these tips to keep your kids content throughout the day.

What to Eat (and Drink)

- Seek out commonly available, kid-friendly food choices such as a *tortilla de patatas* (potato-egg omelette), *bikinis* or *sandwich mixto* (grilled ham-and-cheese sandwich), *empanada de atún, pollo, carne picada,* or *jamón y queso* (savory pastry filled with tuna, chicken, ground beef, or ham and cheese), or *bocadillo* (French-bread sandwich usually filled with meat, cheese, or egg). For breakfast, try *una tostada con mantequilla y mermelada* (toast with butter and jam) or a croissant, along with *zumo natural* (fresh-squeezed orange juice). Fruit, cereal, and yogurt are available at the supermarket.
- Sweet treats popular with little travelers include *churros con chocolate* (fried dough strips with a dense chocolate drink for dipping), *ensaimada* (a Mallorca-style croissant with powdered sugar), *crema catalane* (like a crème brûlée), and *torró/turrón* (a nougat confection).

Where to Eat

- Picnic lunches or dinners work well. Try large grocery stores such as Carrefour Market or Mercadona. Or drop by a *panadería* (bakery), which will likely have baguette sandwiches, pizza by the slice, and empanadas. There are also plenty of tiny, convenient shops with long hours throughout the old town. Near the beach? Head to the market—El Mercat de la Barceloneta—near the Barceloneta Metro stop (closed Sun; Plaça del Poeta Boscà 1, ajuntament.barcelona.cat/mercats). Having snacks on hand can avoid meltdowns (and can help your kids avoid them, too).
- Choose easy eateries. A good, safe (though not exotic) bet is the cafeteria/restaurant at the **$ El Corte Inglés** department store on Plaça de Catalunya (service all day). Quick chain restaurants such as Pans & Company serve reasonably priced *bocadillos* (sandwiches) and fries—and grownups can order a beer.

Barcelona Books for Kids

Get your kids into the spirit of Barcelona with these books about the city and a few of its luminaries. (Also see my recommended books and films list in the appendix, which includes some good choices for teenagers.)

Building with Nature: The Life of Antoni Gaudí (Rachel Rodriguez and Julie Paschkis, 2009). Beautiful, folksy illustrations enliven the biography of Barcelona's most famous architect.

City Trails—Barcelona (Lonely Planet Kids, 2018). Follow Marco and Amelia as they find odd and wonderful secrets off the beaten path, giving quirky insights into the sights and history of Barcelona.

Let's Visit Barcelona!: Adventures of Bella & Harry (Lisa Manzione and Kristine Lucco, 2012). Two Chihuahuas visit Barcelona with their family, learning basic Spanish phrases and visiting famous landmarks.

Mission Barcelona: A Scavenger Hunt Adventure (Catherine Aragon, 2014). This interactive scavenger hunt will keep your youngsters engaged throughout your trip.

Molly and the Magic Suitcase: Molly Goes to Barcelona (Chris Oler and Amy Houston Oler, 2013). With the help of a magic suitcase, Molly and her brother trek to Barcelona in search of adventure.

Pablo Picasso: Meet the Artist (Patricia Geis, 2014). Young readers will enjoy this look at Picasso's art and may just be inspired to create some of their own.

Picasso and Minou (P. I. Maltbie and Pau Estrada, 2005). This beautifully illustrated book tells the story of Picasso and his work through the eyes of his cat, Minou.

A Stroll with Mr. Gaudí (Pau Estrada, 2014). In this fun introduction to Barcelona's architecture, Antoni Gaudí takes a walk through the city, visiting famous landmarks.

CHILDREN

When to Eat

- Catalans eat late—usually about 21:00 or 22:00—and dinner can take two hours. If you're eating late with your kids at a restaurant, bring something to occupy them and seek out places on squares like Plaça Reial where kids can run free while you dine. Catalan children go out and stay out late, so don't worry about your kids disturbing others as they gambol around the plaza.

SIGHTSEEING

The key to a successful Barcelona family vacation is to slow down. Tackle one or two key sights each day, mix in a healthy dose of pure fun at a park or beach, and take extended breaks when needed.

Planning Your Time

- Let your kids make some decisions, such as choosing lunch spots or deciding which stores or museums to visit. Deputize your child to lead you on my self-guided walks and museum tours.
- Older children and teens can help plan sightseeing details, such as what to see, how to get there, and ticketing details.
- Take advantage of Time Out Barcelona's website, which includes kids' activities, shows, and family restaurants (www.timeout.com/barcelona/barcelona-for-kids).
- Don't overdo it. Tackle only one or two key sights a day. Encourage your kids to endure an hour to see a sight, then relent if they've had enough.
- Balance your museum-going with fun and energetic activities, like boating in Citadel Park or biking along the beach.
- Barcelona's sights generally offer free admission to children and reduced admission for students—always ask before buying tickets for your kids.
- Follow this book's crowd-beating tips to the letter. Kids despise long lines even more than you do.
- Public WCs are hard to find: Try museums, ice cream shops, and fast-food restaurants.

Successful Sightseeing

- Get kids engaged in age-appropriate museum fun. Younger kids may enjoy a scavenger hunt approach: Buy postcards of sights in the museum gift shop (or give them this book with its photos) and let them find the art. Museum audioguides are great for older children.
- Bring a sketchbook to a museum and encourage kids to select a painting or statue to draw. It's a great way for them to slow down and observe.
- Seek out kid-friendly museums, such as CosmoCaixa or the Maritime Museum.

Making or Finding Quality Souvenirs

- Buy your child a trip journal and encourage them to write down observations, thoughts, and favorite sights and memories. This journal could end up being your child's favorite souvenir.

- For a group project, keep a family journal. Pack a small diary and a glue stick. While relaxing over ice cream, take turns writing or drawing about the day's events and include mementos such as ticket stubs from museums and postcards.
- Teens might love shopping (or even window-shopping). See the Shopping in Barcelona chapter for fun areas.

MONEY, SAFETY, AND STAYING CONNECTED

Before setting them loose, talk to your kids about safety and money.

- Give your child a money belt (or other clothing with secure secret storage) and an expanded allowance; you are on vacation, after all. Let your kids budget their funds by comparing and contrasting the dollar and euro.
- If you allow older kids to explore a museum or neighborhood on their own, be sure to establish a clear meeting time and place.
- For kids of all ages, it's good to have a "what if" procedure in place in case something goes wrong. If your child has a mobile phone, enable the "Find My Phone" feature in case you get separated. Give your kids a business card from your hotel, along with your contact information and emergency taxi fare. Let them know to ask to use the phone at a hotel if they are lost.
- Teens traveling with a mobile device can keep in touch with friends at home—and European kids they meet—via the same apps they use at home. Readily available Wi-Fi helps keep online time affordable, or consider buying an international data plan (see the "Staying Connected" section of the Practicalities chapter).

Top Kids' Sights and Activities

ATTRACTIONS
Tibidabo

This 100-year-old amusement park (the city's oldest) sits atop the Tibidabo foothills above town; visiting it could easily fill an entire day.

At the top are Disneyland-like rides and some vintage attractions appealing to younger children, teens, and adults alike. Many enjoy the maze of mirrors—you have to wear gloves so the mirrors stay fingerprint-free. Older kids may like modern attractions such as a 4-D cinema show and the Virtual Express roller coaster. Those on a budget can enjoy the entrance labeled *Panoramic views*,

CHILDREN

which allows access to an old-fashioned carousel, the sky-high Ferris wheel perch, and a handful of other classic rides (see page 66).

CosmoCaixa

One of Europe's most advanced science museums, CosmoCaixa features hands-on exhibits, many of which are specifically geared toward small children. Youngsters will love the jungle greenhouse and Antarctic base, while the 3-D planetarium (€6 extra) may entice older kids and teens.

Cost and Hours: €6, free for kids 15 and under; daily 10:00-20:00; Metro: Tibidabo, then hop on bus #196 for one stop or walk about 15 minutes to the museum, Carrer d'Isaac Newton 26; +34 932 126 050, www.cosmocaixa.es.

Barcelona Zoo (Zoo de Barcelona)

This enormous zoo inside Citadel Park first gained fame as the home of Copito de Nieve (Snowflake), the world's only known albino gorilla. The zoo now features tigers, hippos, zebras, Komodo dragons, and more.

Cost and Hours: €13 for kids 3-12, free for kids 2 and under, €22 for teens and adults; hours vary by season, summer hours daily 10:00-20:00, last entrance one hour before closing; Metro: Barceloneta, Ciutadella-Vila Olímpica, Marina, or Arc de Triomf; +34 937 065 656, www.zoobarcelona.cat.

Barcelona Aquarium at Port Vell (L'Aquàrium de Barcelona Port Vell)

Located on the waterfront not far from the Columbus Monument, the aquarium is home to more than 11,000 animals. Its star attraction is the "Oceanarium," a 262-foot underwater glass tunnel that lets you walk beneath schools of deep-sea creatures such as sharks and stingrays. The Port Vell area is an inviting mix of towering sailboats and a steady flow of people on the boardwalk in the midst of daily life; the green space offers room for a picnic or quick rest from sightseeing.

Cost and Hours: €18 for kids 5-10, €10 for kids 3-4, free for kids 2 and under, €25 for ages 11 and older; open Mon-Fri 10:00-19:00, Sat-Sun until 20:00, later in summer; Metro: Drassanes or Barceloneta, Moll d'Espanya del Port Vell, +34 932 217 474, www.aquariumbcn.com.

Magic Fountains (Font Màgica)

This popular, free spectacle uses classic and modern tunes—including film scores—as the soundtrack for a fanciful water show. Built for the 1929 World's Fair and renovated before the 1992 Olympics, it's part of a web of ponds and waterfalls on Avinguda Maria Cristina in Montjuïc—though the fountains sometimes close in

CHILDREN

drought conditions (check ahead to make sure the fountains are running; see page 79).

MUSEUMS AND EXHIBITS
Art Museums
A short visit to some of Barcelona's modern and contemporary art museums could dazzle your kids. Many offer educational programs aimed at children and their families.

Museu d'Art Contemporani (MACBA) houses a vast collection of artwork from the past 50 years and offers lectures, video screenings, and special exhibits covering contemporary culture and art. The museum's square is also a roller-skaters' hangout; it's fun to watch the tricks before going inside (€11, free for kids 13 and under; Mon and Wed-Fri 11:00-19:30, Sat 10:00-20:00, Sun 10:00-15:00, closed Tue; Metro: Universitat or Catalunya, Plaça dels Àngels 1, +34 934 813 368, www.macba.cat).

The **Picasso Museum** gives kids a chance to marvel at the artist's early works (see page 137).

If you feel like venturing outside of the city for a surreal experience, a two-hour drive or train ride will take you to the **Dalí Theater-Museum** in the town of Figueres (see page 247).

Chocolate Museum (Museu de la Xocolata)
Satisfy everyone's sweet tooth while learning the history of traditional Catalan confectionery through a range of kid-friendly exhibits. You'll see chocolate statues of just about anything and everything. Family activities may even include painting with chocolate (see page 57).

Maritime Museum (Museu Marítim de Barcelona)

This museum illuminates the history of Catalunya's rich maritime past from the 13th to the 20th century. Boat aficionados and sailors-to-be enjoy the collection of model boats and seafaring gadgets, as well as the sprawling marina. Museum admission includes the *Santa Eulàlia* (docked on the Moll de la Fusta quay), a historic three-masted schooner from 1918 that was meticulously restored to its original state. It's especially fun to visit on Saturday mornings, when the schooner sails around the harbor—reserve well in advance (see page 46).

CHILDREN

Natural Science Museum (Museu de Ciencies Naturals)
A good choice for any kid interested in nature, this museum—home to more than three million specimens—celebrates the diversity in flora, fauna, and geology in Catalunya and beyond. Its main exhibit, Planet Life, follows the birth of Earth and the evolution of life. A special space, the "Science Nest," has activities designed for preschoolers, but it's open only on the weekends.

Cost and Hours: €6, free for kids 15 and under, free Sun after 15:00, €7 combo ticket with Botanical Gardens; Tue-Sat 10:00-19:00, Sun until 20:00, shorter hours Oct-Feb, closed Mon year-round; Metro: El Maresme-Fòrum, Plaça Leonardo da Vinci 4, +34 932 566 002, www.museuciencies.cat.

Botanical Gardens
Montjuïc is the home of the natural history museum's Botanical Gardens and its Botanical Institute, as well as the Historical Botanical Garden. A network of paths follows the natural terrain, taking visitors past 87 outdoor exhibits known as "phytoepisodes."

Cost and Hours: €5, free for kids 15 and under, €7 combo-ticket with Natural Science Museum; daily June-Aug 10:00-20:00, closes earlier off-season; walk or take bus #150 from Plaça d'Espanya or the Montjuïc funicular from Paral-lel, main entrance between Olympic Stadium and castle—see map on page 68, Carrer Dr. Font i Quer 2; +34 932 564 160, www.museuciencies.cat.

CHILDREN

Olympic and Sports Museum (Museu Olímpic i de l'Esport)
Sports-crazed kids might enjoy this museum, as well as exploring what is left of the adjacent, anticlimactic 1992 Olympic Stadium. The mod-yet-tacky museum offers up several kid-friendly multimedia installations, such as a virtual race against an Olympic athlete, but it ultimately appeals only to Olympics fanatics (see page 74).

Camp Nou Soccer Stadium
"Barça" is to Barcelona what the Cowboys are to Dallas; the city lives and breathes for this top-ranked soccer team. The men's team is playing at the old Olympic Stadium as its home turf gets a much-needed reboot, but Camp Nou remains the destination for a pricey interactive visitors center including memorabilia from past seasons of glory and a preview of the updated stadium. An English audio-guide helps explain the exhibits—and the city's soccer obsession.

The crowded, energetic FC Barcelona superstore (Barça Store) is a cool spot for kids and teens as well. Pick up a scarlet-and-blue jersey or scarf as a souvenir (see page 66).

PARKS AND BEACHES
Citadel Park (Parc de la Ciutadella)
Barcelona's most central park sprawls its grassy fields and large avenues across the grounds of an old fortress and offers plenty for curious kids to discover. Attractions include a giant mammoth statue, a small lake with rental rowboats and duck feeding, a large Baroque fountain (La Cascada), and several outdoor events held throughout the year. The Barcelona Zoo is also accessible from the park.

Horta Labyrinth Park (Parc del Laberint d'Horta)
Away from the city center in an unassuming location lies the most tranquil green space in town. With barely a tourist in sight, the park holds a handful of Neoclassical and Romantic gardens, highlighted by a small central maze. There are more than 20 water features—pools, fountains, reservoirs, canals, and an artificial waterfall—and the tricky labyrinth should provide ample entertainment for kids.

Cost and Hours: €1.50 for kids 5-13, free for kids 4 and under, €2.25 for adults, free on Wed and Sun; daily 10:00-20:00, closes earlier off-season, last entry one hour before closing; Metro: Mundet, then a 15-minute walk; the park is at Passeig dels Castanyers 1, behind a velodrome.

Sant Sebastià, Barceloneta, and Nova Icària Beaches
These are the closest, longest, and busiest beaches (with Sant Sebastià preferred by locals). Both are near the city center, making them a good stop before or after sightseeing. A long boardwalk with food, drink, and ice-cream options lines Sant Sebastià and Barceloneta; on the sand, you'll come upon children's play areas (including one with a cool climbing frame). Expect beach sports such as table tennis, beach volleyball, and the Basque handball game, *pelota*. Look out at the waves, and you'll also spot a surfer or two.

If you don't care for crowds, head instead for the nearby Nova Icària beach; this more tranquil beach is frequented by families. Nova Icària is within walking distance of the 1992 Olympic Marina, a popular place for sailing and boating. All of these beaches are accessible from the Old City area by bus or Metro; see page 82 for directions.

CHILDREN

OTHER EXPERIENCES

Sardana Dance

The easy-to-do *sardana* is a beloved traditional symbol of Catalan unity and pride. Kids may enjoy this spectacle of local culture (see page 7).

Cable Car (El Transbordador Aeri del Port)

This is a fun and scenic ride between the Barcelona waterfront and Montjuïc, providing spectacular views of the city. Note that the car is often crowded and very slow-moving; if there's a long line, it may not be worth the wait (see page 70).

CHILDREN

SHOPPING IN BARCELONA

Barcelona is a fantastic shopping destination, whatever your taste or budget. The streets of the Barri Gòtic and El Born are bursting with characteristic hole-in-the-wall shops and delightful neighborhood boutiques, while the Eixample is the upscale "uptown" shopping district. The area around Avinguda del Portal de l'Angel (at the northern edge of the Barri Gòtic) has a number of department and chain stores.

Most shops are open Monday through Friday from about 9:00 or 10:00 until lunchtime (13:00 or 14:00). After the siesta, they reopen in the evening (16:30 or 17:00) and stay open until 20:00 or 21:00. Large stores and some smaller shops in touristy zones may remain open through the afternoon—but don't count on it. On Saturdays, many shops are open in the morning only. On Sundays, most shops are closed (though the Maremagnum complex on the harborfront is open).

For information on VAT refunds and customs regulations, see the "Money" section of the Practicalities chapter. For clothing size comparisons between the US and Europe, see the appendix.

What to Buy

Home and Design Goods

Consider picking up prints, books, posters, decorative items, or other keepsakes featuring works by your favorite artist (Picasso, Dalí, Miró, Gaudí, etc.). Gift shops at major museums are open to the public (such as the Picasso Museum and Gaudí's La Pedrera) and are a bonanza for art and design lovers. Model-ship builders and nautical buffs will be fascinated by the offerings at the Maritime Museum shop.

In this design-oriented city, home decor shops are abundant

and fun to browse, offering a variety of Euro-housewares unavailable back home. For something more classic, look for glassware or other items with a dash of Modernista style.

Decorative tile and pottery can be a good keepsake. Eixample sidewalks are paved with distinctively patterned tiles, which are sold in local shops.

Foodie Items
Home cooks might enjoy shopping for olive oil, wine, spices (such as saffron or sea salts), high-quality canned foods and preserves, dried beans, and other Spanish food items. Remember, these must be sealed to make it back through US customs. But keep in mind that cured meat can never get past US customs, even if it is vacuum-packed and sealed. Cooks can look for European-style gadgets at kitchen-supply stores.

Torró (or *turrón* in Spanish) is the beloved nougat treat that's traditionally eaten around Christmastime but has become popular anytime.

Market halls are great places to shop for Catalan edibles. The best are La Boqueria (described in the Ramblas Ramble chapter), Santa Caterina (described in the El Born Walk chapter), and Sant Antoni (slightly off the beaten path in El Raval).

Clothing, Jewelry, and Accessories
Department and chain stores can be fun places to browse for clothing—including styles you won't find back home.

An *espardenya* (or *alpargata* in Spanish) is a soft-canvas, rope-soled shoe (known in the US as an espadrille). It originated as humble peasant footwear in the 14th century in the Pyrenean region (including Catalunya, Occitania, and the Basque Country), but has become popular in modern times for its lightweight comfort in hot weather. A few shops in Barcelona still make these the traditional way.

Jewelry shops are popular here. While the city doesn't have a strictly local style, finding a piece with a Modernista flourish gives it a Barcelona vibe.

Accessories crafted from discarded materials into stylish, useful products (such as handbags) sell well in "green" Barcelona.

Catalan Pride
If you're drawn to Catalunya's culture, consider a Catalan flag (gold and red stripes). And if you're a fan of Catalan independence, pick up one with the blue triangle and star.

Sports fans love jerseys, scarves, and other gear associated with the wildly popular Barça soccer team. As you wander, you'll likely see official football team shops. Knockoffs can be found at any tourist gift shop for less.

Shopping Spots

THE OLD CITY

The Barri Gòtic bursts with shops, from international chain stores to creative artisan boutiques. Neighboring El Born is another good area for boutique-hopping (see my El Born Walk chapter, which takes you through the heart of this district and points you to some appealing shopping streets). Keep in mind that many shops are closed during the midafternoon siesta and have shorter hours or are closed altogether on Sundays.

Barri Gòtic Shopping Walk
(From the Cathedral to the Ramblas)

Most visitors going between the cathedral and the Ramblas follow the straight shot along the wide Carrer de la Portaferrissa. This drag is lined with mostly inter-national clothing stores catering to teens and young adults (Zara, Mango, etc.). For a more characteristic route—leading you through far more interesting streets lined with little local shops—plunge into some lanes just to the south. This brief, U-shaped walk is designed to lead you through some of the Barri Gòtic's most enjoyable shopping streets.

• *Begin on* **Plaça Nova,** *the long square in front of the cathedral. At the west end of that square, stand facing the old Roman towers and the big BARCINO letters. Turn 90 degrees to the right, and just to the left of the restaurant (Bilbao Berria "BB"—good for a quick tapas bite with fine seating facing the cathedral), head up the tight lane called...*

❶ **Carrer de la Palla:** This is ideal for antiques, with a half-dozen ancient-feeling shops crammed with mothballed treasures. (You'll also find, on the left, a fenced-in area with fragments of the old Roman walls, which functions today as a schoolyard soccer field at recess time.) Mixed in are a few contemporary art galleries and offbeat shops.

Stay on this street until you reach the fork, marked by the building with ❷ **Caelum,** a casual but classy-feeling café (at #8) selling a wide range of nun-made pastries from convents around Spain. Peruse the boxes of sisterly goodies and consider sticking around for a coffee—either on the charming main floor or down in the cellar.

• *From here, detour left and head down...*

❸ **Carrer dels Banys Nous:** This street curves gracefully south

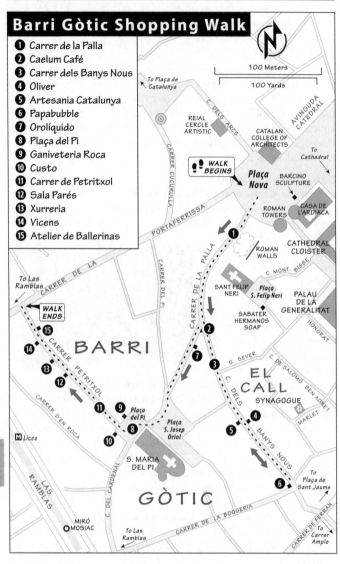

Barri Gòtic Shopping Walk

1. Carrer de la Palla
2. Caelum Café
3. Carrer dels Banys Nous
4. Oliver
5. Artesania Catalunya
6. Papabubble
7. Orolíquido
8. Plaça del Pi
9. Ganiveteria Roca
10. Custo
11. Carrer de Petritxol
12. Sala Parés
13. Xurreria
14. Vicens
15. Atelier de Ballerinas

as it follows the route of the original Roman wall. While you'll have to backtrack a bit, it's another great shopping street with antiques and colorful, locally made attire.

About 100 yards down this street, on the left at #10, the sprawling ❹ **Oliver** shop (selling home decor, women's clothing, and accessories) has the remains of an old Arabic bath in the back. Directly across the lane, ❺ **Artesania Catalunya** (at #11) is a large marketplace run by the city, featuring handmade items from Catalan artisans. You can typically find ceramics, jewelry, leather goods, and accessories, but the artisans and merchandise change every few months. Just beyond that, ❻ **Papabubble** (at #3) is a candy shop where you can watch treats being made the old-fashioned way.

• *Backtrack to Caelum and take a hard left down Carrer de la Palla to another fine shop.*

❼ **Orolíquido:** At #8, this shop's name means "Liquid Gold." Inside you'll find high-quality olive oils from around Spain, along with cosmetics made with olive oil, balsamic vinegars, and other natural products.

• *After another block, you'll pop out on the charming, café-lined Plaça de Sant Josep Oriol, facing the Church of Santa Maria del Pi. Skirt around the right side of the church to find...*

❽ **Plaça del Pi:** While small, this square—named for its *pi* (or pine) tree—has some worthwhile shops. Enjoy checking out ❾ **Ganiveteria Roca,** a cutlery shop selling knives, shaving gear, and other items for your checked luggage (at #3). Nearby is a small branch of the colorful Barcelona clothing designer ❿ **Custo** (at #2). On many days, local food and crafts markets set up on this square.

• *Head up the street immediately left of Josep Roca.*

⓫ **Carrer de Petritxol:** This fun, narrow, characteristic lane (pronounced peht-ree-CHUHL) is decorated with historic tiles. It's a fun combination of fancy jewelry shops and art galleries (such as ⓬ **Sala Parés,** at #5, where Picasso had his first professional exhibition in town—step in and enjoy the latest in 150 years of art exhibits).

For a great *churros con chocolate* break, stop into ⓭ **Xurreria** (#11). Elegant older ladies gather here for the Spanish equivalent of teatime. For a more local treat, try an *ensaimada* (Mallorca-style croissant with powdered sugar) or the *crema catalane* (like a crème brûlée). A few doors further down (at #15) is ⓮ **Vicens,** a fancy sweets shop specializing in *torró.* They offer generous plates of samples, lots of varieties on sale in small quantities, and a warm welcome.

If you're looking for Barcelona ballet flats, you'll find them in a rainbow of colors at ⓯ **Atelier de Ballerinas** (at #18).

• *You'll dead-end onto touristy Carrer de la Portaferrissa. Head one block left to get to the Ramblas, or five blocks right to return to the cathedral. Or retrace your steps, this time poking into side streets to discover more shops.*

More Shops in the Barri Gòtic

The streets described in the above walk are just the beginning. While exploring the many other characteristic lanes of the Barri Gòtic, keep an eye out for these shops.

Sabater Hermanos (abbreviated "Hnos." on the sign) continues a family tradition of making and selling handmade, natural, colorful soaps. The simple but fragrant shop feels like an artisanal Lush. To buy soap and call it a culturally redeemable souvenir, look for the bars shaped like characteristic Barcelona sidewalk tiles (down a small lane opposite the cathedral's cloister at Plaça Sant Felip Neri 1; for location, see the "Barri Gòtic Shopping Walk" map).

Papirum is an inviting, classic, artisan shop selling craft paper, stationery, and handbound blank books (near the Barcelona History Museum at Baixada de la Llibreteria 2, run by Dolores Crespo and family). For location, see the "Barri Gòtic Walk" map in that chapter.

Carrer Ample, the street one block up from the tapas-loaded Carrer de la Mercè (in the lower part of Barri Gòtic—just above the waterfront), feels local but with little bursts of trendy energy. On the other side of the Ramblas (two blocks below Plaça de Catalunya), stroll down skinny **Carrer de Bonsuccés** (it turns into **Carrer d'Elisabets**) and poke into the boutiques along the way.

AVINGUDA DEL PORTAL DE L'ANGEL

Barcelona natives do most of their shopping at big department stores. You'll find these and a high concentration of chain stores on one convenient street: **Avinguda del Portal de l'Angel,** which connects Plaça de Catalunya with the cathedral.

Chain Stores: Chains along this street include Zara, Massimo Dutti (upscale business attire, like Banana Republic), Bershka (teens), Pull and Bear (young adults—sort of the Spanish Gap), Barcelona-based Mango (clothing), Camper shoes (which started in Mallorca), and Women's Secret (the Spanish answer to Victoria's Secret). Most have several locations scattered around the city, and some even have different offerings based on their location (for instance, the Zara in the Barri Gòtic has more casual clothes, while the one along the ritzy Diagonal street emphasizes business attire).

Department Stores: At the top of Avinguda del Portal de l'Angel, Plaça de Catalunya has a gigantic **El Corte Inglés,** with everything you can imagine—clothes, housewares, furniture, electronics, bonsai trees, a travel agency, haircuts, and cheap souvenirs (get the complete list by picking up an English directory at their info desk). It also has a supermarket in the basement and a ninth-floor view cafeteria (Mon-Sat 9:00-21:00, until 22:00 in summer, closed Sun except in

summer). Across the square is **FNAC**—a French department store that sells electronics, music, books, and tickets for major concerts and events (Mon-Sat 9:30-21:00, until 22:00 in summer, closed Sun).

THE EIXAMPLE

This ritzy "uptown" district is home to some of the city's top-end shops (for locations, see the "Eixample Walk" map on page 153). In general, you'll find a lot of big international names along **Passeig de Gràcia,** the main boulevard that runs from Plaça de Catalunya to the Gaudí sights—an area fittingly called the "Golden Quarter" (Quadrat d'Or). Appropriately enough, the "upper end" of Passeig de Gràcia has the fancier shops (Gucci, Luis Vuitton, Chanel, and so on) while the southern part of the street is relatively "low-end." One block to the west, **Rambla de Catalunya** holds more local (but still expensive) options: fashion, home decor, jewelry, perfume, and so on. The streets that connect Rambla de Catalunya to Passeig da Gràcia are also home to some fine shops.

Cubiñá, three blocks east and a block south, is a furniture and home-decor shop—worth a peek for its upscale-mod collection, as well as for the Domènech i Montaner building that houses it (Carrer Mallorca 291).

Farther south, the street called **Consell de Cent** has a variety of art galleries (close to Plaça de Catalunya, roughly between Passeig de Gràcia and Carrer d'Enric Granados). The neighborhood a block west of the Block of Discord is home to a fun kitchen store: **Gadgets & Cuina** (Carrer d'Aragó 249).

And much farther to the west, the broad main boulevard **Diagonal** is another popular shopping zone—especially the stretch between Plaça de Francesc Macià and where it crosses Gran Via de Carles III (at the Maria Cristina Metro stop, near Camp Nou).

LAS ARENAS MALL

While the shops inside it are nothing special, the Las Arenas shopping mall itself is since it fills Barcelona's repurposed bullring on Plaça d'Espanya. It's convenient to combine with a visit to the Montjuïc sights (described in the Sights in Barcelona chapter).

After Catalunya outlawed bullfighting in 2010, the former *plaça de toros* was converted into a modern mall with chain stores, a food court, a view terrace on top, and an escalator that trundles all the way up through its wide-open atrium (daily 10:00-22:00 in summer, 9:00-21:00 in winter, don't pay the small fee to take the exterior elevator—the escalators are free, Gran Via de les Corts Catalanes 373-385).

NIGHTLIFE IN BARCELONA

Like all of Spain, Barcelona is extremely lively after hours. People head out for dinner at 22:00, then bar-hop or simply wander the streets until well after midnight. Some days it seems that more people are out and about at 2:00 in the morning (party time) than at 2:00 in the afternoon (lunch time). The most "local" thing you can do here after sunset is to explore neighborhood watering holes and find your favorite place to enjoy a glass of wine. I've described several parts of town ideally suited to doing just that. For a musical event, consider taking in a serious performance at a fancy venue (such as the Palace of Catalan Music), or opt for a jazz, flamenco, or classical guitar show.

Information: Check out online guides *Time Out Barcelona* (www.timeout.com/barcelona) and *Visit Barcelona* (www.barcelonaturisme.com), both in English with descriptions of each day's main events and ticket information. The TI's culture website is also helpful (www.barcelona.cat/barcelonacultura). Other resources include *See Barcelona* (www.seebarcelona.com) and *Barcelona Metropolitan* (www.barcelona-metropolitan.com).

Palau de la Virreina, an arts-and-culture information office just off the Ramblas, provides details on Barcelona cultural events—music, opera, and theater—and sells last-minute tickets (Tue-Sun 11:00-20:00, closed Mon, on the Rambla of Flowers at Ramblas 99, +34 933 161 000, https://ajuntament.barcelona.cat/lavirreina).

Getting Tickets: Most venues sell tickets through their websites, or you can book through Ticketmaster or Eventbrite. Tickets are also sold at the box offices in the main El Corte Inglés department store and the giant FNAC electronics store (both on Plaça de Catalunya, extra booking fee), and at the ticket desk in Palau de la Virreina (see above).

MUSIC AND DANCE

Concerts

Several classy venues host high-end performances.

The **Palace of Catalan Music** (Palau de la Música Catalana), with one of the finest Modernista interiors in town (see the listing on page 54), offers a full slate of performances, ranging from symphonic to Catalan folk songs to chamber music to flamenco (box office open Mon-Fri 9:00-21:00, Sat 9:30-21:00, Sun 9:30-13:00, Carrer Palau de la Música 4, Metro: Urquinaona, box office +34 932 957 207, www.palaumusica.cat). Look for shows held in the Sala de Concerts in order to see the Modernista main concert hall (not in the Petit Palau hall).

The **Liceu Opera House** (Gran Teatre del Liceu), right in the heart of the Ramblas, is a pre-Modernista, sumptuous venue for opera, dance, children's theater, and concerts (buy tickets online up to one hour before show or in person, Ramblas 51, Metro: Liceu, info +34 934 859 900 www.liceubarcelona.cat).

Another, much less architecturally interesting venue for classical music is **L'Auditori,** the home of the city's orchestra (boxy modern building northeast of Old City at Lepant 150; Metro: Bogatell, Marina, or Monumental; +34 932 479 300, www.auditori.cat).

Some of Barcelona's top sights host good-quality concerts. Try **La Pedrera** (described later under "Performances at Gaudí Sights"), **Casa Batlló, Fundació Joan Miró,** and **CaixaForum;** for details, check their websites.

Touristy Performances of Spanish Clichés

Two famously Spanish types of music—flamenco and Spanish guitar—have little to do with Barcelona or Catalunya but are performed to keep visitors happy. If you're headed to other parts of Spain where these musical forms are more typical (such as Andalucía for flamenco), you might as well wait until you can experience the real deal. But if this is your only stop in Spain, here are some options.

Flamenco: While flamenco is foreign to Catalunya (locals say that it's like going to see country music in Boston), there are some good places to view this unique Spanish artform. Head to **Palau Dalmases,** in an atmospheric old palace courtyard in El Born, for the highest-quality performances I've found (€35 includes a drink; daily at 17:30, 18:45, 20:00, and 21:15; also hosts opera and jazz, Carrer de Montcada 20, +34 660 769 864, www.flamencopalaudalmases.com).

Tarantos, on Plaça Reial in the heart of the Barri Gòtic, puts on brief (30 minutes), riveting flamenco performances several times nightly—an easy and inexpensive way to see it. Performances are in a touristy little bar/theater with about 50 seats (€17; nightly at

Sights Open Late

Many of Barcelona's major sights are open well into the evening. If you'd like to extend your sightseeing day, here's where to do it:

Near the Ramblas
Maritime Museum: Daily until 20:00
Palau Güell: April-Sept Tue-Sun until 20:00
La Boqueria Market: Mon-Sat until 20:30

Barri Gòtic and El Born
Frederic Marès Museum: Sun until 20:00
Barcelona History Museum—Plaça del Rei: Sun until 20:00
Picasso Museum: Tue-Sun until 20:00 in peak season
Santa Caterina Market: Tue and Thu-Fri until 20:00
Church of Santa Maria del Mar: Tue-Sat until 20:30

Eixample and Beyond
Sagrada Família: April-Sept daily until 20:00
La Pedrera (Casa Milà): March-Oct daily until 20:30; also hosts nighttime visits
Casa Batlló: Daily until 20:00; also hosts nighttime visits
Park Güell: April-Oct daily until 22:00 (must enter by 19:30)

Montjuïc and Vicinity
Fundació Joan Miró: April-Oct Tue-Sat until 20:00
Catalan Art Museum: May-Sept Tue-Sat until 20:00
Magic Fountains: Shows run between 20:00 and 22:30 several nights a week (no shows in drought conditions and Jan-Feb)
CaixaForum: Daily until 20:00
Las Arenas Mall: June-Sept daily until 22:00, Oct-May until 21:00, restaurants open late year-round

18:30, 19:30, and 20:30; Plaça Reial 17, https://tarantosbarcelona.com).

Another option is the pricey (and relatively high-quality) **Tablao Cordobés** on the Ramblas (€45 includes a drink, €80 includes mediocre buffet dinner and better seats, 3 performances/day, Ramblas 35, +34 933 175 711, www.tablaocordobes.es).

For flamenco in a concert-hall setting, try one of the Palace of Catalan Music's regular performances (see listing earlier, under "Concerts").

Spanish Guitar: "Masters of Guitar" concerts are offered nearly daily in several locations including the Palace of Catalan

Music. Check the website for upcoming performances (+34 647 514 513, www.maestrosdelaguitarra.com).

Performances at Gaudi Sights

A classy option is a **"Summer Nights at La Pedrera"** concert at Gaudí's Modernista masterpiece in the Eixample. This evening series features live jazz and the chance to see the rooftop illuminated (€38, check website for times and book ahead, +34 932 142 576, www.lapedrera.com).

Casa Batlló offers a "Magic Night" ticket which includes a tour, a rooftop concert, and a glass of *cava* (most nights in peak season at 20:00, €69 Blue ticket, €89 Gold ticket gets you a better seat).

Jazz

Hotel Casa Fuster, a Modernista landmark designed by Lluís Domènech i Montaner, is a luxury hotel that hosts a weekly Woody Allen-inspired jazz night (€40-80, Thu 21:00-23:00, in the basement of Café Vienés, reservations recommended, across Avinguda Diagonal from the Eixample at Passeig de Gràcia 132, +34 932 553 006, www.hotelcasafuster.com).

Jamboree jazz and dance club, right on Plaça Reial, features jazz sets nightly, often at 19:00, in a cellar under brick vaults (check schedule online or stop by, Plaça Reial 17, Metro: Liceu, +34 933 191 789, https://jamboreejazz.com).

Also consider the divey **Harlem Jazz Club** (a couple of blocks off Plaça Reial at Comtessa de Sobradiel 8, +34 933 100 755, www.harlemjazzclub.es).

AFTER-HOURS HANGOUT NEIGHBORHOODS

Most Barcelonans' idea of "nightlife" is hopping from bar to bar with a circle of friends while nibbling tapas and enjoying drinks. The streets are jammed with people. In general, the weekend progression (Thu-Sat) goes like this: dinner at around 22:00; a music club for cocktails and DJ music from midnight; then, at about 2:00 or 3:00 in the morning, hit the discos until dawn. The following neighborhoods let you join in this social ritual.

NIGHTLIFE

El Born

Passeig del Born, a broad parklike strip stretching from the Church of Santa Maria del Mar up to the old market hall, is lined with

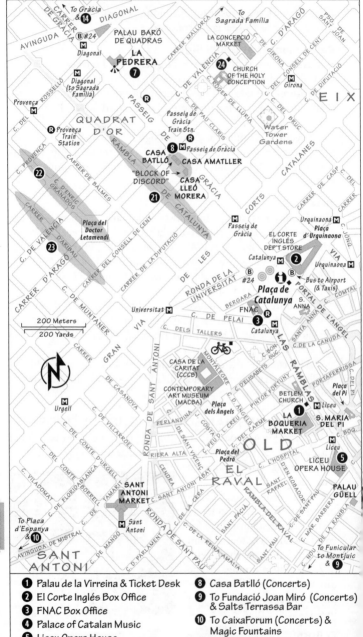

NIGHTLIFE

1 Palau de la Virreina & Ticket Desk
2 El Corte Inglés Box Office
3 FNAC Box Office
4 Palace of Catalan Music
5 Liceu Opera House
6 To L'Auditori
7 La Pedrera (Jazz Concerts)
8 Casa Batlló (Concerts)
9 To Fundació Joan Miró (Concerts) & Salts Terrassa Bar
10 To CaixaForum (Concerts) & Magic Fountains
11 Palau Dalmases
12 Plaça Reial Nightlife
13 Tablao Cordobés

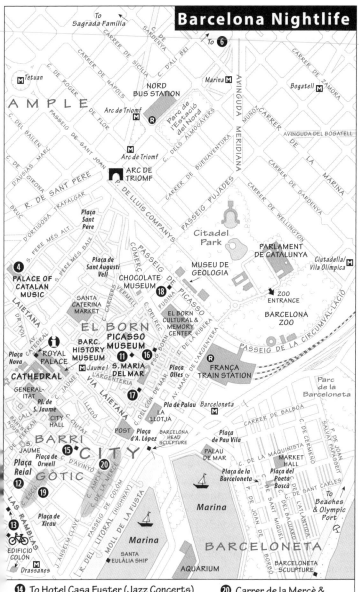

Barcelona Nightlife

To Sagrada Família

To **6**

14 To Hotel Casa Fuster (Jazz Concerts) & Other Gràcia Nightlife

15 Harlem Jazz Club

16 Miramelindo

17 La Vinya del Senyor

18 Aire de Barcelona (Baths)

19 Carrer de Escudellers

20 Carrer de la Mercè & Carrer Ample

21 Rambla de Catalunya

22 Carrer d'Enric Granados

23 Carrer d'Aribau

24 Bar Dow Jones

NIGHTLIFE

inviting bars and nightspots. Wander the side streets for more options.

Right on Passeig del Born is **Miramelindo,** a local favorite—mellow yet convivial, with two floors of woody ambience and a minty aura from all those mojitos the bartenders are mashing up (Passeig del Born 15). **Palau Dalmases,** in the atmospheric courtyard of an old palace, slings cocktails when it's not hosting flamenco shows (described earlier). **La Vinya del Senyor** is a fine place for a glass of high-quality wine on the square in front of the Church of Santa Maria del Mar.

The **Aire de Barcelona** Arab-style thermal baths, across from Citadel Park, are open late and have great style. They are ideal for recovering from a busy day of sightseeing (from €80/person for 1.5 hours, massage also possible; reserve ahead—a week ahead for weeknights, a month ahead for weekends; Paseo Picasso 22, +34 932 204 418, https://beaire.com).

Plaça Reial and Nearby

This elegant-feeling square, just off the Ramblas in the Barri Gòtic, has a trendy charm. It bustles with popular bars and restaurants offering pleasant outdoor tables and inflated prices. Plaça Reial is also home to the **Tarantos** flamenco bar and **Jamboree** and **Harlem** jazz clubs (all described earlier).

While not a great place to eat, this is a fine place to sip a before- or after-dinner drink. **Ocaña,** at #13, has a dilapidated-mod interior, a see-through industrial kitchen that serves up tapas, rickety-chic secondhand tables out on the square, and another cocktail bar downstairs (open nightly, can reserve a table online at www.ocana.cat). Or there's always the student option: Buy a cheap beer from a convenience store (you'll find several just off the square, including a few along Carrer dels Escudellers, just south of Plaça Reial), then grab a free spot on the square, either sitting on one of the few fixed chairs, perched along the rim of the fountain, or simply leaning up against a palm tree.

In addition to the jazz clubs mentioned earlier, you'll find a variety of nightclubs here, including the hip **Sidecar Factory Club** (at #7, often live music, www.sidecar.es).

Wandering the streets near the square leads to other nightlife options. **Carrer de Escudellers** is a significantly rougher scene—a few trendy options are mixed in with several sketchy dives. Much closer to the harbor, **Carrer de la Mercè** (described in the Eating in Barcelona chapter) has its share of salty sailors' pubs and more youthful bars. The next street up, **Carrer Ample,** has a similar scene.

Barceloneta

A broad beach stretches for miles from the former fishermen's quarter at Barceloneta to the Fòrum (see the "Barceloneta & Beaches" map on page 83). Every 100 yards or so is a *chiringuito*—a shack selling drinks and light snacks. Originally these sold seafood, but now they keep locals and tourists well-lubricated. It's a very fun, lively scene on a balmy summer evening and a nice way to escape the claustrophobic confines of the Old City to enjoy some sea air and the day's final sun rays.

Barceloneta itself has a broad promenade facing the harbor, lined with interchangeable seafood restaurants. But the best beach experience is beyond the tip of Barceloneta. From here, a double-decker boardwalk runs the length of the beach, with a cool walkway up above and a series of fine seafood restaurants with romantic candlelit beachfront seating tucked down below. Pricey but well-regarded places featuring high-quality Catalan cuisine are **Agua, Ca la Nuri,** and **Arenal.** Farther along, **Carpe Diem Lounge Club** (a.k.a. CDLC) is a fun Turkish-themed bar with cozy lounging sofas—ideal for a post-dinner drink; later, it becomes an edgier disco.

Around Frank Gehry's glittering fish sculpture (at the former Olympic village) are several popular discos crowded with twentysomethings (including the famous—and exclusive—**Opium Barcelona,** a haunt of Barça footballers and other celebrities). Beyond the beach, at the Olympic port, you'll find more bars with chill-out music (which later turn into livelier discos).

Montjuïc

With a little hustle, in summer it's possible to string together a fun evening of memorable views from the Montjuïc hilltop. For details, see the Montjuïc section on page 67.

Start with sweeping city vistas as you ride the Aeri del Port cable car (catch it at the tip of the Barceloneta peninsula) up to the park's Miramar viewpoint. From there, head up to Montjuïc Castle on foot for more breathtaking views. Finally, wind your way around the hilltop to **Salts Terrassa Bar** (Avinguda Miramar 31), at the diving pool space once used for the 1992 Olympic Games, for sweeping views of the city. Or head down to the **Catalan Art Museum** and reward yourself with a drink at its terrace café—a prime spot for taking in the Magic Fountains show.

NIGHTLIFE

The Eixample

Barcelona's upscale uptown isn't quite as lively or funky as some other neighborhoods, but a few streets have some fine watering holes. Walk along the inviting, parklike **Rambla de Catalunya**, or a couple of blocks over, along **Carrer d'Enric Granados** and **Carrer d'Aribau** (near the epicenter of the Eixample's gay community); all of these streets are speckled with cocktail bars offering breezy outdoor seating. In the opposite direction (east of Passeig de Gràcia), **Bar Dow Jones**—popular with the American expat student crowd—has a clever gimmick: Drink prices rise and fall like the stock market (Carrer del Bruc 97). For locations see the map earlier in this chapter.

Gràcia

A bit farther flung, and more local-feeling because of it, the Gràcia neighborhood sits between the Eixample and Park Güell. Known for its design schools and its international art-house cinema (the Cines Verdi, www.cines-verdi.com/barcelona), it's the unpretentious but intellectual corner of town. Though it lacks the twisty Gothic-lanes ambience of the Old City, Gràcia has the feel of a small town (which it was, before being swallowed up by an expanding Barcelona). It's popular with both local and international students and can be a bit rowdy. The district is even more vibrant in August, when it hosts the Festa Major de Gràcia, with street music everywhere.

The most interesting stretch of Gràcia is squeezed between two Metro stops: Fontana, on the L3 (green) line; and Joanic, on the L4 (yellow) line. Here's a handy bar-crawl route: From the Fontana stop, exit and turn left, heading down the shop-lined Carrer d'Astúries. After crossing the busy Carrer del Torrent de l'Olla, keep going straight two short blocks to **Carrer de Verdi.** You'll find several nightspots up and down this street, and a block over, at **Plaça de la Virreina** (where several places fill the square in front of the church with outdoor tables). From there you can head down Carrer de Torrijos, with more options—including **Café Salambó**, with an Art Deco vibe (at #51). A right turn at Carrer de Ramón y Cajal leads you (in three blocks) to your grand finale, **Plaça del Sol,** the epicenter of Gràcia nightlife.

NIGHTLIFE

BARCELONA CONNECTIONS

This chapter covers Barcelona's airports, main train station, cruise port, and main bus station.

I don't advise driving in Barcelona—thanks to its excellent public transportation and taxis, you won't need a car here, and the parking fees are outrageously expensive.

Connecting with the Rest of Spain—and Beyond: Located in the far northeast corner of Spain, Barcelona makes a good first or last stop for a trip to Spain (or elsewhere in Europe). From the US, it's as easy to fly into Barcelona as it is to land in Madrid, Lisbon, or Paris. Or you could sandwich Barcelona between flights or high-speed rail trips.

Those who plan on renting a car later in their Spain trip can start in Barcelona, take the high-speed train to Madrid (3 hours), sightsee Madrid and Toledo, then pick up a car—cleverly saving on several days' worth of rental fees.

For more on train travel and car rentals in Spain, see the Practicalities chapter.

By Plane

Most flights use the city's primary **Josep Tarradellas Barcelona-El Prat Airport;** a few budget flights use a smaller airstrip 60 miles away, called **Girona–Costa Brava Airport.** Information on both airports can be found on the official Spanish airport website, www.aena.es.

JOSEP TARRADELLAS BARCELONA-EL PRAT AIRPORT

Generally referred to as El Prat, the airport is eight miles southwest of town (code: BCN, www.aena.es). It has two large terminals linked by shuttle buses. Terminal 1 serves Air France, Air Europa, American, British Airways, Delta, Iberia, Lufthansa, United, Vueling, and others. EasyJet, Ryanair, and minor airlines use the older Terminal 2, which is divided into sections A, B, and C.

Terminal 1 and the bigger sections of Terminal 2 (A and B) each have a post box, a pharmacy, plenty of good eateries in the gate areas, and ATMs.

Getting Between El Prat Airport and Downtown

To get downtown cheaply and quickly, take the bus or train (about 30 minutes on either). You can also connect by Metro (more transfers) or taxi (more expensive).

By Bus: At either terminal, follow the yellow and black bus signs to catch the Aerobus (#A1 and #A2, corresponding with Terminals 1 and 2). It makes several stops downtown, including at Plaça de Catalunya and near many of my recommended hotels (returning from downtown, buses leave from in front of El Corte Inglés). Either way it's very easy: Buses depart about every five minutes (runs 24/7, fewer departures after midnight, 30- to 40-minute ride, buy €6.75 ticket at self-service machines or from driver, +34 900 929 692, http://aerobusbarcelona.es).

By Train: The Renfe train (on the "R2 Nord" Rodalies line) leaves from Terminal 2 and involves more walking. Head up the escalators and down the long orange-roofed skybridge to reach the station (2/hour at about :08 and :38 past the hour, 20 minutes to Sants station, 25 minutes to Passeig de Gràcia station—near Plaça de Catalunya; €4.60, purchase from machines at the airport train station). If you're arriving or departing from Terminal 1, you'll need to use the airport shuttle bus to connect with the train station, so allow extra time (10 buses/hour, 7-minute ride between terminals).

Long-term plans call for the Renfe train and eventually the AVE to be extended to Terminal 1. Stay tuned.

By Metro: Given the convenient Aerobus and train options, the Metro doesn't make sense for trips between the airport and downtown. If you do end up on the Metro, here are directions: Take L9 Sud (orange) line from either Terminal 1 or 2 to the Zona Universitària stop, then transfer to the L3 (green) line and ride to a downtown stop (Passeig de Gràcia, Plaça de Catalunya, or Liceu). To reach the airport from downtown via Metro, take line L3 to Zona Universitària, and transfer to line L9 in the direction of Aeroport T1 (runs about every 10 minutes 5:00 until late; 25-30-minute ride). Use the €5.15 *Bitllet Aeroport* ticket or any "Hola BCN!" travel card (other Metro tickets do not cover this trip).

By Taxi: A taxi between the airport and downtown costs

about €40 (including the €4.50 airport supplement). For good service, you can round up to the next euro on the fare—but keep in mind that the Spanish don't generally tip cabbies.

GIRONA–COSTA BRAVA AIRPORT

Some budget airlines use this airport, located 60 miles north of Barcelona near Girona (code: GRO, www.aena.es). If you arrive on a Ryanair flight, you can take a **bus** (#604), run by Ryanair and operated by Sagalés, to the Barcelona Nord bus station (departs airport about 20 minutes after each arriving flight, 1.25 hours, €19.50, +34 902 130 014, www.sagales.com). You can also take a Sagalés bus (#607, about hourly, 30 minutes, €2.75) or a taxi (€25) to the town of Girona, then catch a train to Barcelona (at least hourly, 1.5 hours, €15-20). A taxi between the Girona airport and Barcelona costs at least €130.

CHEAP FLIGHTS

Check the reasonable flights from Barcelona to Sevilla or Madrid (though note that high-speed rail travel to Madrid can be just as fast and, with Avlo trains, cheap as well; see "Train Connections," later in this chapter). **Vueling** is Spain's most popular discount airline (www.vueling.com). Other airlines that fly to Madrid include **Iberia** (www.iberia.com) and **Air Europa** (www.aireuropa.com). For more information on flights within Europe, see the Practicalities chapter.

By Train

Virtually all trains end up at Barcelona's **Sants train station,** west of the Old City. AVE trains from Madrid go only to Sants station.

But many other trains also pass through other stations en route, such as **França station** (between the El Born and Barceloneta neighborhoods), or the downtown **Passeig de Gràcia** or **Plaça de Catalunya** stations (which are also Metro stops—and very close to most of my  recommended hotels). Figure out which stations your train stops at (ask the conductor) and get off at the one most convenient to your hotel.

SANTS TRAIN STATION

Barcelona's big white main train station offers many services. In the large lobby area, you'll find a TI, ATMs, a world of handy shops and eateries, pay WCs, car-rental kiosks, and, in the side concourse, a classy, quiet Sala Club lounge for travelers with first-class reservations. Sants is the only Barcelona station with luggage storage (€6/up to 2 hours, €10/day, daily 7:00-22:00, follow signs to *consigna;* go toward track 14, then exit the main building toward parking lot and go down to level -1).

In the vast main hall is a very long wall of ticket windows. Figure out which one you need before you wait in line (all are labeled in English). Generally, windows 1-5 (on the left) are for local commuter and *media distancia* trains, such as to Sitges; windows 6-7 give information—go here first if you're not sure which window you want; windows 8-19 handle advance tickets for long-distance *(larga distancia)* trains beyond Catalunya; and windows 20-21 sell tickets for long-distance trains leaving today. Take a number and wait for your turn.

Scattered nearby are train-ticket vending machines. The red-and-gray machines sell tickets for local and *media distancia* trains within Catalunya. The purple machines are for national Renfe trains; these machines can also print out reserved tickets if you have a confirmation code. And the orange machines sell local *Rodalies* train tickets. There are usually attendants around the machines to help you.

Getting Downtown: To reach the center of Barcelona, take the Metro or a train. To ride the subway, follow signs for the Metro (red *M*), and hop on the L3 (green) or L5 (blue) line, both of which link to useful points in town. Purchase tickets for the Metro at touch-screen machines near the tracks.

To zip downtown even faster (just 5 minutes), you can take any Rodalies de Catalunya suburban train from track 8 (R1, R3, or R4) to Plaça de Catalunya (departs at least every 10 minutes). Your long-distance Renfe train ticket comes with a complimentary ride on Rodalies, as long as you use it within three hours before or after your Renfe trip. Look for a code on your ticket labeled *Combinat Rodalies* or *Combinado Cercanías.* Go to the orange commuter ticket machines, touch *Combinat Rodalies,* type in your code, and the machine will print your ticket.

TRAIN CONNECTIONS

Unless otherwise noted, all trains listed next depart from Sants station; some trains also stop at other stations more convenient to the downtown tourist zone: França station, Passeig de Gràcia, or Plaça de Catalunya. Figure out if your train stops at these stations (and board there) to save yourself the trip to Sants.

If departing from the downtown Passeig de Gràcia station, where three Metro lines converge with the rail line, you may find the underground tunnels confusing. You can't access the Renfe station directly from some entrances. Use the northern entrances to this station (rather than the southern "Consell de Cent" entrance, which is closest to Plaça de Catalunya).

Train Info: +34 912 320 320, www.renfe.com.

From Barcelona by Train to Madrid: The **AVE** train to Madrid is faster and more comfortable than flying (especially when you consider that you're zipping from downtown to downtown). The train departs at least hourly. The nonstop train is a little more expensive but faster (€130, 2.5 hours) than the train that makes a few stops (€110, 3 hours). Regular reserved AVE tickets can be purchased in advance (often with a discount) at the Renfe website. If you have a rail pass, most trains require paid reservations; see the "Transportation" section of the Practicalities chapter.

Renfe's low-cost high-speed **AVLO** trains offer fares as low as €20 for the Barcelona-Zaragoza-Madrid route. These are a good budget option but come with less leg room and no food service (vending machines only, pay extra for seat reservation and larger suitcases, http://avlorenfe.com).

From Barcelona by Train to: Sitges (departs from both Passeig de Gràcia and Sants, 4/hour, 35 minutes), **Montserrat** (departs from Plaça d'Espanya—not from Sants, 1-2/hour, 1 hour, €25 round-trip, includes cable car or rack train to monastery—see details on page 237), **Figueres** (hourly, 1 hour via AVE or Alvia to Figueres-Vilafant; hourly, 2-3 hours via local trains to Figueres station), **Sevilla** (2/day direct, more with transfer in Madrid, 6-7 hours), **Granada** (5/day via AVE, 1 direct, others transfer in Madrid, 6-8 hours—1.5-hour flight is better), **Córdoba** (4/day direct, 5.5 hours, many more with transfer in Madrid), **Salamanca** (5-6/day, 5-7 hours, change in Madrid from Atocha station to Chamartín or Principe Pio station via Metro or *cercanías* train), **San Sebastián** (2/day direct, 6 hours), **Málaga** (7/day via AVE, 6.5 hours; some with transfer), **Lisbon** (no direct trains—best to fly).

From Barcelona by Train to France: Direct high-speed trains run to **Paris** (2-4/day direct, 7 hours), **Lyon** (2/day, 5 hours, more with change in Perpignan, Narbonne, or Valence), and **Toulouse** (1/day, 3 hours), and there are more connections with transfers.

By Bus

Most buses depart from the Nord bus station at Metro: Arc de Triomf, but confirm when researching schedules (www.barcelonanord. barcelona). Destinations served by Alsa buses (www.alsa.es) include

Madrid and **Madrid's Barajas Airport** (nearly hourly, 8 hours), and **Salamanca** (2 night buses, change in Burgos, 11.5 hours). Moventis Sarfa buses (https://compras.moventis.es) serve many **coastal resorts,** including **Cadaqués** (1-2/day, 3 hours). Reservations are smart for long-distance destinations, especially during the busy summer season.

BUS Garraf leaves from Gran Via de les Corts Catalanes and Plaça d'Espanya in downtown Barcelona to **Sitges** (2/hour, 1 hour, www.busgarraf.cat). One bus departs daily for the **Montserrat** monastery, leaving from Carrer de Viriat near Sants station (1.5 hours, www.autocaresjulia.com, see page 239).

By Cruise Ship

Most cruise ships arrive in Barcelona at the **Moll Adossat/Muelle Adosado** port, about two miles from the bottom of the Ramblas. This port has four modern, airport-like terminals (lettered A through D). From either cruise terminal, it's easy to reach the Ramblas. **Taxis** meet arriving ships outside terminal building exits. To get to the airport, ask for *"tarifa cuatro"*—a €39 flat rate between the airport and the cruise port, all fees included. You can also take a **shuttle bus** to the bottom of the Ramblas, then walk or hop on public transportation to various sights. The return bus to the port leaves from where you were dropped off.

Other Terminals: Two other terminals are far less commonly used: the **World Trade Center,** just off the southern end of the Ramblas (a 10-minute walk from the Columbus Monument), and **Moll de la Costa,** tucked just beneath Montjuïc (ride a shuttle bus to World Trade Center; from there, it's a short walk or taxi ride to the Columbus Monument).

DAY TRIPS FROM BARCELONA

Montserrat • Figueres • Cadaqués • Sitges

Four fine sights are day-trip temptations from Barcelona. Pilgrims with hiking boots head 1.5 hours into the mountains for the most sacred spot in Catalunya: Montserrat. Fans of Surrealism can enjoy a fantasy in Dalí-land by combining a stop at the Dalí Theater-Museum in Figueres (1-2 hours from Barcelona) with a day or two in the classy, often sleepy port-town getaway of Cadaqués (pictured above, an hour from Figueres). Or for a quick escape from the city, head 40 minutes south to the charming and free-spirited beach town of Sitges.

Montserrat

Montserrat—the "serrated mountain"—rockets dramatically up from the valley floor northwest of Barcelona. With its unique rock formations, moun-taintop monastery (also called Montserrat), and spiritual connection with the Catalan people, it's a popular day trip. This has been Catalunya's most im-portant pilgrimage site for a thousand years. Hymns explain how the mountain  was carved by little angels with golden saws. Geologists blame nature at work.

Once upon a time, there was no mountain. A river flowed here, laying down silt that solidified into sedimentary layers of

hard rock. Ten million years ago, the continents shifted, and the land around the rock massif sank, exposing this series of peaks that reach upward to 4,000 feet. Over time, erosion pocked the face with caves and cut vertical grooves near the top, creating the famous serrated look.

The monastery is nestled in the jagged peaks at 2,400 feet, but it seems higher because of the way the rocky massif rises out of nowhere. The air is certainly fresher than in Barcelona. In a quick day trip, you can view the mountain from its base, ride a funicular up to the top of the world, tour the basilica and museum, touch a Black Virgin's orb, hike down to a sacred cave, and listen to Gregorian chants by the world's oldest boys' choir.

Montserrat's monastery is Benedictine, and its 30 monks carry on its spiritual tradition. Since 1025, the slogan *"ora et labora"* ("prayer and work") has pretty much summed up life for a monk here. The Benedictines welcome visitors—both pilgrims and tourists—and offer this travel tip: Please remember that the most important part of your Montserrat visit is not enjoying the architecture but rather discovering the religious, cultural, historical, social, and environmental values fundamental to the Catalan people.

GETTING TO MONTSERRAT

Barcelona is connected to the valley below Montserrat by a convenient **train;** from there, a cable car or rack railway transports you up to the mountaintop. They are similar in cost and travel time, but you have to decide which to take when you buy your ticket in Barcelona—see the "Tickets to Montserrat" sidebar. Altogether, it's about 1.5 hours each way between downtown Barcelona and the monastery.

Other options are **driving** or taking the **bus.**

By Train Plus Cable Car or Rack Railway

Trains to Montserrat leave from Barcelona's Plaça d'Espanya. Take the Metro to Espanya, then follow signs for Montserrat (which show a graphic of a train and the *FGC* symbol—for Ferrocarrils de la Generalitat de Catalunya) through the tunnels to the FGC station. Once there, check the overhead screens or ask for help (staff are usually at the ticket machines) to find the track for train line R5 (direction: Manresa, 1-2/hour—usually at :36 and/or :56).

Hang on to your train ticket; you'll need it to exit the FGC station when you return to Plaça d'Espanya. You'll ride about an hour on the train. For the cable car, get out at the Montserrat-Aeri station; for the rack railway, continue another few minutes to the next station, Monistrol de Montserrat (or simply "Monistrol de M.").

Cable Car or Rack Train? For the sake of scenery and fun, I enjoy the little German-built cable car more than the rack railway. Departures are more frequent (4/hour rather than 1-3/hour on the railway), but because the cable car is small, you may wait a while to get on (up to an hour when crowded). If you dislike heights, take the rack train. If you'd like to try both, buy a one-way ticket to Montserrat including the cable car, and buy the return ticket for the rack railway and train back to Barcelona from the Cremallera station in Montserrat.

Cable Car, from Montserrat-Aeri Station: Departing the train, follow signs to the cable car station (covered by your train or combo-ticket; 4/hour, 5-minute trip, April-mid-Oct daily 9:30-19:00, shorter hours in winter, www.

Tickets to Montserrat

Various combo-tickets cover your journey to Montserrat, as well as some sights there. All begin with the train from Barcelona's Plaça d'Espanya to Montserrat stops that connect to either a cable car or a rack railway—you'll be asked to specify one or the other when you buy your ticket (same round-trip price for either).

The basic option is a **train ticket** to Montserrat (€25 round-trip, includes cable car or rack railway to monastery, find train schedules at www.fgc.cat). Note that if you decide at Montserrat that you want to use the funiculars to go higher up the mountain or to the Sacred Cave, you can buy a €17.85 ticket covering both funiculars at the TI or at either funicular. Two combo-tickets offered by the train company cover transportation and various admissions including the basilica and La Moreneta (€45 **Trans Montserrat** and €65.50 **Tot Montserrat,** www.cremallerademontserrat.cat).

You can get advice about your ticket choice and return schedules in Barcelona at the Plaça d'Espanya train station, where you'll find cable car info booths (daily 9:00-13:30). Then purchase any of these options from a ticket machine—if you need help, ask one of the TI officials standing by in the morning. To use your included round-trip Metro ride to get *to* the station, buy your Montserrat ticket in advance at the Plaça de Catalunya TI. Combo-tickets are also available via the Montserrat TI (www.montserratvisita.com) and the Barcelona TI's online shop (http://bcnshop.barcelonaturisme.com).

---

aeridemontserrat.com). Don't linger on the platform: Make your way to the cable car quickly, as you may have to wait to go up.

On the way back down, cable cars depart from the monastery every 15 minutes; make sure to give yourself enough time to catch a Barcelona-bound train (these leave at :05 and :45 past the hour Mon-Fri, only at :45 Sat-Sun).

Rack Railway (Cremallera), from Monistrol de Montserrat Station: From this station you can catch the Cremallera rack railway up to the monastery (covered by your train or combo-ticket; 1-3/hour, 20-minute trip, www.cremallerademontserrat.cat). On the return trip, trains depart the monastery at :15 past the hour, allowing you to catch the Barcelona-bound train leaving Monistrol de Montserrat at :45 past the hour. The last convenient connection leaves the monastery at 19:15. Confirm the schedule when you arrive. Note that the rack railway has one intermediate stop (Monistrol-Vila, at a large parking garage), but—either coming or going—you want to stay on until the end of the line. There's a good info booth at the Cremallera station (daily 8:00-14:00).

By Car

Once drivers get out of Barcelona (Road A-2, then C-55), it's a short 30-minute drive to the base of the mountain, then a 10-minute series of switchbacks to the actual site (where you can find pay parking). It may be easier to park your car down below and ride the cable car or rack railway up; there's plenty of free parking at the Monistrol-Vila rack railway station (cable car—€8.60 one-way, €13 round-trip; rack railway—€8.10 one-way, €13.50 round-trip, €17.80 version also includes Museum of Montserrat).

DAY TRIPS

By Bus

One bus per day connects downtown Barcelona directly to the monastery at Montserrat (departs from Carrer de Viriat near Barcelona's Sants station daily at 9:15; returns from the monastery to Barcelona at 18:00 June-Sept, at 17:00 Oct-May; €5.10 each way, 1.5 hours, operated by Autocares Julià, https://autocaresjulia.com). Since the other options are scenic, fun, and relatively easy, the only reason to take a bus is to avoid transfers.

Orientation to Montserrat

When you arrive at the base of the mountain, look up the rock face to find the cable car line, the monastery near the top, and the tiny building midway up (marking the Sacred Cave).

However you make your way up to the Montserrat monastery, it's easy to get oriented once you arrive at the top. Everything is within a few minutes' walk of your entry point. All the transit options—including the rack railway and cable car—converge at one big station. Above that are the funicular stations: one up to the ridge top, the other down to the Sacred Cave trail. Across the street is the TI, and above that (either straight up the stairs or up the ramp around the left side) is the main square. To the right of the station, a long road leads along the cliff to the parking lot; a humble farmers market along here sells *mel y mató*, a characteristic Catalan cheese with honey.

Crowd-Beating Tips: Arrive early or late, as tour groups mob the place midday. Crowds are less likely on weekdays and worst on Sundays.

TOURIST INFORMATION

The square below the basilica houses a helpful TI, right across from the rack railway station (daily from 9:00 until just after last train heads down, +34 938 777 701, www.montserratvisita.com). A good audioguide, available only at the TI, describes the general site and basilica (€6.50; €18 includes entrance to museum, bland audiovisual presentation, and book). If you're a hiker, ask for the handout

DAY TRIPS

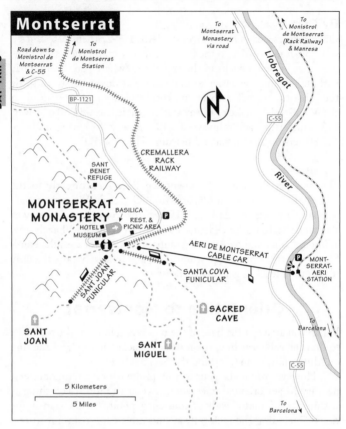

Montserrat

To Montserrat Monastery via road

To Monistrol de Montserrat (Rack Railway) & Manresa

Llobregat

Road down to Monistrol de Montserrat & C-55

To Monistrol de Montserrat Station

BP-1121

C-55

River

CREMALLERA RACK RAILWAY

SANT BENET REFUGE

MONTSERRAT MONASTERY

BASILICA

HOTEL REST. & PICNIC AREA

MUSEUM

AERI DE MONTSERRAT CABLE CAR

MONT-SERRAT-AERI STATION

SANT JOAN FUNICULAR

SANTA COVA FUNICULAR

To Barcelona

SACRED CAVE

SANT JOAN

SANT MIGUEL

C-55

5 Kilometers

5 Miles

To Barcelona

outlining hiking options here. Trails offer spectacular views (on clear days) to the Mediterranean and even (on clearer days) to the Pyrenees.

The audiovisual center (across the street from the TI) provides some cultural and historical perspective. The exhibit—nowhere near as exciting as the mountains and basilica outside—includes a seven-minute video about the mountain's history and the daily lives of the resident monks and a video performance of the Escolania boys choir (€5.50, covered by Trans Montserrat and Tot Montserrat combo-tickets, same hours as TI). La Botiga, the TI's big gift shop, is down the street.

Sights in Montserrat

Montserrat Spin Tour

From the main square in front of the basilica complex, face the main façade and take this spin tour. Like a good pilgrim, face Mary, the high-up centerpiece of the façade. Below her to the left is St.

Benedict, the sixth-century monk who established the rules that came to govern Montserrat's monastery. St. George, the symbol of Catalunya, is on the right (amid victims of Spain's Civil War).

Five arches line the base of the facade. The one on the far right leads pilgrims to the high point of any visit, the Black Virgin (a.k.a. La Moreneta). The center arch leads into the basilica's courtyard, and the arch second from left directs you to a small votive chapel filled with articles representing prayer requests or thanks. Timed tickets are required to enter the basilica and visit La Moreneta; see below.

Now look left of the basilica, where delicate arches mark the 15th-century monks' cloister. The monks have planted four trees here, hoping to harvest only their symbolism (palm = martyrdom, cypress = eternal life, olive = peace, and laurel = victory). Next to the trees are a public library and a peaceful reading room. The big archway is the private entrance to the monastery. Still turning to your left, you'll see the modern hotel and, below that, the glass-fronted museum. Other buildings provide cells for pilgrims. The Sant Joan funicular lifts hikers up to the trailhead (you can see the tiny building at the top). From there you can take a number of fine hikes (described later). Another funicular station descends to the Sacred Cave. And finally, five arches separate statues of founders of the great religious orders. Step over to the arches for a commanding view (on a clear day) of the Llobregat River, meandering all the way to the Mediterranean.

▲▲Basilica

Although there's been a church here since the 11th century, the present structure was built in the 1850s, and the facade dates from 1968. The decor is Neo-Roman-esque, so popular with the Roman-tic artists of the late 19th century. The basilica itself is ringed with interesting chapels, but the focus is on the Black Virgin (La Moreneta) sitting high above the main altar. The monastery began requiring res-ervations and charging admission in 2023 to curb crowding, preserve an atmosphere of prayer, and contrib-ute to the site's upkeep.

Cost and Hours: Basilica—€6, La Moreneta—add €2, must reserve timed-entry ticket online in advance at https://tickets. montserratvisita.com/en; covered by Trans Montserrat and Tot Montserrat tickets; open daily 8:30-18:15.

Visiting the Basilica: Montserrat's top attraction is **La More-**

The History of Montserrat

The first hermit monks built huts at Montserrat around AD 900. By 1025, a monastery was founded. The Montserrat Escolania, or Choir School, soon followed and is considered to be the oldest music school in Europe (they still perform—see "Choir Concert" at the end of "Sights in Montserrat").

Legend has it that in medieval times, some shepherd children saw lights and heard songs coming from the mountain. They traced the sounds to a cave (now called the Sacred Cave, or Santa Cova), where they found the Black Virgin statue (La Moreneta)—making the monastery a pilgrim magnet.

In 1811 Napoleon's invading French troops destroyed Montserrat's buildings, though the Black Virgin, hidden away by monks, survived. Then, in the 1830s, the Spanish royalty—tired of dealing with pesky religious orders—dissolved the monasteries and convents.

But in the 1850s, the monks returned as part of Catalunya's (and Europe's) renewed Romantic appreciation for all things medieval and nationalistic. (Montserrat's revival coincided with the beginning of other institutions born out of rejuvenated Catalan pride: the much-loved FC Barcelona soccer team; Barcelona's Palace of Catalan Music; and even the local sparkling wine, *cava*.) Montserrat's basilica and monastery were reconstructed and became, once more, the strongly beating spiritual and cultural heart of the Catalan people.

Then came Francisco Franco, the dictatorial leader who wanted a monolithic Spain. To him Montserrat represented Catalan rebelliousness. During Franco's long rule, from 1939 to 1975, the *sardana* dance was still illegally performed here (but with a different name), and literature was published in the outlawed Catalan language. In 1970, 300 intellectuals demonstrating for more respect for human rights in Spain were locked up in the monastery for several days by Franco's police.

Once Franco was history, the 1990s brought another phase of rebuilding (after a forest fire and rain damage). The Montserrat community is thriving once again, unafraid to display its pride in the Catalan people, culture, and faith.

neta, the small wood statue of the Black Virgin, discovered in the Sacred Cave in the 12th century. Legend says she was carved by St. Luke (the gospel writer and supposed artist), brought to Spain by St. Peter, hidden away in the cave during the Moorish invasions, and miraculously discovered by shepherd children. (Carbon dating says she's about 800 years old.) "Moreneta" is usually translated as "black" in English, but the Spanish name actually means "tanned." The statue was originally lighter, but it darkened over the centuries from candle smoke, humidity, and the natural aging of its original varnish.

While George is the patron saint of Catalunya, La Moreneta is its patroness, designated as such by the pope in 1881. Pilgrims shuffle down a long, ornate passage leading alongside the church for their few moments alone with the Virgin.

Though Mary is behind a protective glass case, the royal orb she cradles in her hands is exposed. Pilgrims touch Mary's orb with one hand and hold their other hand up to show that they accept Jesus. Newlyweds in particular seek Mary's blessing.

Immediately after La Moreneta, to the right, is the delightful Neo-Romanesque **chapel** where worshippers can sit behind the Virgin and pray. The ceiling, painted in the Modernista style in 1898 by Joan Llimona, shows Jesus and Mary high in heaven. The trail connecting Catalunya with heaven seems to lead through these serrated mountains. The lower figures symbolize Catalan history and culture.

You'll exit by walking along the **Ave Maria Path** (along the outside of the church), which thoughtfully integrates nature and the basilica. Thousands of colorful votive candles are all busy helping the devout with their prayers. Before you leave the inner courtyard and head out into the main square, pop in to the humble little room with the many votive offerings. This is where people leave personal belongings (wedding dresses, baby's baptism outfits, wax replicas of body parts in need of healing, and so on) as part of a prayer request or as thanks for divine intercession.

Museum of Montserrat

This bright, shiny, and cool collection of paintings and artifacts was mostly donated by devout Catalan Catholics. While it's nothing earth-shaking, you'll enjoy an air-conditioned wander past lots of antiquities and fine artwork. Head upstairs first to see some lesser-known works by the likes of Picasso, Caravaggio, Monet, Renoir, Pissarro, Degas, and local Modernista artists (Ramón Casas, Santiago Rusiñol, Isidro Nonell, and Joaquim Mir). One gallery shows how artists have depicted the Black Virgin of Montserrat over the centuries in many different styles. Down on the main floor, you'll see ecclesiastical gear, a good icon collection, and more paintings, including—at the very end—works by Dalí and a few Picasso sketches and prints.

Cost and Hours: €8, covered by Tot Montserrat combo-ticket, daily 10:00-18:15, +34 938 777 745.

▲Sant Joan Funicular and Hikes

This funicular climbs 820 feet above the monastery in five minutes. At the top of the funicular, you are at the starting point of a 20-minute walk that takes you to the Sant Joan Chapel (follow sign for *Ermita de St. Joan*). Other hikes also begin at the trailhead by the funicular (get details from TI before you ascend; basic map

DAY TRIPS

with suggested hikes posted by upper funicular station). For a quick and easy chance to get out into nature and away from the crowds, simply ride up and follow the most popular hike— a 45-minute, mostly downhill loop through mountain scenery back to the monastery. To take  this route, go left from the funicular station; the trail—marked *Monestir de Montserrat*—will first go up to a rocky crest before heading downhill.

Cost and Hours: €9.75 one-way funicular ride, €15 round-trip, €17.85 combo round-trip for both Sant Joan and Santa Cova, covered by Trans Montserrat and Tot Montserrat combo-tickets, goes every 20 minutes, more often with demand.

Sacred Cave (Santa Cova)

The statue known as La Moreneta was originally discovered in the Sacred Cave (or Sacred Grotto), a 40-minute hike down from the monastery (then another 50 minutes back up). The path (c. 1900) was designed by devoted and patriotic Modernista architects, including Gaudí and Josep Puig i Cadafalch. It's lined with Modernista statues depicting scenes corresponding to the Mysteries of the Rosary—a set of prayers that reflect on the life and death of Jesus. While the original Black Virgin statue is now in the basilica, a replica sits in the cave. A three-minute funicular ride cuts 20 minutes off the hike. (The funicular may be closed for repairs— check locally.) If you're here late in the afternoon, check the schedule before you head into the Sacred Cave to make sure you don't miss the final ride back down the mountain. Missing the last funicular could mean catching a train back to Barcelona later than you had planned.

Cost and Hours: €3.90 one-way funicular ride, €6 round-trip, €17.85 combo round-trip for both Sant Joan and Santa Cova, covered by Trans Montserrat and Tot Montserrat combo-tickets, goes every 20 minutes, more often with demand.

Choir Concert

Montserrat's Escolania, or Choir School, has been training voices for centuries. Fifty young boys, who live and study in the monastery itself, make up the choir. The boys sing for only 10 minutes, the basilica is jam-packed, and it's likely you'll see almost nothing.

Cost and Hours: €8, reservation required, generally Mon-Fri at 13:00, choir on vacation late June-late Aug, check schedule and reserve at https://tickets.montserratvisita.com/en/.

Sleeping and Eating in Montserrat

An overnight here gets you monastic peace and a total break from the modern crowds. There are ample rustic cells for pilgrim visitors, but tourists might prefer **$$ Hotel Abat Cisneros.** This three-star hotel with 82 rooms and all the comforts is low-key and appropriate for a sanctuary (half- and full-board available, elevator, +34 938 777 701, www.montserratvisita.com, reserves@larsa-montserrat. com).

Montserrat is designed to feed hordes of pilgrims and tourists. You'll find a cafeteria along the main street (across from the train station) and a grocery store and bar with simple sandwiches where the road curves on its way up to the hotel. In the other direction, follow the covered walkway below the basilica to reach the Mirador dels Apòstols, with a bar, cafeteria, restaurant, and picnic area. The Hotel Abat Cisneros also has a restaurant, and the Montserrat-Aeri train station has a ramshackle but charming family-run bar with outdoor tables, simple food, and views of the mountain and the cable cars. The best option is to pack a picnic from Barcelona, especially if you plan to hike.

Figueres

The town of Figueres (feeg-YEHR-ehs)—conveniently connected by train to Barcelona—is of sightseeing interest mainly for its Dalí Theater-Museum. In fact, the entire town seems Dalí dominated. But don't be surprised if you also see bargain-hunting French shoppers. Some of the cheapest shops in Spain—called *ventas*—are here to lure French visitors.

GETTING TO FIGUERES

Figueres is an easy day trip from Barcelona or a handy stopover en route to France. It has two train stations on opposite sides of town: **Figueres-Vilafant** (served by the high-speed train from Barcelona's Sants station, about hourly, 1 hour, buy in advance) and **Figueres** (served by the less expensive but slower regional train; departs from Barcelona's Sants station or from the Renfe station at Metro: Passeig de Gràcia; hourly, 2.5-3 hours; slightly more expensive *media distancia* trains take closer to 2 hours). If you're on your way to Paris, it's possible to take the high-speed train from Barcelona in the morning, visit the Dalí Theater-Museum, and catch the late-afternoon TGV train (also called "InOui") to Paris. Neither train station has baggage storage, but the bus station (across from

DAY TRIPS

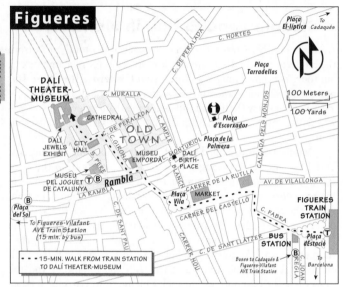

Figueres station) and the Dalí Theater-Museum do. For bus connections to Cadaqués, see "Getting to Cadaqués," later.

Orientation to Figueres

You'll find the town's museums and sights clustered within a couple of blocks of one another—the Rambla shopping street, church, City Hall, toy museum (Museu del Joguet), and Catalan art museum (Museu Empordà)—as well as the only sight that matters for most visitors: the Dalí Theater-Museum.

Tourist Information: The TI is at Plaça de l'Escorxador 2 (Mon-Sat 9:30-18:00, Sun 10:00-15:00, +34 972 503 155, www. visitfigueres.cat). An info desk sometimes opens at the Figueres TGV train station.

Arrival in Figueres: The most important sights are all clearly marked with red directional signs.

To reach the Dalí museum from **Figueres-Vilafant station,** take the Teisa bus in front. Don't delay—buses depart only with the arrival of each train (€1.85, buy ticket from driver, cash only). Get off at the Plaça del Sol stop—ask the driver for map with timetable to plan out your return. From there, it's a five-minute walk uphill to the museum. Taxis charge about €12 to and from the station. If you miss the bus, plan to take a taxi or make the 20-minute walk.

To get to the museum from **Figueres station,** simply follow *Museu Dalí* signs (and the crowds) for the 15-minute walk to the museum. See the map in this section for a suggested route.

Sights in Figueres

DALÍ THEATER-MUSEUM

This ▲▲▲ museum is *the* essential Dalí sight—and, if you like his work, one of Europe's most enjoyable museums, period. Inaugurated in 1974, the Dalí Theater-Museum (Teatre-Musei Dalí) is a work of art in itself. Ever the entertainer and promoter, Dalí personally conceptualized, designed, decorated, and painted it to showcase his life's work. The museum fills a former

theater and contains the artist's mausoleum (his tomb is in the crypt below center stage). It's also a kind of mausoleum to Dalí's creative spirit.

Dalí had his first public art showing at age 14 here in this building when it was a theater, and he was baptized in the church just across the street. He felt sentimental about the place. After the theater was destroyed in the Spanish Civil War (along with most of Figueres— the town was the last Republican stronghold before France), Dalí struck a deal with the mayor:

Dalí would rebuild the theater as a museum to his works, Figueres would be put on the sightseeing map...and the money's been flowing in ever since.

Dalí worked here over many years and personally designed the core of the museum (Rooms 1 through 18). Even the building's exterior—painted pink, studded with golden loaves of bread, and topped with monumental eggs and a geodesic dome—exudes the artist's outrageous public persona. The Dalí Theater-Museum is called the largest Surrealist object in the world.

Cost: €17 (€3 more July-Aug); purchase a timed-entry ticket online in advance. Your ticket includes free entry to the nearby Museu de L'Empordà (Catalan paintings) and discounted entry to the Museu del Joguet de Catalunya (toys).

Hours: July-Aug daily 9:00-20:00; Sept-June Tue-Sun 10:30-18:00, occasionally open Mon—call or confirm online; last entry 45 minutes before closing, +34 972 677 500, www.salvador-dali.org.

Salvador Dalí (1904-1989)

When Salvador Dalí was asked, "Are you on drugs?" he replied, "I am the drug...take me."

Labeled by various critics as sick, greedy, paranoid, arrogant, and a clown, Dalí produced some of the most thought-provoking and trailblazing art of the 20th century. His erotic, violent, disjointed imagery continues to disturb and intrigue to this day.

Born in Figueres to a well-off family, Dalí showed talent early. He was expelled from Madrid's prestigious art school—twice—but formed longtime friendships with playwright and poet Federico García Lorca and filmmaker Luis Buñuel.

After a breakthrough art exhibit in Barcelona in 1925, Dalí moved to Paris. He hobnobbed with fellow Spaniards Pablo Picasso and Joan Miró, along with a group of artists exploring Sigmund Freud's theory that we all have a hidden part of our mind, the unconscious "id," which surfaces when we dream. Dalí became the best-known spokesman for this group of Surrealists, channeling his id to create photorealistic dream images (melting watches, burning giraffes) set in bizarre dreamscapes.

His life changed forever in 1929, when he met an older, married Russian woman named Gala who would become his wife, muse, model, manager, and emotional compass. Dalí's popularity spread to the US, where he (and Gala) weathered the WWII years.

Reservations Recommended: It's important to reserve ahead online for this museum, which can be a mob scene, especially when bad weather drives beach crowds here (they let in no more than 200 people each half-hour). You can make a reservation online as little as two hours in advance—or check the board in front of the ticket window for last-minute availability (you'll pay €1 more) if you arrive *sans* reservation. It may be possible to change your entry time if you arrive ahead of schedule.

Bag Check: The free bag check will have your belongings waiting for you at the exit. It's OK to leave checked backpacks and small suitcases here while you browse the town.

Sightseeing Tip: Much of Dalí's art is movable and coin-operated—bring a few €0.20 and €1 coins and keep an eye out for the machines where you insert them. It's fun to gather other museumgoers in a group to experience these animated works together.

In the prime of his career, Dalí's work became less Surrealist and more classical, influenced by past masters of painted realism (Velázquez, Raphael, Ingres, Vermeer) and by his own study of history, science, and religion. He produced large-scale paintings of historical events (e.g., Columbus discovering America, the Last Supper) that were collages of realistic scenes floating in a surrealistic landscape, peppered with thought-provoking symbols.

Dalí—an extremely capable technician—mastered many media, including film. *An Andalusian Dog* (*Un Chien Andalou*, 1929, with Luis Buñuel) was a cutting-edge montage of disturbing, eyeball-slicing images. He designed Alfred Hitchcock's big-eye backdrop for the dream sequence of *Spellbound* (1945). He made jewels for the rich and clothes for Coco Chanel, wrote a novel and an autobiography, and pioneered what would come to be called "installations." He also helped develop "performance art" by showing up at an opening in a diver's suit or by playing the role he projected to the media—a super-confident, waxed-mustached artistic genius.

In later years, Dalí's over-the-top public image contrasted with his ever-growing illness, depression, and isolation. He endured the scandal of a dealer overselling "limited editions" of his work. When Gala died in 1982, Dalí retreated to his hometown, living his last days in the Torre Galatea of the Theater-Museum complex, where he died of heart failure.

Dalí's legacy as an artist includes his self-marketing persona, his exceptional ability to draw, his provocative pairing of symbols, and his sheer creative drive.

Background

Dalí's art can be playful but also disturbing. He was passionate about the dark side of things, but with his wife, Gala, for balance, he managed never to go off the deep end. Unlike Pablo Casals (the Catalan cellist) and Pablo Picasso (another local artist), Dalí didn't go into exile under Franco's dictatorship. Pragmatically, he accepted both Franco and the Church, and was supported by the dictator. Apart from the occasional *sardana* dance, you won't find a hint of politics in Dalí's art.

You could spend hours here, wandering around and wondering: Is it real or not real? Am I crazy, or is it you? Beethoven is painted with squid ink applied by a shoe on a stormy night. Jesus is made with candle smoke and an eraser. It's fun to see the Dalí-ization of art classics. Dalí, like so many modern artists, was inspired by the masters—especially Velázquez.

❷ Self-Guided Tour

The museum has two parts—the theater-mausoleum and the "Dalí's Jewels" exhibit in an adjacent building. There's no logical order for a visit (that would be un-Surrealistic). Naturally, there's no audioguide (but there is a good museum book for sale and a free map available at the entrance). Dalí said there are two kinds of visitors: those who don't need a description, and those who aren't worth a description. At the risk of offending Dalí, I've written this loose commentary to attach some meaning to your visit.

Courtyard (Ground Floor): Step into the courtyard (with its audience of golden statues) and face the stage (visible through the window wall). You know how you can never get a cab when it's raining? Pop a coin into Dalí's personal 1941 Cadillac and it rains inside the car. Look above, atop the tire tower: That's the boat Dalí enjoyed with his soulmate, Gala—his emotional life preserver, who kept him from going overboard. When she

died, so did he (for his last seven years). Blue tears made of condoms drip below the boat.

Stage/Cupola (Ground Floor): Now cross through the courtyard and go up to the stage. On the left wall, squint at the big digital Abraham Lincoln, and president #16 comes into focus. Approach the painting to find that Abe's facial cheeks are Gala's butt cheeks—or use the coin-operated telescope (at the far end) or your phone's camera to focus on his face.

Treasures Room (Ground Floor): Under Lincoln, a door leads to the **Treasures Room** (Room 4), with the best collection of original Dalí oil paintings in the museum. (Many of the artworks displayed elsewhere in the building are prints.) You'll see Cubist visions of Cadaqués and dreamy portraits of Gala. One portrays her half-nude, as if her arms are a woven basket supporting her exposed breast like a crust of bread. Dalí said, "She has become my basket of bread." In the tiny-but-powerful *Specter of Sex Appeal*, crutches—a recurring Dalí theme—also represent Gala, who kept him supported whenever a meltdown threatened.

Downstairs Crypt (Lower Level): Make your way downstairs, below the stage, and pay respect at the artist's crypt, within dimly lit rooms filled with golden sculptures. True to the irreverent spirit of Dalí, the public toilets are right next to his tomb.

Mae West Room (First Floor): Back upstairs and to the right (as you face the stage), head into the famous Mae West Room (Room 11), a tribute to the sultry seductress. Dalí loved her attitude. Saying things like, "Why marry and make one man unhappy, when you can stay single and make so many so happy?" Mae West was to conventional morality what Dalí was to conventional art. Climb the stairs to the vantage point where the

sofa lips, fireplace nostrils, painting eyes, and drapery hair come together to make the face of Mae West.

If you side-trip up to the second and third floors from here, you can visit Rooms 12-14, where you'll find numbered prints from various book illustrations Dalí did and his private collection of works by other artists who inspired him.

Smoking Lounge (First Floor): Circle around to Room 15, with purple walls, labeled "Palace of the Wind" (just above the entrance). Formerly the

theater's smoking lounge, it displays portraits of Gala and Dalí bookending a Roman candle of creativity. The fascinating ceiling painting shows the feet of Gala and Dalí as they bridge the earth and the heavens. Dalí's drawers are wide open and empty, indicating that he gave everything to his art. It was in this hall that the young Dalí first exhibited his art to the public.

Final Section (First Floor): Circle clockwise around the theater and take a good look at the stage once more, then go through the Bramante's Temple Room, followed by several more exhibits in Rooms 19 to 22. You'll be routed back downstairs and through the gift shop.

Nearby: As you leave the theater through the turnstile gate, hook right around the corner to pop into the adjacent, not-to-be-missed Dalí's Jewels exhibit (*Dalí-Joies,* covered by your theater ticket). It shows sketches and paintings of jewelry Dalí designed, and the actual pieces jewelers made from those surreal visions: a mouth full of pearly whites, a golden finger corset, a fountain of diamonds, and the breathing heart. Explore the ambiguous perception worked into the big painting titled *Apotheosis of the Dollar.* The upstairs section includes the exquisite, jeweled creation titled *Chalice of Life.*

DAY TRIPS

OTHER SIGHTS IN TOWN

While everything else in Figueres pales compared to the Dalí The-ater-Museum, you're right in the heart of town, near a few enjoy-able sights and countless eateries. (Remember, you can check your bag at the Dalí museum and pick it up later.)

A few blocks downhill from the museum, you'll hit the **Ram-bla,** Figueres' grand boulevard, with the **Museu Empordà** (19th-and 20th-century Catalan paintings, free with Dalí ticket, gener-ally open Tue-Sun 10:00-19:00, closed Mon year-round, at Rambla 2). The nearby **Museu del Joguet de Catalunya**—a toy museum—offers a delightful trip back to Grandpa's Catalan childhood with three floors of old playthings (€7, discounted with Dalí ticket, generally Tue-Sat 10:00-18:00, closed Sun-Mon, audioguide-€1, Carrer Sant Pere 1).

Cadaqués

Since the late 1800s, Cadaqués (kah-dah-KEHS) has served as a haven for intellectuals and artists alike. The fishing village's craggy coastline, sun-drenched colors, and laid-back lifestyle inspired Fauvists such as Henri Matisse and Surrealists such as René Magritte, Marcel Duchamp, and Federico García Lorca. Even Picasso, drawn to this en-chanting coastal haunt, painted some of his Cubist works here.

Salvador Dalí, raised in nearby Figueres, brought international fame to this sleepy Catalan port. As a kid Dalí spent summers here in the family cabin, where he was inspired by the rocky landscape that would later be the backdrop for many Surrealist canvases. In 1929, he met his future wife, Gala, in Cadaqués. Together they converted a fisherman's home in nearby Port Lligat into their semipermanent residence, dividing their time between New York, Paris, and Cadaqués. It was here that Dalí did his best work.

In spite of its fame, Cadaqués is mellow and feels off the beaten path. At the easternmost tip of Spain, it's remote, with no train service and only a tiny access road that dead-ends, making it less developed than it might otherwise be. If you want a peaceful beach-town escape near Barcelona, this is it. From the moment you descend into the town, taking in whitewashed buildings and deep blue waters, you'll be struck by the port's tranquility and beauty.

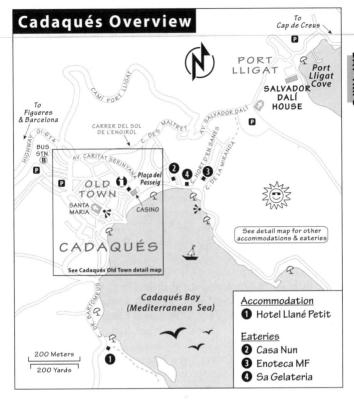

Join the locals playing chess or cards at the cavernous harborfront Casino Coffee House. Have a glass of *vino tinto* or *cremat* (a traditional rum-and-coffee drink served flambé-style) at one of the seaside cafés. Savor the lapping waves, brilliant sun, and gentle breeze.

The Salvador Dalí House at Port Lligat, a 20-minute walk from the Cadaqués town center, is the main sightseeing attraction (reservations required). And at the gateway to Cadaqués, you'll see a Statue of Liberty with both arms raised, based on a Dalí drawing inspired by his visit to New York City. He thought, "Why not two?"

GETTING TO CADAQUÉS

Reaching Cadaqués is very tough without a car. There are no trains and only a few buses a day. A taxi from Figueres is another option.

By Car: Cadaqués is about an hour's drive from Figueres. The road is flat at first, then twists dramatically over a desolate mountain range (with sweeping views over town). As only one small road goes in and out of Cadaqués, you will likely run into traffic during the summer months.

To visit the town center, park in the big lot just above the city—don't try to park near the harborfront. The handiest free parking is on Riera de Sant Vicenç, the long, generally dry riverbed that flows through the center of town (but steer clear on Monday when the town market happens here).

To drive to the Salvador Dalí House, carefully track *Port Lligat* signs at the big, elongated roundabout as you enter Cadaqués (as you approach from Figueres, you'll loop all the way around the roundabout and exit at its top corner—near where you entered). A big parking lot is just past the Salvador Dalí House, an easy five-minute walk along a gravel beach.

By Bus: Moventis Sarfa buses serve Cadaqués from **Figueres** (4/day weekdays, 2/day weekends, 1 hour) and from **Barcelona** (1-2/day, 3 hours). You can buy tickets in Barcelona at the TI on Plaça de Catalunya. Bus info: +34 972 258 713 (Cadaqués), https://compras.moventis.es. On busy summer days, it's wise to buy your ticket in advance.

By Taxi: A one-way taxi from Figueres costs about €75. It's just a little more for a round-trip—including the drive to Port Lligat and a couple of hours' wait. You can arrange a ride over the phone in advance (+34 972 505 043; good Spanish skills help—or ask your hotelier), or in person at the taxi stand on the Rambla in Figueres (from the Dalí Theater-Museum, walk down Carrer Sant Pere to the Rambla). Driver Josep María has an official taxi-and-van service and offers the same rates (book in advance, +34 696 906 476).

Orientation to Cadaqués

TOURIST INFORMATION

The TI is near the waterfront at Carrer Cotxe 2 (July-mid-Sept Mon-Sat 9:00-21:00, shorter hours Sun and off-season plus closed for lunch, +34 972 258 315, www.visitcadaques.org).

HELPFUL HINTS

Electric Golf Carts and Bikes: EcoCar has a handful of electric golf carts and drivers that can take you around, including to the Dalí House in Port Lligat (€4/person) and to the spectacular clifftop views at Cap de Creus (€8/person). They also rent carts and electric bikes by the hour, half-day, or day (cash only, arrange in advance, Avinguda Caritat Serinyana 10, +34 618 883 656, www.ecocarcadaques.com, Diego speaks English).

Local Guide: Simply a delight to be with, **Mercè Donat** organizes tours in and around Cadaqués. Mercè knows everyone and loves to show off her town. For €90, she's all yours for a two-hour town walk. She also does tours with her car (up to

4 people, €150/half-day, €250/day) and can tailor a "Discover Dalí" day (+34 686 492 369, www.rutescadaques.com).

Tourist Train: The tourist train goes around town and to Port Lligat and back, with recorded narration and a few photo stops—including the Dalí House (€11, usually departs at 11:00 and on the hour 15:00-18:00, 1 hour). It also does a loop to the lighthouse at Cap de Creus, where you can enjoy the views for about 20 minutes before returning to Cadaqués (€17, departs at 12:00, 2 hours; for either tour, purchase tickets at the booth in the square just below the casino, +34 653 829 442, www.estrenetdecadaques.cat).

Taxis: There are only two taxis in Cadaqués. Schedule in advance if you need a ride. Pepe speaks just enough English (+34 606 067 015).

Market Day: If you're here on a Monday, be sure to stroll through the sprawling market that fills the paved riverbed through the center of town (Riera de Sant Vicenç) from 8:00 until 14:00.

DAY TRIPS

Cadaqués Walk

Cadaqués has no really important "sights" other than the Dalí House. But the old town is remarkably interesting and easy to miss. Here's a quick eight-point walk. Having strolled this, you can better relax along the harbor knowing you've "done" Cadaqués.

Dalí Statue on Beach: Start near the statue of Salvador Dalí. The artist called Cadaqués home (he lived a 20-minute walk away in the 1920s and 1930s). He did his best work here and put this small town on the map. From the Dalí statue, walk down to the water's edge and survey the harbor. Looking inland, you can see the Hotel La Residencia. This was the only hotel in town when Dalí arrived, and it remains a kind of time warp.

• *Notice the street that runs below grade, beneath a short bridge that's nearly at the water's edge.*

Riverbed Street: This street, just in front of the casino building, really is a paved and usually dry riverbed. A couple of times each year, after big rains, this big drain becomes a raging river, saving the city from flash floods—which washed out several earlier bridges. Old-timers remember previous bridges on this spot, which separates the old town from the new. Traditionally, the bridge was where people hung out on benches, but the new bridge is too narrow to host loungers. Now people make do with the wide windowsills of the casino.

• *Walk over to the casino entrance.*

Casino: This place feels like the timeless clubhouse of the town, where the old boys gather to play cards and pool. Wander

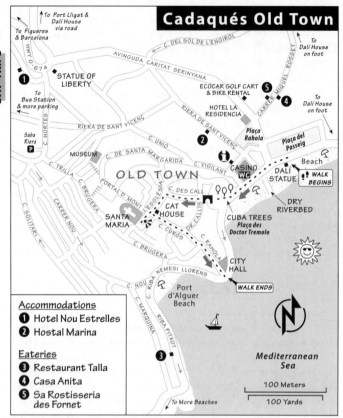

Cadaqués Old Town

To Port Lligat &
Dalí House
via road

To Figueres
& Barcelona

C. DEL SOL DE L'ENGIROL

AVINGUDA CARITAT SERINYANA

To
Dalí House
on foot

HWY. GI-674

1 STATUE OF LIBERTY

ECOCAR GOLF CART & BIKE RENTAL **5**

4

To
Dalí House
on foot

To
Bus Station
& more parking

HOTEL LA RESIDENCIA

RIERA DE SANT VICENÇ

Plaça Rahola

Plaça del Passeig

Saba Riera **P**

C. HORTES

RIERA DE SANT VICENÇ

C. UNIÓ

2

Beach

MUSEUM

C. DE SANTA MARGARIDA

C. VIGILANT

CASINO WC

DALÍ STATUE

WALK BEGINS

C. TRILLA

C. BRUGERA

PORTAL D. MONT

OLD TOWN

C. DES CALL

CAT HOUSE

DRY RIVERBED

CARRER NOU

C. SOLITARI

C. ESGLESIA

SANTA MARIA

C. CUROS

DR. CALLIS

C. RAHOLA

CUBA TREES
Plaça des Doctor Tremolo

C. BRUGERA

C. NOU

NEMESI LLORENS

CITY HALL

C. RIBA

Port d'Alguer Beach

WALK ENDS

C. MARQUINA

RIBA PITXOT

Mediterranean Sea

Accommodations
1 Hotel Nou Estrelles
2 Hostal Marina

Eateries
3 Restaurant Talla
4 Casa Anita
5 Sa Rostisseria des Fornet

3

100 Meters

100 Yards

To More Beaches

inside. There's a public WC next to the pool table. Enjoy the old photos on the walls.

• *Just past the casino is a small park with three...*

Cuba Trees: These stubby "elephant trees" were imported by locals who left Cuba when it won its independence from Spain in 1897. These trees are a reminder that lots of Catalans moved to Cuba in the 19th century and came back home when Spanish rule ended. Just uphill from the top tree are bits of the beloved (and well-used) old bridge benches. From here, try to imagine when Cadaqués was a small walled town filling the bluff above you.

• *Climb uphill to the right, through the archway above, into the...*

Old Town and Jewish Quarter: Stepping through the main gate, you enter a different world. Climb up Carrer des Call, the old Jewish street. There was a strong Jewish community in Spain from the first century until 1492. That's when Christian fanaticism (gone wild with the final Reconquista victory) led to the expulsion of Jews

and Muslims from Catholic Spain. Notice the characteristic slate
~~pavers underfoot.~~

• *Keep climbing until the T-intersection. There, at the top, turn left to
the church.*

Church of Santa Maria: Enjoy the commanding view from
in front of the church (generally open daily 10:00-13:00 & 16:00-
20:00). This spot marks the high point of the old town. If the
church is open, step inside to enjoy its amazing Baroque altar from
the 1700s. Pop a euro into the light box to appreciate this treasure
(and support the church). Carved from pine wood with 365 figures,
it's covered with gold from the Americas. Peter (with the keys) and
Paul (with his trusty sword) are actually part of the doors that lead
into the sacristy. Fishermen paid for this altar—as you're reminded
by the two guys in red and green, dressed as fishermen would have
been in the mid-1700s. Treasures like this throughout Spain survived until the rampant destruction of churches during the civil
war in the 1930s. This altar exists today because industrious locals
built a protective wall in front of it all the way to the ceiling.

• *From the church, walk steeply down Carrer Curós. But first, on the left,
notice the Cat House, a one-woman mission to care for the town's homeless cats. (She lives here with 20 cats and one dog.)*

Carrer Curós, or Gallery Street: This characteristic lane is
lined with art galleries. Near the lower end, local painters show off
by painting the covers on electrical panels.

• *The street bottoms out at City Hall (on the left) and a small terrace
overlooking the harbor.*

City Hall: You're at the Casa de la Vila, or City Hall. The
top of the old city wall here now serves as a balustrade for a view
terrace, and it's a delightful spot to look out for pirates. The last
Barbary pirate raid (from North Africa) was in 1828. You should
be safe.

Sights near Cadaqués

SALVADOR DALÍ HOUSE AND GARDEN

Once Dalí's home and worth ▲▲▲, this house (Casa Salvador
Dalí) in Port Lligat gives fans a chance to explore a labyrinthine
compound. This is the best artist's house I've toured in Europe. It
shows how a home can really reflect the creative spirit of an artistic
genius and his muse. The ambience, both inside and out, is perfect for a Surrealist hanging out with his creative playmate. The
bay is ringed by sleepy islands. Fishing boats are jumbled on the
beach. After the fishermen painted their boats, Dalí asked them to
clean their brushes on his door—creating an abstract work of art he
adored (which you'll see as you line up to get your ticket).

Cost and Hours: House—€15, garden only—€8 (€3 more

July-Aug); mid-June–mid-Sept daily 9:30-20:30; rest of year Tue-Sun 10:30-18:00, often closed Mon—see website. Last tour departs 50 minutes before closing. No bags are allowed in the house; the baggage check is free.

Reservations Required: You must have reservations to visit the house (+34 972 251 015, www.salvador-dali.org). In summer, book at least a few weeks ahead. You must arrive 30 minutes early to pick up your ticket, or they'll re-sell it. Really! For a full visit, see the home (with a timed entry and escorted tour) followed by the garden.

No Reservation? Those without a ticket to the home can easily get a garden ticket and see all the exteriors (including the pool).

Getting There: Parking is free nearby. There is no public bus service to the house, but from Cadaqués you can arrange a ride to and from in an **EcoCar** (see "Helpful Hints," earlier). If arriving by taxi, ask to be dropped in Port Lligat instead of the Cadaqués town center. On foot, the house is a 20-minute, one-mile walk over the hill from Cadaqués to Port Lligat. (The path, which cuts across the isthmus, is straight up and over. It's much shorter than the road.) Follow signs to *Casa S. Dalí.*

Visiting the House

Across from the entry is a wooden boat with a tree growing through it, symbolically connecting earth and sky with the fishermen's culture. A few small-time fishermen still work out of this bay and sell their catch at the pier each morning. (You'll find lockers near the boat.)

Only eight people are allowed inside every 10 minutes. A guide will escort you through the house and give you a brief explanation before turning you loose for a few minutes. (As the content shared is light, talk with your guide for more info.) The entire visit takes 50 minutes. Before or after your tour, enjoy the video that plays in the waiting lounge—with walls covered in Dalí media coverage—just across the lane from the house.

The **house's interior** is left almost precisely as it was in 1982, when Gala died and Dalí moved out—never to return. (He died in 1989.) You'll see Dalí's studio (the clever easel cranks up and down to allow the artist to paint while seated, as he did eight hours a day); the bohemian yet divine living room (complete with a mirror to reflect the sunrise onto their bed each morning); and the painter's study. Like Dalí's art, his home is offbeat, provocative, and fun.

Visiting the Garden

While you'll get a guided tour of Dalí's home, you're on your own in his playful garden—which is where your house tour ends. It's a one-way circle (following numbered signs, 14-20). Here's what to look for:

Dalí's **patio** is where you can enjoy a little playful Dalí hide-and-seek, with crickets in cages, a horseshoe-shaped, slate dining table, and cool corridors leading to the olive garden out back. Enter the **"egg terrace"** to the right (#15, the egg symbolizes fertility), protected from the steady wind. Above, in a niche, is a **sink**—a reminder of Dalí's belief (or joke) that to gain salvation you must be clean. He was ambiguous about his religion. From a platform, you'll view *Christ of the Rubbish*, a huge **statue** (#17) that sprawls on the ground, created from collected junk.

In the **olive grove** (#18), relax on Dalí's six-legged chairs ("they never fall"). And then enjoy a commanding view of the bay, including an island where hippies slept back in the 1960s. At the top of the garden is a theater with video documentaries (rarely with English subtitles).

Descend through Dalí's **"historic garden,"** noting that he preserved this oasis to honor the hard labor and time it took to create. At a little patio you reach a broken eggshell sculpture (symbolizing how Dalí and Gala were "hatched")—climb in for some photo fun.

Now it's party time, and you're poolside. Dalí's penis-shaped **pool** (#20) is surrounded by stylish kitsch (Mae West lips sofa, fountain with cheap Spanish sherry bottles)—decor as eclectic as his circle of friends. Imagine the parties. Dalí hosted lots of hedonism but would himself only observe. That's why Gala had many lovers, and he accepted it. Just beyond the head of the "penis" is the old pre-electric lamp from the lighthouse at Cap de Creus.

Your exit was Dalí's **entry.** Dalí had a national phone booth placed here for the convenience (and expense) of friends who needed to make a call. Notice the white sculpture of a warrior with a small child (see the two little feet) emerging from it. The message: Leave your warrior outside and let your inner child enter.

NEAR CADAQUÉS

Cap de Creus

The top excursion for nature lovers is the easternmost point of mainland Spain—Cap de Creus. The cape, marked by a lighthouse, is a popular nine-mile round-trip hike (get details at the Cadaqués TI). There are swimming coves along the way and a restaurant at the lighthouse. The easy way to get there is via EcoCar or tourist train (see "Helpful Hints," earlier).

Drive to France

Just over the border is the charming French town of Collioure (which seems like Cadaqués' sister city). It's a scenic 1.5-hour drive; you'll pass an evocative abandoned border post along the way—where the Pyrenees mountains hit the Mediterranean.

Sleeping in Cadaqués

$$ Hotel Llané Petit, with 32 spacious rooms (half with view balconies), is a small resort-like hotel with its own little beach, a 10-minute walk south of the town center (some view rooms, air-con, elevator, free breakfast, pay parking, Carrer del Doctor Bartomeus 37, +34 972 251 020, www.llanepetit.com, info@llanepetit.com).

$ Hotel Nou Estrelles is a big, concrete exercise in efficient, economic comfort. Facing the bus stop a few blocks in from the waterfront, this family-run hotel offers 15 rooms at a great value (air-con, elevator, Carrer Sa Tarongeta 3, +34 972 259 100, www.hotelnouestrelles.com, info@hotelnouestrelles.com, Emma).

$ Hostal Marina is run by a local family with care and enthusiasm and has 30 fresh rooms at a great location a block from the harborfront main square (RS%—use code "Rick Steves," some rooms with balcony, family rooms, no elevator, Riera de Sant Vicenç 3, +34 972 159 091, www.hostalmarinacadaques.com, info@hostalmarinacadaques.com, Pau and Isabel).

Eating in Cadaqués

$$$$ Restaurant Talla, grandly situated across from the old town with a harbor view, serves modern Mediterranean top-end cuisine. It has a rustic yet elegant interior and some fine harborside tables outside. Call ahead to reserve a seating at this popular place (daily except winter, Riba Pitxot 18, +34 972 258 739).

$$$ Casa Nun, serving wonderful traditional Catalan dishes and the freshest seafood, has been run by Paco since 1979 (fun photos in the back). Its cozy interior is whitewashed and tiled, and the little front porch gives a few tables great harbor views. Portions are big—don't hesitate to split first courses family-style (closed Mon-Tue, Plaça Portixó 6, +34 676 312 300).

$$ Casa Anita is good for an entertaining meal. You'll sit with others around a big table and enjoy fresh local fish and homemade *helado* (ice cream). There's no menu—you'll just eat what they serve you (closed Mon, Carrer Miquel Rosset 16, +34 972 258 471, Joan and family).

$$$ Enoteca MF is popular for their creative tapas and *raciones*, prepared with local ingredients that they mostly produce or catch themselves (Riba des Poal, +34 972 258 954).

$ Sa Rostisseria des Fornet is a very simple deli designed mostly for takeout but with a couple of humble tables. There's no atmosphere, but it's cheap (you pay by weight), fast, and tasty (Carrer Miquel Rosset 3, +34 972 258 501).

For Dessert: The venerable ice cream shop **Sa Gelateria** faces the harbor (east of the center). Along with gelato, they serve homemade popsicles.

Sitges

Sitges (SEE-juhz) is one of Catalunya's most popular resort towns. Because the town beautifully mingles sea and light, it's long been an artists' colony. Here you can still feel the soul of the Modernistas...in the architecture, the museums, the salty sea breeze, and the relaxed rhythm of life. Today's Sitges is a world-renowned vacation destination among the gay community. Despite its jet-set status, the Old Town has managed to retain its charm. With a much slower pulse than Barcelona, Sitges is an enjoyable break from the big city.

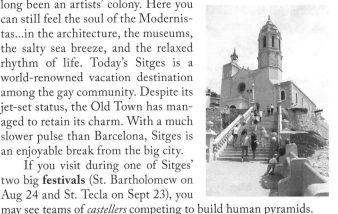

If you visit during one of Sitges' two big **festivals** (St. Bartholomew on Aug 24 and St. Tecla on Sept 23), you may see teams of *castellers* competing to build human pyramids.

To reach Sitges, you can take the train or bus. Southbound trains depart Barcelona from the Sants and Passeig de Gràcia stations (take frequent Rodalies train on the dark-green line R2sud toward Sant Vicenç de Calders, 35 minutes). The **TI** is to the left after you exit the train station. They can provide information about beaches and the town in general (Plaça Eduard Maristany 2, +34 938 944 251, www.sitgesanytime.com). Bus Garraf runs an easy and frequent bus from downtown Barcelona (with stops near the university and Plaça d'Espanya) that stops at Barcelona's airport en route to Sitges (1 hour, www.busgarraf.cat).

Visiting Sitges: Sitges basically has two attractions—its tight-and-tiny Old Town (with a couple of good museums) and its long, luxurious beaches. To head into the heart of town, exit the train station straight ahead and walk down Carrer Francesc Gumà. When it dead-ends, continue right onto Carrer de Jesús, which takes you to the town's tiny main square, Plaça del Cap de la Villa. Cross the square and turn left down Carrer Major ("Main Street"), which after several blocks leads you past the old market hall (now a local exhibition space) and the Town Hall to a beautiful terrace next to the main church.

Take time to explore the **Old Town**'s narrow streets. They're crammed with cafés, boutiques (many closed midday), and all the resort staples. The focal point, on the waterfront, is the 17th-century Baroque-style **Sant Bartomeu i Santa Tecla Church** (not open to the public). The terrace in front of the church will help you get the lay of the land. Poke into the Old Town or take the grand staircase down to the beach promenade.

As an art town, Sitges has seen its share of creative people—look for the sculptures by local artists scattered all over town, then head to the two appealing museums that share one entrance and fee, located just behind the church (closed Mon, www.museusdesitges.cat). The **Museu Maricel,** which began as an eclectic display of art from a local collector, proudly shows works from the 10th century through the first half of the 20th, including pieces by Sitges artists. The **Museu del Cau Ferrat** bills itself as a "temple of Modernism," as collected by local artist and intellectual Santiago Rusiñol. In addition to paintings and drawings, it has ironwork, glass, and ceramics. Also on this square, you'll see **Palau Maricel**—a sumptuous old mansion that's sometimes open to the public on Sunday mornings.

Nine **beaches,** separated by breakwaters, extend about a mile southward from town. Stroll down the seaside promenade, which stretches from the town to the end of the beaches. Anyone can enjoy the sun, sea, and sand, or you can rent a beach chair to relax like a pro. The crowds thin out about halfway down, and the last three beaches are more intimate and cove-like. Along the way, restaurants and *chiringuitos* (beach bars) serve tapas, paella, and drinks. If you walk all the  way to the end, you can continue inland to enjoy the nicely landscaped Terramar Gardens (Jardins de Terramar).

Sleeping in Sitges: Hotel values are not much better in this swanky beach resort than in Barcelona. As this is a party town, expect some noise after hours (request a quiet room). Consider

$$ Hotel Celimar (dated rooms in a classic Modernista building facing the beach, Paseo de la Ribera 20, +34 938 110 170, www. hotelcelimar.com) or the larger **$$ Hotel Medium Romàntic** (an old-fashioned-elegant, quirky place in a sunny villa close to the train station, Sant Isidre 33, +34 938 948 375, www.mediumhoteles. com).

BARCELONA: PAST & PRESENT

Barcelona has thrived for 2,500 years. Its location is ideal: on a gently sloping plain facing the Mediterranean, where east-west sea trade meets the natural north-south highway to northern Europe. In its day, Barcelona has been a Roman retirement colony, a maritime power, a dynamo of the Industrial Age, a cradle for all things modern, and capital of the Catalunya region. Today it cobbles together all these elements into a one-of-a-kind culture.

Keep in mind that Catalunya's history is quite distinct from that of the rest of Spain. Catalans pride themselves on their different language and independent traditions. When the rest of Spain was riding high, Catalunya was often in the doldrums, and vice versa.

The painter Joan Miró said, "We Catalans believe that you must plant your feet firmly on the ground in order to jump high in the air." This optimistic Catalan spirit—earthy but creative—has blossomed again and again through their history. Free spirits like Dalí, Miró, Gaudí, and even Wilfred the Hairy have all come from this small corner of Europe.

PREHISTORY AND ROMAN ORIGINS
(c. 500 BC-AD 500)

The original Iberian inhabitants settled atop Barcelona's hills overlooking the harbor, creating settlements on Montjuïc and around today's Plaça de Sant Jaume. They called their town "Barkeno"—possibly after Hannibal Barca, the Carthagin-

Barcelona Almanac

Population: 1.6 million

Languages: Spanish and Catalan are the two official languages of Catalunya, but Catalan is the preferred language in schools and offices. Catalan is not a dialect of Spanish, but an independent language.

Currency: Euro (€)

City Layout: The tangled Gothic Quarter (Barri Gòtic) lies at the heart of the city, edged by the connected boulevards of the Ramblas. The more orderly Eixample district spreads north of the Old City, while unassuming Barceloneta spills along the seafront. Looking down over it all is the big Montjuïc hill.

Tourist Tracks: More than 32 million people visit Barcelona each year, and more than 8 million stay overnight. The Ramblas sees more than 150,000 people daily. Avinguda del Portal de l'Àngel is Spain's most-walked street, trod upon by 3,500 pairs of feet every hour.

Architecture: Barcelona is home to the Modernista style championed by Catalan architect Antoni Gaudí, whose most famous work is the Sagrada Família church. Nearly 30 of his buildings are scattered throughout the greater Barcelona area.

Fun in the Sun: Until 1992, when the city hosted the Olympic Games, Barcelona had only one small beachfront area, in Barceloneta. Other waterfront property was taken up for industrial purposes. For the Olympics, the seaside was redeveloped, and the city shoreline is now spanned by nine beaches along a three-mile stretch.

Soccer: Futbol Club (FC) Barcelona has the largest privately owned stadium (Camp Nou) in the world, with a seating capacity that will soon top 100,000. Every year, more than 1.5 million people visit its museum.

The Average Jordi: The average Barcelonan is 41 years old, will live to age 81, and is likely Catholic. The majority (59 percent) of Barcelona's residents were born in Catalunya.

ian general who passed through with his war elephants en route to attacking Rome in 218 BC.

In 19 BC, when the (future) Roman Emperor Augustus conquered "Hispania," Barcelona became a busy port, shipping Iberia's produce and wine to the rest of the empire. Roman "Barcino"—a pleasant, sunbathed valley with Mediterranean breezes—also served as a retirement colony for soldiers.

Like most Roman cities, Barcino had a forum in the center of town (today's Plaça de Sant Jaume) and a grid pattern of streets. It was a tight, 30-acre town of some 4,000 inhabitants contained within a wall (the area around today's cathedral). More broadly, the Romans brought Barcelona the Latin language (which became modern Catalan) and a connection to the wider world.

At first, pagan Rome persecuted Christian martyrs (such as Santa Eulàlia). But when Christianity became entrenched, Barcelona's new Christians built their cathedral—the core of today's cathedral—atop the Roman Temple of Jupiter.

PAST & PRESENT

Sights

- Barcelona History Museum (with Roman ruins in basement)
- Temple of Augustus
- Plaça Nova's big, sculpted BARCINO letters and remnants of the Roman wall
- Roman necropolis near the Ramblas
- The cathedral's fourth-century font and Santa Eulàlia's tomb and silver statue

MEDIEVAL GLORY (500-1500)

As the Roman Empire crumbled, Barcelona made a smooth transition, coming under the protection of Romanized Christian Visigoths from Germany. Similarly, when the Moors (Muslims from North Africa) conquered Spain (in 711), Barcelona carried on largely unimpeded. Next (in 801), Charlemagne's son made it part of the Germanic Frankish empire. Barcelona finally came into its own when Frankish Count Wilfred the Hairy (so called because he was; ruled 878-897) declared its independence...launching a golden age.

Wilfred the Hairy's heirs sprouted and grew into powerful sea traders who connected Catalunya to the world. When Count Ramon of Barcelona married Petronila of Aragon in 1137, it united their two realms, creating the powerful kingdom of Aragon.

King Jaume I the Conqueror (1208-1276) acquired rich trading ports across the Mediterranean. He also established the Catalan Generalitat, one of Europe's first parliaments, which still governs the region today. By 1450, the Crown of Aragon ruled

a mercantile empire that stretched from Spain to southern Italy to Greece. Barcelona flourished.

Then came another powerful marriage: In 1469, King Ferdinand II of Aragon married Isabel of Castile. This power couple—the so-called Catholic Monarchs—united the peninsula's two largest kingdoms. They drove the last Moors out, created a unified nation-state, and sent Christopher Columbus to explore new lands. And where did Columbus come first to debrief the Catholic Monarchs upon his return? To Barcelona.

Sights

- Neo-Gothic and medieval motifs in Modernisme (especially the city symbol of St. George slaying the dragon)
- The El Born neighborhood, which flourished during this time
- Catalan Art Museum (excellent Romanesque collection)
- Columbus Monument
- Plaça del Rei and the Royal Palace, where Columbus met Ferdinand and Isabel
- The coffin of Count Ramon in the cathedral
- Plaça de Sant Jaume's Generalitat building and statue of Jaume I
- The churches of Santa Maria del Mar and Santa Maria del Pi, the Chapel of St. Agatha (at the Royal Palace), and the *extra muro* ("outside the walls") Church of Santa Anna
- Montserrat monastery, dating from medieval times

DECLINE (1500-1800)

Ironically, the glorious age of Ferdinand and Isabel also sowed the seeds of Barcelona's decline. Columbus' discoveries opened new Atlantic trade routes that made Barcelona's Mediterranean trade routes obsolete. Meanwhile, the center of royal power slowly shifted from Barcelona to the region midway between Aragon and Castile—the growing city of Madrid. While the rest of Spain enjoyed an unprecedented golden age of fabulous New World wealth, power, and great art, Barcelona became a poor and forgotten backwater.

In 1714, Barcelona suffered a crushing blow. Catalunya had sided against the powerful King Philip V in the War of Spanish Succession, and Philip took revenge. On September 11—a date that is still marked by Catalunya's most sobering holiday—Philip's

PAST & PRESENT

Typical Church Architecture

History comes to life when you visit a centuries-old church. Even if you wouldn't know your apse from a hole in the ground, learning a few simple terms will enrich your experience. Note that not every church has every feature, and a "cathedral" isn't a type of church architecture, but rather a designation for a church that's a governing center for a local bishop.

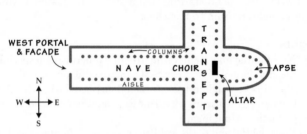

Aisles: Long, generally low-ceilinged arcades that flank the nave

Altar: Raised area with a ceremonial table (often adorned with candles or a crucifix), where the priest prepares and serves the bread and wine for Communion

Apse: Space behind the altar, sometimes bordered with small chapels

Barrel Vault: Continuous round-arched ceiling that resembles an extended upside-down U

Choir: Intimate space reserved for clergy and choir, located within the nave near the high altar and often screened off

Cloister: Covered hallways bordering a square or rectangular open-air courtyard, traditionally where monks and nuns got fresh air

Facade: Exterior of the church's main (west) entrance, usually highly decorated

Groin Vault: Arched ceiling formed where two equal barrel vaults meet at right angles

Narthex: Area (portico or foyer) between the main entry and the nave

Nave: Long central section of the church (running west to east, from the entrance to the altar) where the congregation sits or stands during the service

Transept: One of the two parts forming the "arms" of the cross in a traditional cross-shaped floor plan; runs north-south, perpendicularly crossing the east-west nave

West Portal: Main entry to the church (on the west end, opposite the main altar)

forces overran Barcelona's city walls and massacred the rebels. Catalan independence came to an end.

For the next century, the Spanish crown in Madrid suppressed the Catalan language, culture, and institutions. The Generalitat was disbanded. Trade with the Americas was forbidden. For surveillance and control, the Castilians built an imposing citadel on one side of town and a fortress atop Montjuïc on the other, and ordered that nothing could be built beyond the reach of the fort's cannons. Barcelona spiraled down into a dirty, cramped city contained within its medieval wall.

Sights

- El Born's Monument to Catalan Independence (honoring the victims of September 11, 1714) and Cultural and Memory Center (18th-century archaeological site and exhibits on the 1714 siege)
- Castle of Montjuïc
- Citadel Park (previously the site of the citadel)
- Barceloneta fishermen's quarter (built to house those displaced by citadel construction)
- Betlem Church on the Ramblas (rare example of Baroque)

INDUSTRIAL REVIVAL AND CULTURAL RENAISSANCE (1800-1900)

In the 1800s, Barcelona fomented another revolution—the Industrial Revolution. It harnessed its ample coal reserves and rushing rivers to stoke lucrative textile factories. It imported cotton and shipped the finished cloth abroad from its busy harbor. Workers flocked in from the countryside, and Barcelona's population doubled, reaching a million, with a thriving middle class.

By 1850—while the rest of Spain was a fading colonial shell—Catalunya was humming. In 1854, Queen Isabella II finally loosened Madrid's death-grip, allowing the growing city to tear down the medieval wall and expand northward to create the Eixample neighborhood. Barcelona pioneered modern boulevards, modern plumbing, streetlights, and the first rail line in Spain. The 1888 World's Fair gave the entire city a modern makeover (and the Columbus Monument).

Two cultural movements brought a renaissance of the Catalan language and the arts. First, the Renaixença (roughly 1840-1880) rediscovered Catalunya's historic roots and national identity, similar to the Romantic movements sweeping all of Europe. Writers wrote in Catalan, and artists revived the medieval motifs of Barcelona's 14th-century glory days. This energy flowed naturally into Modernisme (roughly 1890-1910), which continued the love affair with Catalunya's traditions while championing all things modern—things like streetcars and electric lights. The new technology was also meant to be beautiful, and Modernisme is Barcelona's version of the curvy, wistful Art Nouveau style found elsewhere in Europe. As the old city walls came down, Modernista architects like Antoni Gaudí remade the city with fanciful buildings—made of a modern concrete-and-iron substructure but decorated with colorful, playful, medieval motifs.

Sights
- Eixample neighborhood, with the Block of Discord, La Pedrera, and other buildings
- Sagrada Família
- Other Gaudí and Modernista sights

TURBULENT 20TH CENTURY

By the turn of the 20th century, Barcelona was seething with change. Industrialization had made factory owners rich, but the working class was still languishing in dirty slums and unsafe factories. Angry anarchists bombed the Liceu Opera House and vandalized churches, while rioters were shot in the streets.

Barcelona developed a reputation across Spain as a breeding ground for liberals, troublemakers, and nonconformists. In the art world, young Pablo Picasso carried that spirit of rebellion to Paris to break all the rules with Cubism. His fellow Catalan Joan Miró perplexed the masses with his childlike doodles, and Salvador Dalí shocked and astonished with his Surrealistic dreamscapes.

When Spain splintered into its bitter civil war (1936-1939)—pitting democratic Republicans against fascist Nationalists—left-leaning Barcelona became the natural capital of the Republican side. The fascists, under General Francisco Franco (1892-1975), invited Mussolini's Italian air force to bomb Barcelona, killing a thousand citizens. When Barcelona finally fell, the civil war was effectively over. For the next four decades, Franco would rule Spain with an iron fist.

Catalunya was punished. The Generalitat was again abolished and the Catalan president was executed by firing squad. The Catalan language and traditions were suppressed, while "Castilianization" programs promoted the Spanish tongue. You couldn't buy a newspaper in Catalan or hear the people's language spoken on TV. You couldn't dance the *sardana*. Simultaneously, the region was flooded with poor, Castilian-speaking farmers from the rest of Spain looking for work. The city expanded way too fast, throwing up dusty gray concrete buildings amid suburban sprawl.

But underground newspapers and a president-in-exile living in France kept the Catalunya flame alive. Finally, Franco died in 1975, and—on September 11, 1977—millions of Catalan patriots flooded the streets to demand their culture back.

This ushered in a third golden age for Catalunya. The Generalitat and Catalan president returned. Catalan became the sole official language in schools. Barcelona reinvented itself, spiffing up old quarters with new buildings and expanding the Metro system. The Sagrada Família, after nearly a century of false starts, made dramatic progress. The 1992 Summer Olympics brought a renovated Montjuïc and waterfront. As the century turned, Barcelona was embracing the new global economy and stepping out onto the world stage.

Sights

- Picasso Museum
- Fundació Joan Miró, plus Liceu mosaic in the Ramblas, *Woman and Bird* sculpture, and other public works by Miró
- Figueres, hometown of Salvador Dalí
- Cadaqués, a mecca for modern artists
- 1929 World Expo Fairgrounds, including Magic Fountains (at the base of Montjuïc, near Plaça d'Espanya)
- Fresh-looking Montjuïc (with Olympic Stadium) and the rejuvenated waterfront
- *Barcelona Head* sculpture by Roy Lichtenstein, on the waterfront

CATALUNYA TODAY

Barcelona's unique heritage lives on in its vibrant lifestyle amid historic surroundings. With more than 5 million people in its greater metro area, Barcelona is Spain's humming second city. It's Spain's industrial powerhouse, with a GDP second only to the banking center of Madrid. Catalan factories crank out traditional textiles, plus pharmaceuticals, processed foods, and electric

Catalans You May Know

Catalans invented the submarine, assassinated Leon Trotsky, and founded San Diego. Here are some familiar names.

Pablo Picasso (1881-1973): Though he was born in Andalucía (to Spanish, not Catalan, parents) and spent his adult life in France, Picasso's formative teenage years were spent in Barcelona's Barri Gòtic.

Salvador Dalí (1904-1989): The master Surrealist was born in Figueres, spent holidays in Cadaqués, and passed his formative years in Barcelona, where he exhibited his early works and soaked up Gaudí's dreamlike architecture.

Joan Miró (1893-1983): Raised in the Barri Gòtic, he divided his adulthood living between Barcelona and Paris. His whimsical sculptures and ceramics adorn Barcelona.

Antoni Gaudí (1852-1926): Resident of the Barri Gòtic (in his youth), the Eixample (in young adulthood), and Park Güell (in his twilight years). Gaudí designed many of Barcelona's iconic Modernista buildings.

Pau (Pablo) Casals (1876-1973): A world-class cellist who's often described as one of the best musicians ever to pick up the instrument, Casals retired to French Catalunya in protest against Franco.

Bacardi Rum Family: The world-famous rum company was founded in Cuba in 1862 by a man from Sitges; it's now run by his descendants.

Ferran Adrià (b. 1962): This celebrity chef revolutionized cuisine with his innovations in molecular gastronomy.

Antoni Tàpies (1923-2012): Spain's best-known postwar artist is most famous for his distinctive mud-caked canvases.

Pau Gasol (b. 1980) and **Marc Gasol** (b. 1985): These basketball-playing brothers grew up in Barcelona.

Rafael Nadal (b. 1986): From the Catalan-speaking island of Mallorca, this multiple Grand Slam-winning tennis star earned the title "King of Clay" for his dominance on that surface.

vehicles. The ports bustle with container ships, while high-speed trains link Barcelona with Madrid, Paris, and Marseille. The city's highly educated and cosmopolitan populace attracts tech start-ups and a growing service sector. And all this in a stunning Mediterranean setting: No wonder Barcelona often finds itself on "most-livable-cities" lists.

Since a wave of immigration in the early 2000s, Barcelona is changing. Roughly one in four Catalans are either recent immigrants or foreign residents. Still, the local language thrives. Native Barcelonans can switch fluently between Catalan (at home and among friends) and Spanish (the default tongue in public settings).

Politically, Catalunya enjoys a greater level of self-government than other regions in Spain's federal system. The regional government (or Generalitat)—presiding in Gothic splendor on Plaça de Sant Jaume—consists of a president, an executive council, and a unicameral parliament of 135 members. Rather than two dominant political parties, there are many, ranging from far-left to far-right, making coalition-building essential. In general, Catalunya tends to lean further left than Spain as a whole.

Of course, the gorilla that's dominated Catalan politics for decades is independence from Spain. The issue cuts across party lines, so there are both conservative independence parties and liberal ones. Politicians of all stripes leverage the issue to their advantage. Over the years, the ups and downs of the independence movement have simultaneously energized, divided, and exhausted the Catalan people, and it remains a hotly debated topic (see the "Independence for Catalunya?" sidebar on page 130).

Regardless, Catalans are firmly united in one thing: pride in their region. It's one of the defining aspects of Barcelonan culture. Catalan flags drape balconies everywhere. That pride comes out in support for the massively popular men's soccer team, FC Barcelona. Whenever "Barça" plays arch-nemesis Real Madrid (a matchup dubbed "El Clasico"), the soccer pitch becomes the battlefield as these two proud regions fight metaphorically for supremacy.

Despite how modern and progressive Barcelona has become, its history remains everywhere. People still celebrate medieval saints' days and festive traditions. Cinema, TV, and radio keep the Catalan language alive. World-class Catalan writers, artists, and pop musicians create from the unique Barcelona perspective. And every night, cafés and bars ring with the timeless Catalan spirit until the wee hours. Barcelona welcomes the world to share its history.

Sights

- Plaça de Catalunya
- *Sardana* dances in front of the cathedral
- The red-and-gold flag of Catalunya flapping in the breeze

For more on history, consider Europe 101: History and Art for the Traveler, *by Rick Steves and Gene Openshaw (available at www. ricksteves.com).*

PRACTICALITIES

This chapter covers the practical skills of European travel: how to get tourist information, pay for things, sightsee efficiently, find good-value accommodations, eat affordably but well, use technology wisely, and get between destinations smoothly. For more information on these topics, see RickSteves.com/travel-tips.

Travel Tips

Travel Advisories: Before traveling, check updated health and safety conditions, including restrictions for your destination, at Travel.State.gov (US State Department travel pages) and CDC.gov (Centers for Disease Control and Prevention). The Spanish government has an English-language website with all the updated requirements for travel to Spain (www.exteriores.gob.es). The US embassy website for Spain is another good source of information (see later).

While most countries no longer require proof of Covid-19 vaccination for entry, some sights or tours may still have vaccination requirements (check websites). Even if it's not required for your itinerary, it's smart to pack a copy of your vaccine record and/or store a photo of your Covid-19 vaccine card on your phone.

ETIAS Registration: The European Union may soon require US and Canadian citizens to register online with the European Travel Information and Authorization System (ETIAS) before entering Spain and other Schengen Zone countries (quick and easy process). For the latest, check Travel-Europe.europa.eu/etias_en.

Tourist Information: The website for Spain's national tourist office (www.spain.info) is filled with practical information and sightseeing ideas; you can download many brochures and travel guides free of charge. Also see BarcelonaTurisme.com.

In Barcelona, a good first stop is generally at any of its tourist information offices (abbreviated TI in this book; see page 25 for locations). TIs are in business to help you spend money in their town—which can color their advice—but I still swing by to pick up a city map and get info on public transit, walking tours, special events, and nightlife.

Emergency and Medical Help: For any emergency service—ambulance, police, or fire—call **112** (operators typically speak English). If you get sick, do as the locals do and go to a pharmacist for advice. Or ask at your hotel for help—they'll know the nearest medical and emergency services.

Theft or Loss: To replace a passport, you'll need to go in person to an embassy or consulate (see next). If your credit and debit cards disappear, cancel and replace them (see "Damage Control for Lost Cards" on page 280). File a police report, either on the spot or within a day or two; you'll need it to submit an insurance claim for lost or stolen items, and it can help with replacing your passport or credit and debit cards. For help with a lost phone, see "Damage Control for Lost Phones" on page 304. For more information, see RickSteves.com/help.

US Consulates: Nonemergency services by appointment only, +34 932 802 227, after-hours emergency +34 915 872 200 (Passeig de la Reina Elisenda de Montcada 23, https://es.usembassy.gov).

Canadian Consulate: Passport services by appointment only, +34 932 703 614, after-hours emergency in Ottawa—call collect +1 613 996 8885 (Plaça de Catalunya 9, www.spain.gc.ca, click "Consulate of Canada to Spain, in Barcelona").

Time Zones: Spain, like most of continental Europe, is generally six/nine hours ahead of the East/West coasts of the US. The exceptions are the beginning and end of Daylight Saving Time: Europe "springs forward" the last Sunday in March (two weeks after most of North America) and "falls back" the last Sunday in October (one week before North America). For a handy time con-

PRACTICALITIES

verter, use the world clock app on your phone or download one (see www.timeanddate.com).

Business Hours: For visitors, Spain is a land of strange and frustrating schedules. Many businesses respect the afternoon siesta. When it's 100 degrees in the shade, you'll understand why. The biggest museums stay open all day. Smaller ones often close for a siesta. Shops are generally open from about 9:30 to 14:00 and from 17:00 to 21:00, longer for big chain shops or touristy places. Small shops are often open on Saturday only in the morning, and closed all day Sunday.

Watt's Up? Europe's electrical system is 220 volts, instead of North America's 110 volts. Most electronics (laptops, phones, cameras) and appliances (hair dryers, CPAP machines) convert automatically, so you won't need a converter, but you will need an adapter plug with two round prongs, sold inexpensively at travel stores in the US.

Rip Up This Book! Turn chapters into mini guidebooks: Break the book's spine and use a utility knife to slice apart chapters, keeping gummy edges intact. Reinforce the chapter spines with clear wide tape; use a heavy-duty stapler; or make or buy a cheap cover (see the Travel Store at www.ricksteves.com), swapping out chapters as you travel.

Discounts: Discounts for sights are generally not listed in this book. However, seniors (age 65 and over), youths under 18, and students and teachers with proper identification cards (obtain from www.isic.org) can get discounts at many sights—always ask. Some discounts are available only to European citizens.

Online Translation Tips: The Google Translate app converts spoken or typed English into most European languages (and vice versa) and can also translate text it "reads" with your phone's camera. Google's Chrome browser instantly translates websites; Translate.google.com and DeepL.com are also handy.

Going Green: There's plenty you can do to reduce your environmental footprint when traveling. When practical, take a train instead of a flight within Europe, and use public transportation within cities. In hotels, use the "Do Not Disturb" sign to avoid daily linen and towel changes (or hang up your towels to signal you'll reuse them) and turn the air-conditioning off when you leave the room. Bring a reusable shopping tote and refillable water bottle (Europe's tap water is safe to drink). Skip printed materials that you don't plan to keep—get your info online instead. To find out how Rick Steves' Europe is offsetting carbon emissions with a self-imposed carbon tax, see RickSteves.com/about-us/climate-smart.

Travel Insurance

Travel insurance can minimize the considerable financial risks of traveling: accidents, illness, missed flights, canceled tours, lost baggage, theft, terrorism, travel-company bankruptcies, natural disasters, emergency evacuation, and getting your body home in case you die. The decision to buy travel insurance (and how much) depends on your situation. First determine what coverage you already have; many premium credit cards include generous coverage, and other expenses may be covered through your health, homeowners, or rental insurance. Then consider how likely it is that you'll need to change or cancel (for example, if you or a loved one is in frail health), how much of your prepaid trip costs are nonrefundable, and your risk tolerance.

It costs money to buy away the financial risk of travel. The way I see it, if insurance costs 10 percent of your total trip cost, but the chances you'll need it are slim, statistically, you're better off going without. But emotionally, it still might be a good investment. You can compare insurance policies and costs at InsureMyTrip.com.

PRACTICALITIES

Money

Here's my basic strategy for using money wisely in Europe. I pack the following and keep it all safe in my money belt.

Credit Card: You'll use your credit card for purchases both big (hotels, advance tickets) and small (little shops, food stands). Some European businesses have gone cashless, making a card your only payment option. A "tap-to-pay" or "contactless" card is widely accepted and simple to use.

Debit Card: Use this at ATMs to withdraw a small amount of local cash. Wait until you arrive to get euros (European airports have plenty of ATMs); if you buy euros before your trip, you'll pay bad stateside exchange rates. While many transactions are by card these days, cash can help you out of a jam if your card randomly doesn't work and can be useful to pay for things like tips and local guides.

Backup Card: Some travelers carry a third card (debit or credit; ideally from a different bank) in case one gets lost or simply doesn't work.

Stash of Cash: I carry $100-200 in US dollars as a cash backup, which comes in handy in an emergency (for example, if your debit card gets eaten by the machine).

PRACTICALITIES

BEFORE YOU GO

Know your cards. For credit cards, Visa and Mastercard are universal, while American Express and Discover are less common. US debit cards with a Visa or Mastercard logo will work in any European ATM.

Go "contactless." Contactless pay options are now standard in much of Europe. Check to see if you already have—or can get—a tap-to-pay version of your credit card (look on the card for the tap-to-pay symbol—four curvy lines) and consider setting up your smartphone for contactless payment (see next section for details). Both options are more secure than a physical credit card: Instead of recording your credit-card number, a one-time encrypted "token" enables the purchase and expires shortly afterward.

Know your PIN. Make sure you know the numeric four-digit PIN for each of your cards, both debit and credit. Request it if you don't have one, as it may be required for some purchases. Allow time to receive the information by mail—it's not always possible to obtain your PIN online or by phone.

Report your travel dates. Some banks want to know that you'll be using your debit and credit cards overseas, specifically when and where you're headed. Depending on your bank, you can do this either online or over the phone.

Adjust your ATM withdrawal limit. Find out how much you can withdraw daily and ask for a higher daily limit if you want to get more cash at once. Note that European ATMs will withdraw funds only from checking accounts, not from savings accounts.

Find out about fees. For any purchase or withdrawal made with a card, you may be charged a currency conversion fee (1-3 percent) and/or a Visa or Mastercard international transaction fee (less than 1 percent). Shop around; you can compare credit cards on Bankrate.com. Some cards offer lower international fees than others—and some don't charge any at all. If you're getting a bad deal, consider getting a new card. Most credit unions and some airline loyalty cards have low or no international transaction fees.

IN EUROPE
Using Credit Cards and Payment Apps

Tap-to-Pay or **Contactless Cards:** These cards have the usual chip and/or magnetic stripe, but with the addition of a contactless symbol. Simply tap your card against a contactless reader to complete a transaction—no PIN or signature required (except in some cases as a security measure for larger purchases). This is by far the easiest way to pay and is available in much of Europe.

Payment Apps: Just like at home, you can pay with your smartphone or smartwatch by linking a credit card to an app

---

Exchange Rate

1 euro (€) = about $1.10

To convert prices in euros to dollars, add about 10 percent: €20=about $22, €50=about $55. Like the dollar, one euro is broken into 100 cents. Coins range from €0.01 to €2, and bills from €5 to €200 (bills over €50 are rarely used).
Check Oanda.com for the latest exchange rates.

---

such as Apple Pay or Google Pay. To pay, hold your phone near a contactless reader; you may need to verify the transaction with a face scan, fingerprint scan, or passcode. If you've arrived in Europe without a tap-to-pay card, you can easily set up your phone to work in this way.

Will My US Card Work? Usually, yes. On rare occasions, you may run into a situation where your card doesn't work. This is most likely at self-service payment machines (such as transit-ticket kiosks, tollbooths, or fuel pumps). Usually a tap-to-pay card does the trick in these situations. If not, look for a cashier who can process your payment manually, or use cash. Drivers should be prepared to move on to the next gas station if necessary. (In some countries, gas stations sell prepaid gas cards, which you can purchase with any US card.) When approaching a toll plaza or ferry ticket line, use the "cash" lane.

Always Choose to Pay in the Local Currency: During a credit card transaction, the payment terminal will often ask whether you want to pay in US dollars or in the local currency. Always refuse the conversion and *choose the local currency*. While this "service"—called Dynamic Currency Conversion (DCC)—offers the illusion of convenience, it comes with a poor exchange rate and/or higher fees, and you'll wind up losing money.

Using Cash

Cash Machines: European cash machines work just like they do at home—except they spit out local currency instead of dollars. In Europe, the universal term for an ATM is "bankomat"; in Spain, look for a *cajero automático*. The best option is an ATM operated by a bank, which offers local cash calculated at the day's standard bank-to-bank rate. Look for a cash machine marked with a bank logo, and ideally use one just outside a brick-and-mortar bank (in the rare event that you have any issues).

You'll more commonly see cash machines run by exchange or money-transfer companies, which have unfavorable rates, higher fees, or both. These can be marked Euronet, Travelex, Your Cash, and Cashzone—or simply marked generically, as "bankomat" or "ATM." Avoid these unless you enjoy paying too much for your local cash.

Rip-off exchange ATMs are often the only option at airports and train stations. On arrival, consider using a cashless payment option to get downtown, then find a real bank near your hotel to withdraw local currency.

If your debit card doesn't work, try a lower amount—your request may have exceeded your withdrawal limit or the ATM's limit. If you still have a problem, try a different ATM or come back later. When offered the choice to process your transaction in US dollars or the local currency, always choose the local currency for the best rates.

Exchanging Cash: Minimize exchanging money in Europe; it's expensive (you'll generally lose 5 to 10 percent). In a pinch, you can find exchange desks at major train stations or airports. Banks generally do not exchange money unless you have an account with them.

Security Tips

Pickpockets target tourists. Keep your passport and backup cash and cards secure in your money belt, and carry only a day's spending money and one card in your front pocket or wallet.

Before inserting your card into an ATM, inspect the front of the machine. If anything looks crooked, loose, or damaged, it could be a sign of a card-skimming device. When entering your PIN, carefully block other people's view of the keypad.

Avoid using a debit card for purchases. Because a debit card pulls funds directly from your bank account, potential charges incurred by a thief will stay on your account while your bank investigates.

To access your accounts online while traveling, be sure to use a secure connection (see the "Tips on Internet Security" sidebar, later).

Damage Control for Lost Cards

If you lose your credit or debit card, report the loss immediately to your bank (using a secure app) or the following global customer-assistance centers: Visa (+1 303 967 1096), Mastercard (+1 636 722 7111), and American Express (+1 336 393 1111).

You'll need to provide the primary cardholder's identification-verification details (such as birth date, mother's maiden name, or Social Security number). You can generally receive a temporary card within two or three business days in Europe (see RickSteves. com/help for more).

If you report your loss within two days, you typically won't be responsible for unauthorized transactions on your account, although many banks charge a liability fee.

TIPPING

Tipping in Spain isn't as automatic and generous as in the US. For special service, tips are appreciated, but not expected. As in the US, the proper amount depends on your resources, tipping philosophy, and the circumstances, but some general guidelines apply.

Restaurants: If eating at the counter of a tapas bar, there's no need to tip, though it's respectable to round up the bill. At restaurants with table service, if a service charge is included in the bill, add about 5 percent; if it's not, leave 10-15 percent. If paying with a credit card, be prepared to tip separately with cash or coins; credit card receipts don't have a tip line. For more details on tipping in restaurants and tapas bars, see pages 296 and 298.

Taxis: For a typical ride, just round up your fare a bit (for instance, if the fare is €4.85, pay €5). If the cabbie hauls your bags and zips you to the airport to help you catch your flight, you may want to toss in a little more.

Services: For local guides, private drivers, or others who spend several hours with you, and significantly improve the quality of your trip, a healthy tip (of around 10 percent) is not extravagant. In general, if someone in the tourism or service industry does a good job for you, a small tip of a euro or two is appropriate...but not required. If you're not sure whether (or how much) to tip, ask a local for advice.

GETTING A VAT REFUND

Wrapped into the purchase price of your Spanish souvenirs is a value-added tax (VAT) of 21 percent (in Spain, it's called IVA—*Impuesto sobre el Valor Añadido*). You're entitled to get most of that tax back if you purchase more than €90 worth of goods at a store that participates in the VAT-refund scheme. Typically, you must ring up the minimum at a single retailer—you can't add up your purchases from various shops to reach the required amount. (If the store ships the goods to your US home, VAT is not assessed on your purchase.)

Getting your refund is straightforward...and worthwhile if you spend a significant amount.

At the Merchant: Have the merchant completely fill out the refund document (they'll ask for your passport; a photo of your passport usually works). Keep track of the paperwork and your original sales receipt. Note that you're not supposed to use your purchased goods before you leave Europe.

At the Border or Airport: Process your VAT document at your last stop in the European Union (such as the airport) with the customs agent who deals with VAT refunds (allow plenty of extra time to deal with this process and have your purchased items easily accessible for inspection). At some airports, you'll go to a customs office to get your documents stamped and then to a separate VAT refund service (such as Global Blue or Planet) to process the refund. Elsewhere, a single VAT desk handles the whole thing, or you may be able to do it at a self-validation kiosk. (Note that refund services typically extract a 4 percent fee, but you're paying for the convenience of receiving your money in cash immediately or as a credit to your card.) Otherwise, you'll need to mail the stamped refund documents to the address given by the merchant.

CUSTOMS FOR AMERICAN SHOPPERS

You can take home $800 worth of items per person duty-free, once every 31 days. Many processed and packaged foods are allowed, including cheeses, dried herbs, jams, baked goods, candy, chocolate, oil, vinegar, condiments, and honey. Fresh fruits and vegetables and most meats are not allowed, with exceptions for some canned items. As for alcohol, you can bring in one liter duty-free (it can be packed securely in your checked luggage, along with any other liquid-containing items).

To bring alcohol (or liquid-packed foods) in your carry-on bag on your flight home, buy it at a duty-free shop at the airport. You'll increase your odds of getting it onto a connecting flight if it's packaged in a "STEB"—a secure, tamper-evident bag. But stay away from liquids in opaque, ceramic, or metallic containers, which usually cannot be successfully screened (STEB or no STEB).

For details on allowable goods, customs rules, and duty rates, visit Help.cbp.gov.

Sightseeing

Sightseeing can be hard work. Use these tips to make your visits to Spain's finest sights meaningful, fun, efficient, and painless.

MAPS AND NAVIGATION TOOLS

Your best navigation tool is on your phone. **Google Maps** (and similar mapping apps) offers turn-by-turn directions for walking and driving, as well as detailed public transit instructions in most big cities. Simply plug in a destination and instantly get detailed directions for reaching it on foot or by subway, bus, or tram—including where to catch it, how long it takes, where to get off, and how far you'll walk at the other end.

To conserve data, most mapping apps let you download maps in advance (do this when you're on strong Wi-Fi). However, offline maps may not include every feature (most in-city public transit navigation doesn't work offline). For more on how to get online with your phone during your trip, see page 303.

For offline navigation, the maps in this book are concise and simple, designed to help you locate recommended destinations, sights, hotels, and restaurants. In Europe, simple paper maps are generally free at TIs and hotels; maps with more detail are sold at newsstands and bookstores.

PLAN AHEAD

Set up an itinerary that allows you to fit in all your must-see sights. For a one-stop look at opening hours, see "Barcelona at a Glance" (page 42); also see the "Daily Reminder" on page 33.

Don't put off visiting a must-see sight—you never know when a place will close unexpectedly for a holiday, strike, or restoration. Opening days and hours can fluctuate; confirm the latest with the TI or at the sight's official website (listed throughout this book).

Many museums are closed or have reduced hours at least a few days a year, especially on holidays such as Christmas, New Year's, and Labor Day (May 1). A list of holidays is in the appendix; check for possible closures during your trip. In summer, some sights may stay open late. Off-season hours may be shorter.

Going at the right time helps avoid crowds. This book offers tips on the best times to see specific sights. Try visiting popular sights very early or very late. Evening visits (when possible) are usually more peaceful, with fewer crowds (see the "Sights Open Late" sidebar on page 222). Late morning is usually the worst time to visit a popular sight.

If you plan to hire a local guide, reserve ahead by email. Popular guides can get booked up.

Study up. To get the most out of the sight descriptions in this book, read them before you visit.

RESERVATIONS AND ADVANCE TICKETS

Many popular sights in Europe come with long ticket-buying lines. Visitors who buy tickets online in advance (or who have a museum pass covering key sights) can skip the line and waltz right in. Advance tickets are generally timed-entry, meaning you're guaranteed admission on a certain date and time.

For some sights, buying ahead is **required** (tickets aren't sold at the sight and it's the only way to get in). At other sights, buying ahead is **recommended** to skip the line and save time. And for many sights, advance tickets are **available** but unnecessary: At these uncrowded sights you can simply arrive, buy a ticket, and go in.

Don't confuse the reservation options: available, recommended, and required. Use my advice in this book as a guide. Note any

PRACTICALITIES

must-see sights that sell out long in advance and be prepared to buy tickets early. If you do your research, you'll know the smart strategy.

Given how precious your vacation time is, I'd book in advance both where it's required (as soon as your dates are firm) and where it will save time in a long line (in some cases, you can do this even on the day you plan to visit).

You'll generally be emailed a digital ticket with a code that you'll store on your phone to scan at the entrance (if you prefer, you can print it out). At the sight, look for the ticket-holders line rather than the ticket-buying line; you may still have to wait in a security line.

AT SIGHTS

Here's what you can typically expect:

Entering: You may not be allowed to enter if you arrive too close to closing time. And guards start ushering people out well before the actual closing time, so don't save the best for last.

Many sights have a security check. Allow extra time for these lines. Some sights require you to check day packs and coats. (If you'd rather not check your day pack, try carrying it tucked under your arm as you enter.)

At churches—which often offer interesting art (usually free) and a cool, welcome seat—a modest dress code (no bare shoulders or shorts) is encouraged, though rarely enforced.

Photography: If the museum's photo policy isn't clearly posted, ask a guard. Generally, taking photos without a flash or tripod is allowed. Some sights ban selfie sticks; others ban photos altogether.

Audioguides and Apps: I've produced two free, downloadable audio tours for Barcelona that cover many of the sights on my Barcelona City Walk and Eixample Walk; look for the 🎧 in this book. For more on my audio tours, see page 22.

Some sights offer audioguides with dry-but-useful recorded descriptions in English. Often you'll use free Wi-Fi to download the tour to your mobile device on the spot; less frequently you'll borrow or rent a device preloaded with the audio content at the museum. Bring your own plug-in earbuds to enjoy better sound (with a splitter, two can often share one rented device).

Expect Changes: Artwork can be on tour, on loan, out sick, or shifted at the whim of the curator. Pick up a floor plan as you enter and ask the museum staff if you can't find a particular item. Say the title or artist's name, or point to the photograph in this book, and ask, *"¿Dónde está?"* (DOHN-day eh-STAH; meaning, "Where is?").

Services: Important sights usually have a reasonably priced

Sleep Code

Hotels in this book are categorized according to the average price of a standard double room without breakfast in high season.

$$$$	**Splurge:** Most rooms over €200
$$$	**Pricier:** €150-200
$$	**Moderate:** €100-150
$	**Budget:** €50-100
¢	**Backpacker:** Under €50
RS%	**Rick Steves discount**

Unless otherwise noted, credit cards are accepted and hotel staff speak basic English. Comparison-shop by checking prices at several hotels (on each hotel's own website, on a booking site, or by email). For the best deal, *book directly with the hotel.* Ask for a discount if paying in cash; if the listing includes **RS%,** request a Rick Steves discount.

on-site café or cafeteria (handy and air-conditioned places to rejuvenate during a long visit). The WCs at sights are free and generally clean.

Before Leaving: At the gift shop, scan the postcard rack or thumb through a guidebook to be sure you haven't overlooked something that you'd like to see. Every sight or museum offers more than what is covered in this book. Use the information I provide as an introduction—not the final word.

Sleeping

Extensive and opinionated listings of good-value rooms are a major feature of this book's Sleeping sections. Rather than list accommodations scattered throughout a town, I choose hotels in my favorite neighborhoods that are convenient to sightseeing.

My recommendations run the gamut, from dorm beds to luxurious rooms with all the comforts. I like places that are clean, central, relatively quiet at night, reasonably priced, friendly, small enough to have a hands-on owner or manager, and run with a respect for Spanish traditions. I'm more impressed by a handy location and fun-loving philosophy than oversized TVs and a fancy gym. Most of my recommendations fall short of perfection. But if I can find a place with most of these features, it's a keeper.

In Spain, high season *(temporada alta)* is from July to September, while low season *(temporada baja)* runs from November through March. But Barcelona can be busy any time of year. Book your accommodations as soon as your itinerary is set, especially if you want to stay at one of my top listings or if you'll be travel-

Using Online Services to Your Advantage

From booking services to user reviews, online businesses play a big role in planning a trip. Take advantage of their pluses—and be wise to their downsides.

Booking Sites

Booking websites such as Booking.com and Hotels.com offer one-stop shopping for hotels. While convenient for travelers, they're both a blessing and a curse for small, independent, family-run hotels. Without a presence on these sites, small hotels become almost invisible. But to be listed, a hotel must pay a sizable commission...and promise that its own website won't undercut the price on the booking-service site.

Here's the work-around: Use the big sites to research what's out there, then book directly with the hotel. The price will likely be the same as via a booking site, but your money goes to the hotel, not agency commissions. As a savvy consumer, remember: When you book with an online service, you're adding a middleman who takes a cut. To support small, family-run hotels, book direct.

Short-Term Rental Sites

Rental juggernaut Airbnb and other short-term rental sites allow travelers to rent rooms and apartments, often providing more value, space, and amenities than a cookie-cutter hotel. Airbnb fans appreciate feeling part of a neighborhood and getting into a daily routine as "temporary Europeans." Some places are run by thoughtful hosts, allowing you to get to know a local and keep your money in the community, but beware: Others are impersonally managed by large, absentee agencies.

Critics of Airbnb see it as a threat to "traditional Europe." Landlords can make more money renting to short-stay travelers, driving rents up—and local residents out. Traditional businesses

ing during busy times. See the appendix for a list of major holidays and festivals. In Barcelona, trade fairs crop up throughout the year and can send rates soaring (search for trade fair dates at www.firabarcelona.com/en/home).

RATES AND DEALS

I've categorized my recommended accommodations based on price, indicated with a dollar-sign rating (see sidebar). Room prices can fluctuate significantly with demand and amenities (size, views, and so on), but relative price categories remain constant. Hoteliers are encouraged to quote prices with the IVA tax included—but it's smart to ask when you book your room. Additionally, the city of Barcelona levies a tourist tax up to a couple of euros per person per night.

are replaced by ones that cater to tourists. And the character and charm that made those neighborhoods desirable to the tourists in the first place goes too. Some cities have cracked down, requiring owners to obtain a license and to occupy rental properties part of the year (and staging disruptive "inspections" that inconvenience guests).

As a lover of Europe, I share the worry of those who see residents nudged aside by tourists. But as an advocate for travelers, I appreciate the value Airbnb can provide in offering the chance to stay in a local building or neighborhood with potentially fewer tourists.

User Reviews

User-generated review sites and apps such as Yelp and TripAdvisor can give you a consensus of opinions about everything from hotels and restaurants to sights and nightlife. If you scan reviews of a restaurant or hotel and see several complaints about noise or a rotten location, you've gained insight that can help in your decision-making.

As a guidebook writer, my sense is that there is a big difference between the uncurated information on a review site and the vetted listings in a guidebook. A user review is based on the limited experience of one person, who stayed at just one hotel in a given city and ate at a few restaurants there. A guidebook is the work of a trained researcher who forms a well-developed basis for comparison by visiting many restaurants and hotels year after year.

Both types of information have their place, and in many ways, they're complementary. If something is well reviewed in a guidebook and also gets good online reviews, it's likely a winner.

Booking Direct: Once your dates are set, compare prices at several hotels. You can do this by checking hotel websites and booking sites such as Hotels.com or Booking.com. After you've zeroed in on your choice, book directly with the hotel itself, by phone, by email, or on the hotel's website. This increases the chances that the hotelier will be able to accommodate special needs or requests (such as shifting your reservation). When you book direct, the owner avoids the commission paid to booking sites—in exchange, ask if they can give you a discount, a nicer room, or a free breakfast (if it's not already included).

Getting a Discount: Some hotels extend a discount to those who pay cash or stay longer than three nights. And some accommodations offer a special discount for Rick Steves readers, indicated in this book by the abbreviation **"RS%."** Discounts vary: Ask for details when you reserve. Generally, to qualify for this discount, you must book direct (not through a booking site), mention this book when you reserve, show it upon arrival, and sometimes pay cash or stay a certain number of nights. In some cases, you may need to enter a discount code (which I've provided in the listing) in the booking form on the hotel's website. Rick Steves discounts apply to readers with either print or digital books. Understandably, discounts do not apply to promotional rates.

TYPES OF ACCOMMODATIONS
Hotels

In this book, the price for a double room ranges from about $60 (very simple, toilet and shower down the hall) to $400 (maximum plumbing and more), with most clustering at about $150.

Some hotels can add an extra bed (for a small charge) to turn a double into a triple; some offer larger rooms for four or more people (I call these "family rooms" in the listings). If there's space for an extra cot, they'll cram it in for you. In general, a triple room is cheaper than the cost of a double and a single. Three or four people can economize by requesting one big room.

Spain has stringent restrictions on smoking in public places. Smoking is not permitted in common areas, but hotels can designate 10 percent of their rooms for smokers.

Arrival and Check-In: Hotels and B&Bs are sometimes located on the higher floors of a multipurpose building with a secured door. In that case, look for your hotel's name on the buttons by the main entrance. When you ring the bell, you'll be buzzed in.

Hotel elevators are common, though small, and some older buildings still lack them. If stairs are unavoidable, you can ask the front desk for help carrying your bags up.

Most European countries require hotels to collect your name, nationality, and passport number. At check-in, the receptionist might ask for your passport and may keep it for several hours. If you're not comfortable leaving your passport at the desk, bring a copy to give them instead.

If you're arriving in the morning, your room probably won't be ready. Check your bag safely at the hotel and dive right into sightseeing.

In Your Room: Most hotel rooms have a TV and free Wi-Fi, which can vary in strength and quality. Simpler or characteristic places rarely have a TV or a room phone.

Some hotels don't use central heat before November 1 and after April 1 (unless it's unusually cold); prepare for cool evenings if you travel in spring and fall. Summer can be extremely hot. Consider air-conditioning, fans, and noise (since you'll want your window open). Many rooms come with mini refrigerators.

Keep Cool

If you're visiting Spain in the summer, you'll want an air-conditioned room. Most hotel air-conditioners come with a remote control that generally has similar symbols and features: fan icon (toggle through wind power, from light to gale); temperature (20 degrees Celsius is comfortable); louver icon (steady airflow or waves); snowflake and sunshine icons (cold air or heat); and clock ("O" setting: run X hours before turning off; "I" setting: wait X hours to start). When you leave your room for the day, do as the environmentally conscious Europeans do and turn off the air-conditioning.

PRACTICALITIES

Checking Out: While it's customary to pay for your room upon departure, it's smart to settle your bill the day before, when you're not in a hurry and while the manager's there.

Hotelier Help: Hoteliers can be a good source of advice. Most know their city well and can assist you with everything from public transit and airport connections to finding a good restaurant, the nearest launderette, or a late-night pharmacy.

Hotel Hassles: Even at the best places, mechanical breakdowns occur: Sinks leak, hot water turns cold, toilets may gurgle or smell, the Wi-Fi goes out, or the air-conditioning dies when you need it most. Report your concerns clearly and calmly at the front desk.

Light sleepers struggle more in Spain than just about anywhere in Europe. City street noise can be loud (Spaniards are notorious night owls, and traffic can rumble and screech until very late). Bring earplugs, and ask to see your room first. If you suspect night noise will be a problem, request a quiet *(tranquilo)* room in the back, on the courtyard, and/or on an upper floor *(planta alta)*. You'll often sleep better and for less money in a room without a view.

To guard against theft in your room, keep valuables out of sight. Some rooms come with a safe, and other hotels have safes at the front desk. I rarely bother to use one and in a lifetime of travel, I've never had anything stolen from my room.

For more complicated problems, don't expect instant results. Any legitimate place in Spain is legally required to have a complaint book *(libro de reclamaciones)*. A request for this book will generally prompt the hotelier to solve your problem to keep you from writing a complaint. Above all, keep a positive attitude. If your hotel is a disappointment, spend more time out enjoying the place you came to see.

Hostales and Pensiones

Budget hotels—called *hostales* and *pensiones*—are easy to find, inexpensive, and, when chosen properly, a fun part of the Spanish

Making Hotel Reservations

Reserve your rooms as soon as you've pinned down your travel dates. For busy national holidays (and, in Barcelona, trade fairs), it's wise to reserve far in advance (see the appendix).

Requesting a Reservation: For family-run hotels, it's generally best to book your room directly via email or phone. For business-class and chain hotels, or if you'd rather book online, reserve directly through the hotel's official website (not a booking website).

Here's what the hotelier wants to know:
- Type(s) of room(s) you want and number of guests
- Number of nights you'll stay
- Arrival and departure dates, written European-style as day/ month (18/06 or 18 June)
- Special requests (en suite bathroom, cheapest room, twin beds vs. double bed, quiet room)
- Applicable discounts (such as a Rick Steves discount, cash discount, or promotional rate)

Confirming a Reservation: Most places will request a credit-card number to hold your room. If the hotel's website doesn't have a secure form where you can enter the number directly, share this info via a phone call.

Canceling a Reservation: If you must cancel, it's courteous—and smart—to do so with as much notice as possible, especially for smaller family-run places. Cancellation policies can be strict; read

cultural experience. These places are often family-owned and may or may not have amenities such as private bathrooms and air-conditioning. Don't confuse a *hostal* with a hostel—a Spanish *hostal* is an inexpensive hotel, not a hostel with bunks in dorms.

Short-Term Rentals

A short-term rental—whether an apartment, a house, or a room in a private residence—is a popular alternative, especially if you plan to settle in one location for several nights. For stays longer than a few days, you can usually find a rental that's comparable to—and cheaper than—a hotel room with similar amenities. Plus, you'll get a behind-the-scenes peek into how locals live.

Many places require a minimum stay and have strict cancellation policies. And you're generally on your own: There's no reception desk, breakfast, or daily cleaning service.

Finding Accommodations: Websites such as Airbnb, FlipKey, Booking.com, and VRBO let you browse a wide range of properties. In Barcelona, you can check to see if your choice is licensed by visiting FairTourism.barcelona. Alternatively, rental agencies such as InterhomeUSA.com and RentaVilla.com can

From:	rick@ricksteves.com
Sent:	Today
To:	info@hotelcentral.com
Subject:	Reservation request for 19-22 July

Dear Hotel Central,

I would like to stay at your hotel. Please let me know if you have a room available and the price for:
• 2 people
• Double bed and en suite bathroom in a quiet room
• Arriving 19 July, departing 22 July (3 nights)

Thank you!
Rick Steves

the fine print before you book. Many discount deals require pre-payment and can be expensive to change or cancel.

Reconfirming a Reservation: Always call or email to reconfirm your reservation a few days in advance. For B&Bs or very small hotels, I call again on my arrival day to tell my host what time to expect me (especially important if arriving after 17:00).

Phoning: For tips on how to call hotels overseas, see page 305.

provide a more personalized service (their curated listings are also more expensive). For a list of agencies specializing in Barcelona apartment rentals, see page 188.

Before you commit, be clear on the location. I like to virtually "explore" the neighborhood using Google Street View. Also consider the proximity to public transportation and how well connected the property is with the rest of the city. Ask about amenities (elevator, air-con, laundry, Wi-Fi, parking, etc.). Reviews from previous guests can help identify trouble spots.

Think about the kind of experience you want: just a key and an affordable bed...or a chance to get to know a local? Some hosts offer self-check-in and minimal contact; others enjoy interacting with you. Read the description and reviews to help shape your decision.

Confirming and Paying: Many places require payment in full before your trip, usually through the listing site. Be wary of owners who want to take your transaction offline; this gives you no recourse if things go awry. Never agree to wire money (a key indicator of a fraudulent transaction).

Apartments or Houses: If you're staying in one place for several nights, it's worth considering an apartment or rental house.

These can be especially cost-effective for groups and families. European apartments, like hotel rooms, tend to be small by US standards. But they often come with laundry facilities and small, equipped kitchens, making it easier and cheaper to dine in.

Rooms in Private Homes: Renting a room in someone's home is a good option for those traveling alone, as you're more likely to find true single rooms—with just one single bed and a price to match. These can range from air-mattress-in-living-room basic to plush-B&B-suite posh. While you can't expect your host to also be your tour guide—or even to provide you with much info—some are interested in getting to know the travelers who pass through their home.

Other Options: Swapping homes with a local works for people with an appealing place to offer (don't assume where you live is not interesting to Europeans). Good places to start are HomeExchange.com and LoveHomeSwap.com.

Hostels

A hostel *(albergue juvenil)* provides cheap beds in dorms where you sleep alongside strangers for usually under €20-30 per night. Travelers of any age are welcome if they don't mind dorm-style accommodations and meeting other travelers. Most hostels offer kitchen facilities, guest computers, Wi-Fi, and a self-service laundry. Hostels almost always provide bedding, but the towel's up to you (though you can usually rent one). Family and private rooms are often available.

Independent hostels tend to be easygoing, colorful, and informal (no membership required; www.hostelworld.com). You may pay slightly less by booking directly with the hostel. **Official hostels** are part of Hostelling International (HI) and share a booking site (www.hihostels.com). HI hostels typically require that you be a member or else pay a bit more per night.

Eating

Spanish cuisine is hearty, and meals are served in big, inexpensive portions. You can eat well in restaurants for about €15-20—or even more cheaply and more varied if you graze on appetizer-sized tapas in bars.

For listings in this guidebook, I look for restaurants that are convenient to your hotel and sightseeing. When restaurant-hunting, choose a spot filled with locals, not the place with the big signs boasting, "We Speak English." And avoid any restaurant that posts big photographs of its food. Venturing even a block or two off the main drag leads to higher-quality food for a better price.

The Spanish eating schedule—lunch from 13:00 to 16:00, dinner after 21:00—frustrates many visitors. Most Spaniards eat one major meal of the day—lunch *(comida)*—around 14:00, when stores close, schools let out, and people gather with their friends and family for the siesta. Because most Spaniards work until 19:30, supper *(cena)* is usually served at about 21:00 or 22:00. And, since few people want a heavy meal that late, many Spaniards eat a light tapas dinner.

PRACTICALITIES

Generally, no self-respecting *casa de comidas* ("house of eating"—when you see this label, you can bet it's a good, traditional eatery) serves meals at American hours. If you're looking for a "nontouristy restaurant," remember that a spot filled with tourists at 20:00 will be an entirely different—and more authentic—scene at 22:00, when the locals take over.

Survival Tips for Spanish Eating Schedules: To bridge the gap between their coffee-and-roll breakfast and late lunch, many Spaniards eat a light meal at about 11:00 *(merienda)*. This can be a light lunch at a bar or a *bocadillo* (baguette sandwich)—hence the popularity of fast-food *bocadillo* chains such as Pans & Company. Besides *bocadillos,* bars often have slices of *tortilla española* (potato omelet) and fresh-squeezed orange juice. For your main meal of the day, you can either eat a late lunch at a restaurant at around 15:00, then have a light tapas snack for dinner; or reverse it, having a tapas meal in the afternoon, followed by a late restaurant dinner. Either way, tapas bars are the key to eating well at any hour.

RESTAURANT PRICING AND HOURS

I've categorized my recommended eateries based on the average price of a typical main course, indicated with a dollar-sign rating (see sidebar). Obviously, expensive specialties, fine wine, appetizers, and dessert can significantly increase your final bill.

The categories also indicate the personality of a place: **Budget** eateries include street food, takeaway, order-at-the-counter shops, basic cafeterias, and bakeries selling sandwiches. **Moderate** eateries are nice (but not fancy) sit-down restaurants, ideal for a pleasant meal with good-quality food. Most of my listings fall in this category—great for a taste of local cuisine at a reasonable price.

Pricier eateries are a notch up, with more attention paid to the setting, presentation, and (often inventive) cuisine. **Splurge** eateries are dress-up-for-a-special-occasion swanky—typically with an elegant setting, polished service, and pricey and refined cuisine.

Most of my restaurant listings are open daily for lunch and dinner; I've noted exceptions.

> ## Restaurant Code
>
> Eateries in this book are categorized according to the average cost of a typical main course. Drinks, desserts, and splurge items can raise the price considerably.
>
> $$$$ **Splurge:** Most main courses over €25
> $$$ **Pricier:** €18-25
> $$ **Moderate:** €12-18
> $ **Budget:** Under €12
>
> In Spain, takeout food is **$;** a basic tapas bar or no-frills sit-down eatery is **$$;** a casual but more upscale tapas bar or restaurant is **$$$;** and a swanky splurge is **$$$$.**

BREAKFAST

Hotel breakfasts are generally handy, optional, and pricey. Start your day instead at a corner bar or at a colorful café near a market hall. Ask for the *desayunos* (breakfast special, usually only available until noon), which can include coffee, a roll (or sandwich), and juice—much cheaper than ordering them separately. Sandwiches can be either on white bread (called "sandwich") or on a baguette *(bocadillo).*

A basic and standard savory breakfast item is the *tostada* (*torrada* in Catalan)—toasted white bread with olive oil and cured ham, *fuet* (a typical Catalan cured sausage), or cheese. Other options include the *bikini* (grilled ham-and-cheese sandwich) or a slice of *tortilla española* (potato omelet), which is often accompanied by *pa amb tomàquet* (toasted white bread with olive oil, tomato, and salt).

Those with a sweet tooth will find various sweet rolls (*bollos* or *bollería*). If you like a doughnut and coffee in American greasy-spoon joints, try the Spanish equivalent: *churros* (or the thicker *porras*) that you dip in thick hot chocolate or your *café con leche.*

Here are some other key breakfast words (some with their Catalan variant):

Bikini: Grilled ham-and-cheese sandwich (popular in Catalunya)

Bocadillo (bocata) con jamón/queso/mixto: Baguette sandwich with ham/cheese/both

Bocadillo (bocata) mixto con huevo: Baguette sandwich with ham and cheese and an over-easy egg on top

Caracola: "Snail"-shaped pastry, similar to a cinnamon roll

Croissant a la plancha: Croissant grilled and slathered with butter

Palmera: Palm-shaped pastry, like a French *palmier* or "elephant ear"

Pan (pa) de molde/de barra: Bread (sandwich bread/baguette)

Rosquilla: Hard doughnut

Sandwich, tostado: White bread sandwich, toasted

Tortilla española (truita de patates): Potato omelet

SPANISH RESTAURANTS

While Spain's tapas bars offer small plates throughout the afternoon and evening, formal restaurants have a standard à la carte
menu (no tapas) and start their ser-
vice much later than the American
norm. But many eateries blur the
distinction between a bar and a restaurant, boasting both a bar in front
and some sit-down tables in the
back or outside on the *terraza*.

At both restaurants and bars,
smoking is banned in enclosed public spaces.

Ordering: While menus at formal restaurants are generally broken
down by courses or categories, more
casual eateries (and tapas bars) may
feature dishes served in portions called *raciones* (*racions* in Catalan),
or the smaller half-servings, *media-raciones* (*mitja racions* in Catalan). Smaller tapas plates are more commonly served at bars than at
sit-down restaurants.

Typically, couples or small groups can share a few *raciones*,
making this an economical way to eat and a great way to explore
the regional cuisine. Ordering *media-raciones* may cost a bit more
per ounce, but you'll broaden your tasting experience. Two people
can fill up on four *media-raciones*.

For a budget meal in a restaurant, try a *plato combinado* (combination plate), which usually includes portions of one or two main
dishes, a vegetable, and bread for a reasonable price; or the *menú del
día* (menu of the day), a substantial three- to four-course meal that
comes with a drink.

Menus in Barcelona feature lots of seafood, along with local
favorites such as *fideuà* (a kind of Catalan paella made with seafood
and a thin, flavor-infused noodle) and *arròs negre* (black rice cooked
in squid ink). Spanish chefs love garlic and olive oil—many dishes
are soaked in both. You'll see plenty of *jamón* (ham) on menus,
though it is more typically Spanish than Catalan (for more on
jamón, see later). The cheapest meal is a simple *bocadillo de jamón*
(ham sandwich on a baguette), sold virtually everywhere.

Spanish cuisine can be a bit meat-centered for Americans more
accustomed to salads, fruits, and grains. Main meat and fish courses are usually served with only a garnish, not a side of vegetables.
Good vegetarian and lighter options exist, but you'll have to seek
them out. The secret is to choose the creamed vegetable soup, *par-
rillada de verduras* (sautéed vegetables), *ensalada mixta*, or another
green option available as a first course. (Spaniards rarely eat salads

PRACTICALITIES

PRACTICALITIES

Sampling *Jamón*

The staple of Spanish cuisine, *jamón* (hah-MOHN) is prosciut-to-like ham that's dry-cured and aged. It's generally sliced thin (right off the hock) and served at room temperature. *Jamón* can be eaten straight, served in a *bo-cadillo* sandwich, or mixed into a wide variety of dishes. Bars proudly hang ham hocks from the rafters as part of the decor. *Jamón* is more than a food—it's a way of life. Spaniards treasure memories of Grandpa at Christmas, thinly carving a *jamón* supported in a special ham-hock holder, just as Americans savor the turkey carving at Thanksgiving.

Like connoisseurs of fine wine, Spaniards debate the merits of different breeds of pigs, the pig's diet, and the quality of the curing. The two major types of ham are *jamón serrano,* from white pigs whose meat is cured in the mountains of Spain, and the higher-quality *jamón ibérico,* made with the back legs of black-hooved pigs. These Iberian *pata negra* ("black foot") pigs are said to be fatter and happier (slaughtered much later than other pigs), thereby producing particularly fine ham. Another indication of quality is *de bellota,* which means the pig was raised on acorns. *Jamón ibérico de bellota* is, to Spanish eaters, as good as it gets: free-range, black-footed pigs who ate only acorns. (Ham labeled *Jamón ibérico de recebeo* or *de cebo* is still good, but comes from pigs that are grain-fed.)

To sample this delicacy without the high price tag you'll find in bars and restaurants, go to the local market. Ask for 100 grams of top-quality ham (*cien gramos de jamón ibérico;* about €80/kilo, so your *ración* will run about €8), and enjoy it as a picnic with red wine and a baguette. To round out the picnic, also pick up 100 grams each of *salchichón* (salami), *chorizo* (spicy sausage), and *manchego* or *cabrales* cheese, along with some olives and pickles.

as a main course, so they tend to be small and simple—just lettuce, tomatoes, and maybe olives and tuna.) Fruit is often considered a dessert and a healthy choice at the end of a meal.

Tipping: At restaurants with table service, a service charge is sometimes included in the bill (*servicio incluido; servei inclós* in Catalan). In the past, Spaniards traditionally tipped nothing or next to nothing beyond that, but times are changing. There's a growing tendency to tip for good service, especially in cities like Barcelona. Leaving 10-15 percent for excellent service is appreciated. Tip in cash—there's generally no option for adding a tip to your bill when paying with a credit card. At most places, you can leave the tip on the table. At an outdoor café, hand the tip to your server to avoid having it swiped by a passerby.

TAPAS BARS

I can't resist stopping in local tapas bars to munch on tasty small portions of seafood, meat-filled pastries, deep-fried morsels, and other delicious bites (typically costing around €4). Best of all, I can eat well any time of day in a tapas bar.

Chasing down a particular bar for tapas nearly defeats the purpose and spirit of such places—they are impromptu. Just drop in at any lively bar. Some are sit-down, while others are more stand-up.

There is nothing wrong with ordering a tapa or two to start before deciding whether to stay at the same bar or move on. In fact, Spaniards rarely settle into just one place. Part of the joy of eating at a tapas bar is turning it into a mobile feast, visiting two or three bars during a single meal.

The authentic tapas experience is not for shrinking violets. You'll elbow up to a bar crowded with pushy locals, squint at a hand-scrawled chalkboard menu, and try to order from a typically brusque bartender. In some locales, a small, free tapa may be included with your drink. (Notice what locals are being served.) Order your drink first with the expectation of the freebie; then order additional food as you like.

Basque-style bars, which have an array of tapas platters already laid out, are popular in Barcelona and can be less daunting, as you simply point to or grab what you want (see page 190). These tapas are called *pintxos* (or *pinchos*). Note that Barcelona's tapas bars generally don't provide a free, small tapa with the purchase of a drink as may be found elsewhere in Spain.

When to Go: Bars can be extremely crowded with locals, and visitors can find it hard to get in an order—or even find a place to sit. You'll have more room, and get better service, by showing up before the local crowd. Try to be there by 13:30 for lunch and between 20:00 to 20:30 for dinner.

Where to Sit: Eating and drinking at a bar is usually cheapest if you sit or stand at the counter *(barra)*. You may pay a little more to sit at a table *(mesa* or *salón)* and still more for an outdoor table *(terraza)*. Traditionally, tapas are served at the bar, and *raciones* (and

PRACTICALITIES

media-raciones) are served at tables, where food can be shared family style.

It's bad form to order food at the bar, then take it to a table. If you're standing and a table opens up, it's OK to move as long as you signal to the server; anything else you order will be charged at the higher *mesa/salón* price. In the right place, a quiet snack and drink on a terrace is well worth the extra charge. But the cheapest seats sometimes get the best show. Sit at the bar and study the bartenders—they are artists.

Ordering: To figure out what you want, read the posted or printed menu. Use the "Tapas Menu Decoder," later, to sort through your options. You can also just point to items in the display case or at your neighbor's plate to get what you want. Handwritten signs that start out *"Hay"* mean "Today we have," as in *"Hay caracoles"* ("Today we have snails").

Hang back and observe before ordering. When you're ready, be assertive or you'll never be served. To grab the busy bartender's attention, say *"por favor"* (please; *"si us plau"* in Catalan); you can also say *"perdona"* (excuse me; *"perdó"* in Catalan).

Some bars push *raciones* (dinner plate-sized) portions rather than smaller tapas (saucer-sized). Ask for the smaller tapas portions or a *media-ración* (listed as ½ *ración* on a menu)—that way you can try more things.

If you don't know what to order, try an inexpensive sampler plate. Ask for *una tabla de canapés variados* to get a plate of various little open-faced sandwiches. Or ask for a *surtido de* (an assortment of) *charcutería* (a mixed plate of meat) or *queso* (cheese). *Un surtido de jamón y queso* means a plate of different hams and cheeses. Order bread and two glasses of red wine on the right square, and you've got a romantic (and inexpensive) dinner for two.

Paying and Tipping: Don't worry about paying until you're ready to leave; the bartender is keeping track of your tab. To get the bill, ask for *"¿La cuenta?"* (*"El compte?"* in Catalan). If you're sampling tapas at a counter, there's no need to tip (though you can round up the bill).

DESSERTS AND PASTRIES
In Spain, desserts are often an afterthought; here are a few items you may see on menus or in a bakery window:

Arroz con leche: Rice pudding

Bamba de nata: Cream puff

Brazo de gitano: Sponge cake filled with buttercream; literally "Gypsy's arm"

Crema catalana: Catalan take on crème brûlée (Barcelona)

Flan de huevo: Flan (crème caramel)

Fruta de la estación/fruta de temporada: Fruit in season

Helados, variados: Ice cream, various flavors

Mel i mató: Light Catalan cheese with honey (Barcelona)

Músic de fruits secs: Selection of nuts and dried fruits (Barcelona)

Napolitana: Rolled pastry filled with chocolate (similar to French *pain au chocolat*) or *crema* (cream)

Queso: Cheese

Torrijas: Sweet fritters, like French toast, available during Lent and Easter

SPANISH DRINKS
Wine and Spirits

Spain is one of the world's leading producers of grapes, and that means lots of excellent wine, both red *(tinto)* and white *(blanco)*. Major wine regions include Valdepeñas (both red and white wines made in Don Quixote country south of Toledo); Penedès (cabernet-style wines from near Barcelona); Rioja (spicy, lighter reds from the tempranillo grape, from the high plains of northern Spain); and Ribera del Duero (reds from northwest of Madrid).

For a basic glass of red wine, you can order *un tinto.* But for quality wine, ask for *un crianza* (old), *un reserva* (older), or *un gran reserva* (oldest). For good, economical wine, I always ask for **un crianza**—for little or no extra money than a basic *tinto,* you'll get a quality, aged wine.

Cava is Spain's answer to champagne. For variety, consider ordering a **tinto de verano** (red wine with lemon soda—similar to sangria) or try a local **vermut** (vermouth). For nondrinkers, **mosto** is excellent Spanish grape juice that hasn't been fermented (available in both red and white).

Beer

Spaniards rarely ask for a "cerveza." Instead, they usually specify a size or type when ordering, such as a *caña* (small draft beer).

Most places just have the standard local beer—a light lager—on tap. In Barcelona, local options include Estrella Damm, the

PRACTICALITIES

Tapas Menu Decoder

You can often just point to what you want on the menu or in the display case, say *por favor* (Spanish) or *si us plau* (Catalan), and get your food, but these words will help. I've given both Spanish and Catalan (in parentheses), when applicable.

a la parrilla (a la graella)	barbecued
a la plancha (a la planxa)	griddled
aceitunas (olives)	olives
al ajillo	with garlic
albóndigas (mandonguilles)	spiced meatballs with sauce
almejas (cloïsses), a la marinera	clams, in paprika sauce
almendras (ametlles)	almonds (usually fried)
anchoas (anxoves)	cured anchovies (salted or in oil)
atún (tonyina)	tuna
bacalao (bacallà)	cod
bocadillo (entrepà/bocata)	basic baguette sandwich
bombas (bombes)	fried meat-and-potato ball
boquerones (seitons), en vinagre	fresh anchovies, marinated in olive oil, vinegar, and garlic
brocheta (broqueta)	brochette (skewered meat or fish)
calamares fritos (calamars fregits)	fried squid rings
canapé	tiny open-faced sandwich
caracoles (cargols)	small tree snails (May-Sept)
champiñones (xampinyons)	mushrooms
charcutería (xarcuteria)	cured meats
chorizo (xoriço)	spicy sausage
croquetas (croquetes)	croquettes—breaded, fried béchamel with fillings like ham
empanadillas (crestes)	meat or seafood hand pies
ensaladilla rusa (ensalada russa)	potato salad with lots of mayo, peas, and carrots
espinacas, con garbanzos (espinacs, amb cigrons)	spinach, with garbanzo beans
flauta	sandwich on flute-thin baguette
frito (fregit)	fried
fuet	Catalan salami-like sausage
gambas, con cáscara (gambes, amb closca)	shrimp, with shell
gazpacho	cold tomato soup
guiso (estofat)	stew
jamón (pernil)	cured ham (like prosciutto)
judías verdes (mongetes tendres)	green beans

lomo (llom)	pork tenderloin
mejillones (musclos)	mussels
merluza (lluç)	hake (whitefish)
montadito	tapa on bread, mini sandwich in Sevilla
morcilla (botifarró)	blood sausage
morro	pig snout
paella	saffron rice dish with seafood and meat
pan (pa)	bread
patatas bravas (patates braves)	fried potatoes with spicy tomato sauce
pescaditos fritos (peixet fregit)	assortment of fried little fish
pimiento, relleno (pebrot, farcit)	pepper, stuffed
pimientos de Padrón (pebrots de Padró)	fried small green peppers, a few of which are jalapeño-hot
pinchos morunos (pintxos morunos)	skewer of spicy lamb or pork
pisto (samfaina)	mixed sautéed vegetables
pollo, alioli (pollastre, all i oli)	chicken, with garlic olive-oil sauce
pulga, pulguita, or pepito (entrepà petit)	a small baguette sandwich
pulpo (pop)	octopus
queso (formatge)	cheese
queso manchego (formatge manxec)	classic Spanish sheep-milk cheese
rabas (rabes)	squid rings
rabo de toro (cua de bou)	bull's-tail stew (fatty and tender)
revuelto, de setas (remenat, de bolets)	scrambled eggs, with wild mushrooms
salchichón (llonganissa)	salami-like sausage
sandwich (sandvitx)	American-style sandwich on soft bread
sardinas (sardines)	sardines
surtido de (assortit)	assortment of
tabla serrana (assortit d'embotits i formatges)	hearty plate of meat and cheese
tortilla española (truita de patata)	potato omelet
tortilla de jamón/queso (truita de pernil/formatge)	potato omelet with ham/cheese
variado de fritos (peixet fregits)	mix of various fried fish

trendier Moritz, and various craft beers. One of the most-appreciated Spanish lagers is Estrella Galicia, from the Galicia region.

Caña (canya): Small glass of draft beer (7-8 ounces)
Cerveza (cervesa): Beer
Cerveza sin (Cervesa sense): Nonalcoholic beer
Clara con limón/casera: Small beer with lemonade/soda (shandy)
Doble: Typically double the size of a *caña*
Mediana: Bottle of beer (*quinto* is a small bottle)
Sidra: Dry, alcoholic cider
Tubo: Tall, thin glass of beer (about 10 ounces)

Water, Coffee, and Other Nonalcoholic Drinks

If ordering mineral water in a restaurant, request a *botella de agua grande* (big bottle). For a glass of tap water, specify *un vaso de agua del grifo*. If you insist on *del grifo*, not *embotellada* (bottled), you'll usually get it. Note that tap water in Barcelona does not taste particularly good, and some places would rather not serve it to their customers (though it is safe to drink).

Spain's bars often serve fresh-squeezed orange juice. For something completely different, try the sweet and milky *horchata*, traditionally made from *chufa* (a.k.a. tigernuts or earth almonds).

Here are some common additional beverage phrases (with Catalan variants where applicable):

Agua con/sin gas (aigua amb/sin gas): Water with/without bubbles
Café con leche (café amb llet): Espresso with hot milk
Café solo: Shot of espresso, sometimes with hot water added
Cortado (tallat): Espresso with a little milk
Jarra de agua: Pitcher of tap water
Leche: Milk
Refresco (Refresc): Soft drink (common brands are Coca-Cola, Fanta—*limón* or *naranja*, and Schweppes—*limón* or *tónica*)
Té/infusión: Tea
Zumo: Juice
Zumo de naranja, natural: Orange juice, freshly squeezed

Staying Connected

A mobile device is an indispensable tool for efficient travel. Fortunately, staying connected in Europe gets less complicated (and less expensive) each year. You can use your devices much like you do at home, by either getting an international plan or connecting to free Wi-Fi whenever possible. Another option is to buy a European SIM card for your mobile phone. More details are at RickSteves.com/phoning.

Hurdling the Language Barrier

Imported from the Old World throughout the New, Spanish is the most widely spoken Romance language in the world. With its straightforward pronunciation, Spanish is also one of the simplest languages to learn. However, Barcelona adds its own twist: About 75 percent of Barcelonans speak Catalan, the language unique to the Catalunya region. Though all Barcelonans speak Spanish, many locals insist on speaking Catalan first.

Many Barcelonans—especially those in the tourist trade—speak English. Still, many people don't. Locals visibly brighten when you know and use some key Catalan or Spanish words (see "Catalan Survival Phrases" and "Spanish Survival Phrases" in the appendix). Learn the key phrases. Travel with a phrase book, particularly if you want to interact with the Spanish people. You'll find that doors open more quickly and with more smiles when you can speak a few words of the language.

For more tips on hurdling the language barrier, consider the *Rick Steves Spanish Phrase Book* (available at RickSteves. com).

PRACTICALITIES

USING YOUR PHONE IN EUROPE

Here are some budget tips and options.

Sign up for an international plan. To stay connected at a lower cost, sign up for an international service plan through your carrier. Most providers offer a simple bundle that includes calling, messaging, and data. Your normal plan may already include international coverage (for example, T-Mobile's covers unlimited text and low-speed data, plus reasonable per-minute voice calls).

Use free Wi-Fi whenever possible. Unless you have an unlimited-data plan, save most of your online tasks for Wi-Fi (pronounced *wee-fee* in Spanish). Most accommodations in Europe offer free Wi-Fi. Many cafés (including Starbucks and McDonald's) offer hotspots for customers; ask for the password when you buy something. You may also find Wi-Fi at TIs, city squares, major museums, public transit hubs, and airports, and aboard trains and buses.

Minimize the use of your cellular network. The best way to make sure you're not accidentally burning through data is to put your device in "airplane" mode (which also disables phone calls and texts) and connect to Wi-Fi as needed. Turn on your cellular network (or turn off airplane mode) only when you can't find Wi-Fi.

Save large-data tasks for Wi-Fi. If your included data is slow or metered, wait until you're on Wi-Fi to Skype or FaceTime, download apps, stream videos, or do other megabyte-greedy tasks. Using a navigation app such as Google Maps over a cellular net-

---

Tips on Internet Security

Make sure your device is running the latest versions of its operating system, security software, and apps. Next, ensure that your device and apps are password-protected (enable facial recognition where possible). On the road, use only secure, password-protected Wi-Fi. Ask the hotel or café staff for the specific name of their network, and make sure you log on to that exact one.

  If you must access your financial info online, use a banking app rather than accessing your account via a browser, and use a cellular connection, not Wi-Fi. If you're very concerned, consider subscribing to a VPN (virtual private network).

---

work can require lots of data, so download maps when you're on Wi-Fi, then use the app offline.

Limit automatic updates. By default, your device constantly checks for a data connection and updates app content. Check your device's settings menu for ways to turn this off.

Use Wi-Fi calling and messaging apps. Skype, FaceTime, and Google Meet are great for making free or low-cost calls or sending texts over Wi-Fi worldwide. WhatsApp is especially popular with Europeans, and is often the easiest way to communicate with guides, drivers, or other local contacts.

Buy a European SIM card. If you anticipate making a lot of local calls, you need a local phone number, or your provider's international data rates are expensive, consider getting a European SIM card to replace the one in your (unlocked) device. SIM cards are sold at department-store electronics counters, some newsstands (you may need to show your passport), and vending machines. If you need help setting it up, buy one at a mobile-phone shop. Some newer devices may also allow you to download an eSIM from an international provider. There are generally no roaming charges when using a European SIM card in other EU countries, but confirm when you buy.

Damage Control for Lost Phones: Losing your phone can be a significant inconvenience. Before you leave home, make sure your device is set up for automatic cloud backups, and enable the "find my phone" feature (make sure you have access to it from another device, like your travel partner's phone or a laptop). Familiarize yourself with your phone's "lost and lock" mode, which you should enable from another device if your phone goes missing. Report the loss to your mobile carrier; if your phone remains lost, use the "wipe" feature to erase its data.

How to Dial

Here's how to dial from anywhere in the US or Europe, using the phone number of one of my recommended Madrid hotels as an example (915 212 900). If a number starts with 0, drop it when dialing internationally (except when calling Italy).

From a US Mobile Phone
Phone numbers in this book are presented exactly as you would dial them from a US mobile phone. For international access, press and hold the 0 (zero) to get a + sign, then dial the country code (34 for Spain) and phone number.

▶ To call the Madrid hotel from any location, dial +34 915 212 900.

From a US Landline
Replace + with 011 (US/Canada access code), then dial the country code (34 for Spain) and phone number.

▶ To call the Madrid hotel from your home landline, dial 011 34 915 212 900.

From a European Landline
Replace + with 00 (Europe access code), then dial the country code (34 for Spain, 1 for the US) and phone number.

▶ To call the Madrid hotel from a German landline, dial 00 34 915 212 900.
▶ To call my US office from a Spanish landline, dial 00 1 425 771 8303.

From One Spanish Phone to Another
To place a domestic call (from a Spanish landline or mobile), drop +34 and dial the phone number.

▶ To call the Madrid hotel from Barcelona, dial 915 212 900.

More Dialing Tips
Local Numbers: European phone numbers and area codes can vary in length and spacing, even within the same country. Mobile phones use separate prefixes (for instance, in Spain, landlines begin with 8 or 9, and mobile numbers begin with 6 or 7).

Toll and Toll-Free Calls: It's generally not possible to dial European toll or toll-free numbers from a US mobile or landline (although you can sometimes get through using Skype). Look for a direct-dial number instead.

Calling the US from a US Mobile Phone, While Abroad: Dial +1, area code, and number.

More Phoning Help: See HowToCallAbroad.com.

MAIL

For details on sending packages to your own home or to others, visit www.cbp.gov, then select "Travel" and "Know Before You Go." The Spanish postal service works fine, but for quick transatlantic delivery (in either direction), consider services such as DHL (www.dhl.com).

Transportation

Figuring out how to get around in Europe is one of your biggest trip decisions. **Cars** work well for two or more traveling together (especially families with small kids), those packing heavy, and those delving into the countryside. **Trains** and **buses** are best for solo travelers, blitz tourists, city-to-city travelers, and those who want to leave the driving to others. Short-hop **flights** within Europe can creatively connect the dots. Be aware of the potential downside of each option: A car is an expensive headache in any major city; with trains and buses, you're at the mercy of a timetable; flying entails a trek to and from a usually distant airport and leaves a larger carbon footprint.

If your itinerary mixes cities and countryside, my advice is to connect cities by train (or bus) and to explore rural areas by rental car. Arrange to pick up your car in the last big city you'll visit, then use it to lace together small towns and explore the countryside. For more detailed information on transportation throughout Europe, see RickSteves.com/transportation.

TRAINS

Renfe is the Spanish national train system. For information and reservations, visit Renfe.com or dial Renfe's number (+34 912 320 320) from anywhere in Spain. You'll find tips on buying tickets later in this section.

Types of Trains

Trains generally get more expensive as they pick up speed, but all are cheaper per mile than their northern European counterparts. Spain loves to name trains, so you may encounter types of trains not listed here.

The high-speed train called the **AVE** (AH-vay, stands for *Alta Velocidad Española*) whisks travelers between Madrid and Barcelona in less than three hours, and Barcelona and Sevilla in six hours. AVE trains are priced according to their time of departure. Peak hours *(punta)* are most expensive, followed by *llano* and *valle* (quietest and cheapest times). Tickets for these trains typically go on sale two months in advance. AVE trains are almost entirely covered by the Eurail Pass, but the required seat reservations can sell out before you have a chance to buy them in Spain. It's smart to bring your passport (ticket checkers may ask for identification, especially if you have a rail pass).

A related high-speed train, the **Alvia,** runs on AVE lines but can switch to Iberian tracks without stopping.

Avlo is a low-cost version of AVE, running a few times per day between Madrid and Barcelona, Zaragoza, Sevilla, Málaga, and Alicante, with all second-class seating and fewer services (www.avlorenfe.com). Nonrefundable tickets are sold online only (and rail passes are not accepted). Avlo has competition on these routes from **Ouigo Spain** (www.ouigo.com/es/en/destinations), a similar, no-frills version of France's TGV, and **Iryo** (https://iryo.eu/en/), an Italian "Frecciarossa"-style high-speed train with four classes of seating and more frills.

Avant trains are also high-speed—typically about as fast as AVE—but designed for shorter distances. They also tend to be cheaper than AVE, even on the same route. If you're on a tight budget, compare your options before buying.

Intercity and **Media Distancia** trains fall just behind Avant in speed, comfort, and expense. **Cercanías** and **Rodalies** are commuter trains for big-city workers and small-town tourists.

Your ticket for an AVE, Larga Distancia, or Iryo train also allows you to connect by Cercanías, Rodalies, and the Alicante TRAM network within four hours of your ticketed departure and arrival times. Collect a *Combinado Cercanías* ticket at self-service machines and station ticket offices by scanning the bar code or entering the code on your train ticket.

Overnight Trains: Overnight trains are not expected to resume operation in Spain. Their removal leaves no convenient train to/from Portugal (aside from twice-daily service between Vigo and Porto).

Rail Passes

Skip the single-country Eurail Spain Pass: It's unlikely to save you money or time in ticket lines, and rail-pass holders have limited access to necessary seat reservations. If your trip extends beyond Spain, consider the Eurail Global Pass, covering most of Europe (trains crossing the Spanish border only accept passes that cover your entire trip). If you buy separate passes for neighboring countries, note that you'll use a travel day on each when crossing the border.

Renfe offers its own "Renfe Spain Pass," which counts trips instead of calendar days, requires reservations to be made in chronological order, and is sold only on their website. Even with a rail pass, use buses when they're more convenient and direct than trains.

Note that rail-pass holders cannot book seat reservations from home, but only directly at long-distance stations in Spain up to

PRACTICALITIES

Iberia's Public Transportation

departure—if still available. These reservations can sell out well in advance (snapped up by point-to-point ticket buyers), making it difficult to predict whether you'll be able to use a pass at all.

For more detailed advice on figuring out the smartest rail-pass options for your train trip, visit RickSteves.com/rail.

Buying Train Tickets

Trains can sell out, and high-speed AVE ticket prices increase as

your departure date draws closer, so it's smart to buy tickets at least a day in advance—even for short rides. You have several options for buying train tickets: at the station or a Renfe office, at a travel agency, online, or in the Renfe app.

At the Station: Most stations have Renfe ticket machines that take US credit cards (know your PIN). If you need assistance, you'll likely have to wait in a line at a ticket window (and pay a 5 percent service fee). First find the correct line—at bigger stations,

Rail Pass or Point-to-Point Tickets?

Will you be better off buying a rail pass or point-to-point tickets? It pays to know your options and choose what's best for your itinerary.

Rail Passes

A Eurail Spain Pass lets you travel by train in Spain for three to eight days (consecutively or not) within a one-month period. Spain is also covered (along with most of Europe) by the classic Eurail Global Pass.

Discounted rates are offered for seniors (age 60 and up) and youths (ages 12-27). Up to two kids (ages 4-11) can travel free with each adult-rate pass (but not with senior rates). All rail passes offer a choice of first or second class for all ages.

While most rail passes are delivered electronically, it's smart to get your pass sorted before leaving home. For more on rail passes, including current prices and purchasing, visit RickSteves.com/rail.

Point-to-Point Tickets

If you're taking just a couple of train rides, buying individual point-to-point tickets may save you money over a pass. Use this map to add up approximate pay-as-you-go fares for your itinerary, and compare that to the price of a rail pass plus reservations. Keep in mind that significant discounts on point-to-point tickets may be available with advance purchase.

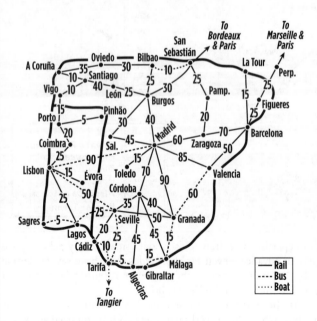

Map shows approximate costs, in US dollars, for one-way, second-class tickets on faster trains.

there might be separate windows for short-distance, long-distance, advance, and "today" *(para hoy)* tickets. You might have to take a number—watch others and follow their lead.

You can also buy tickets or reservations at Renfe offices located in more than 100 city centers. These are more central and multilingual—also less crowded and confusing—than most train stations.

Travel Agency: El Corte Inglés department stores (with locations in most Spanish cities) often have handy travel agencies inside. These can be helpful for those struggling with purchasing train tickets.

Online: Although the Renfe website is useful for confirming schedules and prices, the website sometimes rejects attempts to use a US card (PayPal seems to work better). But with patience and enough Spanish language skill, you may nab an online discount of up to 60 percent (limited seats at these prices, available two weeks to two months ahead of travel). Online vendors with friendlier software include RickSteves.com/rail and Petrabax.com (expect a small fee from either), or use the European vendor TheTrainline. com.

In the App: The Renfe app allegedly offers mobile access to schedules, a journey planner, and ticket-buying options. But the interface is clunky and error-prone; most travelers find it easier to buy tickets online or in person.

BUSES

Bus travel in Spain gives you a glimpse at *España profunda* ("deep Spain"), where everyone seems to know each other and no one's in a hurry. The system can be confusing to the uninitiated, as a number of different companies operate throughout the country, sometimes running buses to the same destinations and using the same transfer points. The aggregator website Movelia.es is a good place to begin researching schedules and companies; local TIs also have bus information for their region.

Among the major companies are Alsa (www.alsa.es), Avanza (www.avanzabus.com), Comes (www.tgcomes.es), and Damas (www.damas-sa.es), but you will see many other regional carriers. Ticket desks are usually clustered within one bus station, and larger stations have a consolidated information desk with all schedules. In smaller stations, check the destinations and schedules posted on each office window.

Remember to double-check the codes on bus schedules to confirm service on the day you want to travel: For example, "12:00S" means 12:00 daily except Saturday. Bus service on holidays, Saturdays, and especially Sundays can be less frequent. Departures are listed under *salidas,* and arrivals are *llegadas.* Whenever possible,

PRACTICALITIES

choose a faster *directo* route over a slower *ruta* option (with more stops along the way).

Some routes can require a transfer; typically (but not always) your onward connection will be run by the originating company. Spend some time at the station upon arrival to check your departure options and buy a ticket in advance if necessary (and possible). If you're downtown, you need a ticket, and the bus station isn't central, save time by asking at the TI about travel agencies that sell bus tickets.

On the Bus: You can (and most likely will be required to) stow your luggage under the bus. Your ticket comes with an assigned seat; if the bus is full, you should take that seat, but if it's uncrowded, most people just sit where they like. Buses are nonsmoking.

Drivers and station personnel may not speak English. Buses generally lack WCs, but they stop every two hours or so for a short break. Drivers announce how long the stop will be, but if in doubt, ask, "How many minutes here?" *("¿Cuántos minutos aquí?")*. Listen for the bus horn as a final call before departure.

RENTING A CAR

It's cheaper to arrange most car rentals from the US, so research and compare rates before you go. Most of the major US rental agencies (including Avis, Budget, Enterprise, Hertz, and Thrifty) have offices throughout Europe. Also consider the two major Europe-based agencies, Europcar and Sixt. Consolidators such as Auto Europe (www.autoeurope.com—or the sometimes-cheaper www.autoeurope.eu) compare rates at several companies to get you the best deal.

Wherever you book, always read the fine print. Check for add-on charges—such as one-way drop-off fees, airport surcharges, or mandatory insurance policies—that aren't included in the "total price."

Rental Costs and Considerations

If you book well in advance, expect to pay roughly $350-500 for a one-week rental for a basic compact car. Allow extra for supplemental insurance, fuel, tolls, and parking. To save money on fuel, request a diesel car. Be warned that international trips—say, picking up in Madrid and dropping off in Lisbon—can be expensive if the rental company assesses a drop-off fee for crossing a border.

Manual vs. Automatic: Cars with manual transmission are more common in Europe and generally cheaper than automatic. If you need an automatic, it's wise to book well in advance. When selecting a car, don't be tempted by a larger model, as it won't be as maneuverable on narrow, winding roads or when squeezing into tight parking lots.

Age Restrictions: Some rental companies impose minimum and maximum age limits. Young drivers (25 and under) and seniors (69 and up) should check the rental policies and rules section of car-rental websites. If you're considered too young or too old, look into leasing (covered later), which has less-stringent age restrictions.

Choosing Pickup/Drop-off Locations: Always check the hours of the location you choose: Many rental offices close from midday Saturday until Monday morning and, in smaller towns, at lunchtime.

When selecting an office, confirm the location on a map. A downtown site might seem more convenient than the airport but could actually be in the suburbs or buried deep in big-city streets. Pedestrianized and one-way streets can make navigation tricky when returning a car at a big-city office or urban train station. Wherever you select, get precise details on the location and allow ample time to find it.

Have the Right License: If you're renting a car in Spain, bring your driver's license. You're also technically required to have an International Driving Permit—an official translation of your license (sold at AAA offices for about $20 plus the cost of two passport-type photos; see www.aaa.com). How this is enforced varies: I've never needed one.

Picking Up Your Car: Before driving off in your rental car, check it thoroughly and make sure any damage is noted on your rental agreement. Rental agencies in Europe tend to charge for even minor damage, so be sure to mark everything. Find out how your car's gearshift, lights, turn signals, wipers, GPS, and fuel cap function, and know what kind of fuel the car takes (diesel is common in Europe). When you return the car, make sure the agent verifies its condition with you.

Car Insurance Options

When you rent a car in Europe, the price typically includes liability insurance, which covers harm to other cars or motorists—but not the rental car itself. To limit your financial risk in case of damage to the rental, choose one of these options: Buy a Collision Damage Waiver (CDW; also called "loss damage waiver" or LDW by some firms) with a low or zero deductible from the car-rental company (roughly 30-40 percent extra), get coverage through your credit card (essentially "free," but more complicated if you need to use it), or get collision insurance as part of a larger travel-insurance policy.

Basic **CDW** costs $15–30 a day and typically comes with a $1,000-2,000 deductible, reducing but not eliminating your financial responsibility. When you reserve or pick up the car, you'll be offered the chance to "buy down" the deductible to zero (for an

PRACTICALITIES

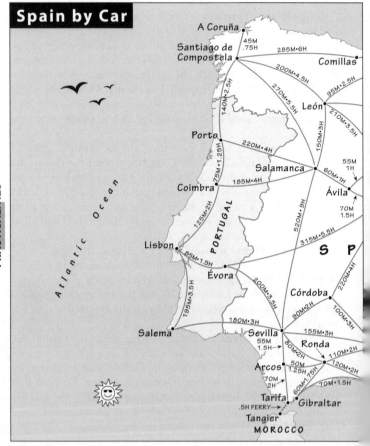

Spain by Car

additional \$10–30/day; this is sometimes called "super CDW" or "zero-deductible coverage").

If you opt for **credit-card coverage,** you must decline all coverage offered by the car-rental company—which means they can place a hold on your card to cover the deductible. In case of damage, it can be time-consuming to resolve the charges. Before relying on this option, quiz your card company about how it works. If you're already purchasing a **travel-insurance policy** for your trip, adding collision coverage can be an economical choice. Both of these options are typically valid everywhere in Europe except the Republic of Ireland and Italy.

For more on car-rental insurance, see RickSteves.com/cdw.

Leasing

For trips of three weeks or more, consider leasing (which automatically includes zero-deductible collision and theft insurance). By

technically buying and then selling back the car, you save money on taxes and insurance. Leasing provides you a brand-new car with unlimited mileage and a 24-hour emergency assistance program. You can lease for as little as 21 days to as long as five and a half months. Car leases must be arranged from the US. One of several companies offering affordable lease packages is Auto Europe.

Navigation Options

If you'll be navigating using your phone, remember to bring a car charger. Most rental cars are equipped with a USB port so you can run your phone's GPS through the dashboard display, but it can also be smart to bring a device mount.

Your Mobile Phone: The mapping app on your phone works fine for navigating Europe's roads. To save on data, most apps allow you to download maps for offline use (do this before you need them, when you have a strong Wi-Fi signal). Some apps—including Google Maps—provide offline route directions, but you'll need data access for current traffic. For more on using a mapping app, see "Using Your Phone in Europe," earlier.

GPS Devices: Most cars come with a dedicated GPS unit, though it's sometimes an add-on cost (about $15-20/day). The unit may come loaded only with maps for its home country; if you need additional maps, ask. Make sure you know how to use the device—and that the language is set to English—before you drive off.

Paper Maps and Atlases: Even when navigating primarily with GPS, I always have a paper map, ideally a big, detailed regional road map. It's invaluable for getting the big picture, understanding alternate routes, and filling in if my phone's GPS stops working. The free maps you get from your car-rental company usually don't have enough detail. It's smart to buy a better map before you go, or pick one up at local gas stations, bookshops, newsstands, and tourist shops.

Driving

Driving in rural Spain is great—traffic is sparse and roads are generally good. But a car is a pain in big cities. Drive defensively. If you're involved in an accident, you will be in for a monumental headache. Spaniards love to tailgate. Don't take it personally; let impatient drivers pass you and enjoy the drive. In smaller towns, following signs to *Centro Ciudad* will get you to the heart of things.

Freeways and Tolls: Spain's freeways come with tolls but save huge amounts of time. Each toll road *(autopista de peaje)* has its own pricing structure, so tolls vary. Near some major cities, you must prepay for each stretch of road you drive; on other routes, you take a ticket where you enter the freeway and pay when you exit. Payment can be made in cash or by credit or debit card (credit-card-only lanes are labeled *"vias automáticas";* cash lanes are *"vias manuales"*).

Because road numbers can be puzzling and inconsistent, be ready to navigate by city and town names. Memorize some key road words: *salida* (exit), *de sentido único* (one way), *despacio* (slow), and *adelantamiento prohibido* (no passing). Mileage signs are in kilometers.

Road Rules: Seatbelts are required by law. Children under 12 must ride in the back seat and use a child's car seat (type varies with age/weight; check with your rental company for details). It's recommended that children over 12 ride in the back when possible.

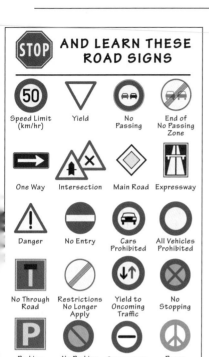

AND LEARN THESE ROAD SIGNS

Speed Limit (km/hr) — Yield — No Passing — End of No Passing Zone

One Way — Intersection — Main Road — Expressway

Danger — No Entry — Cars Prohibited — All Vehicles Prohibited

No Through Road — Restrictions No Longer Apply — Yield to Oncoming Traffic — No Stopping

Parking — No Parking — Customs or Toll Road — Peace

You must put on a reflective safety vest any time you get out of your car on the side of a highway or unlit road (most rental-car companies provide one—check when you pick up the car). Those who use eyeglasses are required by law to have a spare pair in the car.

Be aware of typical European road rules; for example, many countries require headlights to be on at all times, and nearly all forbid handheld mobile-phone use. In Europe, you're not allowed to turn right on a red light unless a sign or signal specifically authorizes it, and on expressways it's illegal to pass drivers on the right. You should also stay in the right lane unless you are passing.

PRACTICALITIES

Ask your car-rental company about these rules, or check the "International Travel" section at Travel.State.gov (enter Spain in the "Learn About Your Destination" box, then click "Travel and Transportation").

Traffic Cops: Watch for traffic radars and expect to be stopped for a routine check by the police. Small towns come with speed traps and corruption. Tickets, especially for foreigners, are issued and paid for on the spot. Insist on a receipt *(recibo),* so the money is less likely to end up in the cop's pocket.

Fuel: Gas and diesel prices are controlled and the same everywhere—about $7 a gallon for gas and $6 a gallon for diesel. Unleaded gas *(gasolina sin plomo)* is either *normal* or *super.* Note that diesel is called *diesel* or *gasóleo*—pay attention when filling your tank. Some pumps are color-coded: Unleaded pumps are green and labeled "E," while diesel pumps (often yellow or black) are labeled "B."

Theft: Thieves easily recognize rental cars and assume they are filled with a tourist's gear. Be sure all your valuables are out of sight and locked in the trunk or, even better, with you or in your room. Parking attendants all over Spain holler, *"Nada en el coche"* ("Nothing in the car"). And they mean it. In cities you can park safely but expensively in guarded lots or garages.

FLIGHTS

To compare flights, begin with an online travel search engine: easy-to-use Google Flights is the top site for flights to and within Europe, Kayak has price alerts, and Skyscanner includes many inexpensive flights within Europe. To avoid unpleasant surprises, before you book, be sure to read the small print about refunds, changes, and the costs for "extras" such as reserving a seat, checking a bag, or printing a boarding pass.

Flights to Europe: Start looking for international flights about four to six months before your trip, especially for peak-season travel. Depending on your itinerary, it can be efficient and no more expensive to fly into one city and out of another.

Flights Within Europe: Flying between European cities is surprisingly affordable. Before buying a long-distance train or bus ticket, check the cost of a flight on one of Europe's airlines, whether a major carrier or a no-frills outfit like EasyJet or Ryanair. Be aware that flying with a discount airline can have drawbacks, such as minimal customer service, time-consuming treks to secondary airports, and a larger carbon footprint than a train or bus.

Flying to the US and Canada: Because security is extra tight for flights to the US, be sure to give yourself plenty of time at the airport (see www.tsa.gov for the latest rules).

Resources from Rick Steves

Begin Your Trip at RickSteves.com

My mobile-friendly **website** is *the* place to explore Europe in preparation for your trip. You'll find thousands of fun articles, beautiful photos, videos, and radio interviews; a wealth of money-saving tips for planning your dream trip; travel news dispatches; a video library of travel talks; our latest guidebook updates (RickSteves. com/update); and the free Rick Steves Audio Europe app. You can also follow me on Facebook, Instagram, and Twitter.

Our **Travel Forum** is a well-groomed collection of message boards where our travel-savvy community answers questions and shares their personal travel experiences—and our well-traveled staff chimes in when they can be helpful (RickSteves.com/forums).

Our **online Travel Store** offers bags and accessories that I've designed to help you travel smarter and lighter. These include my popular carry-on bags (which I live out of four months a year), money belts, totes, toiletries kits, adapters, guidebooks, and planning maps (RickSteves.com/shop).

Our website can also help you find the perfect **rail pass** for your itinerary and your budget, with easy, one-stop shopping for rail passes, seat reservations, and point-to-point tickets (RickSteves. com/rail).

Rick Steves' Tours, Guidebooks, TV Shows, and More

Small Group Tours: Want to travel with greater efficiency and less stress? We offer more than 40 itineraries reaching the best destinations in this book...and beyond. Each year about 30,000 travelers join us on about 1,000 Rick Steves bus tours. You'll enjoy great guides and a fun bunch of travel partners (with small groups of 24 to 28 travelers). You'll find European adventures to fit every vacation length. For all the details, and to book a tour, visit RickSteves.com/tours or call us at +1 425 771 8303.

Books: This book is just one of many books in my series on European travel, which includes country and city guidebooks, Snapshots (excerpted chapters from bigger guides), Pocket Guides (full-color little books on big cities), "Best Of" guidebooks (condensed, full-color country guides), and my budget-travel skills handbook, *Rick Steves Europe Through the Back Door.* A complete list of my titles—including phrase books, cruising guides, and travelogues on European art, history, and culture—appears near the end of this book.

TV Shows and Video Library: My public television series, *Rick Steves' Europe,* covers Europe from top to bottom with over 100 half-hour episodes—and we're working on new shows every year. Watch full episodes for free (RickSteves.com/tv). My free online video library, Rick Steves Classroom Europe, offers a searchable database of short video clips on European history, culture, and geography (Classroom.RickSteves.com).

Monday Night Travel Talks: To raise your travel I.Q., join our virtual travel party every Monday featuring Rick Steves guides discussing European destinations, art, culture, food, travel tips, and more. Join the live events or check out the video recordings (RickSteves.com/mnt).

Audio Tours on My Free App: I've produced 60 free, self-guided audio tours of the top sights in Europe. For those tours and other audio content, get my free **Rick Steves Audio Europe app,** an extensive online library organized by destination. For more on my app, visit RickSteves.com/audioeurope.

Radio: My weekly public radio show, *Travel with Rick Steves,* features interviews with travel experts from around the world. It airs on 400 public radio stations across the US. An archive of programs is available at RickSteves.com/radio.

Podcasts: You can enjoy my travel content via several free podcasts. The podcast version of my radio show brings you a weekly, hour-long travel conversation. My other podcasts include a selection of video clips from my public television show and video recordings of my travel classes (RickSteves.com/podcasts).

APPENDIX

Holidays and Festivals

This list includes selected festivals in Barcelona, plus national holidays observed throughout Spain. Many sights close on national holidays—keep this in mind when planning your itinerary. Before planning a trip around a festival, verify the dates with the festival website, the Spanish national tourist office (www. spain.info), or my "Upcoming Holidays and Festivals in Spain" web page at RickSteves. com/europe/spain/festivals. Also see the "City of Festivals" sidebar on page 36.

Be prepared for big crowds during these holiday periods: Holy Week (Semana Santa) and Easter weekend, Labor Day, Ascension, Pentecost weekend, Assumption weekend, Spanish National Day, Constitution Day, followed closely by the Feast of the Immaculate Conception—both the previous and following weekends may be busy—and Christmas and New Year's Day. Look out for any local holiday that falls on a Tuesday or Thursday—the Spanish will often take Monday or Friday off as well to have a four-day weekend.

Jan 1	New Year's Day
Jan 6	Epiphany (Día de los Reyes Magos)
Mid-Feb	Les Festes de Santa Eulàlia (parades, kid-friendly activities)
March/April	Holy Week: April 13-20, 2025; March 29-April 5, 2026
March/April	Easter Sunday and Monday (some closures): April 20-21, 2025; April 5-6, 2026
April 23	El Día de Sant Jordi (St. George's Day, Barcelona's version of Valentine's Day)
May 1	Labor Day (closures)
May	Ascension: May 29, 2025; May 14, 2026
May/June	Pentecost and Whit Monday: June 8-9, 2025; May 24-25, 2026
May-Sept (Saturdays)	La Festa Catalana (local folk traditions)
May/June	Corpus Christi: June 19, 2025; June 4, 2026
June 24	Festival of St. John the Baptist (bonfires, fireworks)
June-Aug	Música als Parcs (jazz, classical music)
July	Grec Festival (dance, theater, and music)
Mid-Aug	Festes de Sant Roc (Barri Gòtic street festival)
Mid-Aug	Festa Major de Gràcia (music, dancing, food, and drink)
Aug 15	Assumption of Mary (religious festival)
Late Aug	St. Bartholomew Festival, Sitges (carnival, traditional Catalan entertainment)
Sept 11	Catalunya National Day (closures)
Sept 23	St. Tecla Festival, Sitges (fireworks, castellers)
Late Sept	La Mercè Festival (fireworks, parades, music)
Oct 12	Spanish National Day
Nov 1	All Saints' Day
Dec 6	Constitution Day
Dec 8	Feast of the Immaculate Conception
Dec 13	Feast of Santa Lucía
Dec 25	Christmas
Dec 31	New Year's Eve

Books and Films

To learn more about Barcelona's past and present, check out a few of these books or films.

Nonfiction

Barcelona (Robert Hughes, 1992). This is an opinionated journey through the city's tumultuous history, with a focus on art and architecture. *Barcelona: The Great Enchantress* (2004) is a condensed version of Hughes' love song to his favorite city.

Barcelona: A Thousand Years of the City's Past (Felipe Fernandez-Armesto, 1991). A historical and artistic perspective on Barcelona, this book also details the tensions between the city and the rest of Spain.

The Battle for Spain (Antony Beevor, 2006). A prize-winning account of the disintegration of Spain in the 1930s, Beevor's work is the best overall history of the bloody civil war.

Discovering Spain: An Uncommon Guide (Penelope Casas, 1992). Casas, a well-known Spanish cookbook author, insightfully blends history, culture, and food in this personal guide.

Homage to Barcelona (Colm Tóibín, 1990). This rich history of Barcelona includes anecdotes from the author's time in the city.

Homage to Catalonia (George Orwell, 1938). Orwell writes a gripping account of his experiences in the Spanish Civil War fighting Franco's fascists.

Hotel Florida: Truth, Love, and Death in the Spanish Civil War (Amanda Vaill, 2014). In this popular history, Vaill reconstructs events of the Spanish Civil War through the letters, diaries, and photographs of the war correspondents who covered it.

Iberia (James Michener, 1968). Michener's tribute to Spain explores how the country's dark history created a contradictory and passionately beautiful land.

The New Spaniards (John Hooper, 2006). Hooper surveys all aspects of modern Spain, including its transition from dictatorship to democracy, its cultural traditions, and its changing society.

Travelers' Tales: Spain (Lucy McCauley, 1995). This collection of essays from numerous authors creates an appealing overview of Spain and its people.

Fiction

The Carpenter's Pencil (Manuel Rivas, 2001). The psychological cost of Spain's Civil War is at the heart of this unsentimental tale of a revolutionary haunted by his past.

Cathedral of the Sea (Ildefonso Falcones, 2006). A humble medieval *bastaixo* who toils to build the Church of Santa Maria del Mar gradually climbs the social ladder of medieval Barcelona.

The City of Marvels (Eduardo Mendoza, 1986). A young man rises from poverty to wealth and power in 1890s Barcelona.

For Whom the Bell Tolls (Ernest Hemingway, 1940). After covering the Spanish Civil War from Madrid, Hemingway wrote his iconic novel about an American volunteer fighting Franco's fascist forces.

Nada (Carmen Laforet, 1945). This semiautobiographical novel details the experiences of an orphaned university student in post-civil-war Barcelona.

The Queen's Vow (C. W. Gortner, 2012). The life and times of Queen Isabel are vividly re-created in this historical novel.

The Shadow of the Wind (Carlos Ruiz Zafón, 2001). This best-selling thriller is set in 1950s Barcelona; sequels include *The Angel's Game* and *The Prisoner of Heaven*.

Stories from Spain (Genevieve Barlow and William Stivers, 1999). Readers follow nearly 1,000 years of Spanish history in brief short stories printed in Spanish and English.

Films

Barcelona (1994). Two Americans try to navigate the Spanish singles scene and the ensuing culture clash.

Biutiful (2010). A black-market figure and father of two (played by Javier Bardem) learns he has a terminal illness; this film follows him to Barcelona's underground, where he must tie up loose ends.

L'Auberge Espagnole (2002). This comedy-drama chronicles the loves and lives of European students sharing an apartment in Barcelona.

Manuale d'Amore (2005). The four episodes of this film follow the love stories of four couples, with Barcelona and Rome as backdrops.

The Mystery of Picasso (1956). Picasso is filmed painting from behind a transparent canvas, allowing a unique look at his creative process.

Salvador (2006). Barcelona is the backdrop in this story about the life of Salvador Puig Antich, an anarchist and bank robber executed by Franco in the 1970s.

Vicky Cristina Barcelona (2008). In this Woody Allen film, a macho Spanish artist (Javier Bardem) tries to seduce two American women when his stormy ex-wife (Penélope Cruz) suddenly re-enters his life.

Women on the Verge of a Nervous Breakdown (1988). This film, about a woman's downward spiral after a breakup, is one of several piquant Pedro Almodóvar movies about relationships in the post-Franco era. Others include *All About My Mother* (1999), *Talk to Her* (2002), *Volver* (2006), and *Broken Embraces* (2009).

Conversions and Climate

Numbers and Stumblers

- Europeans write a few of their numbers differently than we do. 1 =*1*, 4 =*4*, 7 =*7*.
- In Europe, dates appear as day/month, so Christmas is 25/12.
- Commas are decimal points and decimals are commas. A dollar and a half is $1,50, one thousand is 1.000, and there are 5.280 feet in a mile.
- When counting with fingers, start with your thumb. If you hold up your first finger to request one item, you'll probably get two.
- What Americans call the second floor of a building is the first floor in Europe.
- On escalators and moving sidewalks, Europeans keep the left "lane" open for passing. Keep to the right.

Metric Conversions

A **kilogram** equals 1,000 grams (about 2.2 pounds). One hundred **grams** (a common unit at markets) is about a quarter-pound. One **liter** is about a quart, or almost four to a gallon.

A **kilometer** is six-tenths of a mile. To convert kilometers to miles, cut the kilometers in half and add back 10 percent of the original (120 km: 60 + 12 = 72 miles). One **meter** is 39 inches—just over a yard.

1 foot = 0.3 meter	1 square yard = 0.8 square meter
1 yard = 0.9 meter	1 square mile = 2.6 square kilometers
1 mile = 1.6 kilometers	1 ounce = 28 grams
1 centimeter = 0.4 inch	1 quart = 0.95 liter
1 meter = 39.4 inches	1 kilogram = 2.2 pounds
1 kilometer = 0.62 mile	32°F = 0°C

Clothing Sizes

When shopping for clothing, use these US-to-European comparisons as general guidelines (but note that no conversion is perfect).

Women: For pants and dresses, add 32 in Spain (US 10 = Spanish 42). For blouses and sweaters, add 8 for most of Europe (US 32 = European 40). For shoes, add 30-31 (US 7 = European 37/38).

Men: For shirts, multiply by 2 and add about 8 (US size 15 = European 38). For jackets and suits, add 10. For shoes, add 32-34.

Children: Clothing is sized by height—in centimeters (2.5 cm

APPENDIX

= 1 inch), so a US size 8 roughly equates to 132-140. For shoes up to size 13, add 16-18, and for sizes 1 and up, add 30-32.

Barcelona's Climate

First line, average daily high; second line, average daily low; third line, average days without rain. For more detailed weather statistics for destinations in this book (as well as the rest of the world), check Wunderground.com.

J	F	M	A	M	J	J	A	S	O	N	D
55°	57°	60°	65°	71°	78°	82°	82°	77°	69°	62°	56°
43°	45°	48°	52°	57°	65°	69°	69°	66°	58°	51°	46°
26	23	23	21	23	24	27	25	23	22	24	25

Fahrenheit and Celsius Conversion

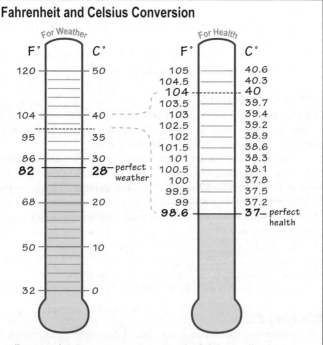

Europe takes its temperature using the Celsius scale, while we opt for Fahrenheit. For a rough conversion from Celsius to Fahrenheit, double the number and add 30. For weather, remember that 28°C is 82°F—perfect. For health, 37°C is just right. At a launderette, 30°C is cold, 40°C is warm (usually the default setting), 60°C is hot, and 95°C is boiling. Your air-conditioner should be set at about 20°C.

Packing Checklist

Whether you're traveling for five days or five weeks, you won't need more than this. Pack light to enjoy the sweet freedom of true mobility.

Clothing

- ❑ 5 shirts: long- & short-sleeve
- ❑ 2 pairs pants (or skirts/capris)
- ❑ 1 pair shorts
- ❑ 5 pairs underwear & socks
- ❑ 1 pair walking shoes
- ❑ Sweater or warm layer
- ❑ Rainproof jacket with hood
- ❑ Tie, scarf, belt, and/or hat
- ❑ Swimsuit
- ❑ Sleepwear/loungewear

Money

- ❑ Debit card(s)
- ❑ Credit card(s)
- ❑ Hard cash (US $100-200)
- ❑ Money belt

Documents

- ❑ Passport
- ❑ Other required ID: Vaccine card, entry visa, etc.
- ❑ Driver's license, student ID, hostel card, etc.
- ❑ Tickets & confirmations: flights, hotels, trains, rail pass, car rental, sight entries
- ❑ Photocopies of important documents
- ❑ Insurance details
- ❑ Guidebooks & maps

Electronics

- ❑ Mobile phone
- ❑ Camera & related gear
- ❑ Tablet/ebook reader/laptop
- ❑ Headphones/earbuds
- ❑ Chargers & batteries
- ❑ Phone car charger & mount (or GPS device)
- ❑ Plug adapters

Toiletries

- ❑ Basics: soap, shampoo, toothbrush, toothpaste, floss, deodorant, sunscreen, brush/comb, etc.
- ❑ Medicines & vitamins
- ❑ First-aid kit
- ❑ Glasses/contacts/sunglasses
- ❑ Face masks & hand sanitizer
- ❑ Sewing kit
- ❑ Packet of tissues (for WC)
- ❑ Earplugs

Miscellaneous

- ❑ Day pack
- ❑ Sealable plastic baggies
- ❑ Laundry supplies: soap, laundry bag, clothesline, spot remover
- ❑ Small umbrella
- ❑ Travel alarm/watch
- ❑ Notepad & pen
- ❑ Journal

Optional Extras

- ❑ Second pair of shoes (flip-flops, sandals, tennis shoes, boots)
- ❑ Travel hairdryer
- ❑ Picnic supplies
- ❑ Disinfecting wipes
- ❑ Water bottle
- ❑ Fold-up tote bag
- ❑ Small flashlight
- ❑ Mini binoculars
- ❑ Small towel or washcloth
- ❑ Inflatable pillow/neck rest
- ❑ Tiny lock
- ❑ Address list (to mail postcards)
- ❑ Extra passport photos

Spanish Survival Phrases

Good morning.	Buenos días.	**bweh**-nohs **dee**-ahs
Good afternoon.	Buenas tardes.	**bweh**-nahs **tar**-dehs
Do you speak English?	¿Habla usted inglés?	**ah**-blah oo-**stehd** een-**glays**
Yes. / No.	Sí. / No.	see / noh
I (don't) understand.	(No) comprendo.	(noh) kohm-**prehn**-doh
Please. / Thank you.	Por favor. / Gracias.	por fah-**bor** / **grah**-thee-ahs
I'm sorry.	Lo siento.	loh see-**ehn**-toh
Excuse me.	Perdone.	pehr-**doh**-nay
No problem.	No hay problema.	noh ī proh-**bleh**-mah
Good. / OK.	Bueno. / Vale.	**bweh**-noh / **bah**-lay
Goodbye.	Adiós.	ah-dee-**ohs**
one / two / three	uno / dos / tres	**oo**-noh / dohs / trehs
four / five / six	cuatro / cinco / seis	**kwah**-troh / **theen**-koh / says
seven / eight	siete / ocho	see-**eh**-tay / **oh**-choh
nine / ten	nueve / diez	**nweh**-bay / dee-**ehth**
How much is it?	¿Cuánto cuesta?	**kwahn**-toh **kweh**-stah
Write it?	¿Me lo escribe?	may loh eh-**skree**-bay
Is it free?	¿Es gratis?	ehs **grah**-tees
Is it included?	¿Está incluido?	eh-**stah** een-kloo-**ee**-doh
Where can I buy / find...?	¿Dónde puedo comprar / encontrar...?	**dohn**-day **pweh**-doh kohm-**prar** / ehn-kohn-**trar**
I'd like / We'd like...	Me gustaría / Nos gustaría...	may goo-stah-**ree**-ah / nohs goo-stah-**ree**-ah
...a room.	...una habitación.	**oo**-nah ah-bee-tah-thee-**ohn**
...a ticket to ___.	...un billete para ___.	oon bee-**yeh**-tay **pah**-rah ___
Is it possible?	¿Es posible?	ehs poh-**see**-blay
Where is...?	¿Dónde está...?	**dohn**-day eh-**stah**
...the train station	...la estación de trenes	lah eh-stah-thee-**ohn** day **treh**-nehs
...the bus station	...la estación de autobuses	lah eh-stah-thee-**ohn** day ow-toh-**boo**-sehs
...the tourist information office	...la oficina de turismo	lah oh-fee-**thee**-nah day too-**rees**-moh
Where are the toilets?	¿Dónde están los servicios?	**dohn**-day eh-**stahn** lohs sehr-**bee**-thee-ohs
men	hombres, caballeros	**ohm**-brehs, kah-bah-**yeh**-rohs
women	mujeres, damas	moo-**heh**-rehs, **dah**-mahs
left / right	izquierda / derecha	eeth-kee-**ehr**-dah / deh-**reh**-chah
straight	derecho	deh-**reh**-choh
When do you open / close?	¿A qué hora abren / cierran?	ah kay **oh**-rah **ah**-brehn / thee-**ehr**-ahn
At what time?	¿A qué hora?	ah kay **oh**-rah
Just a moment.	Un momento.	oon moh-**mehn**-toh
now / soon / later	ahora / pronto / más tarde	ah-**oh**-rah / **prohn**-toh / mahs **tar**-day
today / tomorrow	hoy / mañana	oy / mahn-**yah**-nah

In a Spanish Restaurant

I'd like / We'd like...	Me gustaría / Nos gustaría... may goo-stah-**ree**-ah / nohs goo-stah-**ree**-ah
...to reserve...	...reservar... reh-sehr-**bar**
...a table for one / two.	...una mesa para uno / dos. **oo**-nah **meh**-sah **pah**-rah **oo**-noh / dohs
Non-smoking.	No fumador. noh foo-mah-**dor**
Is this table free?	¿Está esta mesa libre? eh-**stah** eh-stah **meh**-sah **lee**-bray
The menu (in English), please.	La carta (en inglés), por favor. lah **kar**-tah (ehn een-**glays**) por fah-**bor**
service (not) included	servicio (no) incluido sehr-**bee**-thee-oh (noh) een-kloo-**ee**-doh
cover charge	precio de entrada **preh**-thee-oh day ehn-**trah**-dah
to go	para llevar **pah**-rah yeh-**bar**
with / without	con / sin kohn / seen
and / or	y / o ee / oh
breakfast / lunch / dinner	desayuno / almuerzo / cena deh-sah-**yoo**-noh / ahl-**mwehr**-zoh / **seh**-nah
menu (of the day)	menú (del día) meh-**noo** (dehl **dee**-ah)
specialty of the house	especialidad de la casa eh-speh-thee-ah-lee-**dahd** day lah **kah**-sah
tourist menu	menú turístico meh-**noo** too-**ree**-stee-koh
combination plate	plato combinado **plah**-toh kohm-bee-**nah**-doh
appetizers	tapas **tah**-pahs
bread	pan pahn
cheese	queso **keh**-soh
sandwich / soup	bocadillo / sopa boh-kah-**dee**-yoh / **soh**-pah
salad	ensalada ehn-sah-**lah**-dah
meat / poultry	carne / aves **kar**-nay / **ah**-behs
fish / seafood	pescado / marisco peh-**skah**-doh / mah-**ree**-skoh
fruit / vegetables	fruta / verduras **froo**-tah / behr-**doo**-rahs
dessert	postre **poh**-stray
tap water	agua del grifo **ah**-gwah dehl **gree**-foh
mineral water	agua mineral **ah**-gwah mee-neh-**rahl**
(orange) juice	zumo (de naranja) **thoo**-moh (day nah-**rahn**-hah)
coffee / tea / milk	café / té / leche kah-**fay** / tay / **leh**-chay
wine / beer	vino / cerveza **bee**-noh / thehr-**beh**-thah
red / white	tinto / blanco **teen**-toh / **blahn**-koh
glass / bottle	vaso / botella **bah**-soh / boh-**teh**-yah
Cheers!	¡Salud! sah-**lood**
More. / Another.	Más. / Otro. mahs / **oh**-troh
The same.	El mismo. ehl **mees**-moh
The bill, please.	La cuenta, por favor. lah **kwehn**-tah por fah-**bor**
tip	propina proh-**pee**-nah
Delicious!	¡Delicioso! deh-lee-thee-**oh**-soh

For hundreds more pages of survival phrases for your trip to Spain, check out *Rick Steves Spanish Phrase Book*.

Catalan Survival Phrases

Catalan may look similar to Spanish *(castellano)*, but there are important variations in pronunciation. The letters c and z before vowels are pronounced as "s" (unlike the Spanish "th" sound). The letters b, d, r, or t at the end of a word are usually not pronounced (unless the final syllable is stressed). An s between two vowels sounds like a "z."

Hello.	Hola.	**oh**-lah
Do you speak English?	¿Parles anglès?	**par**-luhs ahn-**glays**
Yes. / No.	Sí. / No.	see / noh
I (don't) understand.	(No) entenc.	(noh) ahn-**tehnk**
Please.	Si us plau.	see oos plow
Thank you (very much).	(Moltes) Gràcies.	(**mohl**-tehs) **grah**-see-ehs
I'm sorry. / Excuse me.	Ho sento. / Perdó.	oh **sehn**-too / pehr-**doh**
No problem.	Cap problema.	kahp proh-**blay**-mah
Good.	Bé.	bay
Goodbye.	Adéu.	ah-**day**-oo
one / two / three	uno / dos / tres	**oo**-noo / dohs / trehs
four / five / six	quatre / cinc / sis	**kwah**-trah / seenk / sees
seven / eight	set / vuit	seht / **voo**-eet
nine / ten	nou / deu	**noh**-oo / **deh**-oo
How much?	¿Quant és?	kwahn ehs
Write it?	¿M'ho escriu?	moh ah-**skree**-oo
Is it free?	¿És gratis?	ehs **grah**-tees
Is it included?	¿Està inclós?	eh-**stah** in-**klohs**
Where can I buy / find...?	¿On puc trobar / compar...?	ohn pook troo-**bah** / koom-**prah**
I'd like / We'd like...	Voldria / Voldríem...	vool-**dree**-ah / vool-**dree**-ahm
...a room.	...una habitació.	**oo**-nah ah-bee-tah-see-**oh**
...a ticket to _____.	...una entrada per_____.	**oo**-nah ahn-**trah**-dah pehr _____
Is it possible?	¿És possible?	ehs poh-**see**-blah
Where is...?	¿On està...?	ohn eh-**stah**
...the train station	...l'estació del tren	lah-stah-see-**oh** dahl trehn
...the bus station	...l'estació d'autobuses	lah-stah-see-**oh** dow-toh-**boo**-zehs
...tourist information	...l'oficina de turisme	loo-fee-**see**-nah deh too-**rees**-meh
Where are the toilets?	¿On estan els serveis?	ohn eh-**stahn** ehls sehr-**vays**
men / women	homes / dones	**oh**-mehs / **doh**-nehs
left / right	esquerre / dreta	ehs-**keh**-reh / **dreh**-tah
straight	dret	dreht
At what time does this open / close?	¿A quina hora obre / tanca?	ah **kwee**-nah **oh**-rah **oh**-brah / **tahn**-kah
now / soon / later	ara / aviat / més tard	**ah**-rah / ah-vee-**aht** / mehs tahr
today / tomorrow	avui / demà	ah-**voo**-ee / deh-**mah**
Long live Catalunya!	¡Visca Catalunya!	**vee**-skah kah-tah-**loon**-yah

In a Catalan Restaurant

I'd like / We'd like...	Voldria / Voldríem...	vool-**dree**-ah / vool-**dree**-ahm
...to reserve...	...reservar...	reh-zehr-**vah**
...a table for one / two.	...una taula per una / dues.	
	oo-nah **tow**-lah pehr oo-nah / doo-**ehs**	
Is this table free?	¿Està lliure aquesta taula?	
	eh-**stah** yoo-rah ah-**kwehs**-tah **tow**-lah	
The menu (in English), please.	La carta (en anglès), si us plau	
	lah **kar**-tah (ehn ahn-**glays**) see oos plow	
service (not) included	servei (no) inclós	sehr-**vay**-ee (noh) in-**klohs**
cover charge	preu d'entrada	**preh**-oo dahn-**trah**-dah
to go	per emportar	pehr ehm-por-**tah**
with / without	amb / sense	ahm / **sehn**-seh
and / or	i / o	ee / oh
tapas (small plates)	tapes	**tah**-pahs
daily special	plat del dia	plah dahl **dee**-ah
tourist menu	menú turístic	mah-**noo** too-ree-steek
specialty of the house	especialitat de la casa	
	eh-spah-see-ah-lee-**tah** dah lah **kah**-zah	
combination plate	plat combinat	plah koom-bee-**nah**
half portion	mitja porció	**meet**-yah poor-see-**oh**
breakfast / lunch / dinner	esmorzar / dinar / sopar	
	ehs-mor-**zah** / dee-**nah** / soh-**pah**	
appetizers	entrants	ehn-**trahns**
bread	pà	pah
cheese	formatge	foor-**mah**-jeh
sandwich	entrepà	ehn-trah-**pah**
soup / salad	sopa / amanida	**soh**-pah / ah-mah-**nee**-dah
meat / poultry	carn / aviram	karn / ah-vee-**rahm**
fish / seafood	peix / marisc	paysh / mah-**rees**
fruit / vegetables	fruita / verdures	**froo**-ee-tah / vehr-**doo**-rehs
dessert	postre	**poh**-streh
tap water	aigua (de l'aixeta)	**eye**-gwah (deh lah-**shay**-tah)
mineral water	aigua mineral	**eye**-gwah mee-nah-**rahl**
milk	llet	yeht
(orange) juice	suc (de taronja)	soo (dah tah-**rohn**-zhah)
coffee / tea	cafè / te	kah-**feh** / teh
wine	vi	vee
red / white	negre / blanc	**neh**-greh / blahnk
glass / bottle	copa / ampolla	**koh**-pah / ahm-**poy**-yah
beer	cervesa	sehr-**veh**-zah
Cheers!	¡Salut!	sah-**loo**
More. / Another.	Més. / Un altre.	mehs / oon **ahl**-treh
The same.	El mateix.	ahl mah-**taysh**
The bill, please.	El compte, si us plau.	ahl **komp**-teh see oos plow
tip	propina	proo-**pee**-nah
Delicious!	Boníssim!	boo-**nee**-zeem

INDEX

INDEX

MAP INDEX

Our website enhances this book and turns

Explore Europe

At ricksteves.com you can browse through thousands of articles, videos, photos and radio interviews, plus find a wealth of money-saving travel tips for planning your dream trip. And with our mobile-friendly website, you can easily access all this great travel information anywhere you go.

TV Shows

Preview the places you'll visit by watching entire half-hour episodes of *Rick Steves' Europe* (choose from all 100 shows) on-demand, for free.

ricksteves.com

your travel dreams into affordable reality

Radio Interviews

Enjoy ready access to Rick's vast library of radio interviews covering travel tips and cultural insights that relate specifically to your Europe travel plans.

Travel Forums

Learn, ask, share! Our online community of savvy travelers is a great resource for first-time travelers to Europe, as well as seasoned pros.

Travel News

Subscribe to our free Travel News e-newsletter, and get monthly updates from Rick on what's happening in Europe.

Classroom Europe®

Check out our free resource for educators with 500 short video clips from the *Rick Steves' Europe* TV show.

Pack Light and Right

Gear up for your next adventure at ricksteves.com

Light Luggage

Pack light and right with Rick Steves' affordable, custom-designed rolling carry-on bags, backpacks, day packs and shoulder bags.

Accessories

From packing cubes to moneybelts and beyond, Rick has personally selected the travel goodies that will help your trip go smoother.

Shop at ricksteves.com

Experience maximum Europe

Save time and energy

This guidebook is your independent-travel toolkit. But for all it delivers, it's still up to you to devote the time and energy it takes to manage the preparation and logistics that are essential for a happy trip. If that's a hassle, there's a solution.

Rick Steves Tours

A Rick Steves tour takes you to Europe's most interesting places with great

great tours, too!

with minimum stress

guides and small groups. We follow Rick's favorite itineraries, ride in comfy buses, stay in family-run hotels, and bring you intimately close to the Europe you've traveled so far to see. Most importantly, we take away the logistical headaches so you can focus on the fun.

Join the fun

This year we'll take thousands of free-spirited travelers—nearly half of them repeat customers—along with us on 50 different itineraries, from Athens to Istanbul. Is a Rick Steves tour the right fit for your travel dreams?

Find out at ricksteves.com, where you can also check seat availability and sign up. Europe is best experienced with happy travel partners. We hope you can join us.

See our itineraries at ricksteves.com

A Guide for Every Trip

BEST OF GUIDES

Full-color guides in an easy-to-scan format. Focused on top sights and experiences in the most popular European destinations

Best of England
Best of Europe
Best of France
Best of Germany
Best of Ireland
Best of Italy
Best of Scotland
Best of Spain

COMPREHENSIVE GUIDES

City, country, and regional guides printed on Bible-thin paper. Packed with detailed coverage for a multi-week trip exploring iconic sights and venturing off the beaten path

Amsterdam & the Netherlands
Barcelona
Belgium: Bruges, Brussels, Antwerp & Ghent
Berlin
Budapest
Central Europe
Croatia & Slovenia
England
Florence & Tuscany
France
Germany
Great Britain
Greece: Athens & the Peloponnese
Iceland
Ireland
Istanbul
Italy
London
Paris
Portugal
Prague & the Czech Republic
Provence & the French Riviera
Rome
Scandinavia
Scotland
Sicily
Spain
Switzerland
Venice
Vienna, Salzburg & Tirol

THE BEST OF ROME

me, Italy's capital, is studded with
man remnants and floodlit-fountain
ares. From the Vatican to the Colos-
m, with crazy traffic in between, Rome
onderful, huge, and exhausting. The
ds, the heat, and the weighty history

of the Eternal City where Caesars walked
can make tourists wilt. Recharge by taking siestas, gelato breaks, and after-dark
walks, strolling from one atmospheric
square to another in the refreshing evening air.

red *Pantheon*—which
gest dome until the
rly 2,000 years old
uy over 1,500).

of Athens in the Vat-
odies the humanistic
nce.

gladiators fought
another, entertaining

s Rome *ristoran-*

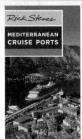

POCKET GUIDES
Compact color guides for shorter trips

Amsterdam
Athens
Barcelona
Florence
Italy's Cinque Terre
London
Munich & Salzburg

Paris
Prague
Rome
Venice
Vienna

SNAPSHOT GUIDES
Focused single-destination coverage

Basque Country: Spain & France
Copenhagen & the Best of Denmark
Dublin
Dubrovnik
Edinburgh
Hill Towns of Central Italy
Krakow, Warsaw & Gdansk
Lisbon
Loire Valley
Madrid & Toledo
Milan & the Italian Lakes District
Naples & the Amalfi Coast
Nice & the French Riviera
Normandy
Northern Ireland
Norway
Reykjavík
Rothenburg & the Rhine
Sevilla, Granada & Southern Spain
St. Petersburg, Helsinki & Tallinn
Stockholm

CRUISE PORTS GUIDES
Reference for cruise ports of call

Mediterranean Cruise Ports
Scandinavian & Northern European
  Cruise Ports

Complete your library with...

TRAVEL SKILLS & CULTURE
*Study up on travel skills and gain
insight on history and culture*

Europe 101
Europe Through the Back Door
Europe's Top 100 Masterpieces
European Christmas
European Easter
European Festivals
For the Love of Europe
Italy for Food Lovers
Travel as a Political Act

PHRASE BOOKS & DICTIONARIES
French
French, Italian & German
German
Italian
Portuguese
Spanish

PLANNING MAPS
Britain, Ireland & London
Europe
France & Paris
Germany, Austria & Switzerland
Iceland
Ireland
Italy
Portugal
Scotland
Spain & Portugal

Credits

RESEARCHER
For help with this edition, Rick relied on...

Cary Walker

Cary discovered international travel during college and has been feeding her wanderlust ever since. A former teacher, she believes that Europe is the best classroom for those who travel with an open mind. When not researching guidebooks or leading Rick Steves' Europe tours, she resides in Dallas with her husband Brian and three well-traveled stepsons.

CONTRIBUTORS
Cameron Hewitt

Cameron Hewitt was born in Denver, grew up in Central Ohio, and moved to Seattle in 2000 to work for Rick Steves' Europe. Since then, he has spent about 100 days each year in Europe—researching and writing guidebooks, blogging, tour guiding, and making travel TV (described in his memoir, *The Temporary European*). Cameron married his high school sweetheart, Shawna, and enjoys taking pictures, trying new restaurants, and planning his next trip.

Gene Openshaw

Gene has co-authored more than a dozen books with Rick, specializing in Europe's art, history, and culture. In particular, their *Europe 101: History and Art for the Traveler* and *Europe's Top 100 Masterpieces* have helped bring European art to life. Gene also writes for Rick's television shows, produces the audio tours, and is a regular guest on Rick's radio show. For public TV, Gene has co-authored two television specials with Rick: *Fascism in Europe* and the ambitious six-hour series *Art of Europe*. Outside of the travel world, Gene has composed an opera called *Matter*, a violin sonata, and dozens of songs. Gene lives near Seattle, where he roots for the Mariners in good times and bad. Check out his latest book on art, travel, and love: *Michelangelo at Midlife*.

ACKNOWLEDGMENTS
Thank you to Risa Laib for her 25-plus years of dedication to the Rick Steves guidebook series.

PHOTO CREDITS

Avalon Travel
Hachette Book Group
1700 Fourth Street
Berkeley, CA 94710

Printed in China by RR Donnelley
Seventh Edition. First printing May 2024.

ISBN 978-1-64171-605-5

For the latest on Rick's talks, guidebooks, tours, public television series, and public radio
show, contact Rick Steves' Europe, 130 Fourth Avenue North, Edmonds, WA 98020, +1 425
771 8303, RickSteves.com, rick@ricksteves.com.

Rick Steves' Europe
Managing Editor: Jennifer Madison Davis
Editorial Group Manager: Cathy Lu
Editors: Glenn Eriksen, Julie Fanselow, Suzanne Kotz, Rosie Leutzinger, Teresa Nemeth,
  Jessica Shaw, Carrie Shepherd, Chelsea Wing
Researcher: Cary Walker
Contributors: Cameron Hewitt, Gene Openshaw
Creative Director: Sandra Hundacker
Maps & Graphics: Orin Dubrow, David C. Hoerlein, Lauren Mills, Mary Rostad

Avalon Travel
Senior Editor and Series Manager: Madhu Prasher
Associate Managing Editors: Jamie Andrade, Sierra Machado
Copy Editor: Kelly Lydick
Proofreader: Elizabeth Jang
Indexer: Stephen Callahan
Production & Typesetting: Lisi Baldwin, Jane Musser, Ravina Schneider
Cover Design: Kimberly Glyder Design
Maps & Graphics: Kat Bennett

COLOR MAPS

Greater Barcelona • Barcelona • Barcelona's Old City
• Barcelona's Eixample • Barcelona's Public Transportation

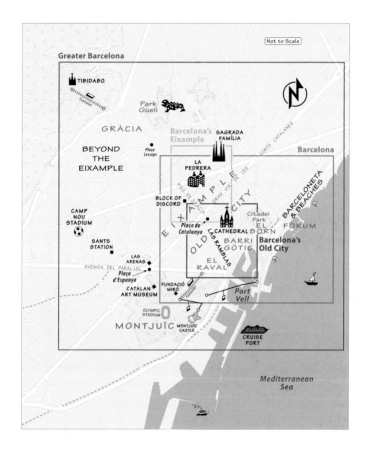

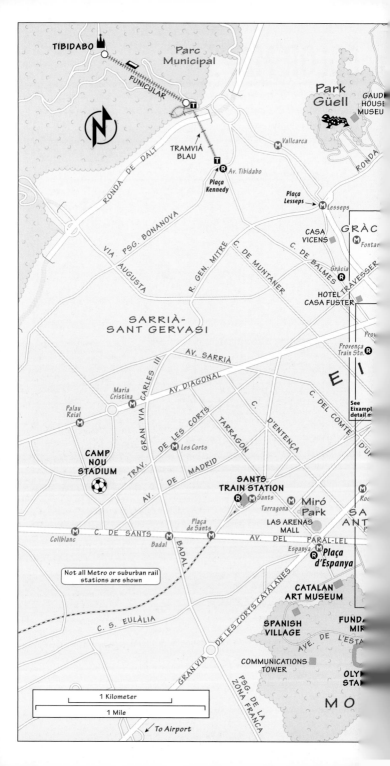

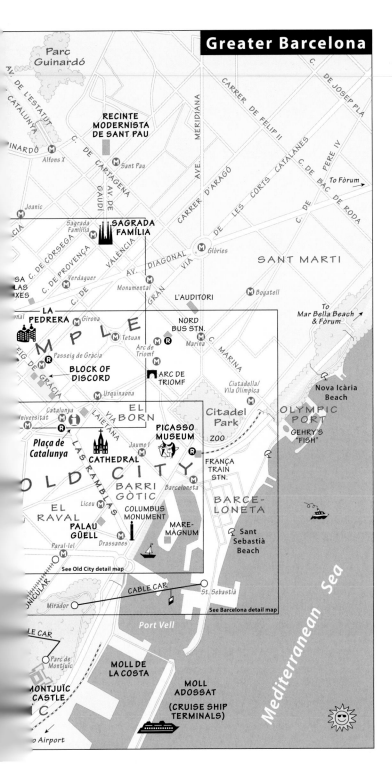

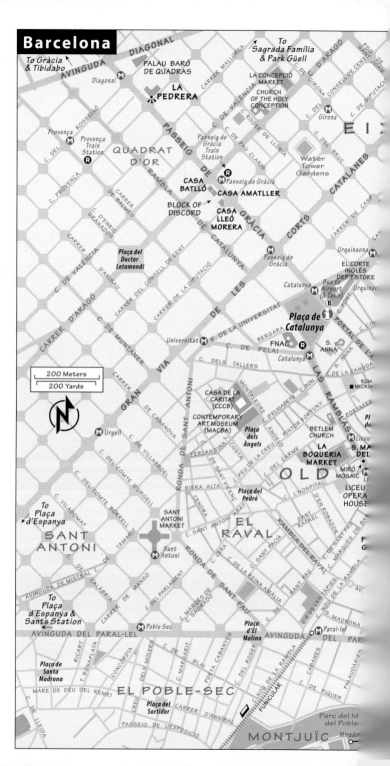

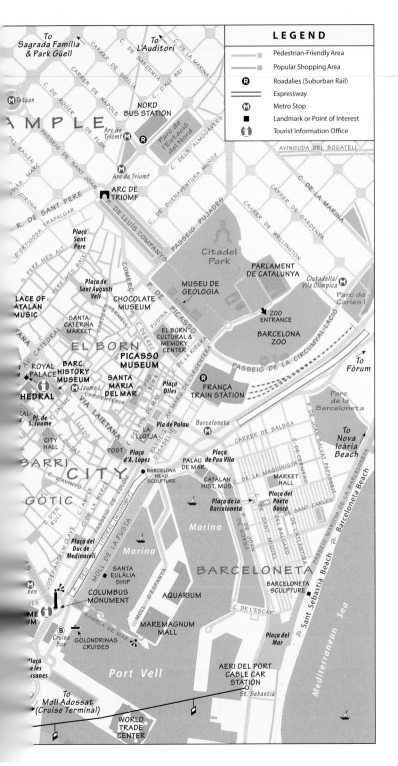

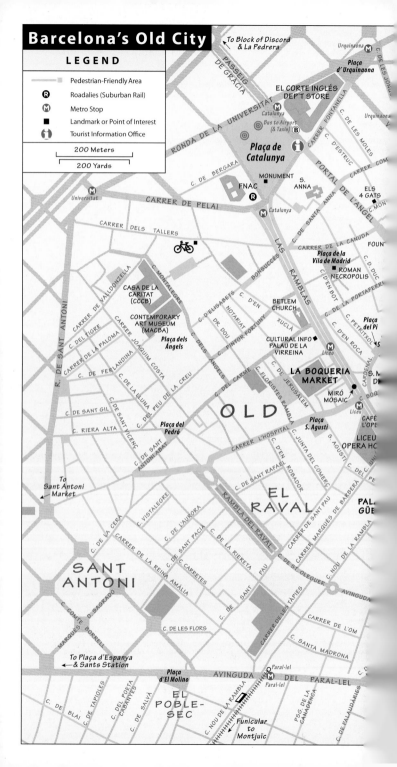

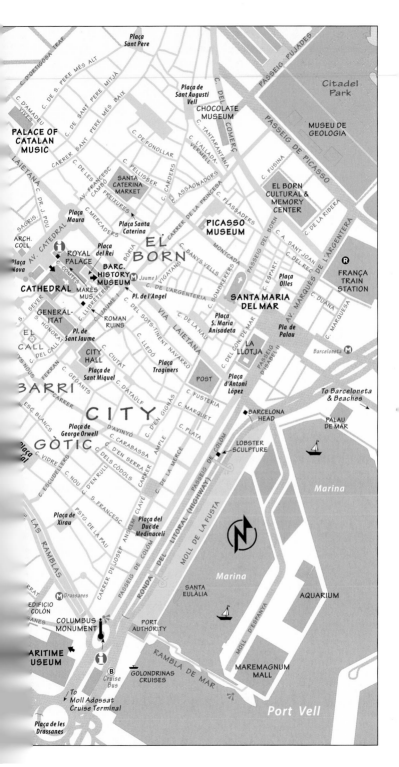

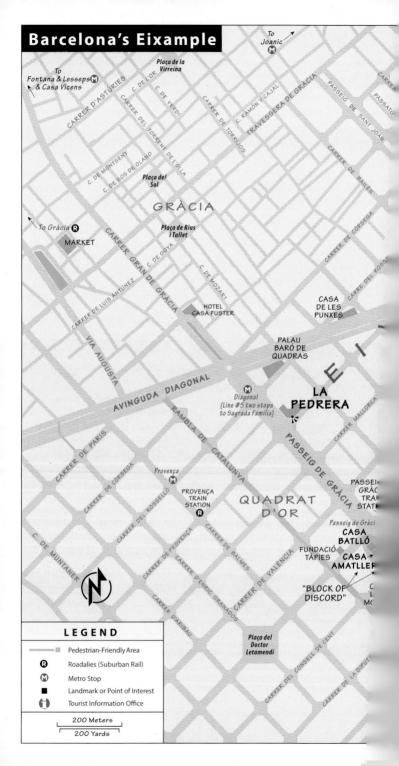

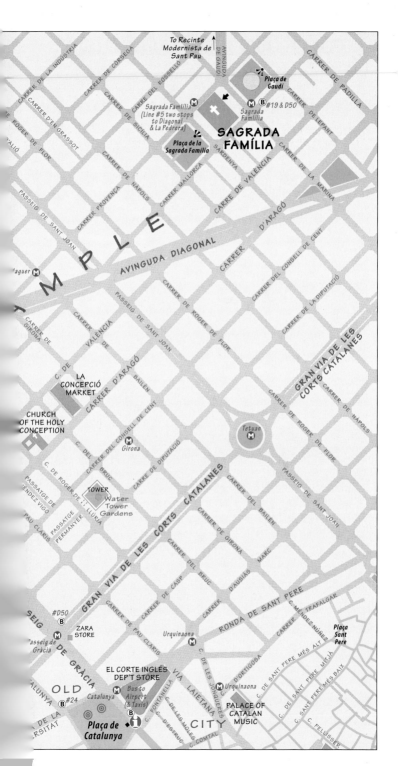

Barcelona's Public Transportation

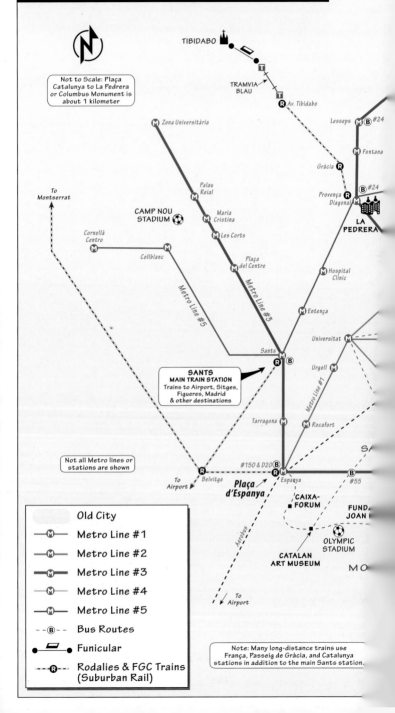